THE

PLEASANTNESS OF

A RELIGIOUS LIFE

OPENED AND IMPROVED;

and

RECOMMENDED TO THE

CONSIDERATION OF ALL,

PARTICULARLY OF YOUNG

PEOPLE.

THE
PLEASANTNESS
OF A RELIGIOUS LIFE

Matthew Henry

Christian Heritage

© 1998 Christian Focus Publications Ltd
ISBN 1 85792 391 X

Published by
Christian Focus Publications Ltd
Geanies House, Fearn, Ross-shire,
IV20 1TW, Scotland, Great Britain.

Contents

INTRODUCTION

I

This write-up of a set of six sermons was Matthew Henry's final literary labour. It was in the press when he died, aged 52, in 1714, and came out shortly after as *The Pleasantness of a Religious Life opened, and proved, and recommended to the consideration of all, particularly of Young People*. J.B. Williams, Henry's biographer, called this an 'attractive title', but I doubt whether many today will find it attractive.

That however is not Henry's fault. The reason this title strikes us as leaden-footed is that during the almost three centuries separating him from us 'pleasantness' has become a weak word, stating only that something is not too bad; 'religious' has become a vague word, covering all faiths and attitudes that involve 'God' or 'gods' (or, nowadays, 'goddesses') at some point; 'consideration' has become a cool word, suggesting thought that is consciously detached rather than committed; and 'young people' has become a patronizing phrase that creates expectations of being talked down to and so turns real young people off. If, however, the latter-day associations of Henry's title discourage us from digging into his book, it will be a pity; for what he is actually writing about, in his smooth, fulsome, and turn-of-the-17th-century style is, the joy of Christian life, and as I usher his book back from obscurity into a world that has welcomed volumes on the joy of cooking and of sex and such like, I cannot help wishing that he had given it that kind of title.

Henry is quite up-front about what he is doing. Working from Proverbs 3:17, which the NIV renders '(wisdom's) ways are pleasant ways, and all her paths are peace,' he first observes that 'nothing draws more forcibly than pleasure', and then lays it down that 'true piety has true pleasure in it'. More fully:

> Pleasure is a tempting thing. What yields delight cannot but attract desire... religion has pleasure on its side... Here is a bait that has no hook under it... a pleasure which God himself invites you to, and which will make you happy, truly and eternally happy... it is certain that there is true pleasure in true religion (p. 49f.).

Henry's aim is to make us see that real Christianity is a journey into joy, always moving us on from one joy to another, and that this is one of many good and strong reasons for being excited and whole-hearted in our discipleship. He makes his point well, and this is how:

First, he lists twelve pleasures that Christians as such enjoy: (1) knowing God and the Lord Jesus Christ; (2) resting in God; (3) being God's child; (4) tasting God's gracious goodness in all creature comforts; (5) relying on God's care; (6) delighting in God; (7) praising God; (8) escaping slavery to our appetites and (9) passions; (10) loving and doing good to others; (11) communing with God constantly; (12) looking forward to heaven's glory.

Then he reviews what God has done to bring sinners joy: made peace for them through the cross; promised them peace plus pleasure; and given them the Holy Spirit, the Scriptures, the ordinances of worship in prayer and song, and the gospel ministry, to bring home to them the blessings prepared for them. He lists those blessings as pardon, assurance, access to God, contentment, the calmness and confidence of a good conscience, and actual foretastes of glory.

Then he confirms what he has said so far by appealing to the facts of Christian experience, which fully verify his argument, and by picturing the Christian life as a journey made pleasant by its worthwhileness, by the gift of strength for travel, by the presence of the Holy Spirit to guard and guide, by good company, delightful terrain, good weather, and ample provisions en route, and by knowing that we shall experience journey's end as home.

Finally, having dismissed the scepticism of the irreligious and the misrepresentations of the morose regarding the delights of devotion, and having countered the idea that the pains of repenting, the demands of self-discipline and self-denial, and the constant experience of opposition, destroy the joy of discipleship, he urges his readers directly, starting from where they are, to enter into the fulness of the spiritual life that he has been describing.

Some things do not change. What Henry wrote nearly three centuries ago, wrapping it up in language that must strike us as old-fashioned, is as true and wise today as ever it was. We too get told, sometimes by our secular friends, sometimes by our own morbid thoughts, that being a Christian is a bleak and burdensome business, and not being a Christian would be more fun; we too, like Henry's first hearers and readers, need to be reminded that it is absolutely not so. Henry's reminder comes from his heart: 'herein, I confess,' he writes, 'I indulge an inclination of my own; for this doctrine of the pleasantness of religion is what I have long had a particular kindness for, and taken all occasions to mention' (p. 20). Christian life, though not a joy ride, is a joy road! As a connoisseur and veteran of spiritual pleasures, Henry will help us verify that today.

II

Who was Matthew Henry, who wrote this precious little book? He was a Silver Age Puritan. Let me explain.

In the world of literary study and history of ideas, a distinction is often drawn between the Golden and Silver Ages of creative movements. The Golden Age is the period in which the pioneers do the creative work, establishing themselves as the masters by the classical, landmark quality of their achievements. The Silver Age follows: it is a period in which those who lead seek first and foremost to follow in the footsteps of the forerunners, laying out, polishing up, and faithfully passing on the tradition of wisdom they have inherited. They dot its i's and cross its t's and develop its details as they go along, and, standing on their predecessors' shoulders, they sometimes top them in clarity and precision of statement; yet they remain conservers rather than creators, and settlers rather than explorers. Their goal is to maintain a heritage, and it is to this end that they dedicate their powers and devote their efforts.

In Christianity, the Golden-Silver distinction applies in different ways, according to one's angle of vision. Thus, from one standpoint you can label Luther's volcanically creative career as the Golden Age of the Reformation, and see the systematizing skill of Calvin and Melanchthon as its Silver counterpart. From another standpoint, the era of Luther, Calvin, Bucer, Martyr, Cranmer, Knox and their colleagues is the Golden Age of reformational theology, and the Puritan theological century from Perkins to Owen, with its continental counterpart from Beza to Turretin, is the Silver Age that succeeded it. From a third standpoint, master teachers of the Christian life like John Newton, Murray McCheyne, C.H. Spurgeon, J.C. Ryle, and Arthur Pink are the Silver Age in relation to the Golden Age of Puritan pioneers such as Perkins, Sibbes, Baxter, Bunyan, Owen, Gurnall, Thomas Goodwin and Thomas Hooker, for mapping the inner realities of the Christian life of faith, hope, and love. And from a fourth standpoint three men whose best work adorns the early eighteenth century should be seen as Silver Age figures in relation to the entire theological and practical output of the Puritan Golden Age that preceded them: namely, Cotton Mather, Isaac Watts, and Matthew Henry. All three are under-appreciated and need to be revalued, but here our focus is on Henry alone.

He was born in 1662, the year in which his godly Puritan father, Philip Henry, was one of two thousand ejected from pastoral ministry in the restored Church of England. His parents grounded him in Puritan beliefs and behaviour patterns (daily prayer, Bible reading, self-watch and self-examination; journal-keeping, and practice of the presence of God; scrupulous morality and generous philanthropy; thorough-going Sabbatarianism, and hard work for the other six days of the week). Precocious, bright, lively and Bible-loving, he never wanted to do anything else with his life other than serve his Lord in pastoral ministry; and in 1687, having passed through a nonconformist academy and read some law in Gray's Inn, he received Presbyterian ordination and began pastoring a congregation in Chester. It grew to over 350 during the 25 years he served it. In 1712, two years before his death, he relocated in Hackney, just outside London.

As a good preacher of the Puritan type, he was much in demand. As a matter of conscience he never refused an invitation to preach if he could possibly accept it, and throughout his ministry he was constantly in some pulpit or other, sometimes three times a day in different places.

Both Sunday services in his own church lasted up to three hours, since he not only preached for an hour from a text but also spent an hour expounding a chapter of the Bible. Out of this practice grew his famous Commentary, which he began to publish in 1704, and of which he completed five volumes, taking him to the end of Acts, before his death. (Friends later composed volume six on the basis of his surviving notes.)

Simple and practical in style while thoroughly scholarly and well-informed for substance, the Commentary remains an all-time classic, standing head and shoulders above any other popular exposition produced either before or since.

III

How should modern readers tune in to *The Pleasantness of a Religious Life*, in order to get the best out of it? This is a necessary question, for Henry assumes much that cannot be taken for granted today, and unless we adjust to this at the outset we may well be left feeling that his material is bland and facile, and does not really speak to our condition – or, putting it more bluntly, that you need to be a pretty old-fashioned person to appreciate such old-fashioned stuff! The following points are made in hope of pre-empting any such reaction.

First, we must get clear on the Puritan understanding of Christianity: which is a connected view of God, of the Bible, of the world, of ourselves, of salvation, of the church, of history, and of the future. Few, it seems, even in Bible-believing churches, grasp this whole picture, and in liberal churches, where attention to scholars' fads and fancies replaces the teaching of the Bible, there is virtually no grasp of it at all. Once, churches taught it to all their children, using catechisms, but not any more. I state it here, therefore, in summary form.

God, who within the unity of his being is intrinsically a society, the Father, the Son, and the Holy Spirit together, and who is infinite, unchanging, and almighty in his wisdom, goodness, and justice, created the universe, and ourselves within it, so that he might love and bless us, and we might love and praise him. But things have gone wrong.

Original sin is the radical distortion of every human being's moral nature, making love and honour to God from our hearts impossible and self-centredness at deepest level inevitable. We sin because we are sinners, and human history, from one standpoint, is original sin writ large.

Jesus Christ the Saviour, the Jew who died, rose, reigns, and will return for retribution to everyone, past, present, and future, is God the Son incarnate, whose death atoned for our sins, whom we trust for forgiveness and acceptance and serve as our living Lord, and who unites us to himself for the renewal of his image in us, dethroning original sin and giving us resources against its down-drag in the process. This is present salvation.

The Holy Spirit, the third divine person, acts for the Father and the Son by convincing us of our sin and need of Christ's reality as Saviour; by drawing us to him in penitent faith through regeneration; by witnessing to our pardon, adoption, and hope of glory; and by progressively working in us Christ-likeness of character as we pursue what is in truth our journey home. This is the application of redemption.

The church is the supernatural society of all regenerate persons united by the Holy Spirit to Jesus Christ, called to worship, witness and work together for Christ's glory, and enriched with stated pastors, sacramental ordinances, and abundant serving abilities, for that purpose. Every Christian belongs to the church as God knows it, needs it as his supportive family, and should fellowship within it committedly in one of its particular local expressions. Christian life is corporate life.

The Bible, the written word of God, is the divine source of knowledge of these things.

Such, in a nutshell, is the Puritan understanding of Christianity, which Henry assumes in his readers.

Second, we must get clear on the antithesis between Puritan Christianity and Western secularism, in both its modernist and post-modernist forms. Where Puritanism looks to the Word of God for self-knowledge and life-guidance, modernity looks with optimism to human reason as expressed in the sciences and philosophies, while post-modernism, of which today's universities are full, tells the modernists with pessimism that their enterprise is hopeless, since what philosophers and scientists, like Christians before them, offer as universal truth is really only an improper venture in mind-control.

Whatever be thought of this claim (does it, for instance, apply to post-modernism itself?), it is clearly as much an expression of secularism as is the modernity it seeks to undermine, and from the battlefield where modernists and post-modernists slug it out the fumes of relativism, scepticism, and despair drift everywhere, producing a mind-set in which nothing seems certain, nothing feels quite worthwhile, and grabbing such pleasures as each moment offers seems the only thing to do. So human nature is devalued, human life is cheapened, human thought is blocked, and we live aimlessly, prompted only by instinct, appetite, and various forms of greed in the manner of what we used to call the lower animals. Our idea of life is of drifting along, and our idea of pleasure stops short at the momentary satisfying of instinctual, sensual, body-based, self-absorbed cravings, urges, and itches. (I grade these according to their strength: an urge is a strong itch, and a craving is a strong urge). This is where our secularism has brought us, and it is a sad story.

In direct antithesis to all aspects of this secular trend stands Henry's forceful recall to the eternal truth – 'true truth', as Francis Schaeffer would have said – about human nature.

The soul is the man.... ('soul' here means personal, conscious, thinking, continuing self). I hope it will be readily granted me, that man is principally to be considered as an intellectual, immortal being, endued with spiritual powers and capacities, allied to the world of spirits; that there is a spirit in man, which has sensations and dispositions of its own, active and receptive faculties, distinct from those of the body: and that this is the part of us, which we are, and ought to be most concerned about; because it is really well or ill with us, according as it is well or ill with our souls. Believe, that in our present state, the soul and the body have separate and contesting interests; the body thinks it is its interest to have its appetites gratified, and to be indulged in its pleasures; while the soul knows it is its interest to have the appetites of the body subdued and mortified, that spiritual pleasures may be the better relished.... Be wise, therefore; be resolute, and shew yourselves men who are actuated and governed by reason, and are affected by things as reason represents them to you: not reason as it is in the mere natural man, clouded, and plunged, and lost in sense; but reason elevated and guided by divine revelation to us, and divine grace in us. Walk by faith, and not by sense (p. 50f.).

Only as we grasp the antithesis between the historic Christian and modern secular approaches to the business of living, and programme ourselves to shake off cultural prejudice and take the Christian, biblical, Puritan view of human nature and human welfare seriously, shall we be able to profit from the flood of wisdom that Henry here pours out as he gets into his stride.

The popular idea of a Puritan has always been of a pharisaical sourpuss who spreads gloom wherever he goes. In fact, however, as the real-life Puritan practised the disciplines of serious Christianity, praying, fasting, keeping his heart, warring against the world, the flesh, and the devil, maintaining an ordered life and doing all the good he could, he found mental pleasure and joy at every turn of the road – in quiet, in tumult, in peace and prosperity, in sorrow and strain – and this is the experience that Henry wants to share and deepen. Thought-control, in re-alising the reality of God present each moment to bless, is the secret, and Henry's discourse, read and re-read, can lead us directly into it. I hope that very many will prove this to be so.

J.I. Packer

TO THE READER

The distinction which the learned Dr. Henry More insists so much upon, in his explanation of the grand mystery of godliness, between the animal life and the divine life, is certainly of great use to lead us into the understanding of that mystery. What was the fall and apostasy of man, and what is still his sin and misery, but the soul's revolt from the divine life, and giving up itself wholly to the animal life? And what was the design of our Redeemer, but to recover us to the divine and spiritual life again, by the influences of his grace? And to this his gospel has a direct tendency: his religion is all spiritual and divine, while all other religions savour of the animal life. 'Christianity,' saith he, 'is that period of the wisdom and providence of God, wherein the animal life is remarkably insulted, and triumphed over by the divine' (Book ii, chap 7) and so far, and no farther, are we Christians indeed, than as this revolution is brought about in our souls. The conflict is between these two. Nothing draws more forcibly than pleasure. In order therefore to the advancing of the interests of the divine life in myself and others, I have here endeavoured, as God has enabled me, to make it evident, that the pleasures of the divine life are unspeakably better, and more deserving, than those of the animal life: were people convinced of this, we should gain our point.

The substance of this treatise was preached last

year in six sermons, in the ordinary course of my
ministry, in which were stated many other reasons
why we should be religious; I was then solicited to
make it public, and now take this opportunity to
prepare it for the press, when, through the good hand
of my God upon me, I have finished my fifth volume
of expositions, before I go about the sixth. And
herein, I confess, I indulge an inclination of my own;
for this doctrine of the pleasantness of religion is
what I have long had a particular kindness for, and
taken all occasions to mention. Yet I would not thus
far have gratified either my friends' request, or my
own inclination, if I had not thought that, by the
blessing of God, it might be of some service to the
common interest of Christ's kingdom, and the common salvation of precious souls.

MH
May 31st 1714

INTRODUCTION

*Her ways are ways of pleasantness,
and all her paths are peace (Prov. 3:17).*

True religion and godliness is often in scripture, and particularly in this book of the Proverbs, represented, and so recommended to us, under the name and character of wisdom (Prov. 1:2, 7, 20; 2:2, 10; 3: 13; Ps. 111:10), because it is the highest improvement of the human nature, and the best and surest guide of human life. It was one of the first and most ancient discoveries of God's mind to the children of men, to the inquisitive part of them, that are in search for wisdom, and would have it at any rate; then, when God made a weight for the winds, and a decree for the rain – when he brought all the other creatures under the established rule and law of their creation, according to their respective capacities – then he declared this to man, a reasonable creature, as the law of his creation (Job 28:25-28) 'Behold, the fear of the Lord, that is wisdom, and to depart from evil', the evil of sin, 'is understanding'.

The great men of the world, that engross its wealth and honours, are pretenders to wisdom, and think none do so well for themselves as they do; but though their neighbours applaud them, and their posterity, that reap the fruit of their worldly wisdom, approve their sayings yet 'this their way is their folly' (Ps. 49:13, 18); and so it will appear, when God himself shall call those fools, who said to their souls, take your ease, in barns full of corn, and bags full of money (Luke 12:20; Jer. 17:11).

The learned men of the world were wellwishers to wisdom, and modestly called themselves lovers of wisdom; and many wise principles we have from them, and wise precepts; and yet their philosophy failed them in that which man's great duty and interest lies, viz, acquainting himself with his Maker, and keeping up communion with him: herein they that 'professed themselves to be wise became fools' (Rom. 1:22), and 'the world by wisdom knew not God' (1 Cor. 1:21). But true Christians are, without doubt, the truly wise men, to whom 'Christ is made of God wisdom' (1 Cor. 1:30) 'in whom are hid', not from them, but for them, 'all the treasurers of wisdom and knowledge' (Col. 2:3). They understand themselves best, and on which side their interest lies, that give up themselves to the conduct of Christ, and his word and Spirit; that consult his oracles, and govern themselves by them, which are indeed the truest oracles of reason (Prov. 9:10). Men never begin to be wise, till they begin to be religious; and they then leave off to be wise, when they 'leave off to do good' (Ps. 36:3).

Now, to recommend to us the study and practice of this true wisdom, to bring us into a willing subjection to her authority, and keep us to a conscientious observance of her dictates, the great God is here by Solomon reasoning with us, from those topics which, in other cases, use to be cogent and commanding enough. It is wonderful condescension, that he who has an indisputable authority over us, thus vouchsafes to reason with us; to draw with the 'cords of a man, and the bands of love' (Hos. 11:4), when he might make use only of the cords of a God, and the bands of the law (Ps. 2:3); to invite us to that by precious promises, which he enjoins upon us by his precepts, and those 'not grievous' (1 John 5:3).

Interest is the great governess of the world; which, when men are once convinced of, they will be swayed by more than by any thing else. Every one is for what he can get, and therefore applies himself to that which he thinks he can get by. The common inquiry is, 'who will show us any good?' We would all be happy, we would all be easy. Now it is here demonstrated by eternal truth itself, that it is our interest to be religious; and therefore religion deserves to be called wisdom, because it teaches us to do well for ourselves: and it is certain, that the way to be happy, that is, perfectly holy, hereafter, is to be holy, that is, truly happy, now. It is laid down for a principle here, 'Happy is the man that findeth wisdom' (Prov. 3:13) that finds the principles and habits of it planted in his own soul by divine grace; that having diligently sought, has at length found that pearl of great price: 'and the man that getteth understanding', reckons himself therein a true gainer. The man that draws out understanding, so the original word signifies; that produceth it, and brings it forth, *Qui profert intelligentiam*; and so the Chaldee reads it. Happy is the man, that having a good principle in

him, makes use of it, both for his own and others'
benefit; that having laid up, lays out.

It is necessary to our being happy, that we have
right notions of happiness; the nature of it, wherein
it consists, what are the ingredients of it, and what
the ways that lead to it: for many keep themselves
miserable by thinking themselves happy, when really they are not; and we have reason to suspect their
mistake concerning themselves, because they mistake so grossly concerning others: they 'call the
proud happy' (Mal. 3:15), they 'bless the covetous,
whom the Lord abhors' (Ps. 10:4). It concerns us
therefore to consider, whence we take our measures
of happiness, and what rules we go by in judging of
it; that we may not covet our lot with those, with
whom we should dread to have our lot; that we may
not say as the Psalmist was tempted to say, when he
looked upon the outward prosperity of worldly people, 'happy is the people that is in such a case'; but
as he was determined to say, when he looked upon
the true felicity of godly people, Happy, thrice
happy, for ever happy, 'is that people whose God is
the Lord' (Ps. 144:15). And as God here saith, whose
judgment, we are sure, is according to truth, 'happy
is the man that finds wisdom'.

The happiness of those that are religious, is here
proved,

1. From the true profit that is to be got by religion.
'Godliness is profitable to all things' (1 Tim. 4:8), it
is of universal advantage. Though we may be losers
for our religion, yet we shall not only be losers by it,
but we shall be unspeakable gainers in the end. They

that trade with wisdom's talents, will find 'the merchandise of it better than the merchandise of silver, and the gain thereof than fine gold', and that it is 'more precious than rubies'. As long since as Job's time it was agreed, that the advantages of religion were such, that as they could not be purchased, so they could not be valued with the gold of Ophir, the precious onyx, or the sapphire; the topaz of Ethiopia 'could not equal them' (Job 28:16, 19). Length of days is in Wisdom's right hand, even life for evermore; length of days, and no shortening of them; 'and in her left hand riches and honour' (Prov. 3:16), yea, 'the unsearchable riches of Christ', and the honour that comes from God, which are true riches, and true honours, because durable, because eternal, and for ever out of the danger of poverty and disgrace.

In all labour there is profit, more or less, of one kind or other, but no profit like that in the labour of religion: they who make a business of it, will find great advantage by it; its present incomes are valuable, and a comfortable honourable maintenance for a soul, but its future recompenses infinitely more so, above what we are able either to speak or think.

2. From the transcendent pleasure that is to be found in it. Here is profit and pleasure combined, which completes the happiness. *Omne tulit punctum, qui miscuit utile dulci*. Those that pursue the gains of the world in wealth and riches, must be willing to deny themselves in their pleasures; and they that will indulge themselves in their pleasures, must be content not to get money, but to spend it. As they that are

covetous know they must not be voluptuous, so they
that are voluptuous leave no room to be covetous;
but it is not so in the profits and pleasures of religion:
here a man may both get and save the spiritual riches
of divine grace, and yet at the same time bathe in a
full stream of divine consolations, and be, neverthe-
less, a holy epicure in spiritual delights, in his laying
up treasure in heaven. The soul may even then dwell
at ease, when it is labouring most diligently for the
meat that endures to external life. This is that which
the text speaks of; and both the profit and pleasure of
religion are put together in the next words 'she is a
tree of life' (verse 18) both enriching and delighting
'to them that lay hold upon her': what gain or
comfort like that of life?

First, We are here assured, that her 'ways are
ways of pleasantness'; not only pleasant ways, but in
the abstract, ways of pleasantness, as if pleasantness
were confined to those ways, and not to be found any
where else: and the pleasantness ariseth not from any
foreign circumstance, but from the innate goodness
of the ways themselves. Or it denotes the exceeding
superlative pleasantness of religion; it is as pleasant
as pleasantness itself; 'They are ways of pleasantness'; it is the word from which Naomi had her name
in the day of her prosperity, which afterwards she
disclaimed (Ruth 1:20). 'Call me not Naomi, pleasant; but Marah, bitter.' Think that you hear Wisdom
saying, on the contrary, 'Call me not Marah, bitter',
as some have miscalled me, 'but call me Naomi,
pleasant'. The vulgar Latin reads it *Viae pulchrae*;
her ways are beautiful ways, ways of sweetness, so

the Chaldee. Wisdom's ways are so; that is, the ways which she has directed us to walk in, the ways of her commandments, those are such, as if we keep close to, and go on in, we shall certainly find true pleasure and satisfaction. Wisdom saith, 'This is the way, walk in it'; and you shall not only find life at the end, but pleasure in the way. That which is the only right way to happiness, we must resolve to travel, and to proceed and persevere in it, whether it be fair or foul, pleasant or unpleasant: but it is a great encouragement to a traveller, to know that his way is not only the right way, but a pleasant way: and such the way to heaven is.

God has told us by Solomon, chapter 2:3, 4, that we must 'cry after knowledge, and lift up our voice for understanding'; that we must seek it, and search for it, must spare no cost or pains to get it: he had told us, that this wisdom would restrain us, both from the way of the evil man, and of the strange woman (chapter 2:12, 16) that it would keep us from all the forbidden pleasures of sense. Now, lest these restraints from pleasure, and constraints to piety and labour, should discourage any from the ways of religion, he here assures us, not only that our pains will be abundantly recompensed with the profits of religion, but the pleasures we forego will be abundantly balanced by the pleasures we shall enjoy.

Secondly, It is added, that 'all her paths are peace'. Peace is sometimes put for all good; here some take it for the good of safety and protection. Many ways are pleasant, they are clean, and look smooth, but they are dangerous, either not sound at bottom, or beset with thieves: but the ways of wisdom have in them a holy security, as well as a holy serenity; and they that walk in them, have God himself for their shield as well as their sun, and are not only joyful in the hope of good, but are, or may be, quiet also from the fear of evil.

But we may take it for the good of pleasure and delight, and so it speaks the same with the former part of the verse: as there is pleasantness in wisdom's ways, so there is peace in all her paths.

1. There is not only peace in the end of religion, but peace in the way. There is not only peace provided as a bed, for good men to lie down in at night, when their work is done, and their warfare is accomplished; they shall then 'enter into peace, rest in their beds' (Isa. 57:2). 'Mark the perfect man, and behold the upright, for the end of that man is peace' (Ps. 37:37) it is everlasting peace; but there is also peace provided as a shade, for good men to work in all day, that they may not only do their work, but do it with delight; for even the work of righteousness, as well as its reward, 'shall be peace' (Isa. 32:17) and the immediate effect of righteousness, as well as its issue at last, quietness and assurance for ever.

It is possible, that war may be the way to peace; *Sic quaerimus pacem*, 'thus we pursue peace', is the best motto to be engraven on weapons of war; but it is the glory of those who are truly religious, that they not only seek peace, but enjoy it: the peace of God rules their hearts, and by that means keeps them: and even while they are travellers, they have peace, though they are not yet at home.

It is the misery of the carnal, irreligious world, that 'the way of peace they have not known' (Rom. 3:17) for they are like the troubled sea; there is 'no peace, saith my God, to the wicked' (Isa. 57:20, 21). How can peace be spoken to them that are not the 'sons of peace' (Luke 10:4, 5) to them that have not grace for the word of peace to fasten upon? They may cry peace to themselves, but there is no true peace either in their way, or in their end: to such I say, as in 2 Kings 9:18, 'What hast thou to do with peace? turn thee behind me'; but in God's name I speak peace to all that are in covenant with the God of peace, to all the faithful subjects of the prince of peace: they have experimentally known the way of peace; and to them I say, Go on, and prosper: go on in peace, for the God of love and peace is, and will be with you.

2. There is not only this peace in the way of religion in general, but in the particular paths of that way: view it in the several acts and instances of it, in the exercise of every grace, in the performance of every duty, and you will find, that what is said of the body of Christianity, is true of every part of it; it is peace.

The ways of religion are tracked as pathways are (Cant. 1:8), we go forth by the footsteps of the flock. It is the good old way, that all have walked in that are gone to heaven before us; and this contributes something to the peace of it: walk in the old way, and you shall 'find rest to your souls' (Jer. 6:16). We go on in our way with so much the more assurance, when we see those going before us, who 'through faith and patience, are now inheriting the promise'; let us but keep the path, and we shall not miss our way.

The Chaldee reads it *Itinera ejus pacifica*; her journeys are peace. The paths of wisdom are not like walks in a garden, which we make use of for diversion only, and an amusement; but like tracks in a great road, which we press forward in with care and pains, as a traveller in his journey, *plus ultra* still, till we come to our journey's end. We must remember, that in the ways of religion we are upon our journey, and it is a journey of business – business of life and death; and therefore we must not trifle, or lose time, but must lift up our feet as Jacob did (Gen. 29:1), 'then Jacob went on his way' (in the margin it is, he lift up his feet) and lift up our hearts as Jehoshaphat did, 'in the ways of the Lord' (2 Chr. 17:6) and not take up short of the end of our faith and hope, not take up short of home: and though the journey is long, and requires all this care and application, yet it is pleasant, it is peace notwithstanding.

In the way of religion and godliness taken generally, there are different paths, according to the different sentiments of wise and good men, in the less weighty matters of the law; but blessed be God, every different path is not a by-path: and if it be not, but keep within the same hedges of divine truths and laws as to the essentials of religion, it may be, it shall be a way of peace; for both he that eateth, and he that eateth not, giveth God thanks (Rom. 14:6) and has comfort in it. If we rightly understand the kingdom of God, the way of wisdom is not meat and drink; and we shall find it to be, which indeed it is 'righteousness and peace and joy in the Holy Ghost' (Rom. 14:17).

3. There is this peace in all the paths of wisdom, in all the instances of pure and undefiled religion; look into them all, make trial of them all, and you will find there is none to be excepted against, none to be quarrelled with; they are all uniform and of a piece: the same golden thread of peace and pleasure runs through the whole web of serious godliness.

We cannot say so of this world, that all its paths are peace; however some of them may pretend to give the mind a little satisfaction, its pleasures have their alloys; that which one thing sweetens, another comes presently and imbitters. But as there is a universal rectitude in the principles of religion (Ps. 119:128), 'I have esteemed all thy precepts concerning all things to be right'; and Proverbs 8:8: 'All the words of my mouth are in righteousness,' saith Wisdom, 'and there is nothing froward or perverse in them'; so there is a universal peace and pleasure in the practice of religion; all our paths, if such as they should be, will be such as we could wish.

The doctrine, therefore, contained in these words, is:

That 'true piety hath true pleasure in it'. Or thus:

The 'ways of religion are pleasant and peaceful ways'.

CHAPTER 1

The Explication of the Doctrine

It is a plain truth which we have here laid down, and
there is little in it that needs explication: it were well
for us, if we would but as readily subscribe to the
certainty of it, as we apprehend the sense and meaning of it. Nor will any complain, that it is hard to be
understood, but those who know no other pleasures
than those of sense, and relish no other, and therefore
resolve not to give credit to it. Those who think, How
can this be that there should be pleasure in piety? will
be ready to question, What is the meaning of this
doctrine? and to call it a hard saying.

You know what pleasure is: I hope you know
something of what the pleasure of the mind is; a
pleasure which the soul has the sensation of. And do
you not know something of what piety is, a due
regard to God above us, and having the eyes of the
soul ever directed unto him; then you know what I
mean when I say, that there is an abundance of real
pleasure and satisfaction in the ways of religion and
godliness.

But to help you a little in the understanding of it,
and to prevent mistakes, observe,

First, That I speak of true piety, and of that as far as it goes.

1. Hypocrites are very much strangers to the delights and pleasures of religion; nay, they are altogether so, for it is a joy which those strangers do not intermeddle with. Counterfeit piety can never bring in true pleasure. He that acts a part upon a stage, though it be the part of one that is never so pleasant, though he may humour the pleasantness well enough, he doth not experience it. The pleasures of God's house lie not in the outer courts, but within the vail. None know what the peace of God means, but those that are under the dominion and operation of his grace; nor can any that deny the power of godliness, expect to share in the pleasures of it. When wisdom enters into thine heart, takes possession of that, and becomes a living active principle there; then, and not till then, it is 'pleasant unto thy soul' (Prov. 2:19). They that aim at no more but the credit of their religion before men, justly fall short of the comfort of it in themselves.

Hypocrites have other things that they delight in, the satisfactions of the world, the gratifications of sense, which put their mouths out of taste to spiritual pleasures, so that they have no pleasure in them. They that have their hearts upon their marketings, are weary of the new moons and the sabbaths (Amos 8:5). With good reason, therefore, doth Job ask, 'Will the hypocrite delight himself in the Almighty?' (27:10). No; his soul takes its ease in the creature, and returns not to the Creator as its rest and home.

Some flashy pleasure a hypocrite may have in

religion, from a land-flood of sensible affections, who yet has not the least taste of the river of God's pleasures. There were those who delighted to know God's ways (Isa. 58:2), they met with some pretty notions in them, that surprised them, and pleased their fancies, but they did not delight to walk in them. The stony ground received the word with joy, and yet received no lasting benefit by it (Luke 8:13) Herod heard John gladly (Mark 6:20). He found something very agreeable in his sermons, and which natural conscience could not but embrace, and yet could not bear to be reproved for his Herodias. A florid preacher, such as Ezekiel was, may be to them as a 'very lovely song of one that can play well on an instrument' (Ezek. 33:32) and yet at the same time, the word of the Lord, if it touch their consciences, and show them their transgressions, is to them a reproach (Jer. 6:10).

They whose hearts are not right with God in their religion, cannot have the pleasure of communion with God; for it is the soul only that converseth with God, and that he communicates himself to; bodily exercise profiteth little (1 Tim. 4:8) and therefore pleaseth little. The service of God is a burden, and a task to an unsanctified unrenewed heart: it is out of its element when it is brought into that air: and therefore instead of snuffing it up, and saying, behold what a pleasure it is! it snuffs at it, and saith, 'behold what a weariness it is!' (Mal. 1:13). Nor can they take any pleasure in communing with their own consciences, or in their reflections; for these are ready upon all occasions to give them uneasiness, by charging them with that which is disagreeable to their profession, and gives the lie to it: and though they cry, Peace, peace, to themselves, they have that within them that tells them, the God of heaven doth not speak peace to them; and this casts a damp upon all their pleasure, so that their religion itself gives them pain, God himself is a terror to them, and the gospel itself condemns them for their insincerity. And in time of trouble and distress, none are so much afraid as the sinners in Zion (Isa. 33:14) the secret sinners there: and fearfulness is the greatest surprise of all to the hypocrites, that are at ease in Zion (Amos 6:1) and think its strongholds will be their security.

And therefore it is that hypocrites cast off religion, and discharge themselves of the profession of it, after they have a while disguised themselves with it, because it doth not sit easy; and they are weary of it. Tradesmen that take no pleasure in their business, will not stick to it long, no more will those that take no pleasure in their religion; nor will any thing carry us through the outward difficulties of it, but the inward delights of it: if those be wanting, the tree is not watered, and therefore even its leaf will soon wither (Ps. 1:3). The hypocrite will not always call upon God, will not long do it, because he will not delight himself in the Almighty (Job 27:10). And this ought not to be a stumbling-block to us. Thus hypocrites in religion prove apostates from it, and the reason is, because they never found it pleasant; they never found it pleasant, because they were never sincere in it, which was their fault, and not the fault of the religion they professed.

Let us therefore take heed, and beware of hypocrisy (Luke 12:1), as ever we hope to find pleasure in religion. Counterfeit piety hath some other end in view, some other end to serve, than that which is the spring of true delight. They who rest in that, hew them out cisterns (Jer. 2:13) that can hold but little water, and that dead; nay, broken cisterns that can hold no water; and how can they expect the pleasure which those have, that cleave to, and continually draw from the fountain of life, and living waters? No, as their principles are, such are their pleasures; as their aims are, such are their joys; they appeal to the world, and to the world they shall go. But let not the credit of religion suffer then, for the sake of those who are only pretenders to it, and so indeed enemies to it.

2. It is possible that true Christians may, through their own fault and folly, want very much of the pleasure of religion; and therefore, I say, true piety, as far as it goes, is very pleasant; as far as it has its due influence upon us, and is rightly understood, and lived up to.

We maintain that wisdom's ways are always pleasant, and yet must own, that wisdom's children are sometimes unpleasant and therein come short of justifying wisdom, in this matter, as they ought to do (Luke 7:35), and rather give advantage to her accusers, and prejudice to her cause. Either they miss these ways, and turn aside out of them, and so lose the pleasure that is to be found in them; or, which is a common case, they refuse to take the comfort which they might have in these ways. They hamper themselves with needless perplexities, make the yoke heavy which Christ has made easy, and that frightful which he designed should be encouraging; they indulge themselves, and then, as Jonah when he was angry, justify themselves in causeless griefs and fears, and think they do well to put themselves into an agony, to be very heavy and sore amazed, and their souls exceeding sorrowful, even unto death, as Christ's was; whereas Christ put himself into such an agony to make us easy.

But let not true piety suffer in its reputation because of this; for though it be called a religious melancholy, it is not so, for that is contrary to the very nature and design of religion, while it shelters itself under the colour of it, and pretends to take rise from it. It is rather to be called a superstitious melancholy, arising from such a slavish fear of God, as the heathens were driven to by their demons and barbarous sacrifices; which is a great injury to the honour of his goodness, as well as a great injury to themselves.

If the professors of religion look for that in the world, which is to be had in God only, and that is perfect happiness; or, if they look for that in themselves, which is to be had in Christ only, and that is a perfect righteousness; or, if they look for that on earth which is to be had in heaven only, and that is perfect holiness; and then fret, and grieve, and go mourning from day to day, because they are disappointed in their expectations, they may thank themselves. 'Why seek they the living among the dead?' (Luke 24:5, 17).

Let but religion, true and pure religion, in all the laws and instances of it, command and prevail, and these tears will soon be wiped away: let but God's servants take their work before them, allow each principle of their religion its due weight, and each practice of it its due place and proportion, and let them not dash one precept of the gospel, any more than one table of the law, in pieces against the other; let them look upon it to be as much their duty to rejoice in Christ Jesus, as to mourn for sin; nay, and more, for this is in order to that; and then we shall not fear, that their sorrows will in the least shake the truth of our doctrine; for as far as religion is carried, it will carry this character along with it, and further it cannot be expected.

Secondly, In true piety I say there is a pleasure; there is that which we may find comfort in, and fetch satisfaction from. There is a *bonum jucundum* as well as *utile*. That is pleasant which is agreeable, which the soul rejoiceth in, or at least reposeth in; or which it relisheth, pleaseth itself with, and desireth the continuance and repetition of. Let a man's faculties be in their due frame and temper, not vitiated, corrupted, or depraved, and there is that in the exercise of religion which highly suits them, and satisfies them; and this pleasure is such as is not allayed with any thing to cast a damp upon it.

1. The ways of religion are right and pleasant; they are pleasant without the allay of injury and iniquity. Sin pretends to have its pleasures, but they are the 'perverting of that which is right' (Job 33:27), they are 'stolen waters' (Prov. 9:17), unjust though

pleasant; but the pleasures of godliness are as agreeable to the rectitude of our nature as they are gratifying to the pure and undebauched desires of it. They
are the ways in which we should go; and the ways in
which, if we were not wretchedly degenerated, we
would go of choice.

They are right, for they are marked out to us by
our rightful Lord, who having given us the being of
rational creatures, has authority to give us a law
suited to our being; and he has done it both by natural
conscience, and by the written word: he hath said,
'This is the way, walk in it' (Isa. 30:21). It is not only
permitted and allowed us, but charged and commanded us to walk in it; he hath sent us as messen-
gers from him to travel this road upon his errand.
They are right, for they lead directly to our great end,
have a tendency to our welfare here and for ever.
They are the only right way to that which is the
felicity of our being, which we shall certainly miss
and come short of, if we do not walk in this way.

But that is not all, they are also pleasant: 'Behold
how good and how pleasant!' (Ps. 133:1). It is the
happiness of those that fear God, that he not only
'teacheth them in the way that he shall choose' (and
we may be sure that is the right way), but also that
'their souls shall dwell at ease' (Ps. 25:12, 13). And
justly may they dwell at ease, who have Infinite
Wisdom itself to choose their way, and guide them
in it. That may be right which is not pleasant, and that
pleasant which is not right; but religion is both:
therefore in the next verse it is compared to the tree
of life. The tree of knowledge was indeed pleasant to

the eyes, and a tree to be desired, but it was forbidden; and therefore religion is called a 'tree of life', which was not only pleasant, but was allowed till sin entered.

2. They are easy and pleasant; pleasant without the allay of toil and difficulty, any more than ariseth from the corruption of our own nature: that indeed makes such opposition, that we have need of arguments; and, blessed be God, we have good arguments to prove the practice of religion easy: but it is more, it is pleasant.

Much less is said than is intended, when we are told that 'his commandments are not grievous' (1 John 5:3). They are not only not grievous and galling, but they are gracious and pleasing. His yoke is easy (Matt. 11:30). The word there used, signifies more than easy, it is sweet and gentle; not only easy as a yoke is to the neck, when it is so well fitted as not to hurt it, but easy as a pillow is to the head when it is weary and sleepy. It is not only tolerable, but very comfortable. There is not only no matter of complaint in the ways of God, nothing to hurt us, but there is abundant matter of joy and rejoicing: it is not only work which is not weariness, but work which is its own wages; such a tree of life, as will not only screen us from the storm and tempest, and feed us with necessary food, but we may sit down under the shadow of it with great delight, and the fruit of it will be 'sweet unto our taste' (Cant. 2:3).

3. They are gainful and pleasant, and have not the allay of expense and loss. That may be profitable, which yet may be unpleasant, and that pleasant,

which afterwards may prove very unprofitable and prejudicial; what fruit have sinners from those things in which they say they have pleasure? (Rom. 6:21.) But religion brings both pleasure with it, and profit after it: the pleasures of religion do not cost us dear; there is no loss by them when the account comes to be balanced.

The gain of this world is usually fetched in by toil and uneasy labour, which is grievous to flesh and blood. The servants of this world are drudges to it; they 'rise up early, sit up late, eat the bread of sorrows' (Ps. 127:2) in pursuit of its wealth. They 'labour and bereave their souls of good' (Ecc. 4:8), but the servants of God have a pleasure even in the work they are to get by, and which they shall be recompensed for.

Besides the tendency that there is in the practice of serious godliness to our happiness in the other life, there is much in it that conduceth to our comfort in this life. David observes it to the honour of religion (Ps. 19:10), that not only after keeping, but in keeping God's commandments there is a great reward; a present great reward of obedience in obedience. 'A good man is satisfied in himself' (Prov. 14:14) that is, in that which divine grace hath wrought in him; and the saints are said to 'sing in the ways of the Lord' (Ps. 138:5) as those that find them pleasant ways.

And the closer we adhere to the rules of religion, and the more intimate our converse is with divine things, the more we live with an eye to Christ and another world, the more comfort we are likely to have in our own bosoms. Great peace have they that 'love God's law' (Ps. 119:165) and the more they love it, the greater their peace is; nay, it is promised to the church, that 'all her children shall be taught of the Lord' (and those whom he teacheth are well taught, and taught to do well) and then 'great shall be the peace of her children' (Isa. 54:13) it shall be entailed upon them: 'Peace like a river', *in omne volubilis aevum*.

Thirdly, I call it a true pleasure: as there is 'science, falsely so called' (1 Tim. 6:20), so there is pleasure falsely so called. One of the ancients (*Damascen Orthod Fid 50:2*) distinguishes between pleasures that have some truth in them, and pleasures that deceive us with a lie in their right hand. Some have said that the school of Epicurus, which is commonly branded and condemned for making pleasure man's chief good, did not mean sensual pleasure, but the pleasure of the mind. And we should be willing enough to admit it, but that the other principles of his philosophy were so atheistical and irreligious. But this we are sure of, that it is a true pleasure which religion secures to us; a pleasure that deserves the name, and answers it to the full. It is a true pleasure, for,

1. It is real and not counterfeit. Carnal worldlings pretend a great satisfaction in the enjoyments of the world and the gratifications of sense: 'Soul, take thine ease,' saith one (Luke 12:19). 'I have found me out substance,' saith another (Hos. 12:8), even 'the life of my hand,' saith a third (Isa. 57:10); 'I have seen the fire,' saith a fourth (Isa. 44:16). 'The wicked

boasts of his heart's desire', but Solomon assures us, not only that 'the end of that mirth is heaviness', but that even 'in laughter the heart is sorrowful' (Prov. 14:13). Both those that make a god of their belly, and those that make a god of their money, find such a constant pain and uneasiness attending their spiritual idolatries, that their pleasure is but from the teeth outward. Discontent at present disappointments, and fear of worse; ungoverned passions, which seldom are made less turbulent by the gratifications of the appetite; and above all, consciousness of guilt, and dread of divine wrath, these give them the lie, when they boast of their pleasures, which, with such allays, are not to be boasted of. They would not be thought to be disappointed in that which they have chosen for their happiness, and therefore they seem to be pleased; they seem to be pleasant, when really their heart, if it knows its own wickedness, cannot but 'know its own bitterness' (Prov. 14:10).

And many of the good things of this world, of which we said, 'These same shall comfort us', prove vexations to us; and we are disappointed in that wherein we most promised ourselves satisfaction. 'If we say our bed shall comfort us', perhaps it is not a bed to rest on, but a bed to toss on, as it was to poor Job, when 'wearisome nights were appointed to him'. Nay, such strangers are we to real pleasure in the things of this life, and so oft do we deceive ourselves with that which is counterfeit, that we wish to live those days of life which we are told will be evil days, and those years of which we are assured that we shall say, 'We have no pleasure in them' (Ecc. 12:1).

But the pleasures of religion are solid, substantial pleasures, and not painted; gold, and not gilded over: these sons of pleasure 'inherit substance' (Prov. 8:21) it is that which is the foundation firm, the superstructure strong, the consolations of God not few, nor small (Job 15:11) while a vain and foolish world 'cause their eyes to fly upon that which is not' (Prov. 23:5). Worldly people pretend to the joy they have not; but godly people conceal the joy they have, as he did that had 'found the treasure hid in the field'. They have, like their Master, 'meat to eat, which the world knows not of' (John 4:32).

2. It is rational, and not brutish. It is the pleasure of the soul, not of sense; it is the peculiar pleasure of a man, not that which we have in common with the inferior creatures. The pleasures of religion are not those of the mere animal life, which arise from the gratifications of the senses of the body, and its appetites; no, they affect the soul, that part of us by which we are allied to the world of spirits, that noble part of us, and therefore are to be called the true pleasures of a man.

The brute creatures have the same pleasures of sense that we have, and perhaps in some of them the senses are more exquisite, and consequently they have them in a much higher degree; nor are their pleasures liable to the correctives of reason and conscience as ours are. Who live such merry lives as the leviathan, who plays in the deep? or the birds that 'sing among the branches' (Ps. 104:12, 26)? But what are these to a man, who, being 'taught more than the beasts of the earth, and made wiser than the fowls of heaven' (Job 35:10, 11) and being dignified above the beasts, not so much by the powers of reason, as by a capacity for religion, is certainly designed for enjoyments of a more excellent nature – for spiritual and heavenly delights. When God made man, he left him not to the enjoyments of the wide world, with the other creatures, but inclosed for him a paradise, a garden of pleasure (so Eden signifies), where he should have delights proper for him; signified indeed by the pleasures of a garden, pleasant trees, and their fruits, but really the delights of a soul which was a ray of divine light, and a spark of divine fire, newly breathed into him from above, and on which God's image and likeness was imprinted. And we never recover our felicity, which we lost by our first parents indulging the appetite of the body, till we come to the due relish of those pleasures which man has in common with angels, and a due contempt of those which he has in common with the brutes.

The pleasures of wisdom's ways may, at second hand, affect the body, and be an advantage to that; hence it is said (Prov. 3:8) to be 'health to the navel, and marrow to the bones'; but its residence is in the 'hidden man of the heart' (1 Pet. 3:4), and its comforts 'delight the soul in the multitude of its thoughts' (Ps. 94:19). It is pleasant to the soul, and makes that like a watered garden. These are pleasures which a man, by the assistance of divine grace, may reason himself into, and not, as it is with sensual pleasures, reason himself out of.

There is no pleasure separate from that of religion, which pretends to be an intellectual pleasure, but that of learning, and that of honour; but as to the pleasure of a proud man in his dignities, and the respects paid him, as Herod, in the acclamations of the crowd. It doth but affect the fancy; it is vain-glory, it is not glory: it is but the folly of him that receives the honour, fed by the folly of them that give it; so that it doth not deserve to be called a rational pleasure; it is a lust of the mind that is gratified by it, which is as much an instance of our degeneracy, as any of the lusts of the flesh are. And as to the pleasure of a scholar, abstracted from religion, it is indeed rational and intellectual; but it is only the pleasure of the mind in knowing truth, and not in its enjoying good. Solomon, that had as much of this pleasure as ever any man had, and as nice a taste of it, yet hath assured us from his own experience, that in much wisdom of this kind is much grief, and 'he that increaseth knowledge increaseth sorrow' (Ecc. 1:18). But the pleasures which a holy soul hath in knowing God, and in communion with him, are not only of a spiritual nature, but they are satisfying; they are filling to the soul, and make a happiness adequate to its best affections.

3. It is remaining, and not flashy and transitory. That is true pleasure, and deserves the name, which will continue with us as a tree of life, and not wither as the green herb; which will not be as the light of a candle, which is soon burnt out, but as that of the sun, which is a faithful witness in heaven. We reckon that most valuable, which is most durable.

The pleasures of the sense are fading and

perishing. As 'the world passeth away' (1 John 2:17), so do the lusts of it: that which at first pleaseth and satisfieth, after a while palls and surfeits. 'As the crackling of thorns under a pot' (Ecc. 7:6), which make a great blaze, and a great noise for a little while, but soon end in soot and ashes, such is the laughter of the fool; the end of his mirth is heaviness. Belshazzar's jollity is soon turned into the utmost consternation; 'the night of my pleasure hath he turned into fear to me' (Isa. 21:4). The pleasures of sin are said to be but 'for a season' (Heb. 11:25) for the 'end of that mirth is heaviness'. As they have no consistence, so they have no continuance. But the pleasures of religion will abide, they wither not in winter, nor tarnish with time, nor doth age wrinkle their beauty; frosts nip them not, nor do storms blast them; they continue through the greatest opposition of events, and despise that time and change, which 'happens to all things under the sun' (Ecc. 9:1). Believers, when they are sorrowful, they are but as sorrowful, for they are 'always rejoicing' (2 Cor. 6:10) and 'Thanks be to God, who always causeth us to triumph' (2 Cor. 2:14). If an immortal soul makes an eternal God its chief joy, what should hinder but that it should 'rejoice for evermore (1 Thess. 5:16) for as the treasure, so the pleasure is laid up there, where 'neither moth nor rust can corrupt, nor thieves break through and steal'. Christ's joy which he gives to those that are his, is joy which 'no man taketh from them' (John 16:22) for it is their heart that rejoiceth. They are the beginning of everlasting pleasures, the earnest and foretaste of them; so that they are, in effect, pleasures for evermore. So then, the great truth which I desire my heart and yours may be fully convinced of, is this: that a holy heavenly life spent in the service of God, and in communion with him, is, without doubt, the most pleasant and comfortable life any man can live in this world.

CHAPTER 2

The pleasure of being religious, proved from the nature of true religion, and many particular instances of it.

The doctrine needs no further explication, nor can have any better than our own experience of it; but the chief part of this undertaking is to prove the truth of it: and O! that God, by me, would set it before you in a true light, so as that you may be all convinced of it, and embrace it as a faithful saying, and well worthy of all acceptation, that a godly life is a pleasant life; so as that we may be wrought upon to live such a life!

Pleasure is a tempting thing: what yields delight, cannot but attract desire; it is next to necessity, so strongly doth it urge. Surely, if we were but fully persuaded of this, that religion hath pleasure on its side, we would be wrought upon by the allurement of that to be religious. It is certainly so, let us not be in doubt of it. Here is a bait that has no hook under it, a pleasure courting you which has no pain attending it, no bitterness at the latter end of it; a pleasure which God himself invites you to, and which will make you happy, truly and eternally happy: and shall not this work upon you?

But we may entertain ourselves and our hearers long enough with discourses of the pleasantness of wisdom's ways, but they will not profit, unless they be mixed with faith. O that we would all mix faith with this truth! that we would yield to the evidence of it!

To make way for the proof of it, I would only desire two things:

1. That you would lay aside prejudice, and give a fair and impartial hearing to this cause, and do not prejudge it. 'He that answers any matter before he hear it, (hear it out), it is folly and shame to him' (Prov. 18:13), especially if it be a matter of great importance and concern to himself; a matter of life and death. Be willing, therefore, to believe, that it is possible there may be, and then I doubt not but to make out, that it is certain there is, true pleasure in true religion.

You have got a notion, it may be, and are confirmed in it by the common cry of the multitude, that religion is a sour melancholy thing, that it is to bid farewell to all pleasure and delight, and to spend your days in grief and your years in sighing: and if we offer anything to the contrary, that it is a pleasant thing, and the best entertainment that can be to the mind, you are ready to say, as Ezekiel's hearers did of him, 'Doth he not speak parables?' (Ezek. 20:49) doth he not speak paradoxes? You startle at it, and start from it as a hard saying, like Nathaniel, when he said, 'Can any good thing come out of Nazareth?' (John 1:46). So you are ready to say, can there be any pleasure in religion? Believe it, sirs, there can be, there cannot but be, pleasure in it.

Do not measure religion by the follies of some that profess it, but do not live up to their profession, nor adorn it: let them bear their own burden, or clear themselves as they can; but you are to judge of things, not persons, and therefore ought not to be prejudiced against religion for their sakes. Nor should you measure it by the ill opinions which its adversaries have of it, or the ill name which they endeavour to put upon it, who neither know it, nor love it, and therefore care not what unjust things they say to justify themselves in the contempt of it, and to hinder others from embracing it but think freely of this matter.

2. That you would admit this as a principle, and abide by it, that the soul is the man: this is the *postulatum* I lay down, in order to the proof of the doctrine; and I hope it will be readily granted me, that man is principally to be considered as an intellectual, immortal being, endued with spiritual powers and capacities, allied to the world of spirits; that there is a spirit in man that has sensations and dispositions of its own, active and receptive faculties distinct from those of the body: and that this is the part of us which we are and ought to be most concerned about; because it is really well or ill with us, according as it is well or ill with our souls.

Believe that, in man's present state, the soul and the body have separate and contesting interests; the body thinks it is its interest to have its appetites gratified, and to be indulged in its pleasures; while the soul knows it is its interest to have the appetites of the body subdued and mortified, that spiritual pleasures may be the better relished: and we are here upon our trial, which of these two we will side with. Be wise, therefore, be resolute, and show yourselves men that are acted and governed by reason, and are affected with things as reason represents them to you not reason, as it is in mere natural man, clouded and plunged, and lost in sense; but reason elevated and guided by divine revelation to us, and divine grace in us. Walk by faith, and not by sense: let the God that made you, and knows you, and wisheth you well, and from whom your judgment must proceed, determine your sentiments in this matter, and the work is done.

Now I shall in the first place, endeavour the proof of this doctrine, by showing you what religion is; wherein it consists; and what those things are which constitute serious godliness: and then you shall yourselves judge whether it be not in its own nature pleasant. If you understand religion aright, you will find that it has an innate sweetness in it, inseparable from it. Let it but speak for itself, and it will recommend itself. The very showing of this beauty in its own features and proportions, is enough to bring us all in love with it.

You shall see the pleasure of religion in twelve instances of it.

First, To be religious, is 'to know the only true God, and Jesus Christ whom he hath sent' (John 17:3). And is not that pleasant? This is the first thing we have to do, to get our understandings rightly informed concerning both the object and the medium of our religious regards, to seek and to receive this light from heaven, to have it diffused through our souls as the morning-light in the air, and to be turned to the impression of it, 'as the clay to the seal' (Job 38:14) and this is a pleasure to the soul that understands itself, and its own true interest. 'Truly the light is sweet, and a pleasant thing it is for the eyes to behold the sun' (Ecc. 11:7); 'it rejoiceth the heart' (Prov. 15:30). Hence light is often put for joy and comfort: but no light is comparable to that of 'the knowledge of the glory of God in the face of Jesus Christ' (2 Cor. 4:6).

This is finding the knowledge we had lost, and must for ever have despaired in finding, if God had not made it known to us by his Spirit: it is finding the knowledge we are undone without, and happy, for ever happy in; for what is heaven but this knowledge in perfection? It is finding the knowledge which the soul would covet and rest in, if it had but recovered itself from the *delirium*, which by the fall it is thrown into. They that sit in darkness, when they begin to be religious, begin to see a great light (Matt. 4:16): and it is a pleasing surprise to them; it is coming into a new world; such a pleasure as none could know so well, as he that had his sight given him though he was born blind. 'Blessed are your eyes,' saith Christ to those whom he had brought into an acquaintance with himself, 'for they see.' 'Apply thy heart to my knowledge,' saith Solomon (Prov. 22:17, 18), 'for it is a pleasant thing if thou keep it within thee.' 'Thou wilt eat honey because it is good' (Prov. 24:13, 14), 'and the honeycomb which is sweet to the taste; so shall the knowledge of wisdom be to thy soul.' Could a learned man, that had hit upon a demonstration in mathematics, cry out in a transport of joy, 'I have found, I have found!' and may not they much more boast of the discovery, that have found the knowledge of the Most High?

There is no pleasure in any learning like that of learning Christ, and the things that belong to our everlasting peace; for that which is known is not small and trivial, is not doubtful and uncertain, is not foreign to us, and which we are not concerned in; which are things that may much diminish the pleasure of any knowledge; but it is great and sure, and of the last importance to us, and the knowledge of it gives us satisfaction: here we may rest our souls. To know the perfections of the divine nature, the unsearchable riches of divine grace, to be led into the mystery of our redemption and reconciliation by Christ, this is food; such knowledge as this is a feast to the soul; it is meat indeed, and drink indeed; it is the knowledge of that which the angels desire to look into (1 Pet. 1:12). If the knowledge of the law of God was so sweet to David, 'sweeter than honey to his taste' (Pss. 19:10; 119:103), how much more so should the knowledge of the gospel of Christ be to us? When God gives this wisdom and knowledge, with it he gives joy to him that is good in his sight (Ecc. 3:26).

I wonder what pleasure or satisfaction those can have in themselves, that are ignorant of God, and Christ, and another world, though they are told there is such a knowledge to be had, and there are those that have it, and it is their continual entertainment.

But thus do men stand in their own light, when they love darkness rather than light.

Secondly, To be religious, is to return to God, and repose in him as the rest of our souls; and is not that pleasant? It is not only for our understandings to embrace the knowledge of him, but our affections to fasten upon the enjoyment of him: it is to love God as our chief good, and to rest in that love; to 'love him with all our heart, and soul, and mind, and might', who is well worthy of all that love, and infinitely more; amiable in himself, gracious to us; who will accept our love, and return it; who hath promised to love those that love him (Prov. 8:17). The love of God reigning in the soul (and that is true religion) is as much a satisfaction to the soul, as the love of the world is a vexation to it, when it comes to be reflected upon, and is found to be so ill bestowed.

How pleasant must it needs be, so far to recover ourselves as to quit the world for a portion and happiness, as utterly insufficient to be so, and to depend upon him to be so, who has enough in himself to answer our utmost expectations? when we have in vain sought for satisfaction where it is not to be had, to seek it and find it where it is? to come from doating upon lying vanities, and 'spending our money for that which is not bread' (Isa. 55:2), to live, and live plentifully upon a God that is enough, a God all-sufficient, and in him to enjoy our own mercies? Did ever any thing speak a mind more easy and better pleased than that of David, 'return unto thy rest, O my soul' (Ps. 116:7)? return to God as thy rest, for in him I am where I would be, in him I have what I

would have: or that (Ps. 16:2, 5, 6), 'O my soul, thou
hast said unto the Lord, thou art my Lord, the portion
of my inheritance, and of my cup'? And then, 'the
lines are fallen to me in pleasant places, and I have
a goodly heritage'? or that (Ps. 73:25), 'Whom have
I in heaven but thee, and there is none upon earth that
I desire in comparison of thee; for when flesh and
heart fail, thou art the strength and joy of my heart,
and my portion for ever'?

We place not religion in raptures and transports;
but without doubt, holy souls that are at home in
God, that have 'made the Most High their habita-
tion' (Ps. 91:9), whose desires are towards him,
whose delights are in him, who are in him as their
centre and element, dwell at ease. None can imagine
the pleasure that a believer has in his covenant-
relation to God, and interest in him, and the assurance of his love: have I taken thy testimonies to be
'my heritage for ever'? (Ps. 119:111) surely they are
the rejoicing of my heart; I cannot be better provided
for. When King Asa brought his people to renew
their covenant with God, it is said, 'they sware unto
the Lord with a loud voice, and with shoutings, and
with trumpets' (2 Chr. 15:14, 15). And all Judah
'rejoiced at the oath, for they had sworn with all their
heart'. When we come to make it our own act and
deed, to 'join ourselves to the Lord in an everlasting
covenant', and are upright with him in it, we cannot
but be pleased with what we have done; it is a
marriage-covenant, it is made with joy (Cant. 2:16),
'My beloved is mine, and I am his'.

Thirdly, To be religious, is to come to God as a

Father, in and by Jesus Christ as Mediator. And is not this pleasant? We have not only the pleasure of knowing and loving God, but the pleasure of drawing nigh to him, and having by faith an humble freedom and intimacy with him (Ps. 65:4), 'Blessed are they that dwell in his courts, they shall be satisfied with the goodness of his house, even of his holy temple'. Religion is described by coming to God; and what can be more agreeable to a soul that comes from him? It is to come to God as a child to his father, to his father's house, to his father's arms, and to cry, Abba, Father. To come as a petitioner to his prince, is a privilege; but to come as a child to his father, is a pleasure: and this pleasure have all the saints, that have received the Spirit of adoption. They can look up to the God that made them, as one that loves them, and has a tender compassion for them, 'as a father has for his children' (Ps. 103:13), and delights to do them good, taking pleasure in their prosperity; as one who, though they have offended, yet is reconciled to them, owns them as his children, and encourages them to call him Father. When he afflicts them, they know it is in love, and for their benefit, and that still it is 'their Father's good pleasure to give them the kingdom' (Luke 12:32). When Ephraim bemoaned himself 'as a bullock unaccustomed to the yoke', God bemoaned him 'as a dear son, as a pleasant child' (Jer. 31:18, 20). And if even prodigals, when penitents, become pleasant children to God, surely they have no reason to be unpleasant to themselves.

But this is not all; it is not only to come to God as

a Father, who 'himself loves us' (John 16:27), but it
is to come to him in the name of Jesus Christ who is
our advocate with the Father; that by these two
immutable things we might have strong consolation,
that we have not only a God to go to, but an advocate
to introduce us to him, and to speak for us. Believing
in Christ is sometimes expressed by rejoicing in
him; for it is a complacency of soul in the methods
which infinite wisdom has taken of bringing God
and man together by a mediator. 'We are the circum-
cision that rejoice in Christ Jesus' (Phil. 3:3), not
only rely upon him, but triumph in him. Paul is not
only not ashamed of the cross of Christ, but he
'glories in it' (Gal. 6:14). And when the eunuch is
brought to 'believe in Christ with all his heart, he
goes on his way rejoicing', highly pleased with what
he has done.

What a pleasure, what a satisfaction is it, to lodge
the great concerns of our souls and eternity (which,
surely, we cannot but have some careful thoughts
about) in such a skilful, faithful hand as that of our
Lord Jesus? And this we do by faith. To cast the
burden upon him who is able to save to the uttermost,
and as willing as he is able, and thus to make
ourselves easy, what a privilege! How is blessed
Paul elevated at the thought of this, 'Who is he that
condemneth? It is Christ that died, yea, rather is risen
again' (Rom. 8:34). And with what pleasure doth he
reflect upon the confidence he had put in Jesus
Christ? (2 Tim. 1:12) 'I know whom I have believed,
and am persuaded that he is able to keep that which
I have committed to him against that day'. They that

know what it is to be in pain for sin, and in care to obtain the favour of God, cannot but know what a pleasure it is to believe in Christ as the propitiation for our sins, and our intercessor with God. How can we live a more pleasant life than to 'live by the faith of the Son of God?' (Gal. 2:20); to be continually depending on him, and deriving from him, and referring all to him; and as we have received him, so to walk in him? It is in believing, that we are 'filled with joy and peace' (Rom. 15:13).

Fourthly, To be religious, is to enjoy God in all our creature-comforts; and is not that pleasant? It is to take the common supports and conveniences of life, be they of the richest, or be they of the meanest, as the products of his providential care concerning us, and the gifts of his bounty to us, and in them to 'taste and see that the Lord is good' (Ps. 34:8), good to all, good to us. It is to look above second causes to the first, through the creature to the Creator, and to say concerning every thing that is agreeable and serviceable to us, this I asked, and this I have from the hand of my heavenly Father. What a noble taste and relish doth this put into all the blessings with which we are daily loaded, our health and ease, our rest and sleep, our food and raiment; all the satisfaction we have in our religions, peace in our dwellings, success in our callings! The sweetness of these is more than doubled, it is highly raised, when by our religion we are taught and enabled to see them all coming to us from the goodness of God, as our great benefactor, and thus to enjoy them richly (1 Tim. 6:17), while those who look no further than the creature, enjoy them very poorly, and but as the inferior creatures do.

Carnal irreligious people, though they take a greater liberty in the use of the delights of sense than good people dare take, and therein think they have the advantage of them, yet I am confident they have not half the true delight in them that good people have; not only because all excesses are a force upon nature, and surfeits are as painful as hunger and thirst, but because, though they do not thus abuse God's good creatures, yet they deprive themselves of the comfort of receiving them from their Father's hand, because they are not affected to him as obedient children. 'They knew not that I gave them corn, and wine, and oil' (Hos. 2:8). They make use of the creature, but, as in Isaiah 22:11, 'they have not looked unto the Maker thereof, nor had respect to him that fashioned it long ago', as good people do, and so they come short of the pleasure which good people have.

Is it not pleasant to taste covenant-love in common mercies? Very pleasant to see the hand of our heavenly Father spreading our table, filling our cup, making our houses safe, and our beds easy? This they do that by faith have their eyes ever towards the Lord, that by prayer fetch in his blessing upon all their enjoyments, and by praise give the glory of them to that mercy of his which endureth for ever. And when thus a continual regard is had to that mercy, an abundant sweetness is thereby infused into all the comforts of this life; for as the wrath and curse of God is the wormwood and the gall (Lam.

3:19) in all the afflictions and miseries of this life; so his loving-kindness is the honey and oil in all the comforts and enjoyments of this life: that is it that is 'better than life' (Ps. 63:3, 5) and which is abundantly satisfying: which puts gladness into the heart beyond the joy of harvest (Ps. 4:6, 7). Then the nations are glad, and sing for joy, when not only the earth yields her increase, but with it God, even 'their own God, gives them his blessings' (Ps. 67:5, 6). And when the church is brought to such a sense of God's grace, as to cry out, 'How great is his goodness, and how great is his beauty?' (Zech. 9:17), it follows, that then corn shall make the young men cheerful; intimating that we have no joy of our enjoyments, no true joy of them, till we are led by these streams to the fountain. 'To the pure, all things are pure' (Titus 1:14) and the more pure they are, the more pleasant they are.

Fifthly, To be religious, is to cast all our cares upon God, and to commit all our ways and works to him, with an assurance that he will care for us. And is not this pleasant? It is a very sensible pleasure to be eased of some pressing burden which we are ready to sink under; and care is such a burden: it is a heaviness in the heart of man which maketh it to stoop. Now true religion enables us to 'acknowledge God in all our ways' (Prov. 3:6) and then depend upon him to direct our steps, and follow his directions, not 'leaning to our own understanding'. It is to refer ourselves, and the disposal of everything that concerns us in this world, to God, and to his will and wisdom, with an entire acquiescence in his award and arbitration: 'Here I am, let the Lord do with me as seemeth good in his eyes' (2 Sam. 15:26).

To be truly godly, is to have our wills melted into the will of God in every thing, and to say amen to it, not only as a prayer, but as a covenant; 'Father in heaven, thy will be done'; 'not as I will, but as thou wilt'. It is to be fully reconciled to all the disposals of the divine providence, and all the methods of divine grace, both concerning others and ourselves; to be satisfied that all is well that God doth, and that it will appear so at last, when the mystery of God shall be finished. And how doth the mind enjoy itself that is come to this! How easy is it! It is not only freed from racking anxieties, but filled with pleasing prospects: fears are hereby silenced, and hopes kept up and elevated. Nothing can come amiss to those who have thus been taught by the principles of their religion to make the best of that which is, because it is the will of God; which is making a virtue of necessity.

What uncomfortable lives do they live, that are continually fretting at that which cannot be helped, quarrelling with the disposals of providence, when they cannot alter them; and thus by contracting guilt as well as by indulging grief, doubling every burden! But how pleasantly do they travel through the wilderness of this world, that constantly follow the pillar of cloud and fire, and accommodate themselves to their lot, whatever it is! that, like Paul, through Christ strengthening them, have learned 'in every state to be content; know how to want, and how to abound' (Phil. 4:11, 12, 13).

THE NATURE OF TRUE RELIGION

Religion brings the mind to the condition, whatever it is, and so makes it easy, because the condition, though it be not in every thing to our mind, is according to God's mind, who in all occurrences 'performeth the thing that is appointed for us' (Job 23:14) and will make 'all things work together for good to them that love him'. When the Psalmist had directed us to 'delight ourselves always in the Lord' (Ps. 37:4, 5), that is, to make our religion a constant pleasure to ourselves, he directs us in order thereunto, to commit our way unto the Lord, to trust also in him that he will bring it to pass, so as that we shall have the desire of our hearts. And when St. Paul had encouraged us to be 'careful for nothing, but in every thing to make our requests known to God', he assures us, that if we do so, 'the peace of God, which passeth all understanding, shall keep our hearts and minds' (Phil. 4:6, 7).

Sixthly, To be religious, is to 'rejoice in the Lord always' (Phil. 3:1; 4:4). And is not that pleasant? It is not only one of the privileges of our religion that we may rejoice, but it is made one of the duties of it: we are defective in our religion, if we do not live a life of complacency in God, in his being, his attributes, and relations to us. It should be a constant pleasure to us, to think that there is a God; that he is such a one as the scripture has revealed him to be, and being infinitely wise and powerful, holy, just, and good; that this God governs the world, and gives law to all creatures; that he is our owner and ruler; that in his hand our breath is; in his hand our times, our hearts, and all our ways are. Thus certainly it is, and thus it must be: and happy they that can please themselves with these thoughts; as those must needs be a constant terror to themselves, who could wish it were otherwise.

They who thus delight in God have always something, and something very commanding too, to delight in; a fountain of joy that can never be either exhausted or stopped up, and to which they may always have access. How few are there that 'live many days, and rejoice in them all' (Ecc. 11:8). Such a thing is supposed indeed, but it is never found true in any but those that make God their joy, the gladness of their joy, as the Psalmist expresseth it (Ps. 43:4), their exceeding joy: and in him it is intended our joy should terminate, when we are bid to 'rejoice evermore' (1 Thess. 5:16).

The conversion of the nations to Christ, and his holy religion, is often prophesied of in the Old Testament, under the notion of their being brought into a state of holy joy (Pss. 96:11; 97:1; 100:1). 'The Lord reigneth, let the earth rejoice, and let the multitude of isles be glad thereof.' 'Rejoice ye Gentiles with his people' (Rom. 15:10). The gospel is 'glad tidings of great joy to all people' (Luke 2:10). When Samaria received the gospel, 'there was great joy in that city' (Acts 8:8) so essential is joy to religion. And the conversation of those that are joined to the Lord, when it is as it should be, is cheerful and joyful: they are called upon to 'walk in the light of the Lord' (Ps. 138:5) and to 'sing in the ways of the Lord' (Isa. 2:5) and to 'serve the Lord their God with joyfulness and gladness of heart in the

abundance of all things' (Deut. 28:47), yea, and in
the want of all things too (Hab. 3:17). 'Though the
fig-tree do not blossom, and there be no fruit in the
vine.' Has God now accepted thee, and thy works in
Jesus Christ, 'go thy way, eat thy bread with joy, and
drink thy wine with a merry heart' (Ecc. 9:7). It is the
will of God that his people should be a cheerful
people, that his Israel should 'rejoice in every good
thing which the Lord their God giveth them' (Deut.
26:11), so that it is their own fault if they have not a
continual feast, and be not made to rejoice with the
outgoings of every morning and every evening; for
the compassions of that God, in whom they rejoice,
are not only constant, but new and fresh daily.

Seventhly, To be religious, is to make a business
of praising God: and is not that pleasant? It is indeed
very unpleasant and much against the grain, to be
obliged continually to praise one that is not worthy
of praise: but what can be more pleasant, than to
praise him to whom all praise is due, and ours
particularly? to whom we and all the creatures lie
under all possible obligations; who is worthy of, and
yet exalted far above all blessing and praise; from
whom all things are, and therefore to whom all
things ought to be? There is little pleasure in praising
one, whom none praise that are wise and good, but
only the fools in Israel: but in praising God we
concur with the blessed angels in heaven, and all the
saints, and do it in concert with them, who the more
they know him, the more they praise him. 'Bless the
Lord ye his angels, and all his hosts': and therefore
with what pleasure can I cast in my mite into such a

treasury! 'Bless the Lord, O my soul!'

There is little pleasure in praising one who will not regard our praises, nor take notice of our expressions of esteem and affection: but when we offer to God the sacrifice of praise continually, according to the obligation which our religion lays upon us, that is, the 'fruit of our lips, giving thanks to his name' (Heb. 13:15) we offer it to one that takes notice of it, accepts it, is well pleased with it, smells a savour of rest from it (Gen. 8:21) and will not fail to meet those with his mercies that follow him with their praises; for he hath said, that they that 'offer praise, glorify him'; such a favourable construction doth he put upon it, and such a high stamp upon coarse metal.

Now, what is it that we have to do in religion but to praise God? We are taken into covenant with God, that we should be to him for a name, and for a praise (Jer. 13:11) are called into his marvellous light, that we should 'show forth the praises of him that called us' (1 Pet. 2:9). And how can we be more comfortably employed? They are therefore 'blessed that dwell in God's house, for they will be still praising him' (Ps. 84:4). And it is a good thing, good in itself, and good for us; it is very pleasant 'to give thanks unto the Lord, and to show forth his praises' (Pss. 135:3; 92:1) for we cannot do ourselves a greater honour, or fetch in a greater satisfaction, than by 'giving unto the Lord the glory due unto his name': it is not only a heaven upon earth, but it is a pledge and earnest of a heaven in heaven too; for if we be here 'every day blessing God' (Ps. 145:2) we shall be praising him for ever and ever; for thus all that shall go to heaven hereafter, begin their heaven now. Compare the hellish pleasure which some take in profaning the name of God, and the heavenly pleasure which others take in glorifying it, and tell me which is preferable.

Eighthly, To be religious, is to have all our inordinate appetites corrected and regulated; and is not that pleasant? To be eased from pain is a sensible pleasure, and to be eased from that which is the disease and disorder of the mind, is a mental pleasure. Those certainly live a most unpleasant uncomfortable life, that are slaves to their appetites, and indulge themselves in the gratifications of sense, though never so criminal; that lay the reins on the neck of their lust, and withhold not their hearts from any joy. The drunkards and unclean, though they are said to give themselves to their pleasures, yet really they estrange themselves from that which is true pleasure, and subject themselves to a continual pain and uneasiness.

The carnal appetite is often overcharged, and that is a burden to the body, and its distemper: when enough is as good as a feast, I wonder what pleasure it can be to take more than enough; and the appetite, the more it is indulged, the more humoursome and troublesome it grows; it is surfeited, but not satisfied; it doth but grow more impetuous, and more imperious. It is true of the body, what Solomon says of a servant (Prov. 29:21), 'He that delicately bringeth up his servant from a child, shall have him become his son', nay, his master, at the length. If we suffer the body to get dominion over the soul, so that the

interests of the soul must be damaged to gratify the
inclinations of the body, it will be a tyrant, as an
usurper generally is, and will rule with rigour; and as
God said to the people (1 Sam. 8:18) when by
Samuel he had showed them the manner of the king
that they chose, when they rejected his government,
'You will cry out in the day because of your king
which ye have chosen you, and the Lord will not
hear': so it is with those that bring themselves into
disorders, diseases, and terrors by the indulgence of
their lusts; who can pity them? they are well enough
served for 'setting such a king over them' – Who
hath woe? who hath sorrow? (Prov. 23:29). None so
much as they that 'tarry long at the wine', though
they think to have the monopoly of pleasure. The
truth is, they that live in these pleasures are 'dead
while they live' (1 Tim. 5:6) and while they fancy
themselves to take the greatest liberty, really find
themselves in the greatest slavery; for they are 'led
captive by Satan at his will' (2 Tim. 2:26) and of
'whom a man is overcome, of the same is he brought
in bondage' (2 Pet. 2:19). And if the carnal appetite
have not gained such a complete possession, as quite
to extinguish all the remains of reason and conscience, those noble powers, since they are not
permitted to give law, will give disturbance; and
there are few that have so full an enjoyment of the
forbidden pleasures of sense, but that they sometimes feel the checks of reason, and the terrors of
conscience, which mar their mirth, as the handwrit-
ing on the wall did Belshazzar's, and make their
lives uncomfortable to them, and justly so, which

makes them the more unhappy. Now, to be religious, is to have the exorbitant power of those lusts and appetites broken; and since they will not be satisfied, to have them mortified, and brought into a quiet submission to the commanding faculties of the soul, according to the direction of the divine law; and this the peace is preserved, by supporting good order and government in the soul.

Those certainly live the most easy, healthful, pleasant lives, that are most sober, temperate, and chaste; that allow not themselves to eat of any forbidden tree, though pleasant to the eye; that live regularly, and are the masters, not the servants of their own bellies (1 Cor. 9:27) that 'keep under their bodies, and bring them into subjection' to religion and right reason; and by laying the axe to the root, and breaking vicious habits, dispositions, and desires, in the strength of divine grace, have made the refraining of vicious acts very easy and pleasant: (Rom. 8:13) 'If through the Spirit we mortify the deeds of the body', we live, we live pleasantly.

Ninthly, To be religious, is to have all our unruly passions likewise governed and subdued: and is not that pleasant? Much of our torment ariseth from our intemperate heats, discontent at the providence of God, fretfulness at every cross occurrence, fear of every imaginary evil, envy at those that are in a better state than ourselves, malice against those that have injured us, and an angry resentment of every the least provocation; these are thorns and briars in the soul, these spoil all our enjoyments, both of ourselves, and of our friends, and of our God too; these make men's lives unpleasant, and they a terror to themselves and to all about them. But when by the grace of God these roots of bitterness are plucked up, which bear so much gall and wormwood, and we have learned of our Master to be 'meek and lowly in heart' (Matt. 11:29) we find rest to our souls, we enter into the pleasant land. There is scarce any of the graces of a Christian, that have more of a present tranquillity and satisfaction, both inherent in them, and annexed to them, than this of meekness. 'The meek shall eat, and be satisfied' (Ps. 22:26), they shall 'inherit the earth' (Matt. 5:5), they shall 'delight themselves in the abundance of peace' (Ps. 37:11) and they shall 'increase their joy in the Lord' (Isa. 29:19) which nothing diminisheth more than ungoverned passion; for that grieves the Spirit of grace, the Comforter, and provokes him to withdraw (Eph. 4:30, 31).

How pleasant is it for a man to be master of his own thoughts, to have a calmness and serenity in his own mind, as those have, that have rule over their own spirits, and thereby are kept in peace! That will break an angry man's heart, that will not break a meek man's sleep.

Tenthly, To be religious, is to dwell in love to all our brethren, and to do all the good we can in this world: and is not that pleasant? 'Love is the fulfilling of the law' (Rom. 13:10); it is the second great commandment to 'love our neighbour as ourselves'. All our duty is summed up in one word, which as it is a short word, so it is a sweet word, *love*. Behold 'how good and how pleasant it is to live in holy love' (Ps. 133:1); it is not only pleasing to God, and amiable in the eyes of all good men, but it will be very comfortable to ourselves: for they that 'dwell in love, dwell in God, and God in them' (1 John 4:16).

Religion teacheth us to be easy to our relations, and to please them well in all things; neither to give nor resent provocations, to bear with their infirmities, to be courteous and obliging to all with whom we converse; to keep our temper, and the possession and enjoyment of our own souls, whatever affronts are given us: and can any thing contribute more to our living pleasantly?

By love we enjoy our friends, and have communion with them in all their comforts, and so add to our own; 'rejoicing with them that do rejoice' (1 Thess. 3:9). By love we recommend ourselves to their love, and what more delightful than to love, and be beloved? Love is the very element of a pure and sanctified mind, the sweet air it breathes in, the cement of the best society, which contributes so much to the pleasure of human life. The sheep of Christ united in flocks by the bond of holy love, lie down together in the green pastures by the still waters, where there is not only plenty, but pleasure. The apostle exhorting his friends to 'be of good comfort' (2 Cor. 13:11) and to go on cheerfully in their Christian course, exhorts them, in order to that, to be of one mind, and to live in peace, and then 'the God of love and peace will be with them'.

And what pleasure is comparable to that of doing good? It is some participation of the pleasure of the eternal mind, who delights to show mercy, and to do good: nay, besides the divinity of this pleasure, there

is a humanity in it; the nature of man, if it be not
debauched and vitiated, cannot but take pleasure in
making others safe and easy. It was a pleasure to Job,
to think that he had 'caused the widow's heart to sing
for joy', had been 'eyes to the blind, and feet to the
lame, and a father to the poor', and that they had been
'warmed with the fleece of his sheep' (Job 29:13, 15,
16; 31:20). The pleasure that a good man hath in
doing good, confirms that saying of our Saviour's
that 'it is more blessed to give than to receive' (Acts
20:35).

Eleventhly, To be religious, is to live a life of
communion with God: and is not that pleasant?
Good Christians being taken into friendship, have
'fellowship with the Father, and with his Son Jesus
Christ' (1 John 1:3), and make it their business to
keep up that holy converse and correspondence.
Herein consists the life of religion, to converse with
God, to receive his communications of mercy and
grace to us, and to return pious and devout affections
to him; and can any life be more comfortable? Is
there any conversation that can possibly be so pleasant as this to a soul that knows itself, and its own
powers and interests?

In reading and meditating upon the word of God,
we hear God speaking to us with a great deal of
condescension to us, and concern for us, speaking
freely to us, as a man doth to his friend, and about our
own business; speaking comfortably to us in compassion to our distressful case; and what can be more
pleasant to those who have a value for the favour of
God, and are in care about the interests of their own

souls? 'When their judges are overthrown in stony places, they shall hear my words, for they are sweet' (Ps. 141:6): the words of God will be very sweet to those who see themselves overthrown by sin, and so they will be to all that love God. With what an air of pleasure doth the spouse say, 'It is the voice of my beloved', and he speaks to me! (Cant. 2:8, 10).

In prayer and praise we speak to God, and we have liberty of speech; have leave to 'utter all our words before the Lord' as Jephthah did his in Mizpeh (Judg. 11:11). We speak to one whose ear is open, is bowed to our prayers, nay, to whom the 'prayer of the upright is a delight' (Prov. 15:8) which cannot but make it very much a delight to them to pray. It is not only an ease to a burdened spirit to unbosom itself to such a friend as God is, but a pleasure to a soul that knows its own extraction, to have such a boldness, as all believers have, to enter into the holiest.

Nay, we may as truly have communion with God in providences as in ordinances, and in the duties of common conversation, as in religious exercises; and thus that pleasure may become a continual feast to our souls. What can be more pleasant, than to have a God to go to, whom we may acknowledge in all our ways, and whom our 'eyes are ever towards' (Ps. 25:15) to see all our comforts coming to us from his hand, and all our crosses too; to refer ourselves, and all events that are concerning us, to his disposal, with an assurance that he will order all of the best? What a pleasure it is to 'behold the beauty of the Lord' in all his works, and to taste the goodness of the Lord in all his gifts; in all our expectations to see every man's judgment proceeding from him; to make God our hope, and God our fear, and God our joy, and God our life, and God our all? This is to live a life of communion with God.

Twelfthly, To be religious, is to keep up a constant believing prospect of the glory to be revealed: It is to set eternal life before us as the mark we aim at, and the prize we run for, and to 'seek the things that are above' (Col. 3:1). And is not this pleasant? It is our duty to think much of heaven, to place our happiness in its joys, and thitherward to direct our aims and pursuits; and what subject, what object can be more pleasing! We have need sometimes to frighten ourselves from sin, with the terrors of eternal death; but it is much more a part of our religion, to encourage ourselves in our duty, with the hopes of that eternal life which God hath given us, that 'life which is in his Son' (1 John 5:11).

What is Christianity, but 'having our conversation in heaven' (Phil. 3:20), trading with the new Jerusalem, and keeping up a constant correspondence with that 'better country, that is, the heavenly', as the country we belong to, and are in expectation of, to which we remit our best effects and best affections; where our head and home is, and where we hope and long to be?

Then we are as we should be, when our minds are in a heavenly frame and temper; then we do as we should do, when we are employed in the heavenly work, as we are capable of doing it in this lower world; and is not our religion then a heaven upon earth? If there be a fulness of joy and pleasure in that glory and happiness which is grace and holiness perfected, there cannot but be an abundance of joy and pleasure in that grace and holiness, which is glory and happiness begun. If there will be such a complete satisfaction in vision and fruition, there cannot but be a great deal in faith and hope, so well founded as that of the saints is. Hence we are said, 'Believing to rejoice with joy unspeakable' (1 Pet. 1:8) and to be 'filled with joy and peace in believing' (Rom. 15:13).

It is the character of all God's people, that they are born from heaven, and bound for heaven, and have laid up their treasure in heaven; and they that know how great, how rich, how glorious, and how well secured that happiness is to all believers, cannot but own, that if that be their character, it cannot but be their unspeakable comfort and delight.

Now, lay all this together, and then tell me, whether religion be not a pleasant thing indeed, when even the duties of themselves are so much the delights of it: and whether we do not serve a good Master, who has thus made our work its own wages, and has graciously provided two heavens for those that never deserved one.

CHAPTER 3

The pleasantness of religion proved, from the provision that is made for the comfort of those that are religious, and the privileges they are entitled to.

We have already found by inquiry (O that we could all say we had found by experience!) that the very principles and practices of religion themselves have a great deal of pleasantness in them, the one half of which has not been told us; and yet the comfort that attends religion, and follows after it, cannot but exceed that which is inherent in it and comes with it. If the work of righteousness be peace, much more is the effect of righteousness so (Isa. 32:17), if the precepts of religion have such an air of sweetness in them, what then have the comforts of it? Behold, happy is the people, even in this world, whose God is the Lord!

We must conclude that they that walk in the ways of holy wisdom, have, or may have, true peace and pleasure; for God hath both taken care for their comfort, and given them cause to be comforted: so that if they do not live easily and pleasantly, it is their own fault.

First, The God whom they serve, hath, in general,

taken care for their comfort, and has done enough to convince them, that it is his will they should be comforted; that he not only gives them leave to be cheerful, but would have them to be so; for what could have been done more to the satisfaction of his family, than he has done for it?

1. There is a purchase made of peace and pleasure for them, so that they come to it fairly, and by a good title. He that purchased them a peculiar people to himself, took care they should be a pleasant people, that their comforts might be a credit to his cause, and the joy of his servants in his work might be a reputation to his family. We have not only 'peace with God through our Lord Jesus Christ' (Rom. 5:1-3) but peace in our own consciences too; not only peace above, but peace within; and nothing less will pacify an offended conscience, than that which satisfied an offended God. Yet this is not all: we have not only inward peace, but we 'rejoice in the hope of the glory of God', and triumph over, nay, we triumph in tribulation.

Think what a vast expense (if I may so say) God was at, of blood and treasure, to lay up for us, and secure to us, not only a future bliss, but present pleasure, and the felicities not only of our home, but of our way. Christ had trouble, that we might have peace – pain, that we might have pleasure – sorrow, that we might have joy. He wore the crown of thorns, that he might crown us with roses, and that lasting joy might be upon our heads. He put on the spirit of heaviness, that we might be arrayed with the garments of praise. The garden was the place of his agony, that it might be to us a garden of Eden; and there it was that he indented with his prosecutors for the disciples, upon his surrendering himself, saying in effect to all agonies, as he did to them, 'If ye seek me, let these go their way' (John 18:8) if I be resigned to trouble, let them depart in peace. This was that which made wisdom's ways pleasantness – the everlasting righteousness which Christ, by dying, wrought out, and brought in. This is the foundation of the treaty of peace, and consequently the fountain of all those consolations which believers are happy in. Then it is, that all the seed of Israel glory, when they can each of them say, 'in the Lord have I righteousness and strength' (Isa. 45:24, 25) and then Israel shall dwell safely, in a holy security, when they have learned to call Christ by his name, 'the Lord our righteousness' (Jer. 23:6). If Christ had not gone to the Father, as our High Priest, with the blood of sprinkling in his hand, we could never have rejoiced, but must have been always trembling.

Christ is our peace (Eph. 2:14, 17), not only as he made peace for us with God, but as he preached peace to them 'that were afar off, and to them that were nigh', and has engaged that his people, whenever they may have trouble in the world, shall have peace in him (John 16:33) upon the assurance of which they may be of good cheer, whatever happens.

It is observable, that in the close of that ordinance which Christ instituted, in the night wherein he was betrayed, to be a memorial of his sufferings, he both sang a hymn of joy, and preached a sermon of comfort; to intimate, that that which he designed in dying for us, was to give us 'everlasting consolation, and good hope through grace' (2 Thess. 2:16), and this we should aim at, in all our commemorations of his death. Peace and comfort are bought and paid for; therefore if any of those who were designed to have the benefit of this purchase, deprive themselves of it, let them bear the blame, but let him have the praise who intended them the kindness, and who will take care, that though his kindness be deferred, it shall not be defeated; for though his disciples may be sorrowful for a time, 'their sorrow shall be turned into joy' (John 16:20).

2. There are promises made to believers of peace and pleasure: the benefits Christ bought for them are conveyed to them, and settled upon them, in the covenant of grace; which is well-ordered in all things (2 Sam. 23:5), for the comfort and satisfaction of those, who have made that covenant 'all their salvation and all their desire'. There it is that light is sown for the righteous, and it will come up again in due time; the promises of that covenant are the wells of salvation, out of which they draw water with joy – the breasts of consolation, out of which, by faith, they suck and are satisfied (Isa. 12:3; 66:11).

The promises of the Old Testament that point at gospel-times, speak mostly of this as the blessing reserved for those times, that there should be great joy and rejoicing (Isa. 35:1; 60:1), 'the desert shall rejoice, and blossom as the rose; arise, shine, for thy light is come'; for the design of the gospel was to make religion a more pleasant thing than it had formerly been, by freeing it both from the burdensome services which the Jews were under, and from the superstitious fears with which the heathen kept themselves and one another in awe; and by enlarging the privileges of God's people, and making them easier to come at.

Every particular believer is interested in the promises made to the church, and may put them in suit, and fetch in the comfort contained in them, as every citizen has the benefit of the charter, even the meanest. What a pleasure may one take in applying such a promise as that, 'I will never leave thee nor forsake thee?' Or that, 'all things shall work together for good to them that love God'? These, and such as these, guide our feet in the ways of peace; and as they are a firm foundation on which to build our hopes, so they are a full fountain from which to draw our joys. By the exceeding great and precious promises, we partake of a divine nature (2 Pet. 1:4), this consists, as well as in any thing else, in a comfortable enjoyment of ourselves; and by all the other promises that promise is fulfilled (Isa. 65:14, 15), 'My servant shall eat, but ye shall be hungry; my servant shall drink, but ye shall be thirsty; my servant shall rejoice, but ye shall be ashamed; my servant shall sing for joy of heart, but ye shall cry for sorrow of heart': and the encouragement given to all the church's faithful friends is made good, 'rejoice ye with Jerusalem, and be glad with her all ye that love her' (Isa. 66:10)

3. There is provision made for the application of that which is purchased and promised to the saints. What will it avail that there is wine in the vessel, if

it be not drawn out? that there is a cordial made up, if it be not administered? Care is therefore taken, that the people of God be assisted in making use of the comforts treasured up for them in the everlasting covenant.

A religious life, one may well expect, should be a very comfortable life; for infinite wisdom has devised all the means that could conduce to make it so: 'what could have been done more for God's vineyard' (Isa. 5:4), to make it flourishing as well as fruitful, than what he has done in it? There is not only an overflowing fulness of oil in the good olive, but golden pipes, (as in the prophet's vision, Zech. 4:12) for the conveyance of that oil to the lamps, to keep them burning. When God would himself furnish a paradise for a beloved creature, there was nothing wanting that might contribute to the comfort of it; in it was planted 'every tree that was pleasant to the sight, and good for food' (Gen. 2:8, 9); so in the gospel there is a paradise planted for all the faithful offspring of the second Adam: a Canaan, a land flowing with milk and honey, a pleasant land, a rest for all the spiritual seed of Abraham. Now, as God put Adam into paradise and brought Israel into Canaan, so he has provided for the giving of possession to all believers, of all that comfort and pleasure that is laid up for them. As in the garden of Eden, innocency and pleasure were twisted together; so, in the gospel of Christ, 'mercy and truth have met together, righteousness and peace have kissed each other' (Ps. 85:10), and all is done that could be wished, in order to our entering into this rest, this blessed *sabbatism* (Heb. 4:3, 9). So that if we have not the benefit of it, we may thank ourselves: God would have comforted us, and we would not be comforted, our souls refused it.

Four things are done with this view, that those who live a godly life may live a comfortable pleasant life; and it is pity they should receive the grace of God herein in vain.

(1) The blessed Spirit is sent to be the Comforter: he doth also enlighten, convince, and sanctify, but he hath his name from this part of his office (John 14:16) he is *the Comforter*. As the Son of God was sent to be the consolation of Israel (Luke 2:25), to provide matter for comfort; so the Spirit of God was sent to be the Comforter, to apply the consolation which the Lord Jesus has provided. Christ came to make peace, and the Spirit to speak peace, and to make us to hear joy and gladness, even such as will cause broken bones themselves to rejoice (Ps. 51:8). Christ having wrought out the salvation for us, the work of the Spirit is to give us the comfort of it; hence the joy of the saints is said to be 'the joy of the Holy Ghost' (1 Thess. 1:6) because it is his office to administer such comforts as tend to the filling us with joy.

God by his Spirit 'moving on the face of the waters', made the world according to the word of his power; and by his Spirit moving on the souls of his people, even when they are a perfect chaos, he 'creates the fruit of the lips, peace' (Isa. 57:19), the product of the word of his promise: if he did not create it, it would never be; and we must not only attend to the word of God speaking to us, but submit to the Spirit of God working upon us with the word.

The Spirit, as a comforter, was given not only for the relief of the saints in the suffering ages of the church, but to continue with the church always to the end, for the comfort of believers, in reference to their constant sorrows both temporal and spiritual; and what a favour is this to the church; no less needful, no less advantageous than the sending of the Son of God to save us, and for which, therefore, we should be no less thankful. Let this article never be left out of our songs of praise, but let us always give thanks to him, who not only sent his Son to make satisfaction for us, for 'his mercy endureth for ever', but sent his Spirit to give satisfaction for us, for 'his grace faileth never'; sent his Spirit not only to work in us the disposition of children towards him, but also to witness to our adoption, and seal us to the day of redemption.

The Spirit is given to be our teacher, and to lead us into all truth, and as such he is a comforter; for by rectifying our mistakes, and setting things in a true light, he silenceth our doubts and fears, and sets things in a pleasant light. The Spirit is our remembrancer, to put us in mind of that which we do know, and as such he is a comforter; for, like the disciples, we distrust Christ in every exigence, because we 'forget the miracles of the loaves' (Matt. 16:9). The Spirit is our sanctifier: by him sin is mortified, and grace wrought and strengthened, and as such he is our comforter; for nothing tends so much to make us easy as that which tends to make us holy. The Spirit is our guide, and we are said to be led by the Spirit, and as such he is our comforter; for under his conduct we cannot but be led into ways of pleasantness, to the green pastures, and still waters.

(2) The scriptures are written 'that our joy may be full' (1 John 1:4) that we may have that joy which alone is filling, and hath that in it which will fill up the vacancies of other joys, and make up their deficiencies; and that we may be full of that joy, may have more and more of it, may be wholly taken up with it, and may come, at length, to the full perfection of it in the kingdom of glory: these things are written to you, not only that you may receive the word with joy at first, when it is a new thing to you, but that your joy may be full and constant. The word of God is the mainpipe by which comfort is conveyed from Christ, the fountain of life, to all the saints. That book which the Lamb that was slain took out of the 'right hand of him that sat on the throne', is that which we are by faith to feed upon and digest, and fill our souls with; and we shall find that it will, like Ezekiel's roll (Ezek. 3:3), 'be in our mouths as honey for sweetness', and the opening of its seals will 'put a new song into our mouth' (Rev. 5:9).

Scripture light is pleasant, much more sweet, more pleasant, than for the eyes to behold the sun: the manner of its conveyance is such as makes it abundantly more so, for God speaks to us after the manner of men, in our own language. The comforts which the scripture speaks to us are the sure mercies of David, such as we may depend upon; and it is continually speaking. The scriptures we may have always with us, and whenever we will, we may have recourse to them; so that we need not be to seek for cordials at any time. The 'word is nigh thee' (Rom. 10:8); in thy house, and in thy hand; and it is thy own fault if it be not in thy mouth, and in thy heart. Nor is it a spring shut up or a fountain sealed; those that compare spiritual things with spiritual, will find the scripture its own interpreter; and spiritual pleasure to flow from it as easily, and plentifully, to all that have spiritual senses exercised, as the honey from the comb. All the saints have found pleasure in the word of God, and those who have given up themselves to be led and ruled by it. It was such a comfort to David in his distress, he should have 'perished in his affliction' (Ps. 119:92); nay, he had the joy of God's word to be his continual entertainment (Ps. 119:54). 'Thy statutes have been my songs in the house of my pilgrimage': thy words were found, saith Jeremiah, and I did eat them, yea did feast upon them with as much pleasure as ever any hungry man did upon his necessary food, or epicure upon his dainties: I perfectly regaled myself with them; and 'thy word was unto me the joy and rejoicing of my heart' (Jer. 15:16): and we not only come short of their experiences, but frustrate God's gracious intentions, if we do not find pleasure in the word of God: for 'whatsoever things were written aforetime, were written for our learning, that we, through patience and comfort of the scriptures, might have hope' (Rom. 15:4).

(3) Holy ordinances were instituted for the furtherance of our comfort, and to make our religion

pleasant unto us. The conversation of friends with each other is reckoned one of the greatest delights of this world; now ordinances are instituted for the keeping up of our communion with God, which is the greatest delight of the soul that is allied to the other world. God appointed to the Jewish church a great many feasts in the year (and but one fast, and that but for one day) on purpose for this end, that they might 'rejoice before the Lord their God', they and their families (Deut. 16:11).

Prayer is an ordinance of God, appointed for the fetching in of that peace and pleasure which is provided for us. It is intended to be not only the ease of our hearts, by casting our burden upon God, as it was to Hannah (1 Sam. 1:18), who, when she had prayed, 'went her way, and did eat, and her countenance was no more sad'; but the joy of our hearts, by putting the promises in suit, and improving our acquaintance with heaven; 'ask, and ye shall receive, that your joy may be full' (John 16:24). There is a throne of grace erected for us to come to; a Mediator of grace appointed, in whose name to come; the Spirit of grace given to help our infirmities, and an answer of peace promised to every prayer of faith: and all this that we might fetch in not only sanctifying, but comforting grace, 'in every time of need' (Heb. 4:16). God's house, in which wisdom's children dwell, is called a house of prayer; and thither God brings them, on purpose to 'make them joyful' (Isa. 56:7).

Singing of psalms is a gospel ordinance, designed to contribute to the pleasantness of our religion;

designed not only to express, but to excite, and increase our holy joy: in singing to the Lord, we make a joyful noise to the rock of our salvation (Ps. 45:2). When the apostle had warned all Christians to take heed of drunkenness, 'be not drunk with wine, wherein is excess', lest they should think, that thereby he restrained them from any mirth that would do them good, he directs them, instead of the song of the drunkard, when the heart is merry with wine, to entertain themselves with the songs of angels: 'Speaking to yourselves (when you are disposed to please yourselves) in psalms, and hymns, and spiritual songs, singing and making melody in your hearts to the Lord' (Eph. 5:18, 19). There is no more of substance in this ordinance, than the word and prayer put together, but the circumstance of the voice and tune being a natural means of affecting our hearts, both with the one and with the other, God in condescension to our state, hath been pleased to make a particular ordinance of it, to show how much it is his will that we should be cheerful, 'Is any merry? let him sing psalms' (Jas. 5:13). Is any vainly merry? let him suppress the vanity, and turn the mirth into a right channel: he need not banish, or abjure the mirth, but let it be holy heavenly mirth, and in that mirth let them sing psalms. Nay, is any afflicted, and merry in his affliction, let him show it by singing psalms, as Paul and Silas did in the stocks (Acts 16:25).

The Lord's day is appointed to be a pleasant day, a day of holy rest, nay, and a day of holy joy; a thanksgiving day (Ps. 118:24), 'this is the day which

the Lord hath made, we will rejoice, and be glad in
it'. The psalm and song for the sabbath-day begins
thus, 'it is a good thing to give thanks to the Lord'
(Ps. 92:1). So far were the primitive Christians
carried in this notion, that the Lord's day was designed for holy triumph and exultation, that they
thought it improper to kneel in any act of worship on
that day.

The Lord's Supper is a spiritual feast; and a feast
(Solomon saith, Ecc. 10:19) is 'made for laughter',
and so was this for holy joy: we celebrate the
memorials of his death, that we may rejoice in the
victories that he obtained, and the purchases he
made by his death; and may apply to ourselves the
privileges and comforts, which by the covenant of
grace are made ours. There we cannot but be glad
and rejoice in him, where we 'remember his love
more than wine' (Cant. 1:4).

(4) The ministry is appointed for the comfort of
the saints; and their guides in the ways of wisdom are
instructed, by all means possible, to make them ways
of pleasantness, and to encourage them to go on
pleasantly in those ways. The priests of old were
ordained for men (Heb. 3:1, 2) and were therefore
taken from among men, that they might have compassion upon the mourners. And the prophets had
this particularly in their commission, 'comfort ye,
comfort ye my people, saith your God, speak ye
comfortably to Jerusalem' (Isa. 40:1).

Gospel-ministers, in a special manner, are
appointed to be the helpers of the joy of the Lord's
people; to be Barnabases, sons of consolation, to

strengthen the weak hand, and the feeble knees, and
to say to them who are of a fearful heart, be strong
(Isa. 35:3, 4). The tabernacles of the Lord of hosts
being amiable, the care of all that serve in those
tabernacles, must be to make them appear so; that
they who compass the altars of God, may find him
their exceeding joy. Thus hath God taken care for the
comfort of his people, so that he is not to be blamed
if they be not comforted; but that is not all:

Secondly, There are many particular benefits and
privileges which they are entitled to, who walk in the
ways of religion, that contribute very much to the
pleasantness of those ways. By the blood of Christ
those benefits and privileges are procured for them,
which speaks them highly valuable; and by the
covenant of grace they are secured to them, which
speaks them unalienable.

1. Those that walk in wisdom's ways are dis-
charged from the debts of sin, and that is pleasant;
they are privileged from arrests (Rom. 8:33), 'Who
shall lay any thing to their charge?' while it is God
that justifies them, and will stand by his own act,
against hell and earth: and he is always near that
justifies them (Isa. 50:8). And so is their advocate
that pleads for them nearer than their accuser, though
he stands at the right hand to resist them; and able to
cast him out, and all his accusations.

Surely, they put a force upon themselves, that are
merry and pleasant under the guilt of sin, for if
conscience be awake, it cannot but have a 'fearful
looking for of wrath'; but if sin be done away, the
burden is removed, the wound is healed, and all is

well: 'son, be of good cheer' (Matt. 9:2): though sick
of a palsy, yet be cheerful, for thy sins are forgiven
thee; and therefore, not only they shall not hurt thee,
but God is reconciled to thee, and will do thee good.
Thou mayest enjoy the comforts of this life, and fear
no snare in them; mayest bear the crosses of this life,
and feel no sting in them; and mayest look forward
to another life without terror or amazement.

The pain which true penitents have experience
of, in their reflections upon their sins, makes the
pleasure and satisfaction they have in the assurance
of the pardon of them doubly sweet; as the sorrow of
a woman in travail is not an allay, but rather a foil to
the joy, that a child is born into the world. No pain
more acute than that of broken bones, to which the
sorrows of a penitent sinner are compared; but when
they are well set, and well knit again, they are not
only made easy, but they are made to rejoice, to
which the comforts of a pardoned sinner are compared. 'Make me to hear joy and gladness, that the
bones which thou hast broken may rejoice' (Ps.
51:8). All our bones, when kept, that not one of them
is broken, must say, Lord, who is like unto thee? but
there is a more sensible joy for one displaced bone
reduced, than for the multitude of the bones that
were never hurt; as for one lost sheep brought home,
than for ninety and nine that went not astray: such is
the pleasure which they have, that know their sins
are pardoned.

When God's prophets must speak comfortably to
Jerusalem, they must tell her 'that her iniquity is
pardoned' (Isa. 40:2). Such a pleasure there is in the

sense of the forgiveness of sins, that it enables us to make a light matter of temporal afflictions, particularly that of sickness (Isa. 33:24), 'The inhabitant shall not say, I am sick, for the people that dwell therein shall be forgiven their iniquity'; and to make a great matter of temporal mercies, when they are thus sweetened and secured, particularly that of recovery from sickness (Isa. 38:17), 'thou hast in love to my soul, cured my body, and delivered it from the pit of corruption, for thou hast cast all my sins behind my back.' If our sins be pardoned, and we know it, we may go out and come in, in peace; nothing can come amiss to us; we may lie down and rise up with pleasure, for, all is clear between us and heaven; thus 'blessed is the man whose iniquity is forgiven'.

2. They have 'the Spirit of God witnessing with their spirits, that they are the children of God' (Rom. 8:16), and that is pleasant. Adoption accompanies justification, and if we have an assurance of the 'forgiveness of our sins according to the riches of God's grace' (Eph. 1:5, 7) we have an assurance of this further comfort, that we were predestinated unto the adoption of children by Jesus Christ. The same evidence, the same testimony that is given of our being pardoned, serves as an evidence and testimony of our being preferred, our being thus preferred. Can the children of princes and great men please themselves with the thoughts of the honours and expectations that attend that relation, and may not the children of God think with pleasure of the adoption they have received (Gal. 4:6), the Spirit of adoption?

and that Spirit is witness to their adoption: and the pleasure must be the greater, and make the stronger impression of joy, when they remember that they were by nature not only strangers and foreigners, but children of wrath, and yet thus highly favoured.

The comfort of relations is none of the least of the delights of this life; but what comfort of relations comparable to this of being related to God as our Father, and to Christ as our elder Brother, and to all the saints and angels, too, as belonging to the same family which we are happily brought into relation to; the pleasure of claiming and owning this relation is plainly intimated in our being taught to cry, 'Abba, Father' (Rom. 8:15); why should it be thus doubled, and in two languages, but to intimate to us the unaccountable pleasure and satisfaction with which good Christians call God Father? it is the strong they harp upon, 'Abba, Father'. With what pleasure doth David's own spirit witness to this; 'O my soul, thou hast said unto the Lord, Thou art my Lord' (Ps. 16:2) and it is more to me that God is mine, than if all the world were mine. But when with our spirits, the Spirit of God witnesseth this too, saying to thy soul, yea, he is thy God, and he owns thee as one of his family, witness what he has wrought both in thee, and for thee, by my hand; what joy doth this fill the soul with! joy unspeakable! especially considering that, as the prophet speaks in the place, in the same heart and conscience, where it was said (and by the Spirit too, when he convinced as a Spirit of bondage) ye are not my people, even there it shall be said unto them, by the Spirit, when he comforts as a Spirit of adoption, 'ye are the sons of the living God' (Hos. 1:10).

3. They have an access with boldness to the throne of grace, and that is pleasant. Prayer not only fetcheth in peace and pleasure, but it is itself a great privilege; and not only an honour, but a comfort, one of the greatest comforts of our lives, that we have a God to go to at all times, so that we need not fear coming unseasonably, or coming too often, and in all places, though as Jonah in the fish's belly, or as David in the depths, or in the ends of the earth (Pss. 130:1; 61:2).

It is a pleasure to one that is full of care and grief to unbosom himself; and we are welcome to pour out our complaint before God, and to show before him our trouble (Ps. 142:1, 2). It is a pleasure to one that wants, or fears wanting, to petition one that is able and willing to supply the wants; and we have great encouragement to make our requests known to God: we have an access with confidence (Eph. 3:12); not an access with difficulty, as we have to great men, nor an access with uncertainty of acceptance, as the Ninevites, 'who can tell if God will return to us'? But we have an access with an assurance that whatsoever we ask in faith, according to his will, 'we know that we have the petitions that we desired of him' (1 John 5:15).

It is a pleasure to talk to one we love, and that we know loves us, and though far above us, yet takes notice of what we say, and is tenderly concerned for us: what a pleasure is it then to speak to God! to have not only a liberty of access, but a liberty of speech, freedom to utter all our mind, humbly, and in faith; 'boldness to enter into the holiest by the blood of Jesus' (Heb. 10:19, 20) and not with fear and trembling, as the high priest under the law entered into the holiest; and boldness to pour out our hearts before God (Ps. 62:8) as one who, though he knows our case better than we ourselves, yet will give us the satisfaction of knowing it from us, according to our own showing. Beggars, that have good benefactors, live as pleasantly as any other people: it is the case of God's people; they are beggars, but they are beggars to a bountiful Benefactor, that is 'rich in mercy to all that call upon him': blessed are they that 'wait daily at the posts of wisdom's doors' (Prov. 8:34). If the prayer of the upright be God's delight, it cannot but be theirs (Cant. 2:14).

4. They have a sanctified use of all their creature-comforts, and that is pleasant. 'The Lord knows the ways of the righteous', and takes cognizance of all their concerns (Ps. 37:23). The steps, yea, and the stops too, 'of a good man are ordered by the Lord'; both his successes when he goes forwards, and his disappointments when he goes backwards; he blesseth the work of their hands; and his blessing makes rich, and adds no sorrow with it (Prov. 10:27); more is implied here than is expressed, it adds joy with it, infuseth a comfort into it.

What God's people have, be it little or much, they have it from the love of God, and with his blessing, and then behold all things are clean and sweet to them (Luke 10:41) they come from the hand of a Father, by the hand of a Mediator, not in the channel of common Providence, but by the golden pipes of the promises of the covenant. Even the unbelieving husband, though not sanctified himself, yet is sanctified by the believing wife (1 Cor. 7:14) and so is the comfort of other relations; for to those who please God, every thing is pleasing, or should be so, and is made so by his favour. And hence it is (Ps. 37:16) that a little that a righteous man has, having a heart to be content with it, and the divine skill of enjoying God in it, is better to him than the riches of many wicked are to them: and that a dinner of herbs where love is, and the fear of the Lord, is better, and yields abundantly more satisfaction, than a stalled ox, and hatred and trouble therewith (Prov. 15:16, 17).

5. They have the testimony of their own consciences for them in all conditions, and that is pleasant. A good conscience is not only a brazen wall, but a continual feast; and all the melody of Solomon's instruments of music of all sorts, were not to be compared with that of the bird in the bosom, when it sings sweet. If Paul has a 'conscience void of offence', though he be 'as sorrowful, yet he is always rejoicing'; nay, and even when he is pressed above measure (2 Cor. 1:8, 12), and has received a sentence of death within himself, his rejoicing is this, even the testimony of his conscience concerning his integrity.

As nothing is more painful and unpleasant, than to be smitten and reproached by our own hearts, to have our conscience fly in our faces, and give us our own; so there is nothing more comfortable, than to be upon good grounds reconciled to ourselves, to prove our own work (Gal. 6:4), by the touchstone of

God's word, and to find it right, for then have we 'rejoicing in ourselves alone, and not in another': for 'if our hearts condemn us not, then have we confidence towards God' (1 John 3:21), may lift up our face without spot unto him, and comfortably appeal to his omniscience: 'Thou, O Lord, knowest me, thou hast seen me, and tried my heart towards thee' (Jer. 12:3). This will not only make us easy under the censures and reproaches of men, as it did Job, 'my heart shall not reproach me', though you do; and Paul, 'it is a very small thing with me to be judged of man's judgment': but it will be a continual delight to us, to have our own hearts say, well done. For the voice of an enlightened, well-informed conscience, is the voice of God; it is his deputy in the soul: the thoughts of the sober heathen between themselves when they did not accuse, yet the utmost they could do was but to excuse, which is making the best of bad; but they who have their hearts 'sprinkled from an evil conscience' by the blood of Christ (Rom. 2:15) are not only excused, but encouraged and commended, for their praise is not of men, but of God.

It is easy to imagine the holy, humble pleasure that a good man has, in the just reflection upon the successful resistance of a strong and threatening temptation, the seasonable suppressing and crossing of an unruly appetite or passion; and a check given to the tongue, when it was about to speak unadvisedly. What a pleasure is it to look back upon any good word spoken, or any good work done, in the strength of God's grace, to his glory, and any way to the advantage of our brethren, either for soul or body! With what a sweet satisfaction may a good man lie down in the close of the Lord's day, if God has enabled him, in some good measure, to 'do the work of the day in the day, according as the duty of the day requires'! We may then eat our bread with joy, and drink our wine with a merry heart, when we have some good ground to hope, that God now accepteth our works through Jesus Christ (Ecc. 9:7).

6. They have the earnests and foretastes of eternal life and glory, and that is pleasant indeed. They have it not only secured to them, but dwelling in them, in the firstfruits of it, such as they are capable of in their present imperfect state (1 John 5:13). These things are written unto you that believe on the name of the Son of God, that ye may know, not only that you shall have, but that you have eternal life; you are sealed with that Holy Spirit of promise (Eph. 1:13, 14), marked for God, which is the earnest of our inheritance; not only a ratification of the grant, but part of the full payment. Canaan, when we come to it, will be a land flowing with milk and honey: in God's presence, there is a fulness of joy and pleasures for evermore (Ps. 16:11). But lest we should think it long ere we come to it, the God whom we serve has been pleased to send to us, as he did to Israel, some clusters of the grapes of that good land to meet us in the wilderness; which, if they were sent us in excuse of the full enjoyment, and we were to be put off with them, that would put a bitterness into them; but being sent us in earnest of the full enjoyment, that puts a sweetness into them, and makes them pleasant indeed.

A day in God's courts, and an hour at his table in communion with him, is very pleasant, better than a thousand days, than ten thousand hours, in any of the enjoyments of sense; but this very much increaseth the pleasantness of it, that it is the pledge of a blessed eternity, which we hope to spend within the vail, in the vision and fruition of God. Sabbaths are sweet, as they are earnests of the everlasting sabbatism, or keeping of a sabbath (as the apostle calls it, Heb. 4:9), which remains for the people of God. Gospel feasts are therefore sweet, because earnests of the everlasting feast, to which we shall sit down with Abraham, and Isaac, and Jacob. The joys of the Holy Ghost are sweet, as they are earnests of that joy of our Lord, into which all Christ's good and faithful servants shall enter. Praising God is sweet, as it is an earnest of that blessed state, in which we shall not rest day or night from praising God. The communion of saints is sweet, as it is an earnest of the pleasure we hope to have in the 'general assembly, and church of the firstborn' (Heb. 12:23).

They that travel wisdom's ways, though sometimes they find themselves walking in the low and darksome valley of the shadow of death, where they can see but a little way before them, yet at other times they are led with Moses to the top of mount Pisgah, and thence have a pleasant prospect of the land of promise, and the glories of that good land, not with such a damp upon the pleasure of it as Moses had (Deut. 34:4), 'Thou shalt see it with thine eyes, but thou shalt not go over thither'; but such an addition to the pleasure of it as Abraham had, when God said to him (Gen. 13:14, 15), 'All the land which thou seest, to thee will I give it'. Take the pleasure of the prospect, as a pledge of the possession shortly.

CHAPTER 4

The doctrine further proved by experience.

Having found religion in its own nature pleasant, and the comforts and privileges so with which it is attended, we shall next try to make this truth more evident, by appealing to such as may be thought competent witnesses in such a case. I confess, if we appeal to the natural man, the mere animal (as the word signifies, 1 Cor. 2:14) that looks no further than the things of sense, and 'receiveth not the things of the Spirit of God, for they are foolishness to him'; such a one will be so far from consenting to this truth, and concurring with it, that he will contradict and oppose it: our appeal must be to those that have some spiritual senses exercised, for otherwise 'the brutish man knows not, neither doth the fool understand this' (Ps. 92:6). We must therefore be allowed the testimony of convinced sinners, and comforted saints; wicked people whom the Spirit hath roused out of a sinful security, and godly people, whom the Spirit has put to rest in a holy serenity, are the most competent proper witnesses to give evidence in this case; and to their experience we appeal.

First, Ask those who have tried the ways of sin and wickedness, of vice and profaneness, and begin to pause a little, and to consider whether the way they are in be right, and let us hear what are their experiences concerning those ways; and our appeal to them is in the words of the apostle, 'What fruit had ye then in those things whereof ye are now ashamed?' (Rom. 6:21). Not only what fruit will ye have at last, when the end of these things is death; or, as Job 21:21, 'what pleasure hath he in his house after him, when the number of his months is cut off in the midst?' but what fruit, what pleasure had ye then, when you were in the enjoyment of the best of it?

Those that have been running to an excess of riot, that have laid the reins on the neck of their lusts, have rejoiced with the young man in his youth, and walked in the way of their hearts, and the sight of their eyes, have taken a boundless liberty in the gratifications of sense, and have made it their business to extract out of this world, whatever may pass under the name of pleasure: but when they begin to think (which they could not find in their hearts to do while they were going on in their pursuit), ask them now what they think of those pleasures which pretend to vie with those of religion, and they will tell you,

1. That the pleasure of sin was painful and unsatisfying in the enjoyment, and which then they had no reason to boast of. It was a sordid pleasure, and beneath the dignity of a man, and which could not be had, but by yielding up the throne in the soul to the inferior faculties of sense, and allowing them the

dominion over reason and conscience, which ought to command and give law. It was the gratifying of an appetite, which was the disease of the soul, and which would not be satisfied, but, like the daughters of the horse-leech, still cried, 'Give, give!'

What poor pleasure hath the covetous man in the wealth of the world! It is only the lust of the eye that is thereby humoured, for what good hath the owner thereof, save the beholding thereof with his eyes (1 John 2:16)? and what a poor satisfaction is that? and yet even that is no satisfaction either; for he that loveth silver will find, that the more he has the more he would have, so that he shall not be satisfied with silver; nay, it fastens upon the mind a burden of care and perplexity, so that the 'abundance of the rich will not suffer him to sleep' (Ecc. 5:10, 11, 12).

Drunkenness passeth for a pleasant sin, but it is a brutish pleasure, for it puts a force upon the powers of nature, disturbs the exercise of reason, and puts men out of the possession and enjoyment of their own souls; and so far is it from yielding any true satisfaction, that the gratifying of this base appetite is but bringing oil to a flame: 'when I awake, I will seek it yet again' is the language of the drunkard (Prov. 23:35).

Contention and revenge pretend to be pleasant sins too, *est vindicta bonum vita jucundius ipsa*; but it is so far from being so, that they are, of all other sins, the most vexatious: they kindle a fire in the soul, and put it into a hurry and disorder; where they are, there is confusion and every evil work. The lusts, from whence not only wars and fightings come

(Jas. 4:1) but other sins are said to war in the members; they not only 'war against the soul' (1 Pet. 2:11), and threaten the destruction of its true interests, but they war in the soul, and give disturbance to its present peace, and fill it with continual alarms.

They that have made themselves slaves to their lusts, will own, that it was the greatest drudgery in the world, and therefore is represented in the parable of the prodigal, by a young gentleman hiring himself to one that 'sent him into his field to feed swine' (Luke 15:15), where he was made a fellow-commoner with them, and 'would fain have filled his belly with the husks' that they did eat. Such a disgrace, such a dissatisfaction is there in the pleasures of sin, besides the diversity of masters which sinners are at the beck of, and their disagreement among themselves; for they that are disobedient to that God who is one, are deceived, serving divers lusts and pleasures, and therein led captive by Satan, their sworn enemy, 'at his will' (Titus 3:3).

2. That the pleasure of sin was very bitter and tormenting in the reflection. We will allow that there is a pleasure in sin 'for a season' (Heb. 11:25) but that season is soon over, and is succeeded by another season that is the reverse of it; the sweetness is soon gone, and leaves the bitterness behind in the bottom of the cup; the wine is red, and gives its colour, its flavour very agreeable, but at the last it 'bites like a serpent, and stings like an adder' (Prov. 23:32). Sin is that strange woman, whose flatteries are charming, but 'her end bitter as wormwood' (Prov. 5:3, 4).

When conscience is awake, and tells the sinner he

is verily guilty; when his sins are set in order before him in their true colour, and he sees himself defied and deformed by them; when his own wickedness begins to correct him, and his backslidings to reprove him, and his own heart makes him 'loathe himself for all his abominations' (Jer. 2:19), where is the pleasure of his sin then? As the thief is ashamed when he is discovered to the world, so are the drunkards, the unclean, when discovered to themselves; and say, Where shall I cause my shame to go? there is no remedy, but I must lie down in it. If the pleasure of any sin would last, surely that of ill-got gain would, because there is something to show for it; and yet though that wickedness be sweet in the sinner's mouth, though he 'hide it under his tongue, yet in his bowels it is turned into the gall of asps' (Job 20:11 etc.). He hath swallowed down riches, but shall be forced to vomit them up again.

Solomon had skimmed the cream of sensual delights, and pronounced not only vanity and vexation concerning them all, even the best, but concerning those of them that were sinful, the forbidden pleasures into which he was betrayed, that the reflection upon them filled him with horror and amazement: I applied my heart, saith he, 'to know the wickedness of folly, even of foolishness and madness'; so he now calls the licences he had taken: he cannot speak bad enough of them, for 'I find more bitter than death, the woman whose heart is snares and nets, and her hands as bands' (Ecc. 7:26). And is such pleasure as this worthy to come in competition with the pleasures of religion, or to be named the same day with them! What senseless creatures are the sensual, that will not be persuaded to quit the pleasures of brutes, when they shall have in exchange the delights of angels!

Secondly, Ask those that have tried the ways of wisdom, what are their experiences concerning those ways. 'Call now if there be any that will answer you, and to which of the saints will you turn?' (Job 5:1). Turn you to which you will, and they will agree to this, that 'wisdom's ways are pleasantness, and her paths peace'. However about some things they may differ in their sentiments, in this they are all of a mind, that God is a good master, and his service not only perfect freedom, but perfect pleasure.

And it is a debt which aged and experienced Christians owe both to their Master, and to their fellow-servants, both to Christ and Christians, to bear their testimony to this truth; and the more explicitly and solemnly they do it, the better: let them tell others what God has done for their souls, and how they have 'tasted that he is gracious' (Ps. 66:16). Let them own to the honour of God and religion, that, as in 1 Kings 8:56, there has not failed one word of God's good promise, by which he designed to make his servants pleasant; that what is said of the pleasantness of religion, is really so: let them 'set to their seal that it is true' (1 John 1:1). Let it have their *probatum est*; we have found it so.

The ways of religion and godliness are the good old ways (Jer. 6:16). Now, if you would have an account of the way you have to go, you must inquire of those that have travelled it, not those who have occasionally stepped into it now and then, but those whose business had led them to frequent it. Ask the ancient travellers, whether they have found rest to their souls in this way, and there are few you shall inquire of, but they will be ready to own these four things from experience:

1. That they have found the rules and dictates of religion very agreeable both to right reason, and to their true interest, and therefore pleasant. They have found the word nigh them, and accommodated to them, and not at such a mighty distance as they were made to believe. They have found all God's precepts concerning all things to be right and reasonable, and highly equitable; and when they did but show themselves men, they could not but consent, and subscribe to the law, that it was good (Rom. 7:16) and there is a wonderful decorum in it.

The laws of humility and meekness, sobriety and temperance, contentment and patience, love and charity; these are agreeable to ourselves when we are in our right mind: they are the rectitude of our nature, the advancement of our powers and faculties, the composure of our minds, and the comfort of our lives, and carry their own letters of commendation along with them. If a man understood himself, and his own interest, he would comport with these rules, and govern himself by them, though there were no authority over him to oblige him to it. All that have thoroughly tried them, will say they are so far from being chains of imprisonment to a man, and as fetters to his feet, that they are as chains of ornament to him, and as the girdle to his loins.

Ask experienced Christians, and they will tell you what abundance of comfort and satisfaction they have had in keeping sober, when they have been in temptation to excess; in doing justly, when they might have gained by dishonesty as others do, and nobody known it; in forgiving an injury, when it was in the power of their hand to revenge it; in giving alms to the poor, when perhaps they straitened themselves by it; in submitting to an affliction when the circumstances of it were very aggravating; and in bridling their passion under great provocations. With what comfort does Nehemiah reflect upon it, that though his predecessors in the government had abused their power, yet 'so did not I, (saith he, Neh. 5:15) because of the fear of God'? and with what pleasure doth Samuel make his appeal (1 Sam. 12:3), 'Whose ox have I taken, or whom have I defrauded?' and Paul his: 'I have coveted no man's silver, or gold, or apparel'. If you would have a register of experiences, to this purpose, read the 119th Psalm, which is a collection of David's testimonies to the sweetness and goodness of God's law, the equity and excellency of it, and the abundant satisfaction that is to be found in a constant conscientious conformity to it.

2. That they have found the exercise of devotion to be very pleasant and comfortable: and if there be a heaven upon earth, it is in communion with God in his ordinances; in hearing from him, and in speaking to him, in receiving the tokens of his favour, and communications of his grace, and returning pious affections to him, pouring out the heart before him, lifting up the soul to him. All good Christians will

subscribe to David's experience (Ps. 73:28), 'It is good for me to draw near to God'; the nearer the better; and it will be best of all, when I come to be nearest of all, within the vail, and will join with him in saying, 'Return unto thy rest, O my soul!' (Ps. 116:7) to God as to thy rest, and repose in him. I have found that satisfaction in communion with God, which I would not exchange for all the delights of the sons of men, and the peculiar treasures of kings and provinces.

What a pleasure did those pious Jews in Hezekiah's time find in the solemnities of the passover, who, when they had kept seven days according to the law in attending on God's ordinances, took counsel together to keep other seven days, 'and they kept other seven days with gladness' (2 Chr. 30:23). And if Christ's hearers had not found an abundant sweetness and satisfaction in attending on him, they would never have continued their attendance three days in a desert place, as we find they did (Matt. 15:32). No wonder then that his own disciples, when they were spectators of his transfiguration, and auditors of his discourse with Moses and Elias in the holy mount, said, 'Master, it is good for us to be here'; here let us 'make tabernacles' (Matt. 17:4). I appeal to all, that know what it is to be inward with God in an ordinance, to worship him in the Spirit, whether they have not found abundant satisfaction in it? They will say with the spouse (Cant. 2:3), 'I sat down under his shadow with great delight, and his fruit was sweet unto my taste'; and with the noble Marquis of Vico, 'Let their money perish with them, that esteem all the wealth and pleasure of this world worth one hour's communion with God in Jesus Christ'. They will own, that they never had that true delight and satisfaction in any of the employments or enjoyments of this world, which they have had in the service of God, and in the believing relishes of that loving-kindness of his which is 'better than life' (Ps. 63:3, 5). These have put gladness into their hearts, more than the joy of harvest, or theirs that divide the spoil. If in their preparations for solemn ordinances they have gone forth weeping, 'bearing precious seed', yet they have 'come again with rejoicing, bringing their sheaves with them' (Ps. 126:6).

3. That they have found the pleasure of religion sufficient to overcome the pains and trouble of sense, and to take out the sting of them, and take off the terror of them. This is a plain evidence of the excellency of spiritual pleasures, that religious convictions will soon conquer sensual delights, and quite extinguish them. So that they become as songs to a heavy heart, for 'a wounded spirit who can bear'? But it has often been found, that the pains of sense have not been able to extinguish spiritual delights, but have been conquered and quite over-balanced by them. Joy in spirit has been to many a powerful allay to trouble in the flesh.

The pleasure that holy souls have in God, as it needs not to be supported by the delights of sense, so it fears not being suppressed by the grievances of sense. They can rejoice in the Lord, and joy in him as the God of their salvation, even then, when the fig-tree doth not blossom, and there is no fruit in the vine (Hab. 3:17, 18) for even then, when in the world they have tribulation, Christ has provided that in him they should have satisfaction.

For this we may appeal to the martyrs and other sufferers for the name of Christ; how have their spiritual joys made their bonds for Christ easy, and made their prisons their delectable orchards, as one of the martyrs called his. Animated by these comforts, they have not only taken patiently, but 'taken joyfully, the spoiling of their goods, knowing in themselves that they have in heaven a better and a more enduring substance' (Heb. 10:34). Ask Paul, and he will tell you (2 Cor. 7:5, 6) even then when he was troubled on every side, when without were fightings, and within were fears, yet he was filled with comfort, and was exceeding joyful in all his tribulation; and that as his sufferings for Christ did increase, his consolation in Christ increased proportionably (2 Cor. 1:5). And though he expects no other but to finish his course with blood, yet he doubts not but to finish his course with joy. Nay, we may appeal to the sick-beds and deathbeds of many good Christians for the proof of this; when wearisome nights have been appointed to them, yet God's statutes have been their songs, their songs in the night (Ps. 119:54). 'I have pain,' said one, 'but I bless God I have peace'; 'weak and dying,' said another, 'but *sat lucis intus*, light and comfort enough within.' The delights of sense forsake us when we most need them to be a comfort to us; when a man is 'chastened with pain upon his bed, and the multitude of his bones with strong pain, he abhorreth bread and dainty meat', and cannot relish it (Job 33:19, 20). But then the bread of life and spiritual dainties have the sweetest relish of all. Many of God's people have found it so: 'this is my comfort in mine affliction, that thy word hath quickened me' (Ps. 119:50). This has made all their bed in their sickness, and made it easy.

The pleasantness of wisdom's ways hath sometimes been remarkably attested by the joys and triumphs of dying Christians, in reflecting upon that divine grace which hath carried them comfortably through this world, and is then carrying them more comfortably out of it to a better. 'What is that light which I see?' said an eminent divine on his deathbed. 'It is the sunshine,' said one that was by. 'No,' replied he, 'it is my Saviour's shine: O the joys! O the comforts that I feel! Whether in the body, or out of the body, I cannot tell: but I see and feel things that are unutterable, and full of glory. O let it be preached at my funeral, and tell it when I am dead and gone, that God deals familiarly with man! I am as full of comfort as my heart can hold.' Mr. Joseph Alleine's life, and Mr. John Janeway's, have remarkable instances of this.

4. They have found, that the closer they have kept to religion's ways, and the better progress they have made in those ways, the more pleasure they have found in them. By this it appears, that the pleasure takes its excellency from the religion; that the more religion prevails, the greater the pleasure is. What disquiet and discomfort wisdom's children have is

owing, not to wisdom's ways, those are pleasant, but to their deviations from those ways, or their slothfulness and trifling in these ways; those indeed are unpleasant, and sooner or later will be found so. If good people are sometimes drooping, and in sorrow, it is not because they are good, but because they are not so good as they should be; they do not live up to their profession and principles, but are too much in love with the body, and hanker too much after the world; though they do not turn back to Sodom, they look back towards it, and are too mindful of the country from which they came out; and this makes them uneasy, this forfeits their comforts, and grieves their Comforter, and disturbs their peace, which would have been firm to them, if they had been firm to their engagements. But if we turn aside out of the ways of God, we are not to think it strange, if the consolations of God do not follow us.

But if we cleave to the Lord with full purpose of heart, then we find the joy of the Lord our strength. Have we not found those duties most pleasant, in which we have taken most pains and most care? and that we have had the most comfortable sabbath-visits made to our souls then, when we have been most in the Spirit on the Lord's day? (Rev. 1:10). And the longer we continue, and the more we mend our pace in these ways, the more pleasure we find in them. This is the excellency of spiritual pleasures, and recommends them, greatly, that they increase with use, so far are they from withering, or going to decay. The difficulties which may at first be found in the ways of religion wear off by degrees, and the work of it grows more easy, and the joys of it more sweet. Ask those that have backslidden from the ways of God – have left their first love, and begin to bethink themselves, and to remember whence they are fallen – whether they had not a great deal more comfort when they kept close to God, than they have had since they turned aside from him; and they will say with that adulteress, when she found the way of her apostasy hedged up with thorns, 'I will go, and return to my first husband, for then it was better with me than now' (Hos. 2:7). There is nothing got by departing from God, and nothing lost by being faithful to him.

CHAPTER 5

The doctrine illustrated by the similitude used in the text, of a pleasant way or journey.

The practice of religion is often, in scripture, spoken of as a way, and our walking in that way. It is the way of God's commandments – it is a highway – the King's highway – the King of kings' highway; and those that are religious, are travelling in that way. The schoolmen commonly call Christians in this world, *viatores*, travellers; when they come to heaven, they are *comprehensores*, they have then attained, are at home; here, they are in their journey – there, at their journey's end. Now if heaven be the journey's end, the prize of our high calling, and we be sure, if we so run as we ought, that we shall obtain that, it is enough to engage and encourage us in our way, though it be never so unpleasant: but we are told that we have also a pleasant road. Now there are twelve things which help to make a journey pleasant, and there is something like to each of them which may be found in the way of wisdom, and those who walk in that way.

First, It helps to make a journey pleasant to go upon a good errand. He that is brought up a prisoner in the hands of the ministers of justice, whatever conveniences he may be accommodated with, cannot have a pleasant journey, but a melancholy one: and that is the case of a wicked man; he is going on, in this world, towards destruction; the way he is in, though wide and broad, leads directly to it; and while he persists in it, every step he takes is so much nearer hell, and therefore he cannot have a pleasant journey; it is absurd and indecent to pretend to make it so; though the way may seem right to a man, yet there can be no true pleasure in it, while the end thereof is the ways of death, and 'the steps take hold on hell' (Prov. 5:5). But he that goes into a far country to receive for himself a kingdom, whatever difficulties may attend his journey, yet the errand he goes on is enough to make it pleasant: And on this errand they go that travel wisdom's ways; they look for a kingdom which cannot be moved, and are pressing forwards in the hopes of it. Abraham went out of his own country, 'not knowing whither he went' (Heb. 11:8), but those that set out and hold on in the way of religion, know whither it will bring them, that it leads to life (Matt. 7:14), eternal life; and therefore in the way of righteousness is life (Prov. 12:28) because there is such a life at the end of it. Good people go upon a good errand, for they go on God's errand as well as on their own; they are serving and glorifying him, contributing something to his honour, and the advancement of the interests of his kingdom among men; and this makes it pleasant; and that which puts so great a reputation upon the duties of religion, as that by them God is served and glorified, cannot but put so much the more satisfac-

tion into them. With what pleasure doth Paul appeal
to God, as the God whom he served 'with his spirit
in the gospel of his Son' (Rom. 1:9)!

Secondly, It helps to make a journey pleasant, to
have strength and ability for it. He that is weak, and
sickly, and lame, can find no pleasure in the
pleasantest walks: how should he, when he takes
every step in pain? but a strong man rejoiceth to run
a race, while he that is feeble trembles to set one foot
before another. Now this makes the ways of religion
pleasant, that they who walk in those ways are not
only cured of their natural weakness, but are filled
with spiritual strength; they travel not in their own
might, but 'in the greatness of his strength', who is
'mighty to save' (Isa. 63:1). Were they to proceed in
their own strength, they would have little pleasure in
the journey, every little difficulty would foil them,
and they would tire presently; but they go forth, and
go on 'in the strength of the Lord God' (Ps. 71:16)
and upon every occasion, according to his promise,
he renews that strength to them, and they mount up
with wings like eagles, they go on with cheerfulness,
and alacrity – they run, and are not weary, they walk
and do not faint (Isa. 40:31). God, with his comforts,
enlargeth their hearts, and then they not only go, but
'run the way' of his commandments (Ps. 119:32).

That which to the old nature is impracticable and
unpleasant, and which therefore is declined, or gone
about with reluctancy, to the new nature is easy and
pleasant. And this new nature is given to all the
saints, which puts a new life and vigour into them,
strengthens them 'with all might in the inner man'

(Col. 1:11) unto all diligence in doing-work, patience in suffering-work, and perseverance in both; and so all is made pleasant. They are 'strong in the Lord, and in the power of his might' (Eph. 6:10): and this not only keeps the spirit willing, even then when the flesh is weak, but makes even 'the lame man to leap as an hart, and the tongue of the dumb to sing' (Isa. 35:6). 'I can do all things through Christ which strengtheneth me' (Phil. 4:13).

Thirdly, It helps to make a journey pleasant to have daylight. It is very uncomfortable travelling in the night, in the black and dark night; 'he that walketh in darkness,' saith our Saviour, 'knoweth not whither he goeth' (John 12:35) right or wrong, and that is uncomfortable; and in another place, 'if a man walk in the night he stumbleth, because there is no light in him' (John 11:10). And this is often spoken of as the miserable case of wicked people, 'they know not, neither will they understand, they walk on in darkness' (Ps. 82:5). They are in continual danger; and so much the more, if they be not in continual fear.

But wisdom's children are all 'children of the light, and children of the day' (1 Thess. 5:5). They 'were sometime darkness, but now are light in the Lord', and 'walk as children of the light' (Eph. 5:8). Truly the light is sweet, even to one that sits still, but much more so to one that is in a journey; and doubly sweet to those who set out in the dark, as we all did! But this great light is risen upon us, not only to please our eyes, but 'to guide our feet into the way of peace' (Luke 1:79). And then they are indeed paths of peace, when we are guided into them, and guided in them by the light of the gospel of Christ. And all that walk in the light of gospel-conduct, cannot fail to walk in the light of gospel-comforts. And it adds to the pleasure of having daylight in our travels, if we are in no danger of losing it, and of being benighted; and this is the case of those that walk in the light of the Lord; for the Sun of Righteousness that is risen upon them, with healing under his wings, shall no more go down, but shall be their 'everlasting light' (Isa. 60:20).

Fourthly, It helps to make a journey pleasant, to have a good guide, whose knowledge and faithfulness one can confide in. A traveller, though he has daylight, yet may miss his way, and lose himself, if he have not one to show him his way, and go before him, especially if his way lies as ours does through a wilderness where there are so many bypaths; and though he should not be guilty of any fatal mistake, yet he is in continual doubt and fear, which makes his journey uncomfortable. But this is both the safety and the satisfaction of all true Christians, that they have not only the gospel of Christ for their light – both a discovering and directing light – but the Spirit of Christ for their guide. It is promised, that he shall guide them into all truth (John 16:13), shall guide them with his eye (Ps. 32:8). Hence they are said to walk after the Spirit, and to be led by the Spirit (Rom. 8:1, 14) as God's Israel of old were led through the wilderness by a pillar of cloud and fire, and the Lord was in it.

This is that which makes the way of religion such

a high way as that 'the wayfaring men, though fools, shall not err therein' (Isa. 35:8). There are fools indeed, wicked ones, who walk after the flesh, that miss their way, and wander endlessly – 'The labour of the foolish wearieth every one of them, because he knoweth not how to go to the city' (Ecc. 10:15) – but those fools that shall not err therein, are weak ones, the foolish things of the world, who in a sense of their own folly, are so wise, as to give up themselves entirely to the conduct of the Spirit, both by conscience and the written word. And if they have done this in sincerity, they know whom they have depended upon to guide them by his counsel, and afterwards to receive them to his glory (Ps. 73:24). These may go on their journey pleasantly, who are promised, that whenever they are in doubt, or in danger of mistaking, or being misled, they shall hear a voice saying to them, 'this is the way, walk in it' (Isa. 30:21).

Fifthly, It helps to make a journey pleasant, to be under a good guard, or convoy, that one may travel safely. Our way lies through an enemy's country, and they are active, subtle enemies; the road is infested with robbers, that lie in wait to spoil, and to destroy; we travel by the lions' dens, and the mountains of the leopards; and our danger is the greater, that it ariseth not from flesh and blood, but spiritual wickednesses (1 Pet. 5:8). Satan, by the world and the flesh, waylays us, and seeks to devour us; so that we could not with any pleasure go on our way, if God himself had not taken us under his special protection. The same Spirit that is a guide to these travellers, is their guard also; for whoever are sanctified by the Holy Ghost, are by him 'preserved in Jesus Christ' (Jude 1), preserved blameless; and shall be preserved to the heavenly kingdom (2 Tim. 4:18), so as that they shall not be robbed of their graces and comforts, which are their evidences for, and earnests of eternal life – they are 'kept by the power of God, through faith unto salvation' (1 Pet. 1:5), and therefore may go on cheerfully.

The promises of God are a writ of protection to all Christ's good subjects in their travels, and give them such a holy security as lays a foundation for a constant serenity. Eternal truth itself hath assured them, that 'no evil shall befall them' (Ps. 91:10), nothing really and destructively evil; no evil but what God will bring good to them out of; God himself hath engaged to be their keeper, and to 'preserve their going out and coming in, from hence-forth and for ever', which looks as far forwards as eternity itself; and by such promises as these, and that grace which is conveyed through them to all active believers, God carries them as upon eagles' wings to bring them to himself (Deut. 32:11). Good angels are appointed for a guard to all that walk in wisdom's ways, to bear them in their arms, where they go (Ps. 91:11) and to pitch their tents round about them where they rest (Ps. 34:7) and so to keep them in all their ways. How easy may they be that are thus guarded, and how well pleased under all events! as Jacob was, who 'went on his way, and the angels of God met him' (Gen. 32:1).

Sixthly, It helps to make a journey pleasant, to

have the way tracked by those that have gone before
in the same road, and on the same errand. Untrodden
paths are unpleasant ones; but in the way of religion,
we are both directed and encouraged by the good
examples of those that have chosen the way of truth
before us, and have walked in it. We are bidden to
follow them, who are now 'through faith and patience'
(those travelling graces of a Christian) inheriting the
promises (Heb. 6:12). It is pleasant to think that we
are walking in the same way with Abraham, and
Isaac and Jacob, with whom we hope shortly to sit
down in the kingdom of God. How many holy, wise,
good men have governed themselves by the same
rules that we govern ourselves by, with the same
views – have lived by the same faith that we live by,
looking for the same blessed hope – and have by it
'obtained a good report' (Heb. 11:2). And we go
'forth by the footsteps of the flock' (Cant. 1:8). Let
us, therefore, to make our way easy and pleasant,
take the prophets for an example (Jas. 5:10). And
being 'compassed about with so great a cloud of
witnesses', like the cloud in the wilderness that went
before Israel, not only to show them the way, but to
smooth it for them – let us run with patience and
cheerfulness, 'the race that is set before us, looking
unto Jesus', the most encouraging pattern of all, who
has 'left us an example, that we should follow his
steps' (Heb. 12:1) and what more pleasant than to
follow such a leader, whose word of command is,
'Follow me!'.

Seventhly, It helps to make a journey pleasant, to
have good company: this deceives the time, and

takes off the tediousness of a journey as much as anything – *amicus pro vehiculo*. It is the comfort of those who walk in wisdom's ways, that though there are but few walking in those ways, yet there are some, and those the wisest and best, and more excellent than their neighbours; and it will be found there are more ready to say, 'we will go with you, for we have heard that God is with you' (Zech. 8:23).

The communion of saints contributes much to the pleasantness of wisdom's way; we have many fellow-travellers, that quicken one another, by the fellowship they have one with another, as 'companions in the kingdom and patience of Jesus Christ' (Rev. 1:9). It was a pleasure to them who were going up to Jerusalem to worship, that their numbers increased in every town they came to, and so they went 'from strength to strength' – they grew more and more numerous – 'till every one of them in Zion appeared before God' (Ps. 84:7), and so it is with God's spiritual Israel, to which we have the pleasure of seeing daily additions of such as shall be saved. They that travel together make one another pleasant by familiar converse; and it is the will of God that his people should by that means encourage one another, and strengthen one another's hands; 'they that fear the Lord, shall speak often one to another' (Mal. 3:16), exhort one another daily, and communicate their experiences; and it will add much to the pleasure of this, to consider the kind notice God is pleased to take of it; he hearkens, and hears, and a book of remembrance is written for those that fear the Lord, and think on his name.

Eighthly, It helps to make a journey pleasant, to have the way lie through 'green pastures', and by 'the still waters', and so the ways of wisdom do. David speaks his experience herein (Ps. 23:2) that he was led into the 'green pastures' the verdure whereof was grateful to the eye, and by 'the still waters', whose soft and gentle murmurs were music to the ear; and he was not driven through these, but made to lie down in the midst of these delights, as Israel when they encamped at Elim, where there were 'twelve wells of water, and threescore and ten palm-trees' (Exod. 15:27). Gospel ordinances, in which we deal much in our way to heaven, are very agreeable to all the children of God, as these 'green pastures', and 'still waters'; they call the sabbath a delight, and prayer a delight, and the word of God a delight. These are 'their pleasant things' (Isa. 64:11). There is a river of comfort in gospel ordinances, 'the streams whereof shall make glad the city of God, the holy place of the tabernacles of the most High' (Ps. 46:4), and along the banks of this river their road lies. Those that turn aside from the ways of God's commandments, are upbraided with the folly of it, as leaving a pleasant road for an unpleasant one. Will a man, a traveller, be such a fool as to leave my fields, which are smooth and even, for a rock that is rugged and dangerous, or for the snowy mountains of Lebanon (Jer. 18:14)? In the margin, 'Shall the running waters be forsaken for the strange cold waters?' Thus are men enemies to themselves, and 'the foolishness of man perverteth his way'.

Ninthly, It adds to the pleasure of a journey, to

have it fair over head. Wet and stormy weather takes off very much of the pleasure of a journey; but it is pleasant travelling when the sky is clear, and the air calm and serene; and this is the happiness of them that walk in wisdom's ways, that all is clear between them and heaven; there are no clouds of guilt to interpose between them and the Sun of Righteousness, and to intercept his refreshing beams – no storms of wrath gathering that threaten them. Our reconciliation to God, and acceptance with him, makes every thing pleasant. How can we be melancholy, if heaven smile upon us? 'Being justified by faith we have peace with God' (Rom. 5:1, 2) and peace from God – peace made for us, and peace spoken to us – and then we rejoice in tribulation. Those travellers cannot but rejoice all the day, who walk 'in the light of God's countenance' (Ps. 89:15).

Tenthly, It adds likewise to the pleasure of a journey, to be furnished with all needful accommodation for travelling. They that walk in the way of God, have wherewithal to bear their charges, and it is promised them that they shall 'not want any good thing' (Ps. 34:10). If they have not an abundance of the wealth of this world – which perhaps will but overload a traveller, and be an encumbrance, rather than any furtherance – yet they have good bills; having access by prayer to the throne of grace wherever they are, and a promise that they shall receive what they ask; and access by faith to the covenant of grace, which they may draw upon, and draw from as an inexhaustible treasury. '*Jehovah-jireh*, The Lord will provide'; Christ our Melchisedec brings forth bread and wine, as Genesis 14:18, for the refreshment of the poor travellers, that they may not 'faint by the way'. When Elijah had a long journey to go, he was victualled accordingly (1 Kgs. 19:8); God will give grace sufficient to his people for all their exercises (2 Cor. 12:9) – strength according to their day, 'verily they shall be fed'. And since travellers must have baiting-places, and resting-places, Christ has provided rest at noon (Cant. 1:7), in the heat of the day, for those that are his; and rest at night too: 'return to thy rest, O my soul'.

Eleventhly, It adds something to the pleasure of a journey to sing in the way: this takes off something of the fatigue of travelling, exhilarates the spirits; pilgrims used it; and God has put a song, a new song into the mouths of his people (Ps. 40:3) even praises to their God, and comfort to themselves. He hath given us cause to be cheerful, and leave to be cheerful, and hearts to be cheerful, and has made it our duty to rejoice in the Lord always. It is promised to those who are brought to praise God by hearing the words of his mouth, that 'they shall sing in the ways of the Lord' (Ps. 138:5) and good reason, 'for great is the glory of the Lord'. How pleasantly did the released captives return to their own country, when they 'came with singing unto Zion' (Isa. 51:11)! And much more Jehoshaphat's victorious army, when they 'came to Jerusalem, with psalteries, and harps, and trumpets, unto the house of the Lord'; 'for the Lord had made them to rejoice over their enemies' (2 Chr. 20:27, 28). With this the travellers may revive one another, 'O come, let us sing unto the Lord'!

Twelfthly, It helps to make a journey pleasant to have a good prospect. The travellers in wisdom's ways may look about them with pleasure, so as no travellers ever could; for they can call all about them their own, even 'the world, or life, or death, or things present, or things to come', in this state, all is yours if you be Christ's (1 Cor. 3:22). The whole creation is not only at peace with them, but at their service. They can look before them with pleasure – not with anxiety and uncertainty, but an humble assurance – not with terror, but joy. It is pleasant in a journey to have a prospect of the journey's end – to see that the way we are in leads directly to it, and to see that it cannot be far off; every step we take is so much nearer it, nay, and we are within a few steps of it; we have a prospect of being shortly with Christ in Paradise; yet a little while, and we shall be at home, we shall be at rest, and whatever difficulties we may meet with in our way, when we come to heaven all will be well – eternally well.

CHAPTER 6

The doctrine vindicated from what may objected against it.

'Suffer me a little,' saith Elihu to Job (36:2), 'and I will show thee that I have yet to speak on God's behalf' – something more to say in defence of this truth, against that which may seem to weaken the force of it. We all ought to concern ourselves for the vindication of godliness, and to speak what we can for it, for we know that it is every where spoken against; and there is no truth so plain, so evident, but there have been those that have objected against it; the prince of darkness will raise what mists he can to cloud a truth that stands so directly against his interest; but 'great is the truth, and will prevail'. Now as to the truth of the pleasantness of religion,

First, It is easy to confront the reproaches of the enemies of religion, that put it into an ill name. There are those who make it their business, having perverted their own ways, to pervert the right ways of the Lord, and cast an odium upon them, as Elymas the sorcerer did, with design 'to turn away the deputy from the faith' (Acts 13:8, 10). They are like the wicked spies, that brought up an evil report upon the promised land (Num. 13:32), as a land that did eat up the inhabitants thereof, and neither could be conquered, nor was worth conquering. The scoffers of the latter days speak ill of religion, as a task and a drudgery; they dress it up in frightful, formidable colours, but very false ones, to deter others from piety, and to justify themselves in their own impiety; they suggest that Christ's yoke is heavy, and his commandments grievous, and that to be religious is to bid adieu to all pleasure and delight, and to turn tormentors to ourselves; that God is 'a hard master, reaping where he has not sown, and gathering where he has not strewed' (Matt. 25:24). There were those of old that thus reproached the ways of God and slandered religion, for they said, 'It is vain to serve God' (Mal. 3:14) – there is neither credit nor comfort in it – 'and what profit is it that we have kept his ordinance, and (observe their invidious description of religion) that we have walked mournfully before the Lord of hosts'; as if to be religious was to walk mournfully, whereas indeed it is to walk cheerfully.

Now in answer to these calumnies we have this to say, that the matter is not so. They who say thus of religion, 'speak evil of the things that they understand not' (2 Pet. 2:12), while 'what they know naturally as brute beasts, in those things they corrupt themselves' (Jude 10). The devil we know was a liar from the beginning, and a false accuser of God and religion, and in this particular presented God to our first parents (Gen. 3:5), as having dealt hardly and unjustly with them, in tying them out from the tree of knowledge, as if he envied them the happiness and pleasure they would attain to by eating of that tree;

and the same method he still takes to alienate men's minds from the life of God, and the power of godliness. But we know, and are sure, that it is a groundless imputation, for 'wisdom's ways are ways of pleasantness, and all her paths are peace'.

Secondly, It is easy also to set aside the misrepresentations of religion which are made by some that call themselves its friends and profess kindness for it. As there are 'enemies of the Lord that blaspheme' (2 Sam. 12:14), so there are among the people of the Lord those that give them great occasion to do so, as David did. How many wounds doth religion receive in the house of her friends – false friends they are, or foolish ones, unworthy to be called wisdom's children, for they do not justify her as they ought, but through mistake and indulgence of their own weakness betray her cause instead of pleading it, and witnessing to it, and confirm people's prejudices against it, which they should endeavour to remove. Some that profess religion are morose and sour in their profession – peevish and ill-humoured – and make the exercises of religion a burthen, and task, and terror to themselves, and all about them, which ought to sweeten the spirit, and make it easy, and candid, and compassionate to the infirmities of the weak and feeble of the flock. Others are melancholy and sorrowful in their profession, and go mourning from day to day under prevailing doubts, and fears, and disquietments about their spiritual state. We know some of the best of God's servants have experienced trouble of mind to a great degree. But as to the former, it is their sin, and let them bear their own burthen, but let not religion be blamed for it; and as to the latter, though there are some very good people that are of a sorrowful spirit, yet we will abide by it, that true piety has true pleasure in it notwithstanding.

But, (1) God is sometimes pleased for wise and holy ends, for a time, to suspend the communication of his comforts to his people, and to hide his face from them, to try their faith, that it may be 'found unto praise, and honour, and glory, at the appearing of Christ' (1 Pet. 1:6, 7) and so much the more for their being a while 'in heaviness through manifold temptations'. Thus he corrects them for what has been done amiss by them, and takes this course to mortify what is amiss in them; even winter seasons contribute to the fruitfulness of the earth. Thus he brings them to a closer and more humble dependence upon Christ for all their comfort, and teacheth them to live entirely upon him. And though 'for a small moment he thus forsakes them' (Isa. 54:7) it is but to magnify his power so much the more in supporting them, and to make his returns the sweeter, for he will gather them 'with everlasting kindness'. Light is sown for them, and it will come up again.

(2) This, as it is their affliction, God's hand must be acknowledged in it – his righteous hand; yet there is sin in it, and that is from themselves. Good people have not the comforts they might have in their religion, and whose fault is it? They may thank themselves – they run themselves into the dark, and then shut their eyes against the light! 'My wounds stink and are corrupt,' saith David (Ps. 38:5) – the

wounds of sin which I gave myself are unhealed, not
bound up, or mollified with ointment. And why? Is
it for want of balm in Gilead, or a physician there?
no, he owns it is 'because of my foolishness'; I did
not take the right method with them. God speaks joy
and gladness to them, but they turn a deaf ear to it,
like Israel in Egypt, that 'hearkened not unto Moses
for anguish of spirit, and for cruel bondage' (Exod.
6:9). But let not the blame be laid upon religion,
which has provided comfort for their souls, but let
them bear the blame whose souls refuse to be comforted, or who do not take the way appointed for
comfort – who do not go through with their repenting
and believing. David owns the reason why he wanted
comfort, and was in pain, and in a toss, was because
he 'kept silence'; he was not so free with God as he
might and should have been; but when he said, 'I will
confess my transgression unto the Lord, he was
forgiven, and all was well (Ps. 32:3-5). Those do
both God and Christ, and themselves, and others, a
deal of wrong, who look upon him with whom they
have to do in religion, as one that seeks an occasion
against them, and counts them for his enemies, and
is extreme to mark what they think, or say, or do
amiss; whereas he is quite otherwise, is slow to
anger, swift to mercy, and willing to make the best
of those whose hearts are upright with him, though
they are compassed about with infirmity; he 'will not
always chide; he doth not delight in the death of them
that die, but would rather they should "turn and
live"' (Ezek. 33:11). Nor doth he delight in the tears
of them that weep – he 'doth not afflict willingly, nor

grieve the children of men' (Lam. 3:33), much less his own children, but would rather they should be upon good grounds comforted. Religion then clears itself from all blame, which some may take occasion to cast upon it from the uncomfortable lives which some lead that are religious.

But, Thirdly, It will require some more pains to reconcile this truth of the pleasantness of religion's ways, with that which the word of God itself tells us of the difficulties which the ways of religion are attended with. We value not the misapprehensions of some, and the misrepresentations of others, concerning religion's ways; but we are sure the word of God is of a piece with itself, and doth not contradict itself. Our Master hath taught us to call the way to heaven 'a narrow way', an afflicted way, a distressed way; and we have in scripture many things that speak it so. And it is true; but that doth not contradict this doctrine, that the ways of wisdom are pleasant; for the pleasantness that is in wisdom's ways, is intended to be a balance, and it is very much an overbalance to that in them which is any way distasteful or incommodious. As for the imaginary difficulties which the sluggard dreams of – 'a lion in the way' – 'a lion in the street' – we do not regard them; but there are some real difficulties in it, as well as real comforts, for 'God hath set the one over-against the other' (Ecc. 7:14), that we might study to comport with both, and might sing, and sing unto God of both (Ps. 101:1).

We will not, we dare not make the matter better than it is, but will allow there is that in religion which at first view may seem unpleasant; and yet doubt not but to show that it is reconcilable to, and consistent with all that pleasure which we maintain to be in religion, and so to take off all exceptions against this doctrine. *Amicae Scripturarum lites, utinam et nostrae!* It were well if we could agree with one another, as well as scripture doth with itself.

There are four things which seem not well to consist with this doctrine, and yet it is certain they do.

First, It is true, that to be religious, is to live a life of repentance, and yet religion's ways are pleasant notwithstanding. It is true, we must mourn for sin daily, and reflect with regret upon our manifold infirmities: sin must be bitter to us, and we must even loathe and abhor ourselves for our corruptions that dwell in us, and the many actual transgressions that are committed by us. We must renew our repentance daily, and every night must make some sorrowful reflections upon the transgressions of the day. But then,

1. It is not our walking in the way of wisdom that creates us this sorrow, but our trifling in that way, and our turning aside out of it. If we would keep close to these ways, and press forwards in them as we ought, there would be no occasion for repentance. If we were as we should be, we should be always praising God, and rejoicing in him; but we make other work for ourselves by our own folly, and then complain that religion is unpleasant; and whose fault is that? If we would be always loving and delighting in God, and would live a life of communion with

him, we should have no occasion to repent of that;
but if we leave 'the fountain of living water', and
turn aside to 'broken cisterns', or the brooks in
summer, and see cause – as doubtless we shall – to
repent of that, we may thank ourselves. What there
is of bitterness in repentance, is owing not to our
religion; and it proves not that there is bitterness in
the ways of God, but in the ways of sin, which make
a penitential sorrow necessary for the preventing of
a sorrow a thousand times worse; for sooner or later
sin will have sorrow. If repentance be bitter, we must
not say, this comes of being godly, but this comes of
being sinful: 'This is thy wickedness, because it is
bitter' (Jer. 4:18). If by sin we have made sorrow
necessary, it is certainly better to mourn now, than
'to mourn at the last' (Prov. 5:11). To continue
impenitent, is not to put away sorrow from thy heart,
but to put it off to a worse place.

2. Even in repentance, if it be right, there is a true
pleasure – a pleasure accompanying it. Our Saviour
hath said to them who thus mourn, not only that they
shall be *comforted*, but that they are *blessed* (Matt.
5:4). When a man is conscious to himself that he has
done an ill thing, and what is unbecoming him, and
may be hurtful to him, it is incident to him to repent
of it: now religion hath found a way to put a sweetness
into that bitterness. Repentance, when it is from
under the influence of religion, is nothing but
bitterness and horror, as Judas' was; but repentance,
as it is made an act of religion – as it is one of the laws
of Christ – is pleasant, as it is the raising of the spirit,
and the discharging of that which is noxious and

offensive. Our religion has not only taken care that penitents be not overwhelmed with an excess of sorrow (2 Cor. 2:7) and swallowed up by it – that their sorrow doth not work death, as the sorrow of the world doth – but it has provided, that even this bitter cup should be sweetened; and therefore we find that under the law, the sacrifices for sin were commonly attended with expressions of joy, and that while the priests were sprinkling the blood of the sacrifices 'to make atonement' (2 Chr. 29:24, 25), the Levites attended with psalteries and harps, for so was the commandment of the Lord by his prophets. Even the day to afflict the soul is the day of atonement; and when we receive the atonement, we joy in 'God through our Lord Jesus Christ' (Rom. 5:1). In giving consent to the atonement, we take the comfort of the atonement. In sorrowing for the death of some dear friend or relation, thus far we have found a pleasure in it, that it hath given vent to our grief of which our spirits were full; so in sorrow for sin, the shedding of just tears is some satisfaction to us. If it is a pleasure to be angry, when a man thinks with Jonah, he doth well to be angry, much more it is a pleasure to be sorry, when a man is sure he doth well to be sorry. The same word in Hebrew signifies both to comfort and to repent, because there is comfort in true repentance.

3. Much more after repentance, there is a pleasure attending it, and flowing from it. It is a way of pleasantness, for it is the way to pleasantness. To them that mourn in Zion – that sorrow after a godly sort – God hath appointed beauty for ashes, and the

oil of joy for mourning (Isa. 61:3). And the more the
soul is humbled under the sense of sin, the more
sensible will the comfort of pardon be; it is wounded
in order to be healed; the jubilee-trumpet sounded in
the close of the day of soul-affliction (Lev. 25:9),
which proclaimed the acceptable year of the Lord,
the year of release – and an acceptable year it is
indeed to those who find themselves tied and bound
with the cords of their sins. True penitents go weeping, it is true, but it is to 'seek the Lord their God'
(Jer. 50:4, 5) – to seek him as their God, and to enter
into covenant with him: and let their hearts 'rejoice
that seek the Lord' (Ps. 105:3) for they shall find
him, and find him their bountiful rewarder. They
sorrow not as 'those that have no hope', but good
hope that their iniquities are forgiven; and what joy
can be greater than that of a pardon to one condemned?

Secondly, It is true, that to be religious is to take
care, and take pains, and to labour earnestly (Luke
13:24) and yet 'wisdom's ways are ways of pleasantness'. It is true, we must *strive* to enter into this way
– must be in an agony, so the word is. There is a
violence which the kingdom of heaven suffers, and
'the violent take it by force' (Matt. 11:12). And when
we are in that way, we must 'run with patience' (Heb.
12:1). The bread of life is to be eaten in the sweat of
our face; we must be always upon our guard, and
keep our hearts with all diligence. Business for God
and our souls is what we are not allowed to be
slothful in, but 'fervent in spirit serving the Lord'
(Rom. 12:11). We are soldiers of Jesus Christ, and

we must endure hardness – must war the good warfare till it be accomplished (2 Tim. 2:3).

And yet even in this contention there is comfort. It is work indeed, and work that requires care; and yet it will appear to be pleasant work, if we consider how we are enabled for it, and encouraged in it.

1. How we are enabled for it, and strengthened with strength in our souls to go on in it, and go through with it. It would be unpleasant, and would go on very heavily, if we were left to ourselves, to travel in our own strength; but if we be acted and animated in it by a better spirit, and mightier power than our own, it is pleasant. If God 'work in us both to will and to do of his good pleasure' (Phil. 2:13) we shall have no reason to complain of the difficulty of our work; for God ordains peace for us, true peace and pleasure, by 'working all our works in us' (Isa. 26:12). We may sing at our work, if our minds be by the Spirit of God brought to it, our hands strengthened for it, and our infirmities helped (Rom. 8:26), and particularly our infirmities in prayer, that by it we may fetch in strength for every service – strength according to the day. Daniel at first found God speaking to him a terror, he could not bear it; but when one like 'the appearance of a man came and touched him' (who could be no other but Christ the Mediator) and put strength into him, saying, 'Peace be unto thee, be strong, yea, be strong', it was quite another thing with him; then nothing more pleasant, 'let my Lord speak, for thou hast strengthened me' (Dan. 10:16-19). Though the way to heaven be uphill, yet if we be carried on in it as upon eagles'

wings, it will be pleasant; and those are so that wait
upon the Lord, for to them it is promised that they
'shall renew their strength'. That is pleasant work –
though against the grain to our corrupt natures – for
the doing of which we have not only a new nature
given us, inclining us to it, and making us habitually
capable of application to it, but actual supplies of
grace sufficient for the doing of it, promised us (2
Cor. 12:9) by one who knows what strength we need,
and what will serve, and will neither be unkind to us,
nor unfaithful to his own word. And it is observable
that when God, though he eased not Paul of the thorn
in the flesh, yet said that good word to him, 'my
grace is sufficient for thee'; immediately it follows,
'therefore I take pleasure in infirmities, in reproaches,
in distresses, for Christ's sake; for when I am weak,
then I am strong'. Sufficient grace will make our
work pleasant, even the hardest part of it.

2. How we are encouraged in it. It is true, we must
take pains, but the work is good work, and is to be
done, and is done by all the saints, from a principle
of holy love, and that makes it pleasant (1 John 5:3),
as Jacob's service for Rachel was to him, because he
loved her. It is an unspeakable comfort to industrious
Christians that they are working together with God,
and he with them – that their Master's eye is upon
them, and a witness to their sincerity – he sees in
secret, and will reward openly (Matt. 6:6). God now
accepteth their works, smiles upon them, and his
Spirit speaks to them 'good words and comfortable
words' (Zech. 1:13) witnesseth to their adoption.
And this is very encouraging to God's servants, as it

was to the servants of Boaz, to have their master come to them, when they were hard at work, reaping down his own fields, and with a pleasant countenance say to them, 'the Lord be with you!' (Ruth 2:4). Nay, the Spirit saith more to God's labourers, 'The Lord is with you'. The prospect of the recompense of reward, is in a special manner encouraging to us in our work, and makes it pleasant, and the little difficulties we meet with in it to be as nothing. It was by having an eye to this, that Moses was encouraged not only to bear the reproach of Christ, but to esteem it 'greater riches than the treasures of Egypt' (Heb. 11:26). In all labour there is profit; and if so, there is pleasure also in the prospect of that profit, and according to the degree of it. We must work, but it is to work out our salvation – a great salvation which, when it comes, will abundantly make us amends for all our toil; we must strive, but it is to enter into life, eternal life; we must run, but it is for an incorruptible crown, the prize of our high calling. And we do not run at an uncertainty, nor fight as those that beat the air; for to him that 'soweth righteousness there shall be a sure reward' (Prov. 11:18) and the assurance of that harvest will make even the seedtime pleasant.

Thirdly, It is true, that to be religious, is to deny ourselves in many things that are pleasing to sense: and yet wisdom's ways are pleasantness for all that. It is indeed necessary, that beloved lusts should be mortified and subdued, corrupt appetites crossed and displeased, which, to the natural man, is like plucking out a right eye and cutting off a right hand (Matt. 5:29). There are forbidden pleasures that must be abandoned, and kept at a distance from; the flesh must not be gratified, nor provision made to 'fulfil the lusts of it' (Rom. 13:14), but on the contrary, we must 'keep under the body, and bring it into subjection' (1 Cor. 9:27); we must crucify the flesh, must kill it, and put it to a painful death. The first lesson we are to learn in the school of Christ is to deny ourselves (Matt. 16:24) and this must be our constant practice; we must use ourselves to deny ourselves, and thus take up our cross daily. Now, will not this spoil all the pleasure of a religious life? No, it will not; for the pleasures of sense, which we are to deny ourselves in, are comparatively despicable, and really dangerous.

1. These pleasures we are to deny ourselves in, are comparatively despicable; how much soever they are valued and esteemed by those who live by sense, and know no better, they are looked upon with a generous contempt by those who live by faith, and are acquainted with divine and spiritual pleasures. And it is no pain to deny ourselves entitled to better, more rational, and noble, and agreeable, the delights of the blessed spirits above. The garlic and onions of Egypt were doated upon by those that knew not how to value either the manna of the wilderness, or the milk and honey of Canaan (Num. 11:5); so the base and sordid pleasures of sense are relished by the depraved and vicious appetites of the carnal mind; but when a man has learned to put a due estimate upon spiritual pleasures, those that are sensual have lost all their sweetness, and are become the most insipid things in the world; have no pleasure in them,

in comparison with that far greater pleasure which excelleth. Is it any diminution to the pleasure of a grown man, to deny himself the toys and sports which he was fond of when he was a child? No, when he became a man, he 'put away childish things'; he is now past them, he is above them, for he is acquainted with those entertainments that are manly and more generous. Thus mean and little do the pleasures of sense appear to those that have learned to delight themselves in the Lord.

2. They are really dangerous – they are apt to take away the heart. If the heart be set upon them, they blind the mind, debauch the understanding and conscience, and in many quench the sparks of conviction, and of that holy fire which comes from heaven, and tends to heaven. They are in danger of drawing away the heart from God; and the more they are valued and coveted, the more likely they are to 'pierce us through with many sorrows', and to 'drown us in destruction and perdition'; to deny ourselves in them, is but to avoid a rock, upon which multitudes have fatally split themselves. What a diminution is it to the pleasure of a safe and happy way on sure ground, which will certainly bring us to our journey's end, to deny ourselves the false and pretended satisfaction, of walking in a fair but dangerous way that leads to destruction? Is it not much pleasanter travelling on a rough pavement, than on a smooth quicksand? Where there is a known peril, there can be no true pleasure, and therefore the want of it is no loss or uneasiness. What pleasure can a wise or considerate man take in those entertainments, in

which he has continual reason to suspect a snare and a design upon him, any more than he that was at a feast could relish the dainties of it, when he was aware of a naked sword hanging directly over him by a single thread? The foolish woman, indeed, calls the 'stolen waters' sweet, and 'bread eaten in secret' pleasant (Prov. 9:17, 18); but those find no difficulty, or uneasiness in denying them, who 'know that the dead are there, and her guests are already in the depths of hell'. Therefore, however the corrupt heart may find some reluctancy in refusing those forbidden pleasures, we may say of it as Abigail did of David's denying himself the satisfaction of being revenged on Nabal; afterwards this shall be 'no grief unto us, nor offence of heart' (1 Sam. 25:31).

Fourthly, It is true, that 'we must through much tribulation enter into the kingdom of God' (Acts 14:22), that we must not only deny ourselves the pleasures of sense, but must sometimes expose ourselves to its pains; we must take up our cross when it lies in our way, and bear it after Christ; we are told, that 'all, that will live godly in Christ Jesus, must suffer persecution', at least they must expect it, and get ready for it; bonds and afflictions abide them – losses in their estates – balks in their preferment – reproaches and contempts – banishments, death must be counted upon – and will not this spoil the pleasure of religion? No, it will not; for

1. It is but light affliction at the worst, that we are called out to suffer, and, 'but for a moment', compared with the 'far more exceeding and an eternal weight of glory' that is reserved for us (2 Cor. 4:17),

with which the 'sufferings of this present time are not worthy to be compared' (Rom. 8:18). All these troubles do but touch the body, the outward man, and the interests of that; they do not at all affect the soul; they break the shell, or pluck off the husk, but do not bruise the kernel. Can the brave and courageous soldier take pleasure in the toils and perils of the camp, and in jeoparding his life in the high places of the field, in the eager pursuit of honour, and in the service of his prince and country: and shall not those who have the interests of Christ's kingdom near their hearts, and are carried on by a holy ambition of the honour that comes from God, take a delight in suffering for Christ, when they know that those sufferings tend to his honour, and their own hereafter? They that are 'persecuted for righteousness sake', that are reviled, and have all manner of evil said against them falsely, because they belong to Christ, are bidden not only to bear it patiently, but to rejoice in it, and to be 'exceeding glad, for great is their reward in heaven' (Matt. 5:11, 12), every reproach we endure for Christ, will be a pearl in our crown shortly.

2. As those afflictions abound for Christ, so our 'consolation also aboundeth by Christ' (2 Cor. 1:5). The more the waters increased, the higher was the ark lifted up; the more we suffer in God's cause, the more we partake of his comforts; for he will not be wanting to those whom he calls out to any hardships more than ordinary for his name's sake. The Lord was with Joseph in the prison, when he lay there for a good conscience; and those went from the council

'rejoicing, that they were counted worthy to suffer shame' for Christ's name – were honoured to be dishonoured for him (Acts 5:41).

Thus the extraordinary supports and joys which they experience, that patiently suffer for righteousness sake, add much more to the pleasantness of the ways of wisdom, than the sufferings themselves do, or can, derogate from it; for the sufferings are human, the consolations are divine. They suffer in the flesh, but they rejoice in the spirit; they suffer for a time, but they rejoice evermore; and 'this their joy no man taketh from them'.

CHAPTER 7

The application of the doctrine.

Concerning this doctrine of the pleasantness of religion's ways, I hope we may now say as Eliphaz doth of his principle, 'Lo! this, we have searched it, so it is' (Job 5:27), it is incontestably true, and therefore we may conclude as he doth, 'hear it, and know thou it for thy good'; know thou it for thyself, so the margin reads it, apply it to thyself, believe it concerning thyself, not only that it is good, but that 'it is good for me to draw near to God' (Ps. 73:28) and then only we hear things and know them for our good, when we hear them and know them for ourselves.

Three inferences, by way of counsel and exhortation, we shall draw from this doctrine:

First, Let us all then be persuaded, and prevailed with to enter into, and to walk in these paths of wisdom, that are so very pleasant; this is what I principally intend in opening and proving this truth. Most people would rather be courted than threatened to their duty. Much might be said to frighten you out of the ways of sin and folly, but I would hope to gain the same point another way, by alluring you in the ways of wisdom and holiness. This comes to invite you to a feast which the Lord of hosts hath in the gospel, made to all nations (Isa. 25:6) and to all in the nations, and to you among the rest, for none are excluded, that do not by their unbelief exclude themselves – 'a feast of fat things full of marrow, of wines on the lees well refined' – delights for souls infinitely transcending the delicacies of sense; you are welcome to this feast; 'come, for all things are now ready'; come, eat of wisdom's bread and drink of the wine that she hath mingled (Prov. 9:5). Is a life of religion such a sweet and comfortable life, why then should not we be religious? if such as these be the ways of wisdom, why should not we be travellers in those ways? Let this recommend to us a life of sincere and serious godliness, and engage us to conform to all its rules, and give up ourselves to be ruled by them. It is not enough to have a good opinion of religion, and to give it a good word; that will but be a witness against us, if we do not set ourselves in good earnest to the practice of it, and make conscience of living up to it.

I would here, with a particular and pressing importunity, address myself to you that are young; to persuade you, now in the days of your youth – now in the present day – to make religion your choice and your business; and I assure you, if you do so, you will find it your delight. God, by his grace, convince you of the real comforts that are to be had in real godliness, that you may be drawn cheerfully to Christ with these cords of a man, and held fast to him with these bands of love! 'My son (saith Solomon to his little scholar, Prov. 24:13, 14) eat thou honey, because it is good; and the honeycomb which is sweet to thy taste'; he doth not forbid him the delights of sense, he may use them soberly and moderately and with due caution; but remember that, 'so shall the knowledge of wisdom be to thy soul, when thou hast found it'; thou hast better pleasures than these to mind and pursue, spiritual and rational ones; and instead of being made indifferent to those, we should rather be led to them, and quickened in our desires after them by these delights of sense, which God gives us to engage us to himself, and his service.

The age of youth is the age of pleasure, you think you may now be allowed to take your pleasure: O that you would take it, and seek it there, where alone it is to be had, and that is in a strict observance of the laws of virtue and godliness. Would you live a pleasant life, begin betimes to live a religious life, and the sooner you begin, the more pleasant it will be; it is best travelling in a morning. Would you rejoice, O young people in your youth, and have your hearts to 'cheer you in the days of your youth' (Ecc. 11:9)? Do not walk in the way of your corrupt and carnal hearts, but in the way of God's commandments; for he knows what is good for you better than you do yourselves. Do not walk in the sight of your eyes, for the eyes are apt to fly 'upon that which is not' (Prov. 23:5), but live by faith, that faith which being 'the substance of things hoped for, and the evidence of things not seen' will lead you to that which is; for wisdom makes those that love her to inherit substance, and fills their treasures (Prov. 8:21) and thence ariseth their true satisfaction.

That which I would persuade you to, is to walk in the way of wisdom – to be sober-minded – to be thoughtful about your souls and your everlasting state, and get your minds well-principled, and well-affected, and well-inclined; 'wisdom is the principal thing, therefore get wisdom, and, with all thy getting, get understanding' (Prov. 4:7). That which I would persuade you with, is the pleasantness of this way; you cannot do better for yourselves than by a religious course of life. 'My son, if thine heart be wise, my heart shall rejoice, even mine' (Prov. 23:15, 16), 'yea, my reins shall rejoice, when thy lips', out of the abundance of thine heart, speak right things; but that is not all, not only my heart shall rejoice, but thy own shall. I wish you would see, and seriously consider the two rivals that are making court to you for your souls, for your best affections – Christ and Satan – and act wisely in disposing of yourselves, and make such a choice as you will afterwards reflect upon with comfort. You are now at the turning time of life, turn right now, and you are made for ever. Wisdom saith (Prov. 9:4, 16), 'Whoso is simple let him turn in' to me, and she will cure him of his simplicity; Folly saith, 'Whoso is simple let him turn in' to me, and she will take advantage of his simplicity: now let him come whose right your hearts are, and give them him, and you shall have them again more your own. That you may determine well between these two competitors, for the throne in your souls:

First, See the folly of carnal, sinful pleasures, and abandon them; you will never be in love with the pleasures of religion, till you are persuaded to fall out with forbidden pleasures. The enjoyment of the delights of sense suits best with that age – the appetite towards them is then most violent – mirth, sport, plays, dainties are the idols of young people, they are therefore called 'youthful lusts' (2 Tim. 2:22). The days will come, 'the evil days', when they themselves will say they have no pleasure in them, like Barzillai (2 Sam. 19:35), who, when he is old, can no more relish what he eats and what he drinks. O that reason, and wisdom, and grace, might make you as dead to them now, as time and days will make you after a while! Will you believe one that tried the utmost of what the pleasures of sense could do towards making a man happy; he 'said of laughter, it is mad, and of mirth what doth it?' and that 'sorrow is better than laughter' (Ecc. 2:2; 7:3). Moses knew what the pleasures of the court were, and yet chose rather to 'suffer affliction with the people of God' than to continue in the snare of them (Heb. 11:25) and you must make the same choice; for you will never cordially embrace the pleasures of religion, till you have renounced the pleasures of sin; covenant against them, therefore, and watch against them.

If you would live, and go in the way of understanding, you must 'forsake the foolish' (Prov. 9:6) take heed of the way both of the evil man, and of the 'strange woman; avoid it, pass not by it, turn from it, and pass away' (Prov. 4:14). Look upon sinful pleasures as mean and much below you; look upon them as vile and much against you; and do not only despise them, but dread them, and hate even the garments spotted with the flesh.

Secondly, Be convinced of the pleasure of wisdom's ways, and come and try them. You are, it may be, prejudiced against religion as a melancholy thing, but as Philip said to Nathaniel (John 1:46), 'Come and see.' Believe it is possible that there may be a pleasure in religion, which you have not yet thought of. When religion is looked upon at a distance, we see not that pleasure in it which we shall certainly find when we come to be better acquainted with it. Peter Martyr, in a sermon, illustrated this by this comparison (and it proved a means of the conversion of the Marquis of Vico): he that looks upon persons dancing at a distance, would think they were mad; but let him come nearer, and observe how they take every step by rule, and keep time with the music, he will not only be pleased with it, but inclined to join with them. Come and take Christ's yoke upon you, and you will find it easy; try the pleasure there is in the knowledge of God and Jesus Christ, and in converse with spiritual and eternal things – try the pleasure of seriousness and self-denial – and you will find it far exceeds that of vanity and self-indulgence. Try the pleasure of meditation on the word of God, of prayer, and praise, and sabbath-sanctification, and you will think you have made a happy change of the pleasure of vain and carnal mirth for these true delights. Make this trial by these four rules:

1. That man's chief end is to glorify God, and enjoy him. Our pleasures will be according to that

which we pitch upon and pursue as our chief end; if we can mistake so far, as to think it is our chief end to enjoy the world and the flesh, and our chief business to serve them, the delights of sense will relish best with us; but if the world was made for man, certainly man was made for more than the world; and if God made man, certainly he made him for himself: God then is our chief good, it is our business to serve and please him, and our happiness to be accepted of him. And if so, and we believe so, nothing will be a greater pleasure to us, than that which we have reason to think will be pleasing to him. If we do, indeed, look upon God as our chief good, we shall make him our chief joy, our exceeding joy (Ps. 43:4); if we consider that we were made capable of the pleasure of conversing with God in this world, and seeing him and enjoying him in another, we cannot but think that we wretchedly disparage ourselves, when we take up with the mean and sordid pleasures of sense as our felicity, especially if we forego all spiritual and eternal pleasures for them – as certainly we do, and give up all our expectations of them, if we place our happiness in these present delights; and we are guilty of a greater absurdity than that which profane Esau was guilty of, who 'for one morsel of meat sold his birthright' (Heb. 12:16).

2. That the soul is the man, and that is best for us, that is best for our souls. Learn to think meanly of this flesh by which we are allied to the earth and the inferior creatures; it is formed out of the dust; it is dust, and it is hastening to the dust; and then the

things that gratify it will not be much esteemed as of any great moment; 'meats for the belly, and the belly for meats, but God shall destroy both it and them', and therefore let us not make idols of them. But the soul is the noble part of us, by which we are allied to heaven and the world of spirits; those comforts therefore which delight the soul are the comforts we should prize most, and give the preference to, for the soul's sake. Rational pleasures are the best for a man.

3. That the greatest joy is that which a stranger doth not intermeddle with (Prov. 14:10). The best pleasure is that which lies not under the eye and observation of the world, but which a man has and hides in his own bosom, and by which he enjoys himself, and keeps not only a peaceable, but a comfortable possession of his own soul, though he doth not by laughter, or other expressions of joy, tell them the satisfaction he has. Christ had meat to eat which the world knew not of (John 4:32) and so have Christians, to whom he is the bread of life.

4. That all is well that ends everlastingly well. That pleasure ought to have the preference which is of the longest continuance. The pleasures of sense are withering and fading, and leave a sting behind them to those that placed their happiness in them; but the pleasures of religion will abide with us; in these is continuance (Isa. 64:6), they will not turn with the wind nor change with the weather, but are meat which endures to everlasting life. Reckon that the best pleasure which will remain with you, and stand you in stead when you come to die; which will help to take off the terror of death, and allay its pains. The

remembrance of sinful pleasures will give us killing terrors, but the remembrance of religious pleasures will give us living comforts in dying moments. They that live over Belshazzar's revels, may expect to receive the summons of death, with the same confusion that he did, when 'the joints of his loins were loosed, and his knees smote one against another' (Dan. 5:6), but they that live over Hezekiah's devotions may receive it with the same composure that he did, when with a great deal of satisfaction he looked back upon a wellspent life: 'Now, Lord, remember how I have walked before thee in truth, and with a perfect heart' (Isa. 38:3).

Secondly, Let us, that profess religion, study to make it more and more pleasant to ourselves. We see how much is done to make it so, let us not receive the grace of God herein in vain. Let them that walk in wisdom's ways taste the sweetness of them, and relish it. Christ's service is perfect freedom, let us not make a drudgery of it, nor a toil of such a pleasure. We should not only be reconciled to our duty, as we ought to be to our greatest afflictions, and make the best of it, but we should rejoice in our duty, and sing at our work. If God intended that his service should be a pleasure to his servants, let them concur with him herein, and not walk contrary to him. Now in order to the making of our religion pleasant to us more and more so, I shall give seven directions:

1. Let us always keep up good thoughts of God, and carefully watch against hard thoughts of him. As it is the original error of many that are loose and careless in religion, that they think God altogether

such a one as themselves (Ps. 50:21), as much a
friend to sin as themselves, and as indifferent whether
his work be done or no, so it is the error of many that
are severe in their religion, that they think God, like
themselves, a hard Master; they have such thoughts
of him, as Job had in an hour of temptation, when he
looked upon God as seeking occasions against him,
and numbering his steps, and watching over his sins,
and taking him for his enemy (Job 13:24; 14:16). As
if he were extreme to mark iniquities, and implac-
able to those that had offended, and not accepting
any service that had in it the least defect or imperfec-
tion. But the matter is not so, and we do God and
ourselves a great deal of wrong, if we imagine it to
be so; what could have been done more than God has
done, to convince us that he is gracious, and merciful, slow to anger, and ready to forgive sin when it is
repented of? 'I said I will confess my transgression
unto the Lord, and thou forgavest' (Ps. 32:5) and was
ready to accept the services that came from an
upright hand. He will not always chide nor contend
for ever. So far is he from taking advantages against
us, that he makes the best of us: where the spirit is
willing, he accepts that, and overlooks the weakness
of the flesh. Let us deal with him accordingly; look
upon God as love, and the God of love, and then it
will be pleasant to us to hear from him, to speak to
him, to converse with him, and to do him any service.
It is true, God is great, and glorious, and jealous, and
to be worshipped with reverence and holy fear; but
is he not our Father, a tender gracious Father? Was
not God, in Christ, reconciling the world to himself'

(2 Cor. 5:19) and to all his attributes and relations to us, by showing himself willing to be reconciled to us not withstanding our provocations? See him, therefore, upon a throne of grace, and come boldly to him, and that will make your service of him pleasant.

2. Let us dwell much, by faith, upon the promises of God. What pleasant lives should we lead, if we were but more intimately acquainted with those declarations which God has made of his good will to man, and the assurances he has given of his favour, and all the blessed fruits of it to those who serve him faithfully! The promises are many, and exceeding great and precious, suited to our case, and accommodated to every exigence; there are not only promises to grace, but promises of grace – grace sufficient; and these promises are all 'yea and amen in Christ'. What do these promises stand in our Bibles for, but to be made use of? Come then, and let us apply them to ourselves, and insert our own names in them by faith; what God said to Abraham, 'I am thy shield' (Gen. 15:1). I am *El-shaddai* – a God all-sufficient (Gen. 17:1). What he said to Joshua, 'I will never fail thee nor forsake thee' (Josh. 1:5) he saith to me. What he saith to all that love him, that 'all things work together for good to them' (Rom. 8:28), and to all that fear him, that no good thing shall be wanting to them (Ps. 34:10) he saith to me; and why should not I take the comfort of it? These promises, and the like, are wells of salvation, from which we may draw water with joy; and breasts of consolation, from which we may suck, and be satisfied; they will be both our strength, and our song in the house of our

pilgrimage. So 'well-ordered is the covenant of grace in all things, and so sure' (2 Sam. 23:5) that if having laid up our portion in it, and so made it all our salvation, we would but fetch our maintenance from it, and so make it all our desire and delight, we should have in it a continual feast, and should go on our way rejoicing (Ps. 119:111).

3. Let us order the affairs of our religion with discretion. Many make religion unpleasant to themselves, and discouraging to others, by their imprudent management of it; making that service to be a burden by the circumstances of it, which in itself would be a pleasure; doing things out of time, or tasking themselves above their strength, and undertaking more than they can go through with, especially at first, which is like putting new wine into old bottles (Matt. 9:17) or like over-driving the flocks one day (Gen. 33:13). If we make the yoke of Christ heavier than he has made it, we may thank ourselves that our drawing in it becomes unpleasant. Solomon cautions us (Ecc. 7:16) against being righteous overmuch, and making ourselves overwise, as that by which we may destroy ourselves, and put ourselves out of conceit with our religion; there may be overdoing in well-doing, and then it becomes unpleasant. But let us take our religion as Christ hath settled it, and we shall find it easy. When the ways of our religion are ways of wisdom, then they are ways of pleasantness; that wisdom which dwells with prudence. Wisdom will direct us to be even and regular in our religion, to take care that the duties of our general and particular calling, the business of our

religion, and our necessary business in the world, do not interfere or intrench upon one another. It will direct us to time duty aright; for every thing is beautiful and pleasant in its season (Ecc. 3:11) and work is then easy, when we are in frame for it.

4. Let us live in love, and keep up Christian charity, and the spiritual communion of saints: if we would be of good comfort, we must be of one mind (2 Cor. 13:11) and therefore the apostle presseth brotherly love upon us, with an argument taken from the consolations in Christ (Phil. 2:1) that is, the comfort that is in Christianity. As ever you hope to have the comfort of your religion, submit to that great law of it, 'walk in love'; for behold how good, and how pleasant it is – how good in itself and pleasant to us – for 'brethren to dwell together in unity'. The more pleasing we are to our brethren, the more pleasant we shall be to ourselves. Nothing makes our lives more uncomfortable than strife and contention. 'Woe is me that I dwell among those that hate peace' (Ps. 120:5, 6) it is bad being among those that are disposed to quarrel, and worse having in ourselves a disposition to quarrel. The resentments of contempt put upon us are uneasy enough, and contrivances to revenge it much more so. And nothing makes our religion more uncomfortable, than strifes and contentions about that. We forfeit and lose the pleasure of it, if we entangle ourselves in perverse disputings about it. But by holy love we enjoy our friends, which will add to the pleasure of enjoying God in this world. Love itself sweetens the soul, and revives it, and as it is the loadstone of love,

it fetcheth in the further pleasure and satisfaction of being beloved, and so it is a heaven upon earth; for what is the happiness and pleasure of heaven, but that there love reigns in perfection? Then we have most peace in our bosoms, when we are most peaceably disposed towards our brethren.

5. Let us be much in the exercise of holy joy, and employ ourselves much in praise. Joy is in the heart of praise, as praise is the language of joy; let us engage ourselves to these, and quicken ourselves in these. God has made these our duty, by these to make all the other parts of our duty pleasant to us; and for that end we should abound much in them, and attend upon God with joy and praise. Let us not crowd our spiritual joys into a corner of our hearts, nor our thankful praises into a corner of our prayers, but give both scope and vent to both. Let us live a life of delight in God, and love to think of him as we do of one whom we love and value. Let the flowing in of every stream of comfort lead us to the fountain; and in every thing that is grateful to us, let us 'taste that the Lord is gracious'. Let the drying up of every stream of comfort drive us to the fountain; and let us rejoice the more in God for our being deprived of that, which we used to rejoice in. Let us be frequent and large in our thanksgiving; it will be pleasant to us to recount the favours of God, and thus to make some returns for them, though poor and mean, yet such as God will graciously accept. We should have more pleasure in our religion, if we had but learned 'in every thing to give thanks' (1 Thess. 5:18) for that takes out more than half the bitterness of our

afflictions, that we can see cause even to be thankful for them; and it infuseth more than a double sweetness into our enjoyments, that they furnish us with matter for that excellent heavenly work of praise; 'sing praises unto his name, for it is pleasant', comfortable, as well as comely (Ps. 135:3).

6. Let us act in a constant dependence upon Jesus Christ. Religion would be much more pleasant, if we did but cleave more closely to Christ in it, and do all in his name. The more precious Christ is to us, the more pleasant will every part of our work be; and therefore *believing* in Christ is often expressed by our *rejoicing* in him (Phil. 3:3). We may rejoice in God, through Christ, as the Mediator between us and God; may rejoice in our communion with God, when it is kept up through Christ; may rejoice in hope of eternal life, when we see 'this life in his Son; he that hath the Son, hath life', that is, he has comfort (1 John 5:11, 12). There is that in Christ, and in his undertaking and performances for us, which is sufficient to satisfy all our doubts, to silence all our fears, and to balance all our sorrows. He was appointed to be the consolation of Israel, and he will be so to us, when we have learned not to look for that in ourselves, which is to be had in him only, and to make use of his mediation in every thing wherein we have to do with God. When we rejoice in the righteousness of Christ, and in his grace and strength – rejoice in his satisfaction and intercession – rejoice in his dominion and universal agency and influence, and in the progress of his gospel, and the conversion of souls to him – and please ourselves with prospects

of his second coming – we have then a joy, not only which no man taketh from us, but which will increase more and more; and of the increase of Christ's government, and therefore of that 'peace, there shall be no end' (Isa. 9:7). Our songs of joy are then most pleasant, when the burthen of them is 'none but Christ', 'none but Christ'.

7. Let us converse much with the glory that is to be revealed. They that by faith send their hearts and best affections before them to heaven, while they are here on this earth, may in return fetch thence some of those joys and pleasures that are at God's right hand. That which goes up in vapours of holy desire, though insensible, in 'groanings which cannot be uttered' will come down again in dews of heavenly consolations, that will make the soul as a watered garden. Let us look much to the end of our way, how glorious it will be, and that will help to make our way pleasant. This abundantly satisfies the saints, and is the fatness of God's house on earth (Ps. 36:8, 9). This makes them now to drink of the river of God's pleasures, that with him is the fountain of life, whence all these streams come, and in his light they hope to see light – everlasting light. By frequent meditations on that rest which remains for the people of God (Heb. 4:3), we now enter into that rest, and partake of the comfort of it. Our hopes of that happiness through grace would be very much strengthened, and our evidences for it cleared up insensibly, if we did but converse more with it, and the discoveries made of it in the scripture. We may have foretastes of heavenly delights, while we are

here on earth – clusters from Canaan, while we are yet in this wilderness – and no pleasures are comparable to that which these afford. That is the sweetest joy within us, which is borrowed from the joy set before us; and we deprive ourselves very much of the comfort of our religion, in not having our eye more to that joy. We rejoice most triumphantly, and with the greatest degrees of holy glorying, when we 'rejoice in hope of the glory of God' (Rom. 5:2). In this our heart is glad, and our glory rejoiceth (Ps. 16:9).

Thirdly, Let us make it appear, that we have, indeed, found wisdom's ways to be pleasantness, and her paths peace. If we have experienced this truth, let us evidence our experiences, and not only in word, but in deed, bear our testimony to the truth of it. Let us live as those that believe in the sweetness of religion, not because we are told it, but because we have tasted it (1 John 1:1).

'If so be then (to borrow the apostle's words, 1 Pet. 2:3) we have tasted that the Lord is gracious', if we have, indeed, found it a pleasant thing to be religious,

1. Let our hearts be much enlarged in all religious exercises, and all instances of gospel-obedience. The more pleasant the service of God is, the more we should abound in it. When God enlargeth our hearts with his consolations, he expects that we should run the way of his commandments – that we should exert ourselves in our duty with more vigour, and press forward the more earnestly towards perfection. This should make us forward to every good work, and

ready to close with all opportunities of serving God, and doing good; that which we take a pleasure in, we need not to be twice called to. If indeed the hearts of those 'rejoice that seek the Lord' (Ps. 105:3), then when God saith, 'seek ye my face', how steadily should our hearts answer at the first word, 'thy face, Lord, will I seek' (Ps. 27:8)! And how glad will they be, when it is said unto us, 'let us go unto the house of the Lord'? (Ps. 122:1). This should make us forward to acts of charity, that there is a pleasure in doing good; and we shall reflect with comfort upon it, that we have done something that will turn to the honour of God and our own account. This should make us lively in our duty; the heart fixed in hearing the word, and in prayer and praise. Those that take delight in music, how doth it engage them! How do all the marks of a close application of mind appear in their countenance and carriage! And shall not we by our attending on the Lord without distraction, make it to appear, that we attend upon him with delight, and are in our element when we are in his service? Let this be my rest for ever; here let me 'dwell all the days of my life' (Ps. 27:4). This should keep us constant and unwearied in the work and service of God. What is really our delight, we are not soon weary of. If we delight in approaching to God, we will seek him daily, and make it our daily work to honour him. If meditation and prayer be sweet, let them be our daily exercise; and let this bind our souls with a bond to God, and the sacrifice as with cords to the horns of the altar. With this we should answer all temptations to apostasy: Shall I quit so good a

THE APPLICATION OF THE DOCTRINE

master, so good a service? Entreat me not to leave Christ, or turn from following after him: for it is good to be here. 'Let us make here three tabernacles' (Matt. 17:4). Whither else shall we go, but to him that has 'the words of eternal life'.

2. Let our whole conversation be cheerful, and melancholy be banished. Are the ways of religion pleasant? Let us be pleasant in them, both to ourselves, and to those about us. As for those who are yet in a state of sin and wrath, they have reason to be melancholy, let the sinner in Zion be afraid, be afflicted; joy is forbidden fruit to them; what have they to do with peace? 'Rejoice not, O Israel, for joy as other people, for thou hast gone a whoring from thy God!' (Hos. 9:1). But those who, through grace, are called out of darkness into a marvellous light, have cause to be cheerful, and should have hearts to be so. 'Arise, shine, for thy light is come' (Isa. 60:1). Is the Sun of righteousness risen upon us? Let us arise, look forth as the morning with the morning. That comfort which Christ directs to our souls, let us reflect back upon others. And as our light is come, so is our liberty. Art thou loosed from the bands of thy neck? O captive daughter of Zion, 'awake, awake; put on thy strength, O Zion! put on thy beautiful garments, and shake thyself from the dust, arise and sit down, O Jerusalem' (Isa. 52:1, 2).

Though vain and carnal mirth is both a great sin and a great snare, yet there is a holy cheerfulness and pleasantness of conversation, which will not only consist very well with serious godliness, but greatly promotes it in ourselves, and greatly adorns it and recommends it to others. 'A merry heart,' Solomon saith, 'doth good like a medicine' (Prov. 17:22), and maketh fat the bones; while a broken spirit doth hurt like a poison, and drieth the bones. Christians should endeavour to keep up a cheerful temper, and not indulge themselves in that which is saddening and disquieting to the spirit; and they should show it in all holy conversation, that those they converse with, may see they did not renounce pleasure, when they embraced religion. I am sure, none have so much reason to rejoice as good people have, nor so much done for them to encourage their joy; and therefore, to allude to that of Jonadab to Ammon, 'why art thou, being the king's son, lean from day to day?' (2 Sam. 13:4). Are we in prosperity? therefore let us be cheerful, in gratitude to the God of our mercies, who expects that we should serve him 'with joyfulness, and gladness of heart, for the abundance of all things' (Deut. 28:47) and justly takes it ill if we do not.

Are we in affliction? yet let us be cheerful, that we may make it appear our happiness is not laid up in the creature, nor our treasures on earth. If it is the privilege of Christians to rejoice in tribulation, let them not throw away their privilege, but glory in it, and make use of it. Let the joy of the Lord that hath infused itself into our hearts, diffuse itself into all our converse. 'Go thy way, eat thy bread with joy, and drink thy wine' (Ecc. 9:7), nay, if thou shouldst be reduced to that, drink fair water, 'with a merry heart', if thou hast good ground to hope that in Christ Jesus, God now accepteth thy works; and this 'joy of the Lord will be thy strength'.

3. Let us look with contempt upon the pleasures of sense, and with abhorrence upon the pleasures of sin. The more we have tasted of the delights of heaven, the more our mouths should be put out of taste to the delights of this earth. Let not those who have been feasted with the milk and honey of Canaan, hanker after the garlic and onions of Egypt. Let us keep at a distance from all forbidden pleasures; there is a hook under those baits – a snake under the green grass – a rock under those smooth waters, on which multitudes have split. We must so dread the drunkard's pleasure, as not to 'look upon the wine when it is red' (Prov. 23:31), so dread the pleasures of the adulterer, as not to 'look upon a woman to lust after her' (Matt. 5:28), for these pleasures of sin not only are but for a season, but at the last they 'bite like a serpent, and sting like an adder'. Either spiritual pleasures will deaden the force of the pleasures of sin, or the pleasures of sin will spoil the relish of spiritual pleasures. Let us keep up a holy indifferency even to the lawful delights of sense, and take heed of loving them more than God. The eye that has looked at the sun, is dazzled to every thing else. Have we beheld the beauty of the Lord? let us see and own how little beauty there is in other things. If we be tempted to do any thing unbecoming us, by the allurements of pleasure, we may well say, offer these things to those that know no better; but we do, and will never leave fountains of living water, for cisterns of puddle water.

4. Let not our hearts envy sinners; envy ariseth

from an opinion that the state of others is better than our own, which we grudge and are displeased at, and wish ourselves in their condition. Good people are often cautioned against this sin: 'be not thou envious against evil men, neither desire to be with them' (Prov. 24:1; Ps. 37:1) for if there be all this pleasure in religion, and we have experienced it, surely we would not exchange condition with any sinner, even in his best estate. Envy not sinners their outward prosperity, their wealth and abundance, which puts them into a capacity of having all the delights of sense wound up to the heights of pleasureableness: though they lie 'upon beds of ivory' (Amos 6:4- 6) and 'stretch themselves upon their couches, and eat the lambs out of the flock, and the calves out of the midst of the stall, that chant to the sound of the viol, drink wine in bowls', and anoint themselves with the chief ointments, yet those have no reason to envy them, whose souls dwell at ease in God – who are fed with the bread of life, the true manna, angels' food, and drink of the water of life freely – that make melody with their hearts to the Lord, and are made to hear from him joy and gladness, and have received the anointing of the Spirit. If we have relished the delights of religion, we will say as David, 'Let me not eat of their dainties' (Ps. 141:4). Envy not sinners the liberty they take to sin; they can allow themselves in the full enjoyment of these pleasures, which we cannot think of without horror, but have not we then the enjoyment of those pleasures which are infinitely better, and which they are strangers to? We cannot have both, and of the two, are not ours, without dispute, preferable to theirs, and why then should we envy them? Their pleasures are enslaving, ours enlarging; theirs debasing to the soul, ours ennobling; theirs surfeiting, ours satisfying; theirs offensive to God, ours pleasing to him; theirs will end in pain and bitterness, ours will be perfected in endless joys; and what reason then have we to envy them?

5. Let not our spirits sink, or be dejected, under the afflictions of this present time. We disparage our comforts in God, if we lay too much to heart our crosses in the world; and therefore, hereby let us evidence, that being satisfied of God's loving-kindness, we are satisfied with it. Let us look upon that as sufficient to balance all the unkindnesses of men. They that value themselves upon God's smiles, ought not to vex themselves at the world's frowns. The light of God's countenance can shine through the thickest clouds of the troubles of this present time; and, therefore, we should walk in the light of the Lord, even then when as to our outward condition we sit in darkness. We manifest that we have found true delight and satisfaction in the service of God, and communion with him, when the pleasure of that will make the bitterest cup of affliction, that our Father puts into our hand, not only passable but pleasant; so that, like blessed Paul, when we are as sorrowful, yet we may be always rejoicing, and may take pleasure in infirmities and reproaches, because, though for the present, they are not joyous but grievous, yet when afterwards they yield the peaceable fruit of righteousness, they become not

grievous, but truly joyous. 'Blessed is the man whom thou chastenest.'

6. Let the pleasures we have found in religion, dispose us to be liberal and charitable to the poor and distressed. The pleasing sense we have of God's bounty to us, by which he has done so much to make us easy, should engage us bountifully to distribute to the necessities of saints, according to our ability, not only to keep them from perishing, but to make them easy; and that they may rejoice as well as we. Cheerfulness that enlargeth the heart, should open the hand too. Paul observes it concerning the churches of Macedonia, who were ready to give to the relief of the poor saints at Jerusalem, that it was the abundance of their joy, their spiritual joy, their joy in God, that 'abounded unto the riches of their liberality' (2 Cor. 8:2). When the people of Israel are commanded to rejoice in every good thing which God had given them (Deut. 26:11, 12) they are commanded also to give freely to 'the Levite, the stranger, the fatherless, and the widow, that they may eat, and be filled'. And when upon a particular occasion they are directed to 'eat the fat, and drink the sweet' (Neh. 8:10) at the same time they are directed to 'send portions to them, for whom nothing is prepared', and then the joy of the Lord will be their strength. By our being charitable, we should show that we are cheerful; that we cheerfully taste God's goodness in what we have, and trust his goodness for what we may hereafter want.

7. Let us do what we can to bring others to partake of the same pleasures in religion that we have tasted,

especially those that are under our charge. It adds very much to the pleasure of an enjoyment, to communicate of it to others, especially when the nature of it is such, that we have never the less, but the more rather, for others sharing in it. What good tidings we hear that are of common concern, we desire that others may hear them, and be glad too. He that has but found a lost sheep, 'calls his friends and neighbours to rejoice with him' (Luke 15:6), much more he that has found Christ, and found comfort in him; who can say, not only come rejoice with me, but come and partake with me; for yet there is room enough for all, though never so numerous, enough for each, though never so necessitous and craving. When Samson had found honey in the carcase of the lion (Judg. 14:8) he brought some of it to his parents, that they might partake with him; thus when we have found a 'day in God's courts better than a thousand', we should invite others into those courts, by telling them 'what God has done for our souls' (Ps. 66:16) and how willing he is to do the same for theirs, if they in like manner apply themselves to him. When Andrew with a surprising pleasure had found the Messiah (John 1:41, 45) he cannot rest till he has brought his brother Peter to him; nor Philip till he hath brought his friend Nathanael. They that are feasted with the comforts of God's house, should not covet to eat their morsel alone; but be willing to communicate of their spiritual things.

8. Let us be willing to die, and leave this world. We have reason to be ashamed of ourselves, that we who have not only laid up our treasure above, but

fetch our pleasures thence, yet are as much in love with our present state, and as loath to think of quitting it, as if our treasure, and pleasure, and all were wrapt up in the things of sense and time. The delights of sense entangle us and hold us here; these are the things that make us loath to die, as one said, viewing his fine house and gardens. And are these things sufficient to court our stay here, when God calls to 'arise and depart, for this is not your rest' (Mic. 2:10)?

Let us not be afraid to remove from a world of sense to a world of spirits, since we have found the pleasures of sense not worthy to be compared with spiritual pleasures. When in old age, which is one of the valleys of the shadow of death, we can no longer relish the delights of the body, but they become sapless and tasteless, as they were in Barzillai, yet we need not call those evil days, and 'years in which we have no pleasure', if we have walked and persevered in wisdom's ways; for if so, we may then in old age look back with pleasure upon a life well spent on earth, as Hezekiah did, and look forward with more pleasure upon a life to be better spent in heaven. And when we have received a sentence of death within ourselves, and see the day approaching, the pleasure we have in loving God, and believing in Christ, and in the expressions of holy joy and thankfulness, should make even a sick-bed and a deathbed easy; the saints shall be joyful in glory, and shall sing aloud upon their beds (Ps. 149:5), those beds to which they are confined, and from which they are removing to their graves, their beds in the darkness.

Our religion, if we be faithful to it, will furnish us with living comforts in dying moments, sufficient to balance the pains of death, and take off the terror of it; and to enable us to triumph over it, 'O death! Where is thy sting?' Let us then evidence our experiences of the pleasures of religion, by living above the inordinate love of life, and fear of death.

Lastly, Let us long for the perfection of these spiritual pleasures in the kingdom of glory. When we come thither, and not till then, they will be perfected; while we are here, as we know and love but in part, so we rejoice but in part, even our spiritual joys here have their damps and allays – we mix tears and tremblings with them; but in heaven, there is a fulness of joy without mixture, and pleasures for evermore, without period or diminution. Christ's servants will there 'enter into the joy of their Lord', and it shall be 'everlasting joy' (Isa. 35:10). And what are the pleasures in the way of wisdom, compared with those at the end of the way? If a complacency in the divine beauty and love be so pleasant while we are in the body, and are absent from the Lord, what will it be when we have put off the body, and go to be present with the Lord? If a day in God's courts, and a few minutes spent there in his praises, be so pleasant, what will an eternity within the veil be, among them that dwell in his house above, and are still praising him? If the earnest of our inheritance be so comfortable, what will the inheritance itself be?

Now wherever there is grace, it will be aiming at, and pressing towards its own perfection; it is a 'well of water springing up to eternal life' (John 4:14). This therefore we should be longing for. Our love to God in this world is love in motion, in heaven it will be love at rest. O when shall that sabbatism come, which 'remains for the people of God'! Here we have the pleasure of looking towards God, 'O when shall we come, and appear before him'! Our Lord Jesus, when at his last passover, which he earnestly desired to eat with his disciples, he had drank of the fruit of the vine, he speaks as one that longed to 'drink it new in the kingdom of his Father' (Matthew 26:29). It is very pleasant to serve Christ here, but to depart and to be with Christ, is far better. 'Now are we the sons of God' (1 John 3:2), and it is very pleasant to think of that: but 'it doth not yet appear what we shall be', something there is in reserve, of which we are kept in expectation. We are not yet at home, but should long to be there, and keep up holy desires of that glory to be revealed, that we may be quickened as long as we are here, to press towards the mark for the prize of the high calling.

Their lips were only an inch apart, distracting Cy from his duty to protect her.

All that registered was Kellie's warmth and beauty, seducing him into wanting a taste of her. It was wrong to give in to his desire, but he'd passed a threshold where chemistry had taken over. He could no more stop what was happening than he could prevent himself from being swept into a vortex.

When his mouth closed over hers, he heard a small moan, then she was giving him access as if she couldn't stop herself either. For a minute he forgot everything while the wonder of her response took hold. One kiss became another and another until it all merged into a growing need that set them on fire.

He'd never known this kind of ecstasy before. Maybe it was because of the danger surrounding them that the experience of holding and kissing her had surpassed any pleasure he'd known.

THE TEXAS
RANGER'S BRIDE

BY
REBECCA WINTERS

MILLS
BOON

Published in Great Britain 2015
by Mills & Boon, an imprint of Harlequin (UK) Limited,
Eton House, 18-24 Paradise Road, Richmond, Surrey, TW9 1SR

© 2015 Rebecca Winters

ISBN: 978-0-263-25156-2

23-0815

Harlequin (UK) Limited's policy is to use papers that are natural, renewable and recyclable products and made from wood grown in sustainable forests. The logging and manufacturing processes conform to the legal environmental regulations of the country of origin.

Printed and bound in Spain
by CPI, Barcelona

Rebecca Winters, whose family of four children has now swelled to include five beautiful grandchildren, lives in Salt Lake City, Utah, in the land of the Rocky Mountains. With canyons and high alpine meadows full of wildflowers, she never runs out of places to explore. They, plus her favorite vacation spots in Europe, often end up as backgrounds for her romance novels, because writing is her passion, along with her family and church.

Rebecca loves to hear from readers. If you wish to e-mail her, please visit her website, www.cleanromances.com.

Dedicated to Christopher R. Russell,
a military warrior from Texas who has
become a cherished friend.
This is for you, Sarg.

Chapter One

"This is Tammy White and you're listening to Hill Country Cowboy Radio broadcasting from Bandera, Texas, the Cowboy Capital of the World!

"Oh boy, have we got a lineup for you on this Labor Day weekend, including the star of the Bandera Rodeo, Kellie Parrish from Austin, Texas, our state's hopeful to win the National Barrel Racing Championship in Las Vegas come December. She'll be our guest in the second segment of our show.

"Now hear this. All you cowgirls out there, listen up and hold on to your Stetsons because we have some jaw-dropping, gorgeous, bronco-busting, homegrown cowboys in studio. But that's not the best part. They're four of our famous, legendary Texas Rangers, the pride of the great state of Texas! I've asked my buddy Mel from the fire department to be on hand in case I go into cardiac arrest. It's not every day I'm surrounded by such hunky men. They're not only easy on the eyes, but they wear the star and put their lives on the line every day to protect us.

"Welcome, gentlemen. How come we're so lucky

that four of you were willing to be interviewed? Judging by the way you were laughing when you came into the booth, does it mean you're good friends both on and off duty?"

The men all looked at Cy. Their captain in the Austin office had asked him to be the spokesman for this interview. None of them wanted to do it, but the boss insisted it was important for the Rangers to have a positive public presence. Cy had to cowboy up.

"Yup. The four of us share a very unique bond."

"We want to hear all about it, but first why don't you introduce yourselves and tell us where you're from?"

"Sure. I'm Cyril Vance and call Dripping Springs home." Kit took his turn next. "Ranger Miles Saunders from Marble Falls." Vic followed. "Ranger Stephen Malone. I grew up in Blanco." Cy nodded to Luckey on the other side of Vic. "I'm Ranger James Davis from Austin."

"Ladies, it's too bad this isn't television! You'd eat your hearts out if you were sitting where I am. Through the Hill Country grapevine the station learned that a lot of Rangers are in Bandera to help celebrate Jack Hays Days. You'll see them riding their horses in tomorrow morning's parade. It would be hard to believe that anyone in the state of Texas doesn't know the name Jack Hays. But just in case you don't, we want to hear from you why the name of Jack Hays stirs the hearts of every Texan, particularly those of the Rangers."

"I'll take this," Vic volunteered. "When Sam Houston was reelected to the presidency in December 1841, he recognized the effectiveness of the Rangers. And on

January 29, 1842, he approved a law that officially provided for a company of mounted men to 'act as Rangers.' As a result, 150 Rangers under Captain John Coffee 'Jack' Hays were assigned to protect the southern and western portions of the Texas frontier. Houston's foresight in this decision proved successful in helping to repel the Mexican invasions of 1842, as well as shielding the white settlers against Indian attacks over the next three years."

Vic turned to Kit. "You tell the rest."

"Be happy to. Jack Hays was responsible for improving the quality of recruitments and initiating tough training programs for the new Rangers, as well as initiating an esprit de corps within his command.

"The Paterson Colt six-shooters had just been invented and Captain Hays and his men were fortunate to be armed with these weapons instead of single shotguns. When the Comanche attacked Captain Hays and his company of forty in Bandera Pass in 1842, they were defeated."

"Gentlemen? I found a quote from Walter Prescott Webb, a twentieth-century US historian who said, 'Their enemies were pretty good…the Texas Rangers had to be better.' Do you Rangers still use those old six-shooters? If not, what kind of weapons do you carry?"

Luckey spoke up. "We use a variety that includes the .357-caliber SIG Sauer, the .45-caliber Colt automatic, the SIG Sauer P226 pistol, the Ruger mini-14 automatic rifle and the Remington 12-gauge shotgun."

"There are dozens of questions I want to ask, but

since you're pressed for time, why don't you tell our listeners why the four of you are particularly close?"

Cy nodded. "When I joined the Rangers, I didn't know any of the men in the company. On my application, I'd mentioned that I was a descendant of one of the men in Captain Jack Hays's company of forty. During my interview with our captain at company H, he told me there were three other Rangers in our company who could also trace their ancestry back to the original company of forty."

"Wow!"

"Wow is right. He got the four of us together. The rest was history."

"Imagine that. What a remarkable coincidence! You guys are the real thing. It's in your genes. Kind of gives you gooseflesh."

Kit chuckled. "That's one way of putting it. I can't remember a time when I didn't want to be a Texas Ranger. The pride my family felt for our heritage was instilled in me."

"It looks like none of you could escape your destiny."

Luckey grinned. "We wouldn't want to."

"I heard a rumor that everyone at Ranger headquarters has nicknamed you four 'the Sons of the Forty.' That's heady stuff."

"We don't mind," Vic stated. "But it gives us a lot to live up to."

"I'd say you're doing a spectacular job. According to your captain, the governor of our state gave you citations six months ago for your capture of a drug cartel ring on the most-wanted list. Do the four of you always work together on a case?"

Cy shook his head. "No. It's a very rare occurrence that we have an opportunity to do something big together, but we help each other out from time to time. Each case is different."

"Cowboys and cowgirls? Our station is honored that these Texan heroes have taken time out of their busy lives to let us know a little bit more about them. I have it on good report from your captain that the Sons of the Forty will be leading other Rangers on horseback from all over the state in the parade tomorrow. That will be the chance for you ladies to feast your eyes on the best of the best! Thank you for coming in. It's been a Hill Country thrill for me and everyone listening."

"Thank *you*," they said in a collective voice.

KELLIE GOT OUT of her truck in front of the radio station, pressed for time. She'd just driven in from Amarillo over three hundred miles away, where she'd made a decent time in the rodeo the night before. But it wasn't the low score she'd wanted. The fact that she didn't get the best time had little to do with her skill or her horse's.

Since she'd been on a five-state, pro rodeo racing circuit over the past five weeks, she'd been deeply unsettled by a guy who'd been following her from venue to venue among Montana, Oregon, Utah, New Mexico and Texas.

He'd come up to her after her win in Pendleton, Oregon, and asked her out on a date. She told him she was married in order to put him off. When she drove to Utah for the Eagle Mountain Rodeo, there he was again while she was brushing down her horse after her event. He was hoping she'd changed her mind and would go out with him.

She warned him that if he ever came near her again, she'd call the police. At the same time she signaled to her horse handler, Cody. He walked over to find out what was wrong and the stalker took off.

Cody was taking care of her horse Starburst, the one she'd brought on this circuit along with her champion palomino, Trixie, who was the best horse Kellie had ever owned. Trixie had helped her get to the Pro National Rodeo Finals, which were held in December. It was only three months away and she didn't need any kind of problems that would cause her to lose focus.

The stalker had so frightened her, she'd stuck with her rodeo buddies for the rest of the night. Later on in Albuquerque, New Mexico, she found a note on her truck window that said she couldn't avoid him forever and accused her of lying about being married. That told her this man had mental problems, and that put her on edge. She kept the note to show the police.

Afraid this wacko might turn up in Amarillo, she'd bunked with her good friend Sally, who was married to Manny Florez, one of the bull riders in the rodeo. Cody stayed with her horses and looked after them.

After one more rodeo tomorrow night in Bandera, she would drive straight to her parents' ranch in Austin instead of going home to her town house. Together they'd go to the police. But right now she needed to get through this radio show and then put her horse through some exercises.

She'd left the animal in the horse trailer at the RV park on the outskirts of town with Sally and her husband. For the time being they were her protection.

Trying to conquer her fear of the man stalking her, she headed toward the entrance of the radio station and collided with the first of a group of tall, jean-clad men in Stetsons and cowboy boots coming out the door.

"Oh—I'm sorry." She stepped back, shocked by a dart of male awareness that passed through her at the contact. "I didn't see where I was going."

"No problem, Ms. Parrish." His eyes were a piercing midnight blue. "Good luck at the rodeo tomorrow evening. We'll be rooting for you." He tipped his white hat to her.

"Thank you," she murmured as they headed to a van in the parking area.

Kellie had met hundreds of cowboys in all shapes and sizes over her years pursuing her dream to get to the Finals. She'd dated quite a few, nothing serious. But these four were exceptionally good-looking. The man she'd brushed against had momentarily caused the breath to freeze in her lungs. Why hadn't *he* been the one to ask her out on a date in Oregon? She might have been a fool and said yes without knowing anything about him.

Stunned by her immediate attraction, she hurried inside the building afraid she was late. The receptionist told her to walk straight back to the broadcast booth.

"Oh, good. I'm glad you're here. We're on a station break. I'm Tammy White. You're even more beautiful in person. Thanks for doing the show. You're one of our state's biggest celebrities."

"Maybe with a few rodeo fans."

"You're too modest. Your appearance here is making my day."

"Thanks, Tammy." Kellie shook hands with her and sat down. "I barely got here in time."

"I don't suppose you bumped into the Sons of the Forty while you were on your way in here?"

Kellie blinked. "I actually did bump into one of them. Wait—aren't they the Texas Rangers who brought down a drug cartel recently? It was all over the news."

"Yup. You had the luck of getting to see them up close and personal." *Up close and personal is right.* "I swear if I weren't married…" Kellie knew exactly what she meant. The man with the deep blue eyes was a Texas Ranger!

Kellie couldn't believe it, except that she could. With his rock-hard physique and rugged features, he looked as if he could handle anything. Come to think of it, he had been wearing a badge over his Western shirt pocket. But she'd been so mesmerized by his male charisma, nothing much else registered.

"Okay, Kellie. We'll be live in seven seconds. Ready?"

"No. I'm no good behind a microphone." Her mind was still on the striking Ranger. Her body hadn't stopped tingling with sensation.

"Don't worry. Leave it all to me. This is going to be fun."

It would be fun if it weren't for the menace lurking

somewhere out there. Thank heaven for Sally and her husband, who were letting her stay in their trailer with them tonight and tomorrow night. Monday morning she'd take off at dawn.

She couldn't get back home fast enough to tell her parents what had been happening and go to the police. Kellie had put off telling them about this, hoping the man would give it up, because she didn't want her folks worrying about her. But she'd gotten a call in the middle of the night last night, which was the last straw. Her stalker was potentially dangerous, and that terrified her.

CY'S CAPTAIN, TJ HORTON, walked into his office Monday morning. The veteran Ranger now sported a head of gray hair, but he still looked tough enough to take on any fugitive and win. "It's good you're back."

"I'm just finishing up some paperwork on my last case."

"I've got a new one I'd like you to look over. It just came up. Come on into my office."

"Sure." He followed him down the hall. The captain told him to shut the door and take a seat. Cy could tell something was up.

TJ sat back in his swivel chair with his hands behind his head and smiled at him. "You men did the department proud over the weekend. I listened to your contribution on Hill Country Cowboy Radio. Whether you liked it or not—" nope, none of them liked it "—she made you guys out as the poster boys of the department. You're now known as the Famous Four. I thought that might happen, but good publicity never hurts in an age when law enforcement takes a lot of unfair hits. The favor you did for me personally was much appreciated."

"Anything to help, sir."

"I heard a *but* in there. Next year I'll pick another bunch to carry the flag."

"That's a relief."

TJ chuckled, but then leaned forward with a serious expression. "The police turned over a case to our office this morning. It's high profile and the victim could be in serious danger. Because the case has crossed state lines, they feel our department is better equipped to deal with it. I'd like your take on this one." He handed him a folder.

Cy nodded and opened it. The name Kellie Parrish leaped out at him. *She* was the person in danger?

With her silvery-gold hair and cornflower-blue eyes, the barrel racer was a knockout. Under other circumstances he would have liked to hang around the radio station and listen to her interview. She'd been on his mind ever since he'd seen her a few days ago.

He scanned the folder's contents. She was being pursued by a stalker. He'd followed Ms. Parrish across her latest five-state racing schedule. She'd given the lieutenant a description of the man and a typewritten note he'd left on her truck windshield.

The most alarming aspect of the case was the fact that this stalker had phoned her cell phone as recently as the middle of Friday night. She'd been asleep in her friend's trailer in Bandera before driving to Austin this morning. Terrified, she'd gathered her parents and come straight to police headquarters.

Cy let out a low whistle. "I met her coming in the radio station as we were leaving on Friday. We watched her perform at the rodeo Saturday night. She had the second-best time."

"That's not only an amazing coincidence, but fortuitous. It isn't often you already have prior knowledge of the victim, so you understand what kind of threat she's been living with."

Especially when he'd found her incredibly attractive.

The hairs lifted on the back of his neck. Cy couldn't remember the last time he'd had this strong a feeling for a woman in passing. Because of the stress of the job, he didn't have much time for dating and hadn't been out with anyone for at least four months. After watching Ms. Parrish's performance at the rodeo, he'd admired her skill and found himself wondering how to go about getting to know her better. Not in his wildest dreams had he thought it would happen like this.

TJ kept on talking. "The police chief told me her parents met her at the station. They're well-heeled ranchers from southeast Austin who are demanding protection for their daughter and are willing to pay for it. Ms. Parrish is a prominent athlete. I've already ruled out a possible kidnapping scheme with a plan to collect a ransom or she would likely have been abducted at her first stop in Montana. Her parents want her to quit the rodeo circuit and stay with them until this lowlife is caught. She's their only child."

Cy got it. Ms. Parrish was their precious baby.

He shifted his attention from the file to his boss. "If you could have seen the way she rides, you'd know she would never agree to that." Even under so much stress, she'd put in a terrific time at the Bandera Rodeo. "Otherwise, I'm certain she would have quit the circuit in Pendleton when he first showed up and returned to Austin to contact the police. Several of her competitors headed for the championship in Las Vegas were also in Bandera competing. My bet is on her winning the whole thing."

TJ shook his head. "In order for that to happen, she would need full-time bodyguards on the circuit with her. Her parents can afford it. I'll call them now and ask them to bring her back to headquarters so you can talk to her. When you've got a feel for what you're dealing with, let me know how you want to handle this case."

"TJ? Send her in to me first. Then I'll talk to her folks." Parents had their own ideas about what should be done. It simplified things to talk to the victim without anyone else in the room. "I'll let you know when I want them to join us."

His boss nodded in understanding.

"Until they arrive I'll dig up some more background information on her. I'd better get to it." Cy got to his feet and headed for his own office. He'd start with the personal information listed on her website and go from there. Uncanny how he'd already planned to look at her site when he got the chance, just to learn more about her.

"Let's see what turns up on you, Ms. Parrish."

He typed it in and sat back. Seconds later, there she was astride her palomino, lying low over her horse as it was racing straight down the alley. Pure poetry.

Kellie Parrish
Born: Austin, Texas, on February 14, 1990
Residence: Austin, Texas
Dad: Bronco Parrish—3-time NFR Bull Rider Champion
Mom: Nadine Parrish—Barrel Racer Finals 4 times
Horses: Smokey, Walnut, Miss Pandora, Crackers, Farley, Starburst, Trixie
Joined Pro Rodeo at age 11
Total Earnings: $2,103,775
Wrangler NFR Qualification: 10
College National Finals Qualification: 2
National High School Rodeo Finals Qualifications: 4
Pro Wrangler Finals winner, Oklahoma City, OK: 3
Women's Pro Rodeo Association member

Cy read her blog, keeping track of the dates of the entries for July and August. She'd archived her previous blogs. Her ardent fans wanted to know all about her. How come she wasn't married yet? Did she have a boyfriend?

She'd answered that she preferred to keep her private life private, but she was friendly and encouraging to those trying to become barrel racers themselves. She urged them to click to her online clinic for pointers. That woman was so busy, Cy didn't know how she had time to breathe.

She'd put her rodeo schedule for the season on a separate page. There were links to the WPR Association and all the social media accounts. In other words, her life was pretty well an open book and prime fodder for the degenerate who'd targeted her. Talk about a sitting duck! A gorgeous one.

His eyes went back to her personal stats. The questions some of the commentors asked about her personal life had grabbed his attention. Some of them might have been sent by the stalker. An idea on how to handle this case had started to form in his mind. He reached for the phone to arrange for their department's sketch artist to be on hand when she came in. They needed a picture to run through the criminal database, which could access the files from every state in the union to come up with a match.

There was no telling how long the creep had been stalking other women or when his sick fantasy about Ms. Parrish had started. She'd been traveling the circuit for a number of years. He could have seen her anywhere at any time. But he'd approached her for the first time in Oregon only four weeks ago. Cy would start there.

In case this man was a serial stalker or worse, he wanted a list of every known stalking incident in the Pendleton area in the past year. While he waited for the Parrish family to arrive at headquarters, he put through a call to the Pendleton police department. He asked them to fax him the names of stalking victims and their descriptions of the men menacing them, whether their cases had been solved or were still open. One of those descriptions might match up with the man Kellie Parrish had described.

Restless, Cy went to the cubbyhole down the hall they called a lunchroom and poured himself a cup of coffee while he waited. He had dozens of questions to ask. Vic walked in on him. Their eyes met.

"Guess who's in the boss's office."

His pulse raced for no good reason. *She's here.* Kellie Parrish had made an impact on all the guys. "I already know. A stalker's after her."

His friend's black brows shot up. "You got the case?" Cy smiled. "How come that never happens to me?" Vic poured himself some coffee. "If you need help…"

"Thanks. I'll let you know." Cy took his mug back to his office.

Before long, TJ appeared at the door with her. She was probably five foot seven without her cowboy boots. "I believe you two have already met. Ms. Parrish? Meet one of our agents, Cyril Vance."

Cy got to his feet and shook her hand. "It's a pleasure to meet you again, Ms. Parrish, even if it is under harrowing circumstances."

Fear had darkened the blue of her eyes. "I hope you forgive me for bumping into one of the Sons of the Forty. I'm the one who's honored." TJ had disappeared.

"Please sit down."

"Thank you." She'd dressed in jeans and a creamy-colored Western shirt. Beneath the overhead light, her neck-length wavy hair had that silvery-gold metallic sheen he found stunning. So were her face and the rest of her curvaceous figure. Absolutely stunning.

"Can I get you coffee or a soft drink?"

"Neither, thanks."

"I'm going to record our conversation if that's all right with you."

"Of course."

"I have the notes taken by the police. It says here this stalker last contacted you by phoning in the middle of the night."

"Yes. That was Friday," she said, tight-lipped. "I don't know how he knew my cell number."

"How many people have you given it to?"

"My parents, closest friends, my cousin Heidi and of course my horse handler, Cody."

"Tell me about him."

"He's been my closest horse friend since middle school. We've both had our dreams. I was going to win the PRO Finals Rodeo this year and teach barrel racing. He was going to help me and then run a stud farm. Cody is engaged and plans to get married after Finals."

He nodded. "When you fill out forms of any kind, do you list it as your contact number?"

"No. It's not written anywhere. I always give out my parents' number. No...wait. I did give my cell phone number to a friend, Olivia Brown, who works at the Women's Pro Rodeo Association in Colorado Springs, Colorado. She used to ride with our Blue Bonnet Posse, but her husband was transferred to Colorado Springs, so she got a job with the rodeo association there."

"I'll want to talk to her. Now I'll need a list of your friends and cousin, and their phone numbers. Here's some paper."

"All right." She got right to work. When she'd finished, she looked up.

He took the list from her. "Thank you. What did the stalker say on the phone?"

She bit her lip. "'You lied about having a husband. Don't you know it's not nice to lie?' Then he hung up."

"Was there just the one call that night?" She nodded. "Now let's talk about everything that happened the first time this man made contact with you."

She shuddered visibly. "It was right after the barrel-racing event and awards. I was in the process of removing the saddle from Trixie when I heard an unfamiliar male voice from behind call me by my first name. I turned around to discover a total stranger invading my space. A lot of guys have approached me over the years wanting a date, so it wasn't unusual."

Cy could believe it.

"I don't mean to sound full of myself. It's just part of what goes on during the racing circuit, and I've always taken it in good fun before turning them down. But this was different. He came too close. After telling him no, he just stood there with a smile that made my stomach churn. Something about him wasn't right."

"Could you tell if he'd been drinking?"

"No. I couldn't smell alcohol. I was holding the saddle in front of me with both hands and I told him I was married, hoping he'd get the message and go away. When he calmly told me to prove it, I would have thrown the saddle at him and called security, but a couple of friends happened to walk over and he disappeared. I didn't see him again until I drove to Utah for the next rodeo at Eagle Mountain a week later."

"You drive a truck and horse trailer?"

"Yes. I live in the trailer while I'm on the road. My

horse handler drives his own truck and trailer carrying one of my other horses."

"Do you own a car?"

She nodded. "A four-door white Toyota sedan. I keep it at the condo when I'm gone."

"Do you own or rent?"

"Rent. After I leave the rodeo circuit, I'll be buying my own place."

"Where's the parking?"

"The double-car garage is in back, but there's parking in front."

"Is it in a complex?"

"It's a two-story town house with neighbors on either side of me."

Cy paused long enough to buzz the artist to come to his office, and then he turned to her. "We need a picture of this man. Without a photograph we'll have to rely on your eyes. Our department artist has a singular gift."

She clasped her hands together. "All right."

"While we wait for him, I want you to think back. Before Pendleton, have you ever had the slightest suspicion that someone had targeted you?"

"No. Never."

That sounded final. Jim showed up at the door with a sketch pad and electric eraser pencil. "Come on in, Jim. Ms. Parrish, our state's reigning barrel-racing champion, is being stalked. Let's see what you can work up."

"Sure." He sat in the chair next to Kellie, eyeing her in male appreciation. "It's a privilege to meet you, Ms. Parrish. We'll start with a sketch. I could use the computer, but a sketch can tell you things the computer can't. Don't get nervous or frustrated. You may think this won't work, but in three out of ten cases a culprit has been caught through a sketch. I'll work from the eyes on out. Shall we get started?"

She nodded and answered one question after another while he sketched. They worked together while he refined his drawing.

Cy asked her for a more thorough description while Jim was working.

"He looks like the guy next door. You know, someone's brother. Maybe late twenties. Kind of lean. Okaylooking. Nutty-brown hair that curls. Short-cropped. Maybe five-ten, but he was wearing cowboy boots. Weighs probably 150 to 160 pounds. Brown eyes. He wore jeans and a different pullover the second time I saw him."

Jim kept working at the sketch and showed her what he'd done. She said, "His nose was a little thinner." After fixing it he asked her to take another look. "What do you think?"

"You truly do have a gift. It's remarkably accurate."

"We try."

Cy took the drawing from him. The guy bore a superficial resemblance to Ted Bundy, the serial killer from several decades back, but he kept the observation to himself. "That's great work, Jim. We'll go with this to put in the Integrated Automated Fingerprint Identification System. Thank you."

"You're welcome." He turned to Kellie. "All bets are on you winning the championship in December."

"Thank you so much."

"If anyone can catch him, Ranger Vance can. See you, Cy."

When Jim left the office, she looked at Cy. "You're called Cy?"

"Short for Cyril." *Don't get sidetracked.* "Your next rodeo is in South Dakota in two weeks, but I understand your parents want you to quit the circuit."

"Yes, but since we talked with the police, Dad has told me he'll hire some bodyguards for me so I can continue to compete."

Cy shook his head. "That won't work. We want to draw out this stalker and arrest him. He'll know if you have people protecting you. That will change the way he has to operate. It will hinder our efforts and prolong the time you're forced to live in terror."

Her eyes clouded. "I don't want to give up competition, not when I'm so close to the Finals in December. Isn't there another way?"

Yes, but he didn't know if she'd consider it. He knew her parents would raise objections.

"There's always another way. If you'll excuse me for a moment, I'll be right back." He left the office and headed for TJ's, knocking on the open door.

His boss's head lifted. "Come on in."

Cy shut the door and sat down. "Where are her parents?"

"In the reception area. Have you got an angle on this case yet?"

He nodded and brought him up-to-date. Then he told him his idea. TJ didn't say anything at first. That didn't surprise Cy. "I know it's unconventional."

"Unconventional? Hell, Cy. It's unorthodox and unheard-of in this department."

"But it could work. This way she could continue winning rodeos."

Another few minutes passed before TJ said, "I'll admit it's brilliant. You realize the two of you will be walking a very thin line."

Yup. Cy knew exactly what he meant and he wasn't talking about the culprit. "I'll need another Ranger working with me. Whoever you can spare."

His eyes squinted. "You think she'll agree?"

"Probably not, but it's worth finding out. She's had the world championship in her sights since she was eleven years old. If she says no, then I'll know I was wrong to think she'd do anything to achieve her goal."

He nodded slowly. "All right. You bring her in here and I'll send for her parents. She doesn't need their permission, but they'll have to be in on this from the start or it won't work. I'll make sure all three of them are fingerprinted before they leave the building today."

"Right."

Chapter Two

Cy's plan was bold. But no matter how many ways he could think of to attack the problem, he kept coming back to his first idea.

"Ms. Parrish?" he spoke to her from the doorway. She got to her feet. "If you'll come with me, we're going to meet in the captain's office with your folks."

They walked down the hall, where Cy met Kellie's parents. She took after her father in height and coloring. From her mother she'd inherited her good looks and figure. He shook their hands.

TJ invited everyone to sit down. "Ranger Vance has looked at every aspect of this case and has come up with a strategy. Every so often our Rangers plan a sting and go undercover. It's a very effective way to flush out a criminal. Your daughter's case presents a challenge because no one wants to see her quit the barrel-racing circuit when she's so close to winning the championship in Las Vegas." He glanced at Cy. "Tell them your thinking."

Cy got to his feet. "You could hire bodyguards. But it would probably cause the culprit to stay away for a time, not *go* away. We want this stalker to be put away permanently, and ASAP. The best thing to do is flush him out."

"That makes sense to me," her father said.

"What if he's followed me here to this office?" Kellie sounded anxious, but was still keeping her composure. Cy admired her for that.

"I'm sure he's done that and a lot of other things. He knows where you and your parents live. He knows your rodeo schedule, your phone number. He knows your routine and enjoys frightening you. But we're going to turn the tables on him and produce the husband he doesn't believe exists."

Those blue eyes rounded in shock.

"A husband is different from a bodyguard who goes with you everywhere. A husband and wife have their moments of separation. While I'm not with you, one of my team will be guarding you from a distance.

"To set this up, you'll announce your secret through your blog. I've read through it. Your fans have pressed you over and over again to reveal if there's a special man in your life. After telling them all this time that your life is private, you're going to tell them that you recently married a cowboy. Furthermore you are looking forward to a long honeymoon after the Finals in Las Vegas.

"By putting the announcement out on the internet, it will prove to the world you are telling the truth. Of course, this stalker still won't believe you because you've been his fantasy for a long time and he doesn't live in anyone's reality but his own. I still have yet to discover if he's a psychotic who has lost all connection to his world, or a psychopath with a serious mental disorder. But in either case he'll be enraged when he reads your blog.

"I can assure you he's been reading it for as long as he's been stalking you, and so far there's been no mention of a husband. He thinks he's safe. I have no doubt that some of the people making comments about your personal life on your blog have come from this lowlife."

At that observation she paled.

"It will torture him that you really could be married. He thinks he knows everything about you and won't be able to stand the fact that he could be wrong. That will bring him out of lurk mode. When he does that, it will be his big mistake.

"We have no idea of his place of birth or where he lives. He could be from Austin and followed you all the way to Oregon to begin his reign of terror. You can be sure he has already cased your condo and your parents' ranch and knows every move you make. The Pendleton police are sending me a list of stalking victims in the Pendleton area in case there's a way to link him to your case.

"If he'd wanted to kidnap you to compel your parents to pay a ransom, it would have already happened. So we can conclude money is not his motive. Though you didn't see him in Albuquerque, we know he was out there somewhere putting a note on your windshield and phoning you in the middle of the night in Bandera. According to your schedule, you have another rodeo in South Dakota in two weeks. For the time being I imag-

ine you'll be training here in Austin every day until
you leave. He's probably planning to do something to
you while you're not on the road. Remember—he feels
invincible."

When she heard Cy's assessment of the situation, he
noticed she'd lowered her head, causing the strands of
her molten hair to catch the light from overhead.

"So far you've had your handler and other people
around while you've been taking care of your horses.
But he'll assume you'll be alone in your condo part of
the time for the next two weeks. The beauty of this plan
is that when he comes after you, I'll be there watching
for him. When he makes his move, he'll discover your
husband on the premises. Do you have any questions?"

Now was the time for Kellie to tell him she couldn't
go along with his plan. He held his breath, waiting for
her parents to voice their objections. Instead, her mother
looked at her daughter with an anxious expression.

"His plan sounds solid, but how do you feel about
it, honey?"

He watched Kellie nervously moisten her lips. "I'm
thankful I won't have to be alone." She looked up at Cy.
"Even if it means everyone will think I'm married, I
want that disgusting creature caught." Her voice shook.

TJ sent Cy a silent message. *I'll be damned.*

"Before you go home with your parents, I'll need
your key to the condo and your phone, Ms. Parrish."

"All right." Her hands trembled as she rummaged
in her purse for those items and handed them to him.

"What's the code to get into the garage?" She told
him. "Keep your mailbox key."

"Oh. Okay."

He looked at his watch. "Give me six hours, then all of you come to the condo with any luggage you took on the road and I'll let you in. Pick up your mail on the way in, but don't go through it. Act as normally as you can. We'll talk details inside your condo so we're all tuned in to the same channel."

Kellie's father shook Cy's hand again. "Our daughter didn't tell us what had been happening to her until this morning. It's a nightmarish situation and we're very grateful that you're willing to take her case. We'll all be praying this plan works."

"Thank you for helping her," Kellie's mother said with tears in her eyes.

"It's our job and I'm happy to do it. I'll see you later."

He watched Kellie walk out with them. Cy knew in his gut that this stalker didn't want money. He wanted to do her harm. She'd said he looked as if he was in his late twenties. He wondered how many women before Kellie had already been terrorized by him. The stalker fit the general profile for a predator who was usually from eighteen to thirty.

After they left TJ's office, Cy turned to his boss. "Her condo is in West Austin. I'm going to need help to set things up before they arrive."

"This is a high-priority case. Vic just finished a case and is in the building right now. I'll ask him to assist you before assigning him a new case."

Nothing could have pleased him more. "Thanks, TJ." There wasn't a lot of time. They'd have to assemble a team fast.

Not long after he'd returned to his office to send the artist's sketch to the database, Vic walked in. "I'm all yours." He planted himself on a corner of the desk. "That stint on the radio must have put the boss in a good mood."

"It was so important to him, he actually went along with my plan."

"Which is?"

"Outrageous, but Ms. Parrish agreed to it, too, rather than leave the circuit. She wants to win that championship. I figured she would put her desire to achieve her lifelong goal over her fear of this stalker. We're going to pretend to be married so I can protect her day and night."

"What?" Vic's black eyes narrowed. He got to his feet. "You're kidding me."

Cy gave his friend a sharp look. "Can you think of a better way to get the job done?"

They'd known each other a long time. "Hell, no. It's genius, but—"

"But it doesn't hurt that she's a beautiful woman, right?" He couldn't help but read his friend's mind. "I've examined my motives and have decided that even if she were someone else, it wouldn't make a difference. She's been working her whole life to achieve her goal. For her to quit now would be the end of her dreams, not only for this year, but maybe forever. Anyone with her kind of skill and drive deserves all the help she can get."

"I agree with you."

"This guy is a creep who's been tormenting her for a month. She told him she was married so he'd leave her alone. All that did was fan the flames, so I've decided it's time she produced a husband. I want to catch this stalker, Vic, and believe this is the best way to capture his attention and nab him."

"Where do you want to start?"

"We'll get a surveillance team set up in the van to monitor her when I can't be with her." Cy handed him the sketch.

Vic studied it for a minute. "You know who he looks like?"

"Yup, but let's not go there. In case he's camped out by her condo, you and I will impersonate roofers so we can get in around the back of the building through her garage without him suspecting anything. I want to lift any fingerprints we can find. We'll rig the interior with a camera. Let's move."

He folded her list of names and numbers and put it into his pocket. The note she'd given the police needed to go down to the lab. He already had a list a mile long of things to be done before she arrived with her parents. They'd need wedding rings.

KELLIE CHECKED HER watch as her father drove them to the front of her condo in her parents' Volvo sedan. Six thirty p.m. She still couldn't believe what she'd agreed to. She and the striking Texas Ranger had to pretend to be married starting tonight!

What have I done? She closed her eyes. *You've done what's necessary to survive.*

"Come on, honey. Let's go in and have dinner. You haven't eaten all day."

"I couldn't." But her parents had insisted on picking up some barbecue for all of them.

She hadn't had an appetite since this first started. As for sleep… Nothing seemed real. That monster could have been following them from the ranch. She almost expected him to suddenly appear at the mailbox.

The normal number of bills had stacked up. She put the mail into her purse before getting back in the car. Her mom had been over to her condo several times this past month to water her plants and make sure everything was all right. Thank goodness the Ranger would find her house clean and in good shape. There were times when it looked a mess.

She eyed the condo. No one would know the secret it was holding. If everything had gone as planned, then the Ranger was inside. A vision of the way he'd looked when she'd bumped into him in Bandera was indelibly impressed in her mind. He was a man whose aura gave the impression he could deal with anything or one. Her pulse raced at the realization they would be spending time together.

Kellie got out of the car and hurried up the front steps ahead of her parents. He must have heard them because he opened the door to let them in.

"Hi." His deep voice filtered through to her insides.

Kellie looked up at him. "Hi." He'd changed into a dark blue sport shirt and jeans. His eyes matched his shirt. Outside the radio station, he'd been wearing his white Stetson. But in his office as well as now, the light in the living room illuminated the sun-bleached tips of his wavy light brown hair.

Her mother was carrying the food. "I've brought dinner for all of us."

The Ranger smiled and took the bag from her. "Thank you, Mrs. Parrish. How did you know I'm starving?"

The way the corners of his eyes crinkled sent a surprising curl of warmth through Kellie, who put her purse on a chair. While he and her mother went to the kitchen, she turned to help her father carry her bags upstairs to the bedroom. That was when she saw that another couch had been added to the living room. Everything had been rearranged so it would fit.

As they passed the guest bedroom upstairs, she saw some of the Ranger's things on the bed. She avoided her father's eyes and continued to her room.

"Are you okay, Kellie?"

"I don't know what I am yet, but knowing this Ranger is here to protect me is all that's helping keep my sanity right now."

Her dad gave her a big hug. "I'm relieved, too. The captain told me Ranger Vance was one of the men who brought down the drug cartel earlier in the year. He says there's no one better, and I believe him. Come on. Let's go back down and hear what this Ranger has to say."

Kellie nodded. "I'll be there in a minute." She needed to pull herself together.

He kissed her forehead and left. She took time to freshen up in the bathroom before joining everyone at the dining room table. When the Ranger saw her, he stood. "I'm sure it's strange for you to feel like a guest in your own home."

"I'm too thankful you're here to think about it."

He sat back down. "These ribs are delicious. Thank you. I work better on a full stomach. Tonight I'm going to help your daughter draft her marriage announcement message for her blog. By ten it will be out on the internet. As her parents, you'll be bombarded with questions from everyone who knows you. I want you to tell them that Kellie and I met on the circuit. It was love at first sight and we couldn't stand to wait, so we were privately married before her rodeo performance in Montana.

"Tell people there will be a wedding reception for us at the ranch in December, after Finals. Don't say any more or any less. We'll worry about explanations after this stalker is caught."

This is really happening. She eyed her parents, who agreed to do exactly as he said. He had a way of instilling confidence and trust.

He looked at them. "From here on out, Kellie is going to do what she would do if there were no threat. The three of you will carry on with your lives while I work behind the scenes. No one is to know about this case except the four of us and my team."

"Sally and Cody know a man was bothering me."

"I talked with both of them earlier in the day. They won't be telling anyone about this."

Kellie's father thanked him again. "I think it's time we left the two of you alone so you can get on with your plans. Come on, Nadine."

They both got up from the table. Kellie jumped up to hug them. "I'll call you all the time so you're not worried."

"We love you, honey."

"We do," her father said in a gruff voice and gave her a bear hug. "Do everything the Ranger says."

"I promise." She walked them to the front door. "I love you. Thank you for being the best parents on earth."

"I won't let anything happen to her," the Ranger assured them before they left the condo. The conviction in his voice prevented Kellie from breaking down.

Kellie shut the door and hurried past him to clear the table. He helped put everything in the waste bin while she wiped down the top. "If you want to get started on the blog piece, we can do it here."

"Sounds good, but let's sit down for a minute and lay the groundwork."

She nodded and followed his suggestion. He sat across from her. "First of all, I'd like you to call me Cy and I'll call you Kellie. Next, we need to make this real." He reached in his shirt pocket and set three rings on the table. After putting the larger gold band on the ring finger of his left hand, he said, "Go ahead and see if they fit."

With trembling fingers, she picked up the engagement ring with a beautiful one-carat diamond. She slid it on and it was a surprisingly good fit. So was the gold wedding band. The moment was surreal.

"How do they feel, Mrs. Vance?"

Her head flew back. Their gazes fused for a moment. *It feels too natural.* "Fine."

"Will they bother you when you ride?"

She blinked. "No. My right hand does most of the work."

"Good. Let's discuss the living arrangements. I plan

to sleep downstairs and had the team bring over a hide-a-bed couch. If you don't mind, I'll use the half bath on this floor, but I'll shower upstairs when you're not here. For the time being I'll use the guest room to store my clothes and equipment."

In the next breath he pulled a pair of latex gloves from his back pocket and put them on.

"Why don't you bring me the mail? I'll go through it in case this stalker has sent you a message to frighten you further."

At the thought, her body broke out in a cold sweat. Kellie went into the living room to get her purse and brought it to the table. After she opened it, he reached inside and took out the bills.

He went through the pile one piece at a time. "Let me know if you see something odd."

She shook her head. "It's the usual bills and ads."

He kept going. When he came to a *Cowboy Times* magazine, he held it up by the spine. Two cards fell out along with a three-by-five white envelope. He picked up the letter. There was no return name or address. Her name and address had been typed on the front. "This was postmarked from Austin on the same day he approached you in Eagle Mountain."

Kellie felt her stomach drop while she watched him open it. He spread out the eight-by-ten piece of folded paper. The word *liar* jumped out at them in big letters. She gasped. The stalker had cut them out of some magazine and had glued them on.

"This is going to the forensics lab. It's my opinion that over the years this man has had a string of broken relationships, maybe a failed marriage, and feels betrayed. He has no friends or anyone he's emotionally connected to. Every time he finds a new target, he convinces himself it's love. When nothing works out, he goes into a rage because every woman turns out to be a liar."

"I wonder how many other women he's done this to."

"Who knows, but it stops with you. I noticed you have a laptop upstairs. Why don't you bring it down and we'll get started on your announcement?"

"I'll be right back." When she brought it down a minute later, she noticed he'd put the letter in a plastic bag and had discarded the gloves. He'd also produced a laptop she'd seen lying on the hide-a-bed.

"I'd like to access more of your archives while you work on what you want to say."

"I'll send them to your computer." He gave her his address.

They worked side by side. She wrote something, then deleted it and started again. After several attempts she got into the blog-writing mode and allowed herself to go with the flow.

"How's it coming?" His deep voice broke the silence, but it continued to resonate inside her.

"It's almost there. I'll send you a copy in a minute to see what you think. After I've denied any involvement with a man, it's going to have to be convincing." She read over what she'd written so far.

Hi, all my faithful rodeo fans out there! I'm back from my last rodeo in Bandera, Texas, and won't be competing until two weeks from now in Rapid City, South Dakota, where I'll start out my Midwest circuit. My times have been up and down lately. But that's because something thrilling has happened to me in my personal life.

So many times you've asked me if I have a boyfriend or if I plan to get married one day. I've always said that my love life was private. But I can't keep quiet about this any longer. I did find the man of my dreams while I've been on the rodeo circuit. It was love at first sight for this gorgeous hunk of a cowboy. He's bigger than life to me and my hero in more ways than one.

We decided we couldn't stand to wait to get married until Finals in December. So we tied the knot in a private ceremony before my competition in Pendleton, Oregon. I'm so happy to be his wife, I go around in a daze. It's little wonder I've been unable to concentrate. Trixie thinks I'm a little crazy, bless her heart. It's a miracle she puts up with me and knows how to kill the cans in spite of me.

All of you know I always had a rule that I wouldn't allow a man to throw me off my game while I was riding the circuit. No distractions for me. No siree. But I hadn't met my husband when I said that. The second I looked into his eyes, my world changed in an instant. He's the prince I dreamed about when I was a little girl. He's the great man I'd hoped to meet while traveling the circuit around this great country of the USA.

We'll have a wedding reception after Finals. I'll post some pictures. You'll all swoon when you see him!

PS: Of course I want to win the championship, but

winning the love of my husband surpasses all else. I'm the luckiest cowgirl on the planet and grateful for all of you who constantly send me your support. Long live the rodeo!

Kellie saved the file and pushed the send button. In order to make her blog convincing, she'd had to put her heart into it. But while she waited for his opinion, heat crept into her cheeks. "I just sent you the announcement. While you check it for changes, I'll get a cola. Would you like one?"

"Sure. Thanks."

"Let me know what you think," she said and left the room.

CY OPENED THE file and started to read. His heart thudded when he came to the lines "The second I looked into his eyes, my world changed in an instant. He's bigger than life to me and my hero in more ways than one." The more he read, the harder his heart pounded.

"What do you think?" She put a cold can of cola in front of him. "I know it's probably too much, but I realize this has to convince my readers."

He opened his drink and swallowed half of it in one go. "I agree it's over-the-top, but it sounds like it came from the heart. When that creep reads this, it will push his buttons to the limit. The only correction is to delete Pendleton and put in Glasgow, Montana. That was your event before you left for Oregon. We don't want him to think his appearance in Pendleton had anything to do with the timing of your marriage."

She pulled the laptop in front of her and made the change. "I should have thought of that." Kellie smiled at him. "That's why you're one of the Sons of the Forty! Okay. It's done."

"Go ahead and post it. Now we wait. I wouldn't be surprised if your fans respond in droves and overload your website."

Cy finished off his drink and got up from the table to toss it in the wastebasket. He'd left her phone on the counter and brought it to her. "I checked your phone. The only call you received in the middle of the night came from a throwaway phone and couldn't be traced. I want you to continue to answer your phone.

"I've set it up with an app so you can record an incoming call. I'll walk you through this. It's easy." He pulled his own cell phone from his shirt pocket. "I'll call you. After you've answered, press Four and it will start recording. Ready?"

"Yes."

He pressed the digit that had programmed her number. She let it ring three times, then clicked on. "Hello?"

Cy nodded, letting her know to press the number four digit.

"Hi, Kellie. Did you just get back from Bandera?"

"I drove in this morning."

"How's Trixie?"

"She's at the ranch getting some TLC."

"I bet you wish you were with her."

"Tomorrow I'll drive out there and we'll go for a ride."

"Sounds fun. Talk to you later."

He held the phone away from his ear. "Now click End Call. The recording is downloaded to your iPhone and displayed on the screen. Tap the recording icon to listen. You can also trim the recording as needed by dragging the edge of the file on the screen."

She followed his directions and suddenly they heard their conversation while seeing it at the same time. A natural smile broke out on her lips. Good grief, she was beautiful. "Technology is amazing."

"In your case it's crucial. I want every word recorded when he phones you again."

"Do you think he'll try soon?"

Cy nodded. "If I don't miss my guess, he won't be able to hold back, not after what you've put on your blog."

"I'm afraid to talk to him." He noticed her shiver. "I don't think I'll be able to sleep tonight."

"Tell you what. Why don't you go upstairs and get ready for bed? Then come down here to sleep on the couch for tonight. I'll be nearby on the other couch. If he calls, I'll be right here. Try to get him to talk about why he thought you were lying to him. Anything he says could give us a clue about him."

"You wouldn't mind? I'm behaving like a baby."

"You're behaving like a woman who's being stalked. But I admire you for not giving in to your fear. That's what he wants. He's been watching you for a month if not longer and still doesn't believe you're married. But the blog entry will force him to reveal himself. The phone allows him a voice connection to you. Keep him on long enough for our voice experts to analyze it."

"What do you mean?"

"Vocal oscillations convey so much about the speaker. But more important, our experts will be able to tell if he's a Texan. A Texas accent stands apart from the rest of the South in that it has a twist that is a blending of the major features of the Deep South and Upper South."

"I didn't know that."

He nodded. "The drawl of the Lower South has more influence in East Texas, while the 'twang' of the Upper South has left a greater imprint on West Texas. In South Texas, particularly, the Spanish and Mexican characteristics are heavily combined with that of the others. Once we get a recording of his voice to the experts, they can tell us if he's from here or another state or region entirely. If we can pinpoint where he's from, it could be a great help."

"Then I'll try to keep him on the phone. Excuse me while I run upstairs to get ready."

"Take your time. We've got all night."

Cy planned to stay in the clothes he was wearing. Tomorrow he'd shower and change while she was out at her parents' ranch.

While she was upstairs, he sat down to see if there were any responses to her blog yet. A low whistle escaped when he counted seventy responses already. He scrolled through each one. When he came to the end, he was satisfied none of them was her stalker. It was touching to read how much her fans cared about her and appreciated her help through her online rodeo tips. But they were all excited about her marriage.

He opened up the archives. There were literally hundreds of entries on her blog site. It amazed him. She was definitely a star in her own right and an obvious favorite. He knew she had dozens of awards, but she didn't keep them here. Probably at the ranch. One thing he knew about her already. There wasn't a narcissistic bone in her lovely body.

While he read through a few more entries, she padded into the kitchen in bare feet wearing a blue robe. Beneath it she wore pajamas with Texas Longhorns on them. She'd brought down a blanket and pillow.

Cy had to be careful not to stare. "I take it you're a football fan."

"These are from my parents last Christmas."

"My dad gave me a pair of the same pajamas two years ago." They both laughed.

As she came closer, her smile faded. "Has that lunatic sent a response yet?"

"No. But you now have four hundred hits. Your eager fans want pictures and don't want to wait until December."

Without saying anything, Kellie walked into the living room and lay down on the couch, propping up her pillow and covering herself with the blanket. Cy checked his watch. It was ten to eleven. He picked up her cell phone and put it on the coffee table in front of her.

Once he'd made up the hide-a-bed, he went back to the dining room for her laptop. After turning off the overhead lights, he turned on a lamp in the living room and sat down next to it so he could continue to read the responses as they came in.

"When are *you* going to sleep?"

He liked it that she was concerned enough to ask and flicked her a glance. "Don't worry about me."

She sat up. Her disheveled hair gleamed in the soft light. "I don't know how to begin to thank you for what you're doing for me."

"It's my job."

"A horrible one," she said in a shaky voice. "Every day on the news you hear about some stalking victim found in a landfill—"

"Don't go there." Cy stopped her cold. "Nothing's going to happen to you."

"But who protects *you*?"

He smiled to himself. "I have a team that backs me up. My buddy Vic, one of the men you saw coming out of the radio station with me, is helping on your case."

She lay back down. "You're all remarkable."

"Save your thanks until after we've caught him."

Chapter Three

Kellie had no doubt he'd get the job done, but Cy Vance was too modest for words. That was part of the charm of the man who was growing on her with every passing second. His rugged profile stood out in the lamplight. He'd stretched out in the chair with his hard-muscled legs crossed at the ankles.

She'd been around cowboys all her life. Some of them were more attractive than others. Some had great builds. Others were loaded with talent in the arena. Still others had engaging personalities. But this Texas Ranger had all of those qualities and more. He'd been put together in such a way no one could compare to him.

Impatient with herself for concentrating on the attractive Ranger, she turned over so she faced the back of the sofa. She needed sleep. Desperately. Knowing he was right across the room from her gave her a sense of comfort she hadn't felt since her first encounter with the stalker. How unbelievable was it that the Ranger she'd bumped into in Bandera had come into her life at the most precarious moment of her existence?

When her cell phone suddenly rang, she jerked upright. Kellie flung herself around, staring at her phone in terror.

"It's all right." Cy's deep voice was reassuring. "What does the caller ID say?"

She took a shaky breath. "It's my best friend, Kathie."

"Go ahead and talk to her. Put it on speaker."

Kellie reached for it and clicked on. "Kathie?"

"Hi! I know it's late, but I had to call you. Good grief, Kellie. Is it really true that you're married?"

Her gaze locked with Cy's. "Yes. How did you hear?"

"Patty told me she read it on your blog tonight. How come you didn't tell me?"

Oh dear. Kellie heard the hurt in her voice. Now for the lie… But this lie was going to save her life and it took away her guilt. "It happened while I was on the circuit and there was no time." That part was true. "Look, Kathie. It's a long story and—"

"And your husband wants your attention. Is he right there?"

At that remark Cy's eyes smiled. Kellie felt a fever coming on. "Yes. We just got in from Bandera. I'll tell you all about it later."

"He must really be something for you to get married so fast you didn't even have your parents there."

"W-we couldn't bear to wait any longer."

"Whoa. I'll hang up now, but I expect a detailed report later. You know what I mean."

Embarrassment brought the heat in waves. "Thanks for calling. We'll talk. I promise." She clicked off and put the phone back on the coffee table.

Cy closed the laptop and put it on the floor. He leaned forward with his hands clasped between his knees. "Kathie is one of the names on the list you gave me. Who is she?"

"My best friend in our group. Sally, my other friend, is a part of it, too."

"What group is that?"

"There are about thirty of us who ride for pleasure, but serve as volunteers in case of any kind of local emergency."

His brows lifted. "Do you have a name?"

"We're the Blue Bonnet Posse."

"That's right. You mentioned one of your friends from the group who moved to Colorado Springs. Come to think of it, I have heard of the posse. Weren't you the ones who found that autistic child who'd wandered away from home last year?"

"That one, and a lost Boy Scout. The police department calls our leader when they need volunteers to do a search in the outskirts of Austin."

"No doubt you're kept busy. Those lucky parents must be indebted to you. I'm impressed."

"It's our job." She echoed his earlier words to her.

"Touché." He reached down and pulled off his cowboy boots. She watched him turn out the lamp and stretch out on the hide-a-bed. It couldn't be that comfortable, and he hadn't even changed. He lay on his back with his hands behind his head.

She forced herself to look away. But no sooner had she curled on her side hoping to fall asleep than the phone rang again. Still petrified, but less startled this time, she reached for the phone.

"Put the speaker on," Cy reminded her.

She nodded. It was her father and she clicked on. "Hi, Dad. I've got the phone on speaker."

"Forgive me for calling this late, but your mom and I want to make certain you're all right."

Her gaze drifted to Cy. "I'm fine. Really. The news is out. Kathie just called me."

"We got a call from your cousin Heidi. She read your blog and couldn't believe it."

"I know this is going to come as a shock to everyone who knows me."

"They care about you. It's a tribute to the wonderful woman you are."

"Spoken like a biased parent."

"We love you, Kellie." His voice sounded gruff with emotion. "Tell that Ranger we can't thank him enough."

She looked at Cy's silhouette in the semidarkness. "He knows how you feel. All I do is thank him."

"We're expecting you for lunch. Good night, honey."

"You get a good sleep, Dad. Cy is keeping me perfectly safe. Love you." She hung up the phone and hugged her pillow.

The next time she had cognizance of her surroundings, she heard the phone ringing. Immediately her adrenaline brought her to a sitting position. The second she realized there was no name on the caller ID, she felt bile rise in her throat. Cy had already hunkered down at the coffee table, urging her to pick up and press the recording app.

Her body shook as she reached for the phone. Doing as Cy asked, she clicked on. "Hello?"

"I knew you got home today. How did you like my letter?"

Her eyes closed tightly. "How did you get my phone and address?"

"That was easy as skinning a cat."

She shuddered. "What do you want? I told you I'm married."

"I saw what you wrote on your blog. You think I'd believe that crap? You're a liar!" He shouted the last word.

"You think I'd lie to all my fans and friends? If that's true, then why do you keep phoning a liar?"

"Because you deserve to be taught a lesson you'll never forget."

"Did your girlfriend lie to you?"

"They all lie. When I get through with you, you'll wish you'd never been born, Kellie girl."

"My husband's going to have a lot to say about that."

"Liar, liar, liar, liar, liar, liar!" The line went dead.

Kellie was trembling so hard she dropped the phone. Cy retrieved it and clicked on the recorded conversation. She'd forgotten to put on the speakerphone. His jaw hardened as he listened to the recording.

"That was rage we heard just now. He's afraid you might be telling the truth. You handled him perfectly and kept him on long enough to record his voice patterns. I'll be going into headquarters tomorrow. I'll drop off the letter at the forensics lab and take your phone to our voice expert to see what he can do with it."

He checked his watch. "It's only four in the morning.

Why don't you go up to your bed? If he phones again, I'll let it ring. You need more sleep."

"What about you?"

"I'm fine."

"Even if you aren't, you'd never tell me. Thank you." She grabbed her pillow and blanket before going upstairs.

CY HAD SPOKEN prophetic words. The phone rang every half hour until eight on Tuesday morning. Then it stopped. He made breakfast with the groceries he and Vic had bought yesterday. While he devoured eggs and bacon, he phoned Vic on his phone. His friend answered before the second ring.

"What's up?"

"The stalker phoned her at four this morning. We were able to get a decent recording. When I'm back in the office, I'll have the lab analyze it. I'm headed there as soon as she leaves for her parents' ranch. I assume she'll be gone most of the day."

"The team will take turns monitoring her."

"Good. Where did you leave a car for me?"

"Walk down the alley behind the town houses to the corner. It's a Subaru parked in front of the third house on the right with a for-sale sign. The key is in the usual place."

"Do you think the lab has the results on the fingerprints we lifted yesterday?"

"Maybe. Stan said they'd hurry it."

"With all the bases covered, let's hope this nut case makes his move soon."

"Did you get any sleep last night?"

"Afraid not, but I will today after I get back from the lab. Kellie will probably be gone most of the day. I'll tell her to call me when she's coming back."

"You can level with me," he said in a quiet voice. "How's it going?"

He took a deep breath. "The easy answer is, nothing's going on that shouldn't."

Just then Kellie came walking into the kitchen dressed in Levi's jeans and a short-sleeved yellow blouse. She was a vision and he lost his train of thought.

"Cy? Are you still with me?"

"Yeah."

"I was just saying I can't wait to hear your difficult answer."

Neither could Cy, but this was pure business and that was the way it would stay. "Got to go. Thanks for your help. I'll catch up with you later at the office." He clicked off and stood to greet her. "Good morning. How do you feel?"

"Thanks to you I was able to go right to sleep."

"That's good news."

"But I bet you didn't get a wink." Her eyes had filled with concern.

"I'll make up for it later. Sit down and I'll serve you breakfast."

"I could smell the bacon. I should have gotten up to do it. Fixing food for me isn't your job."

"But you need more sleep than I do after what you've been through this last month." He put a plate of food

in front of her and poured coffee for both of them before sitting down.

"Thank you, Cy." She ate a piece of bacon. "Yum.
Crisp, just the way I like it. Were there any more phone
calls from him after I went to bed?"

Cy eyed her directly. "He rang on the half hour eight
times. I let it ring every time. Your marriage announcement has set him off, exactly the reaction I'd counted on."

"Did he leave messages on the voice mail?" There
was a tremor in her voice.

"Yes, but you don't need to hear them. I'm taking
your laptop and phone into the lab today, but I'll bring
them back." The stalker probably had a stack of prepaid
phone cards, but there might be a time when he had to
use a pay phone that could be traced.

Her brows furrowed. "You think they're too awful
for me to hear?"

"No. They were more of the same. He was ranting
like before."

She sat back in the chair. "Then you really didn't
get any sleep."

"I'll catch up today while you're at the ranch. Someone on the team will be monitoring you every time you
leave your condo. A member of the crew will follow
you. If you have any concerns, call me on your parents' phone. This is my cell number." He wrote it on
the paper napkin.

"While I clean up the kitchen, I'd like you to get on
your laptop. Post a new message on your blog. Say that
you've read the messages and you're overwhelmed by
all the good wishes. Then start to read any messages

that have come since last night. I'm curious to see if he's posted anything. It's my hope he's so angry he might explode and give himself away."

As he cleared the table, she reached for her laptop and opened her blog file. "I don't believe it! Hundreds more messages have been added since last night."

"That's not surprising. Your online tips about barrel racing have won you a loyal audience. Everyone's intrigued about your new relationship."

She lifted her eyes to him. Along with her silver-gold hair, her eyes were a deeper blue this morning and dazzled him. "The fans want to hear about *you*, not me. If they knew you were one of the Sons of the Forty, they'd go crazy and you'd be forced to go into the witness protection program."

With those words his pulse sped up. "Hiding out with you is virtually the same thing."

He loaded the dishwasher. Cy had been a bachelor for so long in his own house, he was used to doing his own cooking and housekeeping. He felt right at home in her kitchen. "Why don't you start reading and see if there's a message that strikes a different chord with you?"

"It'll take me some time."

If they'd met under different circumstances, nothing would have pleased him more than to have whole days and nights with her with no life-threatening issue to deal with. But he had a case to solve and needed to get to headquarters pronto. As he was finishing up, he heard her cry out in alarm.

"What did you read?" He walked over to the table and stood behind her so he could see what had disturbed her. In looking over her shoulder, he could breathe in her fragrance from the shower.

"It's this one sent at eight twenty this morning."

"That's when the phone calls stopped. Read what it says."

"'I bet you're making it up that you have a husband. Why do you enjoy being a tease? No one would watch you in the rodeo if they knew you were such a liar.'" She let out a quiet gasp.

Without thinking, Cy put his hands on the back of her chair. He could tell she was trembling. "I'm going to stop him, Kellie. This morning he made his biggest mistake so far by posting this message on the blog. When I'm at the office, we'll trace it to its source. With every misstep, we're closer to catching him."

She nodded without turning around. He quickly removed his hands and walked over to the kitchen counter where he'd put her phone. He heard her chair legs scrape the tile and turned in her direction.

"I know you're anxious to get going, Cy. I'll run upstairs for my purse and leave for the ranch."

"I'll walk you out to the garage." While he waited for her, he put her phone in his pocket.

The door to the garage was located at the other end of the kitchen. He unlocked it and turned on the garage light where her white Toyota sedan stood parked. He and Vic had checked it for fingerprints yesterday.

When she came out, he opened the driver's side door for her. Once she was inside, he asked her for the remote. "I need it to get in and out with my own car. I'll let you in when you come back from the ranch."

Her eyes played over him as she handed it to him. "Where is it?"

"Parked around the block. Try to enjoy the day, Kellie. You'll be constantly watched. Call me from your parents' when you're ready to come home."

"I will. Have a good day yourself. Be careful," she whispered.

He took a quick breath. "You don't have to worry about me."

"But I do, and I *will*."

It had been a long time since a woman he cared about had been concerned about him. Her unexpected smile revealed the spirit inside her that had dominated her life and made her a champion. He admired her passion for life.

As she started the engine, he pressed the remote so the garage door would open. After she'd backed out, he retrieved his phone and alerted the surveillance team that she was leaving the condo.

Once he couldn't see her, he hurried inside for her laptop and the bagged letter. After he had everything he needed, he left through the garage, closed it with the remote and walked down the alley to the end. Eight-foot-high heavy-duty vinyl privacy fencing ran the length of the alley to separate the backyards of another set of town houses. It was a gorgeous September day, probably sixty-five degrees out.

He found the SUV and took off for headquarters. On the way to his office he stopped by the lab to leave Kellie's phone and laptop plus the letter. Stan came out to talk to him. "TJ said this is high priority. I'll get working on everything now and give you a ring later."

"Thanks, Stan. I need you to do something else for me. I want Rafe to analyze this stalker's voice and see what he can figure out."

"I'll ask him to work on it now and take a late lunch."

"I'd appreciate that. I don't see Janene. When she comes in, ask her to find out the IP for the person who sent Ms. Parrish the message on her blog. I've flagged it."

"Sure. I'll put it on her desk."

"Thanks. See you later."

Cy took off for his office upstairs. On the way down the hall, Vic saw him and called him into his office. "I've been waiting for you. I've got stuff to show you that will blow your mind. Look what the database brought up from the sketch you entered."

Intrigued by Vic's excitement, Cy grabbed a chair and sat next to him. "Thirty-two matches came up on the computer."

"Is there one from Oregon?"

"No."

"My first hunch was wrong, then," Cy muttered. "How about Utah, Montana, New Mexico or Texas?"

"None of those states."

Damn.

"Give me a second. I'm refining these for exact similarities."

Cy watched the screen. They both made sounds when two faces came up. After studying them he exclaimed,

"They're the same person with different rap sheets. How in the hell did that happen?"

Dean Linton Michaels, aliases Dan Linton, Dan Michaels, Michael Linton, Mick Linton, Delinn Michael, twenty-eight, latest known address in Flossmoor, Illinois, is wanted for the murder of two women. The first account is for the stalking and strangulation of a twenty-four-year-old woman, Lucinda Rosen, in Chicago, Illinois. The second account a year later is for the stalking and strangulation of a nineteen-year-old woman, Mary Ferrera, in Memphis, Tennessee. Charges include Aggravated Kidnapping, Unlawful Flight to Avoid Prosecution, Aggravated Sexual Assault. No. 10 on the FBI's most wanted list.

Vic darted him a glance before he scrolled down. "Take a look at this rap sheet."

Lines marred Cy's features as he found himself looking at what appeared to be the exact same man. This one had longer hair.

Andrew Dunham, aliases Denny Andrew, Andy Dunham, Drew Denning, Donny, twenty-eight, latest known address in New Orleans, Louisiana, is wanted for First-Degree Murder in the stalking and strangulation death of a twenty-three-year-old woman in Charleston, South Carolina, thirteen months ago. Charges include Aggravated Kidnapping, Unlawful Flight to Avoid Prosecution, Aggravated Sexual Assault.

Cy shook his head. "It's amazing how closely these two men resemble the sketch. There has to be a mistake since both pictures have to be the same person. Three murders in three years. Kellie needs to see these pictures. If he's the same man and the one she can identify... Let's get on the phone to the agents working those cases while we figure this out."

Over the next two hours they held phone conferences with the FBI agents from Illinois, Tennessee and South Carolina. In all three instances, the agents praised the Rangers for their detective work on Kellie's case and pledged their help.

After Cy's last call, he waited until Vic got off the phone. "I've sent both sets of fingerprints to Stan to verify if it's the same man. They say every person has a double somewhere in the world."

"I wonder if that's really true," Vic murmured.

"Who knows? I need to learn as much as I can before I show Kellie these photos. Even though the artist was able to find us a match, maybe he only bears a superficial resemblance to the man she saw." He printed out both photos. After folding them, he put them in his pocket. "Want to go down to the lab with me?"

Vic jumped up. "Try to keep me away."

When they entered the lab, Stan told them to come around to the table where he was working. They passed Rafe's office. He looked up. "I'm working on this voice analysis. Give me until tomorrow."

"Sure."

They moved toward Stan.

"You got some good prints lifted from the condo and

the car," he said. "Several belong to the victim, and several others belong to the mother. One partial print you lifted from one of the buttons of the keypad for the garage doesn't match anyone's."

Cy eyed Vic. "That's interesting. Maybe we'll find the person who left it. Right now we've got a new puzzle for you to solve. I just sent you the photos and fingerprints of two wanted fugitives who appear to be the same man from the IAFIS data base. But if they're the same man, why didn't the computer pick it up?"

"Let me see." Stan pulled up the information on the computer.

"Their cases have been built from two different areas of the country with different names. Their photos closely match Jim's sketch of the man stalking Kellie. How long will it take you to determine if both pictures are of the same man?"

"Give me a few minutes and I'll check right now." He put both sets of prints up on the screen and used his loupe and counter. He examined them for a while, and then his head came up. "Well, what do you know? Those men aren't the same person. This is a case of identical twins, but as you know there's no such thing as identical fingerprints."

Cy sucked in his breath. "That means both brothers are killers."

Vic looked equally stunned.

"It happens," Stan murmured. "Come close and I'll show you." He pointed to the subtle differences. "Fingerprints are not entirely a genetic characteristic. They are a part of a 'phenotype,' which means they are determined by the interaction of an individual's genes and the intrauterine environment. One fetus in the womb has different hormonal levels, nutrition, blood pressure, position and growth rate of the fingers at the end of the first trimester.

"Minor differences in fingerprints arise from random local events during fetal development. The genes determine the general characteristics of the patterns of fingerprints. However, inside the uterus, finger tissue comes in contact with the amniotic fluid, other parts of the fetus and the uterus.

"Some experts point out, for example, that touching amniotic fluid during the six to thirteen weeks of pregnancy significantly changes the patterns of a fetus's fingerprints.

"Overall, identical twins' fingerprints tend to be similar, but there always will be subtle differences making even their fingerprints unique. That's why there was no match."

Cy unconsciously furrowed his hair with his fingers. He felt the same as years ago when his chest had been stomped on by a bull. "If one of these twin brothers was the man who'd targeted Kellie, how am I going to tell her there are two of them? Hell, Vic. What if they work together and committed all three murders?"

"Maybe that's why the letter in her mailbox had been posted by the one brother here in Austin four days ago while the other brother trailed her all the way home from Oregon."

He eyed Vic. "The murders of the three women were committed a year apart at different places, making it possible that they'd worked in tandem." Cy's body broke out in a cold sweat.

Vic clapped his shoulder. "Take it easy. I know where your thoughts are headed, but it's too early in the process to go there. Like you said, maybe she'll say these photos don't look enough like the man who harassed her in Pendleton to make a definite identification. We know mug shots as well as sketches can be deceiving."

"Yeah. I know," he said in a wooden voice. He turned to Stan. "Do you think that partial print from her condo is substantial enough for you to detect if it matches one of these fingerprints?"

"That will take some time. I'll see what I can do with it."

"Thanks, Stan. Give me a ring no matter what you find. I'll be up in my office for a while longer."

"I'll go with you." Vic walked out of the lab with him.

In the space of a few minutes, Cy felt the full weight of this case to protect Kellie. During his career as a Ranger, he'd never been personally involved like this before. As the captain had warned him, this was a different kind of case for Cy. *You two will be walking a very thin line.*

Cy had no idea he could feel this gutted over the gravity of her situation. He couldn't think of her as just any woman who needed help. His feelings were more complicated than that, but he had an obligation to keep this situation straightforward. Yes, he was attracted to her and admired her great talent, but he couldn't allow that to interfere with his judgment and work ethic.

When they reached his office, Vic looked at him and said, "Go home, Cy. You haven't slept for twenty-four hours and won't be any good on this case without sleep."

"You're right. I'll leave now." He glanced at his watch. It was one thirty. "Kellie will be coming home this evening. I want to be there when she drives in. Thanks for everything, Vic."

"Hey—just doing my job."

"You do a lot more than that, and now I've got another favor to ask."

"Anything."

"Pick up her phone from Stan when he's done with it. I'll get it from you later."

"What's your next move?"

"If Kellie identifies this man as the one who approached her, I'm going to fly to Colorado Springs early in the morning and take her with me. She said she gave her cell-phone number to a friend of hers who works in the office of the Women's Pro Rodeo Association. The stalker had to get her cell phone number from someone.

"I checked out her friends and horse handler while we were at the town house yesterday. They haven't given her phone number to anyone, so I'm going to check out a hunch. We'll be back by evening at the latest. Keep a close eye on her place while we're gone."

"Will do."

"Thanks, Vic."

Cy left the building and hurried out to the car. He couldn't get to Kellie's town house fast enough. Once he'd parked in the garage, he rushed through the house to the upstairs bathroom for a shower and shave. After putting on a clean pair of jeans and a T-shirt in the guest bed-room, he felt better. All he needed now was some food.

He ate a couple of peanut-butter sandwiches and drank half a quart of milk. After putting his phone on the floor next to him, he collapsed on the hide-a-bed. He'd catch a couple of hours before she phoned. Cy had her garage-door opener and would have to let her in.

It felt as if he'd barely sacked out when his phone rang. He reached down for it and saw that his mother was on the line. In the midst of everything, he'd forgotten to tell his family that he'd gone undercover on a new case and wouldn't be available for a while.

That wasn't like him to let something so important slide. As he lay there, he realized he needed to get his act together in a hurry. Biting the bullet, he clicked on.

"Hi, Mom. How are you and Dad?"

"We're fine, darling. The point is, how are you?"

"I'm well, but I'm on a new case and have gone undercover."

"Oh, Cyril—we never see you anymore."

He knew his mother worried about the career he'd chosen, and she never failed to complain about it. But right now he didn't give her the chance.

"Sorry about that, but it's the nature of the job. I promise I'll leave messages to let you know I'm all right."

"I guess that means you can't come to the engagement party we're planning for Beth and Tom on Sunday night."

"I wish I could, but I'll have to wait to see them after this case is solved." He had to solve it. "Give everyone my love. I promise to call you soon."

Cy hung up and lay back again, letting out a heavy sigh. His sister was marrying Thomas Adamson in six weeks. He was an up-and-coming attorney in the law firm Cy's great-grandfather had established in Dripping Springs. Cy was meant to join the business, but law had never held any interest for him. He preferred law enforcement.

After high school, he'd gone the rounds with his father more times than he could count. To make matters worse, halfway through college he'd broken his engagement to a young woman whom his parents really wanted him to marry. He wasn't anyone's favorite son.

Cy fell back to sleep until the phone rang again. A look at the caller ID showed Bronco Parrish. It was Kellie's father. She was calling from the ranch. He clicked on and said hello.

"Hi" came her slightly breathless greeting.

"Are you coming home now?"

"Yes. I'll be there in ten minutes."

"I'll be waiting and open the garage door for you."

"Thank you. See you soon."

It was a long ten minutes. Unable to stand it any longer, he hurried through the house to the garage and opened it while he waited for her. His pulse picked up speed when he saw her drive in next to his Subaru SUV and turn off the engine. She got out of the car and walked toward him with a look that led him to believe she was relieved to see him.

He was relieved, too. Night had already fallen.

Chapter Four

"How's Trixie?" Cy asked after Kellie walked past him into the kitchen.

"Happy to be home. We had a good ride."

He shut and locked the door. "Have you eaten dinner?"

She swung around. "Yes." Her eyes searched his. "Any news yet?"

"Why don't we sit at the table? I have something to show you."

Kellie swallowed hard and sank down onto the nearest chair. He sat opposite her and pulled a paper out of his pocket. "The sketch Jim made was run through the IAFIS criminal database. This is what resulted."

He unfolded it and placed it in front of her. Her gasp filled the kitchen's interior. "That's the man! But his hair is longer here and he looks a little thinner than I remember."

Cy pulled out another paper and unfolded it. The second he put it in front of her, she jumped to her feet. "This one is exactly like I described to you and the artist. His hair is short here."

"There's no doubt in your mind?"

She stared at him. "I'm positive both photos are of the same man who approached me in Pendleton."

"That's all I need to know."

Kellie sat back down again. The photos had caused the blood in her veins to chill.

"We can thank God you came into the police station yesterday before anything happened to you."

Her hand went to her mouth. "It's the same man, so why are there different sets of names for him?"

He pocketed the papers. "It turns out they are identical twins."

She could hardly breathe. *"Twin murderers?"*

"I suspect they work together, but the FBI agents I spoke to didn't realize it until the forensics lab discovered that their prints weren't exactly the same. It would explain why you could receive a letter postmarked from Austin at the same time he approached you in Eagle Mountain."

Kellie buried her face in her hands, trying to comprehend it. The next thing she knew, he'd put a cup of coffee in front of her. "Drink this. You need it."

She took a deep breath and sat back in the chair. "Thank you." For a few minutes she sipped the hot liquid while she tried to absorb what she'd just learned.

"Tomorrow morning I'd like you to fly to Colorado Springs with me. Your friends have sworn they've never given out your cell-phone number to a soul. But if your friend at the Women's Pro Rodeo Association has put your number into the computer, that may explain where these men got it."

"You mean they hacked their computer?"

"I don't know. That's what I want to find out. You've been with that association for several years. These men know your rodeo schedule. Your name is on file with them. I'm curious to know if your friend kept your cell phone number to herself or put it in the computer, never thinking about it. Maybe she even saw him."

Kellie thought back. "When I gave it to her, she knew never to give it to anyone else."

"That was before she moved. Chances are she didn't put it in the system, but I need to find out."

She marveled at the way his mind worked. "What are you thinking?"

He leaned back in the chair drinking his coffee. "These stalkers are cunning. In order to talk to you, the one who approached you had to have done his homework. What you put on your website about belonging to the Women's Pro Rodeo Association might have given him an idea I want to explore."

Kellie had a feeling he hadn't told her everything. "What time do you want to leave?"

"At 5:30 a.m. We have a 7:00 a.m. flight. If we get our business done fast, you'll be back here in time to put your horse through some maneuvers before evening. This will be our first venture in public as a married couple, so we'll behave as man and wife when we reach Colorado."

Man and wife. A tremor ran through her body. He'd anticipated every question and had answered them before she could even think.

"Then I'm going to get ready for bed now."

"Before you go upstairs, I want you to walk out to the mailbox and bring in any mail you find. Don't worry. One of the team will be watching you. I'll be waiting by the front door."

She got this sick feeling in her stomach over the idea that the stalker might have been near her condo today. Reaching in her purse for her keys, she left the town house and took the short walk to retrieve her smattering of mail from the box.

After she returned, she walked over to the table and put it down. There were three ads, a catalog of home decor furnishings and a five-by-seven white envelope with nothing written on the front. When she saw that it didn't have a stamp, she froze.

"When does your mail normally come?"

"Between two and three."

"The stalker may have come after to slip this into your box."

"You think he had a key?"

"These criminals are professionals and have tools, but we're going to find out."

Cy put on gloves and picked it up. After opening the flap, he pulled out a black-and-white glossy photograph of Kellie taken in a beauty salon. She was sitting in a chair with a drape around her neck. Her head had been cut out and it fell on the table. The word *liar* had been printed on the back of it.

"I don't believe it!"

He gave her a probing glance. "Where was this taken?"

"At a beauty salon here in Austin where I go to get my hair styled."

"How long ago?"

"Right before I left for Montana, about five and a half weeks ago."

"You're sure about the timing?"

"Yes. Normally I wear cowboy boots all the time and I always get my hair done later in the day. But that particular morning I had an early appointment and I put on those sandals before I left for the salon because I was in a hurry."

"What time was your appointment?"

"Eight thirty in the morning."

"Do you remember the date?"

"It was a Wednesday. I had to leave right after to make it to Glasgow in time for the rodeo on Saturday, August 2."

"That meant you were in the salon on July 30. How big is the place?"

"It does a lot of business. The Blue Gardenia is on Third Street downtown."

"I've heard of it. Do men get their hair cut and styled there, too?"

"Yes." She shuddered. "That means he was in there watching me. He probably has dozens of pictures of me. It's sickening and depraved."

"Stay strong, Kellie. We're going to catch him."

A moan escaped her. "What about his twin?"

When she looked at him, the dark blue of his eyes seemed to have turned black. "Him, too. Go on up to bed and set your alarm. We'll leave for the airport at five thirty. Before we walk out the door, I'll turn on the camera over the kitchen door on the garage side."

"You think he'll come while we're gone?"

"I'm not sure."

He obviously had more work to do she wasn't privy to, so she got up from the table. "I don't know how to thank you for what you're doing. Your life is in danger, too."

"But this is my job. One I like, though no one in my family does."

"What did they want you to be?"

"An attorney like my father and his father and his father before him."

So Cy was the lone wolf... His own person. She liked that about him very much.

"When this whole ghastly ordeal is over, I'll tell your family personally that you have the undying gratitude from me and my family for coming to my rescue."

His intense gaze continued to hold hers. "That's nice to hear. Now try to get some sleep and leave the worrying to me."

THE SECOND SHE disappeared upstairs, Cy phoned the crew in the surveillance van. "Lyle? The stalker put an envelope in Kellie's mailbox today. There are eight tenants using that box. Did anyone approach it you can't identify?"

"Yes. A woman with dark brown hair. I checked with the landlord of the property. He's never seen her."

A *woman*. "Strange. What time did the camera record it?"

"Four twenty."

That was after the mail had been delivered. "Send me a picture."

"There are three of them. Doing it right now."

As they came through his phone, he studied them. The person was dressed in a woman's business suit with low heels. She would be the same height Kellie had described for the stalker. Any view of the face gave only a partial glimpse. The lab could magnify the images for a better look.

"Lyle? Send these to forensics for enlargements."

"Will do."

"Tomorrow I'll be in Colorado Springs part of the day with Ms. Parrish. That'll give the stalker time to case the town house. He may try to get in to find out if a man lives here with her. Maybe the stalker's twin will show up, too. It's possible they dress in drag part of the time. Keep me posted."

"Sure thing."

Cy ended the call and phoned Vic. "It's possible one of the twins has been dressing up as a woman. I'm sending you the photos taken by Ms. Parrish's mailbox. Go over to the Blue Gardenia beauty salon on Third Street when it opens tomorrow. Show these pictures to everyone who works there. I'm curious if one of the employees can identify our stalker, who likely used his phone camera to take a picture of Kellie getting a haircut." Cy gave him the time and date. "If you get any information from one of the workers at the salon, let me know.

"Then I want you to call around to the places where you can buy a wig. Take those mug shots with you.

The photograph taken of Kellie was snapped almost six weeks ago. See if our stalker purchased one or two wigs in different colors during the month of July and get a copy of the receipt. It's a long shot, but do what you can."

"I'll try everything including places that sell theatrical makeup. He could have posed as an actor needing makeup and a wig."

"Exactly. Thanks, Vic."

"When will you get back from Colorado Springs tomorrow?"

"I'm not sure. Kellie needs to exercise her horses, so I'll drive her to her parents' after we get off the plane. But I'll phone you."

On WEDNESDAY MORNING Kellie got out of the rental car and walked alongside Cy as they entered the building that housed the WPRA in Colorado Springs. She welcomed the warm seventy-nine-degree temperature. Conscious she was playing a part as Cy's new wife, she'd worn a flirty skirt and dressy blouse with high heels to play up her feminine side. It felt good to put on something besides jeans and cowboy boots.

"May I help you?"

"I'm here to see a friend who works here," Kellie told the attractive, twentyish-looking receptionist who hadn't taken her eyes off Cy from the moment they'd walked in the foyer. In a business suit and tie, he'd drawn the attention from a lot of women during their flight.

"Her name is Olivia Brown." Kellie prodded the younger woman in case she hadn't heard her the first time.

"Oh, sure. She's the one who moved here from Texas and works in the membership auditor's office. I'll ring her. You know? You kind of sound like her."

Kellie happened to glance at Cy, who was smiling at her rather than the receptionist. Even his eyes smiled, sending a charge of electricity through her body.

"Olivia wants to know your name."

Gathering her wits, she said, "Tell her it's a friend from the Blue Bonnet Posse."

The receptionist passed it on and suddenly red-haired Olivia came running down the east hallway. "Kellie!" she called out and ran up to give her a hug. "I can't believe it!" She turned to the girl at the desk. "Janie? This is the very famous Kellie Parrish! She's going to win the barrel-racing championship at Finals in Las Vegas this December."

"Wow." Janie's eyes had rounded in surprise.

"One could hope," Kellie murmured in an aside.

"Who's the stud?" Olivia whispered.

Kellie's heart was palpitating out of her chest. "I'd like you to meet my new husband, Cyril Vance."

"You got *married*?" Her voice came out more like a squeak.

"We did," Cy said and shook her hand.

"I announced it on my blog."

"Let me see." Olivia grabbed Kellie's left hand, then whistled. "Gorgeous." She looked up. "I haven't had a chance to read it yet. Oh, how wonderful. Congratulations!" She hugged her again. "Come on down to my office. I'm dying to know what brings you two here. If you're on your honeymoon, I can't figure out how come I'm lucky enough to deserve a visit."

Cy cupped Kellie's elbow and squeezed it as they followed Olivia down the hall.

"Come on in and sit down. Do you two want coffee or soda?"

"Nothing, Olivia. We ate before coming here, but thank you. There's a specific reason why we're here. I'll let Cy explain. My husband is a Texas Ranger working on a case that involves me."

After a five-minute explanation, there were no more smiles coming from Olivia. He showed her a paper that included both mug shots. "These men are identical twins. Do you recognize either of them?"

"No. I've never seen them."

"Do me a favor and show this to everyone who works here. If they've seen them, phone me immediately." He wrote his work number on the paper. "If one of these men had come around here, it could have been as far back as a year ago."

"I'll do it today." She looked at Kellie. "You poor thing. I'm ill over what you've just told me. Let me get into the records on the computer. I always update the information on a file when rodeo results come in. I've been here eighteen months. If I added your cell phone, I don't remember doing it."

"Does everyone on the staff have equal access to the files?"

"No. Only certain of us have the password to get into them." She opened the file.

Kellie wasn't aware she'd been holding her breath

until Olivia looked at them with a pained expression on her face. "Oh no—I *did* put your number in next to your parents' number. I remember now. I put it there for me, never dreaming anyone would ever see this file but me."

"Please don't worry about it, Olivia."

"It could be a blessing in disguise." A somber look had stolen over Cy's features. "Do you know the company that cleans this building?"

"Yes. It's called Grayson Janitorial Services."

"When do they clean?"

"At night after nine."

Kellie turned to him. "You think the stalker pretended to be a janitorial worker and got into the computer?"

"Maybe. If he's cyber savvy, it's a distinct possibility he broke in." His gaze swerved to Olivia. "We're going to go there now and talk to the owner."

"Let me give you the address." Olivia looked it up on the computer and wrote it down on some scratch paper to give to him.

"Thank you. Before we leave, I need one more piece of information. What company services your computers?"

"It's Standard Computer Services."

"We'll find it. Thank you, Olivia. Your help has been invaluable."

"I wish I could have helped you more. I pray you catch that stalker. It's too horrible."

"Cy is keeping me sane," Kellie confessed. "Give my best to your husband. We'll talk soon." They hugged once more before Cy escorted her out of the room and down the hall to the entrance.

"Good luck!" Janie called out. "I hope you win."

"Thank you."

They walked outside and Cy helped her into their rented Buick sedan. Using the Google mapping system, they drove across town to Grayson Janitorial.

Kellie glanced at Cy. "I know Olivia was upset that she'd put my cell number in the database."

"As I said, if this helps me trace the stalker's steps, it could uncover valuable information. It's like putting a puzzle together. Every piece I find forms the picture. If I'm on the wrong trail, we'll head over to Standard Computer Services. Maybe they sent out a technician to the WPRA who resembles our stalker."

Once Cy had parked the car, he took her arm and they entered the business. The store was filled with janitorial supplies. He flashed his credentials in front of the man at the counter.

"I need to speak to the owner."

"Just a minute." The man made a phone call. "A Texas Ranger is out here needing to talk to you."

When he hung up, he told them to walk around the counter and through the closed door to the back office. The middle-aged owner got up from his seat behind the desk and shook their hands. Cy wasted no time pulling out another paper and showing it to the owner.

"Have you ever hired either of these men to work for you? It could have been as far back as six months to a year ago. I'm following up a lead on a case. I understand your company cleans the offices of the WPR Association."

"That's right." The other man studied the mug shots before shaking his head. "I'm the only person who hires and assigns the work for my employees. I've never seen these men."

"What if one of your employees took a friend along while he or she worked?"

"That's against the rules, but I'll talk to my crews. Can I keep this paper?"

"I want you to. I'll write my work number on it in case you have information for me. Thank you."

Cy put an arm around Kellie's back as they left the office. It felt so natural, she didn't think about it until they'd reached the car. While he looked up the address for the computer company on his phone, she glanced at the striking man behind the wheel. She wondered if he could be aware of her in the same way she was of him. When she'd introduced him as her husband to Olivia, she'd felt a sense of pride. *Because you're attracted to him, Kellie, and you're getting too comfortable around him.*

He started the car and drove to another part of the city, where he parked in the lot next to the building reserved for Standard Computer Services.

"Cy? If you want, I'll wait here while you go inside."

His head turned to her, impaling her with those dark blue eyes. "Until I arrest the stalker, I'm not letting you out of my sight."

The way he said it caused a shiver to run through her body. "I just thought—"

"It's my job to keep you safe," he broke in. "I brought you to Colorado to introduce me to Olivia. There's no way I'd leave you sitting alone in this car."

Of course he wouldn't! A killer was after her.

She undid the seat belt and got out of the car before he could come around to help her. For a minute she'd been so concentrated on him and so worried he sensed her attraction to him, she'd said something that had probably made him question her mental capacities. *Get a grip, Kellie.*

He accompanied her inside the building. When he made inquiries, one of the guys working the counter showed them to the manager's office. It was like déjà vu. After introductions, Cy asked the manager to search through their work orders for the WPR Association going back a year.

"This will take me a minute."

"That's all right. I want you to be thorough." While they waited, Cy pulled another paper out of his pocket.

"It looks like we've sent our technicians out there four different times."

"Tell me the dates."

Kellie heard him mention January, April, June and July.

"Do you send one technician at a time?"

"Almost always."

Cy handed him the paper. "Have either of these men worked for your company within the last year? Take your time."

The manager took it from him. Within seconds he looked up at Cy. "This one with the longer hair. His name was Denny Denham." Kellie let out a soft gasp. "He applied for work in April, but only stayed until the end of June."

"Denny Denham has many aliases. He's on the FBI's most wanted list and killed a woman." The manager dropped his jaw in shock.

Kellie's heart thudded painfully. Cy's hunch had paid off. At this point she was in awe of his genius.

"Why did he quit?"

"He said his mother was in a hospital in Michigan and needed him."

"Was he a good tech?"

"Very good. I didn't like losing him."

"Was he the tech sent to the WPRA offices on any of the dates you gave me while he was still working for you?"

"I'll have to go through the signed receipts. It'll take me a few minutes."

"Go ahead."

Cy flashed Kellie a smile meant to encourage her that they were on the right track. He could have no idea of the emotions that smile stirred up inside her.

The manager looked at Cy. "Denny signed the work order for June 20. It was right after that he had to quit work."

The set of Cy's hard jaw spoke volumes. "I want to see his application."

"I'll print it out."

Cy took the paper and stood to shake the manager's hand. "You've been very helpful on this case. Thank you."

The manager still looked dazed as they left the office. Once in the car, Cy started the engine. "I've got everything I came for. We'll head back to Austin in time for you to get in some training with your horses. En route to the airport would you like to stop for a hamburger at a drive-through?"

"That sounds good."

"I got lucky today. That always gives me an appetite."

"It's not luck, Cy. You're brilliant. Didn't you want to study his work application before we left?"

"I'll pore over it with Vic after we get back. It'll be filled with lies, but maybe there'll be something in it that will be valuable to the agents working on the other murder cases."

She stared out the window. "That poor manager looked shattered. Surely he did a background check."

"I have no doubt of it. The trouble with criminals is that they're human beings just like everyone, and for most of the time they drift in and out of the shadows without anyone realizing it until it's too late."

Kellie's gratitude for Cy and all he was doing caused her throat to swell. "I'll never be able to thank you enough, and don't tell me it's nothing."

A low chuckle came out of him. "I wasn't going to. Since taking your case, I've become a husband. I never dreamed it was such a responsibility."

"You're probably sorry you got involved to this extent."

"I wouldn't have done it if it wasn't exactly what I felt needed to be done."

"But I feel guilty because it makes it difficult for you to have a personal life."

"Don't worry about that. I've had a personal life and barely escaped getting married."

Her head swung toward him. "Seriously?"

He nodded. "Her name was Eileen Richards. We were engaged, but it didn't feel right to me and I broke it off."

"How long ago?"

"I was twenty-one and halfway through undergraduate school."

Kellie imagined he was in his early thirties now. "That's young."

"Yup. But my parents and her parents were all for it. As I told you before, they had my life planned out to be an attorney. To everyone's displeasure, once I'd said goodbye to her, I left school and signed up with the Austin police department. I discovered I didn't want to defend criminals, I wanted to catch them."

"Thank heaven," she whispered. "How long have you been a Ranger?"

"Almost three years and I've never regretted my decision. To answer your next question, Eileen is married to a successful businessman. According to my mother, she's expecting her second child, and I couldn't be happier about it."

Neither could Kellie.

Once they'd eaten a quick lunch, they dropped off the rental car and caught their flight back to Austin. They walked to the short-term parking for Cy's car and headed for her parents' ranch.

"We made good time, Cy. It's only four o'clock."

"That's why I wanted to get away early this morning."

She gave him directions and soon he'd pulled up in front of their ranch house. "Would you like to come in? I know my parents would like to talk to you."

"Another time and I will, but I've still got a lot of business to do. Don't forget that one of the crew always keeps you in his sights."

"I know. I'll ask my parents to drive me to the town house tonight."

"Give me a call. I'll be waiting for you."

He had no idea what that meant to her, but he was probably tired of hearing it and she could tell he was anxious to leave. She climbed out of the car and hurried to the front door. Opening it, she called out, "Mom?"

"In the kitchen, darling."

Kellie wheeled around and waved to Cy. He waved back and drove off. She stared after him, wishing she didn't feel strange when his car disappeared. As if she'd lost something.

Her mom gave her a hug. "You're back earlier than I would have expected."

She took a deep breath. "Cy accomplished what he needed. Where's dad?"

"He's out in the pasture, but he'll be back by six."

"Then I'll have enough time to do some training drills with Trixie before dinner."

Her mother followed her up the stairs to her old bedroom. "What happened today?"

Kellie walked over to the dresser where she kept

her older clothes and pulled out a top and some jeans. "He found out how the stalker got my cell-phone number." While she changed outfits, she told her mom everything. "He's so amazing, I couldn't believe it. Talk about methodical. His mind works differently than the average person's.

"I found out his parents wanted him to go into law, but he broke his engagement to this girl and left college to join the Austin police department. He knew what he wanted and went after it. Now he's a Texas Ranger." She stared at her mom. "He can be formidable, but it's cloaked in sophistication. He told me he was going to catch this stalker."

Her mother eyed her pensively. "You believe in him."

"Utterly. He's incredible. I've never met anyone like him."

"No. Neither have I. Your cousin wants to hear all about him."

Kellie nodded. "I'll call her tonight when I get back to the town house. Has anyone else phoned?"

"Yes. Besides many of your friends, news of your marriage has prompted the *Statesman* and the *Chronicle* to get in touch with you for a story and a photo op. Even Tammy White from Hill Country Cowboy Radio is asking for another interview. She said you were a dark horse for pretending that you didn't know Cyril Vance when you were already married to the gorgeous Texas Ranger."

Heat crept into her face. "What did you tell everyone?"

"That you'd get in touch with them when you had time."

"Thanks, Mom. You're an angel." She pulled on a pair of cowboy boots she kept in her closet. "I've got to get out there so Trixie won't think I've abandoned her. See you in a little while."

She flew out of the room and down the stairs. Once she left the house, she ran all the way to the barn. But her thoughts weren't on Trixie. They were concentrated on the man who'd be at the town house later tonight to let her in. She found she was breathless just thinking about it.

Chapter Five

Pleased to discover that Vic was already at the town house, Cy drove into the garage, anxious for them to share information. His friend was dressed in the roofer uniform he'd worn the other day. He'd parked the roofing truck near the end of the alley.

"You got back earlier than I'd thought," Vic said as Cy entered the kitchen.

"That's because I found the information I wanted." He removed his jacket and tie and laid them over one of the chair backs, then he grabbed a soda from the fridge. "Do you want a cola?"

"Sure." They both took a long drink. "I brought Kellie's phone back, but she'll have to wait for her laptop," Vic informed him.

He saw it lying on the table. "Good. She'll be glad to have it." Cy reached for it and checked the messages. The stalker had sent three more. He put on the speaker-phone so Vic could hear them, too. It was more of the same enraged vitriol.

Cy swallowed more of his drink. "I have news. Kellie's friend put her cell-phone number in the WPR Association's database. After some searching I discovered that a Denny Denham worked for Standard Computer Services as a tech in Colorado Springs starting in April of this year. He was called out on a problem at WPRA and signed the work order June 20. After that, he quit his job on the excuse he needed to be with his sick mother in Michigan."

Vic's whistle sang throughout the kitchen. "I talked to Rafe. Get this. He said the voice on Kellie's phone meets the criteria for a person from Virginia Beach or Charleston, South Carolina."

"A long way from Texas," Cy mused aloud. "Charleston's the place where one of the victims was killed."

"Yup. The minute I heard that, I started a search of all identical twin boys born in both the Virginia Beach area and the Charleston area over the time period I've estimated. I'm waiting for them to get back to me."

"You do great work. At this point I'm wondering where these killers saw Kellie and decided to target her. Until now they've operated in the other half of the US."

"You'll figure it out. In the meantime Stan told me that he couldn't get a good read on the half fingerprint from the garage-door pad."

Cy's eyes closed for a minute. "That was a long shot. Did the woman show up at the mailbox today?"

"No. Nothing went on around the town house. It's a waiting game now."

"I'm pretty sure he'll break in one of these nights, possibly even tonight after he sees Kellie's parents drop her off. I'll be waiting for him."

"Or them," Vic added. "The crew will cover the front of the condo. I'll be out in back."

"Any news on the IP address of the email sent to Kellie?"

Vic shook his head. "Janene's still working on the source. Tor hidden services mask their locations behind layers of routing. But she got into a site called 'hangman' and discovered the owner had left the administrative account open with no password. She logged in and is still digging around. As soon as I hear from her, I'll let you know."

"Good." Cy reached into his pocket and pulled out the paper from the computer services company. "This is the application the stalker filled out to get hired for work at the computer company."

They sat down at the table to study it. Cy let out a harsh laugh. "Look at that reference. As I told Kellie, it's full of lies. Two years at another computer company in Omaha, Nebraska, before he moved to Colorado Springs?"

"I'll call the number and see who answers." Vic pulled out his cell phone and tried it, then put the phone to Cy's ear. "You may have reached this recording in error. You can try again or call your operator." Vic hung up.

Cy rubbed his eyes with the palms of his hands. "No doubt he used his brother, who set up a phony address and phone to send the referral. These killers get around, Vic. They've got money to operate. Most likely smash-and-grab stuff, unless they're living off a family death benefit of some kind. I'll email this to the agents on the East Coast."

"Depending on what goes on here tonight, I'll track things down tomorrow." Vic checked his watch. "Tell you what. I'm going to leave to get me a bite to eat. But I'll let you know when I'm back for the rest of the night."

"I can't do this without you." Cy walked him to the back door. After Vic left, he phoned TJ to check in and catch him up on the latest.

"If two of them break in, you may need more backup."

"Vic and the crew have us covered."

"I'll put two more Rangers on alert anyway," his boss said before Cy heard the click.

A second later his phone rang. The caller ID said Nadine, Kellie's mother. He picked up. "Kellie?"

"Hi." The small tremor in her voice brought out his protective instincts.

"Is all well with you and your horses?"

"They're in fine form." She'd ignored his question about herself. The tension had to be getting to her. "I just wanted you to know my parents are driving me home now. We should be there in five minutes."

"Good. Before you come in the house, check your mailbox."

"I will. See you soon." She hung up.

He got up from the table and walked into the living room while he prepared himself for what might happen tonight. If the stalker suspected Kellie had been telling the truth about a husband, he might lie low so she would think the menace had gone away. But neither he nor his twin would ever go away. One thing about a sociopath. Once he'd fixated on his victim, he'd dog her to the bitter end no matter how long it took. With two sociopaths working together, they were a lethal combination.

He ground his teeth, hoping both of them showed up. Once they were taken down, Kellie could get on with her life. So could he...

While he was trying to imagine what that would be like now that he'd met her, he heard her key in the lock. In order not to frighten her, he moved to the kitchen so she'd see him when she walked in. After she locked the door behind her, she turned around.

He noticed she was wearing her riding clothes and boots. Kellie's eyes flew to his. She held up a couple of catalogs. "This was all I found in the box." She put them on the kitchen table.

Cy thumbed through them, but there was no envelope hiding inside the pages. He looked up. "Have you eaten dinner?"

"Ages ago."

"Why don't you sit down and tell me what's wrong? Did something happen you need to talk to me about?"

Her chin lifted. "What's wrong is that you're putting your life on the line for me," she said in a voice shaking with emotion.

He cocked his head. "Would you rather someone else were doing this job? It can be arranged."

"No!" she cried out. "No," she said in a softer tone and looked away. "That isn't what I meant at all."

"Then what *did* you mean?" came his deep, almost-seductive voice.

She folded her arms to her waist. "Situations like this shouldn't happen to anyone, but I know they do. Horrible things happen all the time, all over the world, and a handful of men and women like you are courageous enough to make the bad people go away. There isn't a way to repay you for what you have to face twenty-four hours a day in order to protect someone like me."

Cy put his hands on one of the chair backs. "I get my payment every time I lock up a criminal and throw away the key. There's no satisfaction like it."

"Then you're an amazing breed of man."

"That's exactly what I was thinking about you when I saw you perform in Bandera. Only a few exceptional women have the patience and the skills to work year in and year out to thrill the thousands of people who can only dream about what you do on your horse. The heart of a champion is inside you. All I could do watching you at the rodeo was sit back and marvel."

She eyed him with a frank stare. "What you do and what I do aren't comparable, but I appreciate the compliment."

"It was heartfelt."

"You enjoy the rodeo?"

"All my life."

Her eyes lit up. "Really?"

"I love it. Growing up we had horses and always went to the rodeo. I still keep my horse on my parents' small ranch and ride when I have time. Like most of my friends when I was young, I thought it would be fun to try bull riding and calf roping. But our pitiful attempts that ended in pain and suffering let me know it takes a lot more than just wanting to do it. You know…like possessing the skill, like being born to it, like having the guts to go at it again and again."

Her chuckle delighted him. "That's my father."

"Some of us have it. Some of us don't."

"Instead, you face a terrifying human enemy with no thought for your own life."

Cy laughed. "Don't be deceived. I give a lot of thought to my own life, believe me."

Her smile slowly faded. "I've given a lot of thought to your life, Ranger Vance. Please take care of yourself." The throb in her voice resonated inside him. "It's almost ten o'clock. Unless you need me for anything, I'm going to go upstairs."

He reached for her phone and handed it to her. "You can have this back. Forensics got what they needed from it, but they still have your laptop. I've removed all the messages."

She gripped it. "Did they find a voice match?"

"Yes."

"A Texan accent?"

"No. The stalker sounds like certain people who live in either Virginia Beach or Charleston, South Carolina."

Kellie's surprise over the news caused her to groan. "Charleston was the place where he killed one of his victims."

"Listen to me, Kellie. If I have anything to do with it, there won't be any more."

She nodded. "As I told my mother earlier today, I believe in you. Now I'm going to call some of my friends who left messages with my mom."

"After you do that, turn the ringer off. If the stalker intends on calling you tonight, I don't want you bothered by him. You need sleep."

A pained expression broke out on her face. "What are you going to do?"

"Coordinate with my backup crew."

She slid him an anxious glance. "You think something might happen tonight?"

He watched a nerve throbbing at the base of her throat. Cy was determined to make her fear go away. "If not tonight, perhaps tomorrow night or the next. Either way we'll be ready."

"Then I'll say good-night."

"If you need me, phone me. But by no means come downstairs until I let you know it's all right."

"Okay." She held his gaze for a moment longer before she went upstairs. Soon after, Cy's phone rang. It was Vic.

"I'm walking down the alley to the garage."

"I'll open it."

"Did you know the boss has supplied extra backup?"

"He told me."

"Chris and Jose will be in a taxi in the alley. Lyle and the rest of the crew are in place."

"Good. We're set. This is the window of time the stalker has been waiting for. I'm counting on his making a move any night this week. Next week he knows she'll be leaving for Colorado. If he thinks she could be married, he's got to find out and get rid of her husband before he takes her off someplace and strangles her. He'll need his brother."

"Yup."

"See you in a minute."

Cy hung up and went out to the garage. He lifted the door partway. In less than a minute, Vic came crouching in before Cy lowered it. They both walked through the garage and kitchen to the living room.

"Has Kellie gone to bed?"

"As far as I know."

"How's she handling it?"

"The woman is tough. I'm beginning to understand why she's such a fierce competitor in the arena. That's the only reason this setup is working."

"I think it's more a case of the right two people being thrown together."

Cy knew where his friend was going with that remark, but now wasn't the time. "The thing I keep wondering about is why this pervert targeted Kellie specifically. Her beauty provides one obvious answer. But there's more to it than that. Nothing we've learned so far, not even after collaborating with the FBI agents back east, has shed any light. I'm trying to find the missing link."

"Maybe it will have to come after we catch them."

"You're right." He glanced at Vic. "What do you say we do this in shifts? I'll take the first watch." He fixed the hide-a-bed so Vic could stretch out when he was ready. "Since we know there's no side or back door to this place, my hunch is he'll come in through the garage with a device to let himself in the door into the kitchen."

Vic nodded. "That makes the most sense. The fence isn't that high. He'll be able to scale it easily. I did a patrol of the town houses on the other side of the alley. The tenants don't have garages and park their cars in covered parking across their street. If someone wanted to hide out, they'd have to jump the fence from this alley into one of the backyards and wait so they wouldn't be seen."

After talking strategy for a while, Vic lay down. Cy turned out all the lights in the condo before going into the kitchen. He took out his .357-caliber SIG Sauer and put it on the table. After pouring himself a hot mug of coffee, he sat down in front of his laptop in the dark. Time to catch up on the paperwork for Kellie's case while he could still remember times and details of their trip to Colorado.

Once he'd finished, he went back to Kellie's website and scrolled through her scheduled events, starting with the first rodeo of this year. To his shock he discovered she'd entered the Salem, Virginia, Annual Stampede on January 9. His adrenaline surged.

She'd gone back east!

Cy should have thought about that before now, but he'd been so concentrated on the months since the stalker had appeared, only now had he started to explore all the possibilities.

After consulting a Virginia map, he saw that Salem was on the opposite side of the state from Virginia Beach.

He scrolled down quickly. More shocks. She'd ridden in the Walterboro, South Carolina, Rodeo two weeks after leaving Virginia. Cy looked up the South Carolina map. Walterboro was only forty minutes away from *Charleston*.

Were the stalkers born in Charleston? Did they call it home when they weren't victimizing women? Vic was still waiting to hear back on the identical twins most likely born there or the Virginia Beach area. His friend was asleep, so Cy would have to wait to discuss the idea with him later.

Needing to do something with all the energy flooding his system, he kept scrolling for more information. On the first weekend of February she rode in the Chatsworth, Georgia, Rodeo. Mid-February she entered the rodeo in Memphis, Tennessee, where another murder had taken place.

In March she'd participated in rodeos throughout the Midwest before returning to Austin via a rodeo in Hampton, Arkansas, and another one in Fort Worth, Texas. But his mind kept going back to the Walterboro Rodeo.

If for some reason the stalkers had gone to the rodeo that night, they would have seen Kellie, who had the best time during the performance that night. That might have been the place they first decided she'd be their next target.

Unless—and it was a big *unless*—they were born in Walterboro or the surrounding area. Were Cy's thoughts leaping to improbable conclusions because of the voice match Rafe had found? Could he rely on such a science to provide answers?

Impatient with himself for wanting to find Kellie's stalker so badly he was starting to cross that line TJ had warned him about, he got up to pace the kitchen. He didn't want to take the time to fix another pot of coffee, so he opted for a soda from the fridge. No sooner had he sat down again than his phone rang. It was ten to three. A check of the caller ID told him it was Jose.

"What's going on?"

"I've got my night-vision goggles trained on a masked figure wearing a dark pullover and pants walking in the alley toward you. Can't tell if it's a man or a woman."

"Don't do anything. Let's see what happens, then close in." He hung up and called to Vic, who sprang off the couch and joined him. "Jose has spotted someone in a mask walking in the alley in this direction."

Vic nodded and drew out his weapon. While he hunkered under the table, where he had a direct view of the doorway, Cy flattened himself against the wall on the other side of the door.

They remained in position ten long minutes before Cy heard the sweet telltale sound of someone picking the lock, probably with a paper clip and tension wrench. If Kellie hadn't gone to the police, the scenario happening to her now would have ended her life. As he geared up for the takedown, a rush such as he'd never known took over.

All of a sudden the door opened. Cy came at the killer from behind and put a headlock on him, forcing him to the floor. The stalker let go with a stream of venom while he fought with the strength of a man high on drugs. Cy felt him bite his arm. It took Vic's help to subdue him long enough to handcuff his hands behind his back and ankle cuff him.

Cy rolled his body over and pulled the mask off his head. There was the face of the man in the picture with the longer hair. He leaned over him. "Surprise, Denny, or whoever the hell you are. Was it Donny, Andy or Drew who strangled the woman in Charleston? I'm the husband you and your twin didn't think existed. You're under arrest for the stalking of Kellie Parrish."

By now Vic was on the phone to the rest of the crew. Within seconds Kellie's town house was filled with agents. Cy took the greatest pleasure in reading him his Miranda rights before he was hauled out to the van.

THE SOUNDS OF men's raised voices had brought Kellie awake. She shot out of bed and dressed quickly in a top and jeans. Cy had told her not to go downstairs. But whatever had been going on below, she couldn't stay up here and not know what was happening. She hurried out of her bedroom and flew down the stairs straight into Cy's arms.

He must have been on his way up to her because he caught her to him, hugging her hard before he held her away from him. "We caught the twin with the longer hair, Kellie. For the sake of practicality, we'll call him Denny. In time we'll catch his brother and you'll never have to be afraid again."

The information he relayed filled her with such relief, she could barely find words. "If anything had happened to you…" Her voice sounded raw.

"Nothing did."

"That's not true. There's blood on your forearm."

"He bit me."

"Let me see." She pushed the sleeve of his shirt up

to his elbow. "You need to go to the ER for stitches and a tetanus shot. You could be infected already."

"The bleeding has stopped. I'll take care of it later. Right now we need to talk." He ushered her over to the couch, where they could sit.

The warmth of his body stayed with her. "I know what you're going to tell me. This isn't over yet."

"No, it isn't." In the soft lamplight, his chiseled jaw stood out in stark relief. "We don't know if his brother was watching what went down here tonight from a distance, or if Denny planned to kidnap you and take you to his brother at another location. What we *do* know is that when the brother we'll call Dan realizes Denny has been arrested or isn't around anymore, his rage will escalate and he'll come after you himself to finish the job. Dan is the one who approached you in Pendleton."

Kellie kneaded her hands. "When he finds out you exist—maybe he believes it now—his hatred toward you is what frightens me."

He gave her arm a squeeze. "Nothing's going to happen to either one of us. Why don't you go upstairs and phone your parents? Tell them that one of the brothers is now in custody, and we're hoping to catch the other one soon. It will be a great relief to them."

"I know." She looked into his eyes. "Are you going to get your arm looked at now?"

"I'll do it after I run by headquarters. Vic will stay here while I'm gone so you'll be safe. I want you to go back to bed and we'll see each other tomorrow."

"It already is tomorrow."

His lips twitched. When he did that, her heart skipped a beat. "So it is."

"Cy?"

"What is it?"

Terrified she might give in to the impulse to kiss him and humiliate herself, she got up from the couch. "Thank you. There should be a better way to tell you how I feel, but I can't think what it is. Please get that arm examined." Before she blubbered all over the place, she left the living room and hurried up the stairs.

She wished she could go with him, but that was ridiculous. He was a Ranger and had business to take care of. He'd just taken down one of the FBI's most wanted criminals. Cy had done his job and needed to finish up.

Kellie sank down on the side of her bed. The trouble was, she'd come to look at him as someone much more than an officer of the law. They'd agreed to a fictional marriage to trap the killers, but tonight she didn't feel like a fictional character.

You'd like to be his real wife. Admit it, Kellie.

Appalled by the admission, and shocked that her feelings could run this deep so quickly, she phoned her parents. They were thankful Cy seemed to have accomplished a miracle so fast, and both were overcome with emotions. After they hung up, she got into bed, hoping she could fall asleep. When the phone rang again, she was surprised to discover it was already seven thirty.

She glanced at the screen on her cell, but there was no accompanying ID.

It was the stalker. He'd left a message. She listened to it.

"You're still lying about having a husband. I saw the police drag my brother out of your garage to their van. You're all going to be so sorry for what you've done. Just wait and see what I've got planned."

He'd been watching the whole time.

She phoned Cy immediately, but it went to his voice mail. She told him about the stalker's message before hanging up.

At this point she was wide-awake. The man who'd invaded her space in Pendleton was still out there, and now it was Cy who wouldn't be safe. Her fear for him was greater than ever.

While she waited for him to call back, she showered and washed her hair. After a quick blow-dry, she put on jeans and a plum-colored cotton sweater. Once she'd pulled on her cowboy boots, she was ready for the day.

As she went downstairs, her phone rang. She checked the caller ID. It was Cy!

With a racing pulse, Kellie clicked on and heard "Good morning."

"The same to you. Did you get any sleep?"

"A little. How about you?"

"Don't worry about me. I heard your message. It means he was hiding behind the fence. Don't leave the town house. I'll be over as soon as I can." She heard the click.

Kellie put the phone on the counter. She needed something to do and started to fix breakfast. In case he hadn't eaten yet, she made enough for both of them. Before long she heard the garage door lifting and ran to open the kitchen door for him.

He levered himself from his car wearing a brown Western shirt and jeans. Kellie had a hard time keeping her eyes off his hard-muscled physique. As he came inside, she could smell his soap from the shower and noticed he was clean shaven. Those deep blue eyes zeroed in on her. His piercing gaze sent warmth through her body. "Something smells good."

Yes, it does. That's you.

"It was my turn to fix breakfast for us. Sit down at the table and I'll serve you."

"I won't say no. I'm starving."

"Since I know you haven't had any sleep in twenty-four hours, you need food to keep you going." She got them started on eggs and bacon, topping it off with toast and coffee.

"This is delicious. Thank you."

"You're welcome. Let me look at the bite on your arm."

He flashed her a lazy smile before rolling up his sleeve. She was relieved to see a dressing had covered it. "I told you I watch out for myself."

"I'm glad you had a doctor look at it."

He rolled the sleeve back down. They were both being polite, but it was like trying to avoid the elephant in the room. He eyed her over the rim of his coffee mug. The gold wedding band on his ring finger gleamed in the overhead light, bringing her straight to the point.

"Cy? We have to talk about our situation."

"Agreed. You go first."

She took a deep breath. "That call this morning made me realize that you and I don't have to pretend to be married any longer. The whole point was to flush out the stalker. Now that he's been arrested and his brother watched what went on—probably from behind the fence—there's no more need for you to stay here.

"Last night my dad said he's going to hire some bodyguards for me as soon as tomorrow. In the meantime I'll let the landlord know I'm moving to my parents' ranch, so my condo will be available for a new renter. That will free you to get on with other Ranger work. We have no idea when the stalker will strike again, let alone when he'll be caught. It could take a long time and you're needed for other important cases."

When Cy didn't say anything, she drank more of her coffee. "It's fortunate that no one knows your name, so no explanations are necessary. After the second brother is arrested, then I'll post the truth about the twin brothers on my blog and explain that the fake marriage was announced to lay a trap that worked brilliantly."

Starting to get unnerved by his silence, she took the rings off her finger and put them on the table. "Take these back to headquarters along with any equipment you've left here. And please thank the other men in your crew for protecting me. They'll never know how grateful I am."

He went on drinking his coffee. Why didn't he say something?

Since they'd finished eating, she got up and cleared the table before putting the dishes in the dishwasher.

"Kellie? If you've said everything you wanted to say, come and sit down while I tell you what I'd prefer to see happen, but it's up to you."

What did he mean? The hairs on her neck started to prickle as she did his bidding.

"I was in a meeting early this morning with the captain. I'm still assigned to your case until it's solved. There's no work more important for the department than for me to put away another killer on the list of America's most wanted. Though we've caught one killer, his twin is on the loose and more dangerous to you than ever.

"Since he knows his brother has been arrested, he's angrier than ever. Until he makes his move, and I expect it will be sooner than later, it'll make my job easier if we stay married so *I* can be your bodyguard. At this point I want us to be visible like any married couple. It will taunt him so much, he'll make a mistake. That's what I'll be waiting for. But if you'd rather your father hired bodyguards who would take turns living here, our department will provide backup. The decision is yours."

Kellie didn't need to think. His suggestion thrilled her so much she could hardly find words. But how to tell him without giving herself away?

"Since you already have a plan, let's not deviate from it now."

She struggled for breath. "Only if you're sure."

"Give me your hand." When she extended her arm, he put the rings in her palm. "Put these back on."

Her heart started to run away with her. Not only because of his touch, but because it meant she wouldn't have to say goodbye to him. Not yet anyway...

"Now, if you don't mind, I'm going to stretch out on the hide-a-bed and get some sleep. To put your mind at ease, Lyle and the crew are outside and will remain on watch until tomorrow."

He got up from the table. "Later today we'll drive out to your parents' ranch and go riding together. I want to watch the famous Kellie Parrish in action. When our stalker phones again, and I know he will, let him leave messages and I'll listen to them later."

And with that, she watched him leave the kitchen, feeling more comforted than ever that her Texas Ranger was here.

Chapter Six

Cy walked into the living room, where he took off his cowboy boots. When he'd proposed that Kellie announce their marriage on her blog, he'd thought she would never agree to it. But she went along with the plan and had her parents' blessing.

Just now he'd assumed she'd put the brakes on this latest strategy. To his astonishment, it didn't happen.

Who knew how long the case might go on. Cy did know exactly how his family was going to react when he told them that he and Kellie were pretending to be man and wife. They were worried he'd never get married and continually tried to line him up with a promising match. The party for his sister coming up on Sunday was another excuse for his parents to introduce him to a new woman.

Because of his undercover role as Kellie's husband, any matchmaking on their part would have to be put on hold. They'd be forced to give up trying to manage his love life while he was still working on her case. Nothing would frustrate them more. Or please him more. In fact he was tempted to take her to the party with him on Sunday.

What was today? Thursday? Was it only last Friday when they'd collided outside the radio station in Bandera? Since she'd come into his world, he'd lost track of time. How could it be that already he couldn't comprehend his life without her?

With a relieved sigh, he stretched out on the bed and turned on his side facing the wall. His body felt as if it weighed a thousand pounds, but the capture of Denny Denham had done a lot to lighten his mood. He could actually go to sleep knowing that when he woke up, he'd be with Kellie, who wasn't going anywhere without him. Later today they'd go riding together. He could hardly wait.

The next time he was cognizant of his surroundings, it was four thirty in the afternoon. He'd been sleeping on his stomach. When he turned over, there she was on the couch across from him, curled up with a book. Their eyes met. Hers were smiling.

Uh-oh. "If I snored, don't tell me about it."

"It will be my secret. But I want to know who Sylvia is."

Cy started to chuckle and sat up. "I don't believe it."

"Believe what?" She smiled broadly, illuminating his world. "It seems you've been carrying around a secret. A little while ago you muttered something like, 'Dammit. Where are you, Sylvia?'"

He couldn't hold back his laughter and moved his pillow so she could see his gun. "*That* is Sylvia."

She put the book down. "You call your gun Sylvia?"

"Yup. She goes everywhere I go, but sometimes when I'm dreaming, I find myself looking for her."

Laughter burst out of Kellie. "You gave it a woman's name. Why not a man's?"

"That's an interesting question. I really don't know."

"Was Sylvia an old girlfriend?"

"No such luck," he teased. "When I was a little boy, my father took me to the barbershop in Dripping Springs for my haircuts. The older man had a picture of his wife, who'd died, on the wall. He called her Sylvia. I guess it stuck in my mind to come out later. Some of my colleagues give their weapons a name."

She nodded. "Just like some pilots name their planes. My grandfather had an old car he called Elvira."

Curious, he asked, "Did you name all your horses?"

Kellie let out a sigh. "No, but one day I'd love it if Trixie gave birth to a little filly I could name and raise."

She could have been talking with the same kind of love she would have for her own baby. He wondered what plans she had for the future. "How long do you intend to compete?"

"After the Finals in December, I'm quitting the circuit. It's a demanding life and I've already been in it so long."

That was news to him. "What will you do?"

"This is a low-cost rental. I've been saving all my earnings and plan to buy a small ranch where I can run my own business of training future barrel racers. I have my eye on several properties that have been put out on the market. That way I can be involved with the rodeo, but on the other end."

He sucked in his breath, marveling over her ambition. "From the amount of fans who flood your website for training tips, I have no doubt you'll be so busy you'll have to turn some away."

"All in good time, I hope."

Enjoying this too much, Cy sat up and pulled on his cowboy boots before he got to his feet. He stared down at her. "Speaking of your website, I happened to look at your schedule before Montana and noticed you competed in rodeos back east."

"Yes. As I told you, Sally's husband, Manny, is a bull rider and we decided to enter those rodeos for points. It was also a fun vacation."

Cy rubbed the side of his jaw. "Since the stalkers were operating in the East, it occurred to me one of them would have seen you perform, possibly in Virginia or more likely in South Carolina. We know Charleston was one of the murder scenes. Since Walterboro is only forty minutes away, I'm thinking he might have gone to that rodeo and decided you were his next victim."

"I had the best time in the ratings that night," she murmured.

"The spotlight was on you. It makes perfect sense. We hope to pinpoint the exact location of their births in one of those two areas. It's possible they maintained a home there."

A delicate frown marred her brows. "To think they might have been following me since January…"

"While Dan tracked you all the way until he showed up in Oregon, his brother broke into the files at the WPRA and obtained your cell-phone number. But remember that there's only one of them now and I'm going to catch him. Excuse me for a minute while I freshen up, then we'll leave for your parents' ranch."

He put the gun in his side-waist holster. After making the bed, he left the living room and went upstairs to the guest bedroom. He shut the door and phoned Vic, who picked up on the second ring. "I wondered when I'd hear from you."

"I was catching up on some sleep."

"Which plan did Kellie go with?" Vic had been in on the meeting with TJ.

Cy stopped pacing. "I gave her a choice."

"And?"

"We're going to carry on as we have been."

"In other words she doesn't want anyone else being her bodyguard. Between you and me, the captain's worried you're going to lose your focus."

His jaw hardened. "Is that what you think, too?"

"It doesn't matter what I think."

"The hell it doesn't!"

"Honestly?" Vic questioned. "I've worked with you for three years and trust you with my life. If you think your plan is the best way to keep her safe and catch this predator, I back you all the way."

"Thanks, Vic. I'm going to need your help."

"You've got it."

"We're leaving for her parents' ranch in a few minutes so she can exercise her horses. The crew will be watching the condo while we're gone."

"While you do that I'm going to see if I can get any information out of our prisoner."

"If he talks, it'll be lies."

"Yup. But coming down off his latest fix, he might make a mistake that could be valuable. I'll catch up with you later. Watch your back, Cy."

"Always."

He clicked off and reached for his Stetson.

CY DROVE THEM up to the barn. Kellie got out and headed for the entrance. Cy followed and they walked over to the first stall. "Trixie? I want you to meet a very important person." Kellie's palomino nickered and her ears pointed. "This is Cy. He's going to ride Paladin while we do some circles."

Clearly Cy was no stranger around horses as he rubbed her nose and forelock. "I watched you perform in Bandera, Trixie. You're a champion just like your owner." Her horse nudged him in the chest, causing him to smile at Kellie. When he did that, she forgot where she was or what she was doing.

They moved to the next stall. "This is Paladin, one of Dad's geldings. He's a big bay who loves a good ride. *And* he likes Trixie. When they're out in the pasture, he follows her around."

Cy's eyes gleamed. "I can see why. She's a beauty. Who says romance doesn't exist among our four-legged friends?"

"The only trouble is, he can be annoying and she runs from him."

He burst into that rich male laughter she loved so much. "So she likes her independence."

"At times. But then there are others and she rests her head on his neck."

"Sounds like a mercurial female. I'll do my best to control him."

This close to Cy, darts of awareness shot through her body. Together they picked out their saddles and bridles, then carried them to the stalls. Kellie heard a nicker from another stall.

"Starburst? I haven't forgotten you, but it's not your turn."

A grin broke out on Cy's face. "You talk to them like they're human."

"To tell the truth, I like them better than a lot of humans."

"Amen to that."

Before long they were both mounted. One glance at the gorgeous male astride the bay and she was in danger of melting on the spot. The only way she could describe her condition was that she was in a state of euphoria being with him like this.

He was a natural on a horse and took firm command of Paladin, yet displayed a gentleness that won Kellie's respect and admiration. She decided he could do anything. They rode out to the pasture as if this was something he did every day. Though she hadn't seen him ride in the Bandera parade, she could imagine him with the other three Rangers carrying the flag.

After riding some distance, she headed for the outdoor arena. Cy followed at a slower pace and pulled to a stop. Her pulse raced because he was watching her.

Once inside, Kellie began her routine and made perfect circles with Trixie, always using a little inside leg. She made certain her horse's back feet went in the same track as her front feet. After a few minutes she walked her around, then changed to a trot so she could stand in the stirrups to build up the strength in her legs.

To transition from high speed to stops was part of the routine. So was the exercise of backing up, then calling to her horse to stop. While Kellie was building up her own leg muscles, the exercises were helping Trixie strengthen her hindquarters.

Finally she led her over to the fence and did a few more stops, causing Trixie to use her back hocks and stifles. The routine built the vital control necessary for barrel racing. "Good girl," she called to her horse and patted her neck.

In the background she could hear clapping. When she looked over her shoulder, she saw Cy on Paladin, walking toward them. Beneath his white cowboy hat, his dark blue eyes traveled over her, filling her with warmth. "I wouldn't have missed that expert performance for anything."

"Did you hear that, Trixie? Such high praise coming from one of our famous Texas Rangers." To cover her emotions, she gave her horse another couple of loving pats. "I think you've had a good enough workout for today. It's going to be dark pretty soon. Let's head back to the barn." She glanced at Cy. "I try not to overdo it with her. It's important I make an effort to change her daily routine. Tomorrow I'll work with Starburst for a while."

They rode back in companionable silence. After watering the horses, they put them to bed. On their way out to the car, he asked about her parents.

"They're so thankful you caught one of the stalkers, they decided to attend an important dinner tonight. Otherwise they'd be here to ask you to stay for dinner. But let's go inside anyway to freshen up before we leave for the condo."

In a few minutes they went back to his car. He helped her in and got behind the wheel. "I'm in the mood for a good meal. Have you ever eaten at the Watering Hole? It's only a few miles from here."

He was finally asking her to do something a couple would do, but she couldn't consider this a date in any sense of the word. Cy was hungry and needed to eat. Somehow Kellie had to rein in her thoughts that were growing out of control.

They'd been thrown together because of a life-threatening situation and nothing more. But it was getting harder and harder to remain objective when she was so attracted to him. *It's more than attraction, Kellie. A lot more.*

"I've been there many times," she answered. "Their charbroiled steak is the best in Austin."

"That was easy."

Yes. Way too easy. She was under the Ranger's spell.

Luckily it was the kind of restaurant where you could come as you were. The place was always crowded. While they waited in the lounge area to be called to their table, Anita Wall, one of the women in the Blue Bonnet Posse, made a beeline for Kellie and gave her a hug. "It's so good to see you. I heard you got married. You've got to introduce me."

This was what happened when you went out in public. "Anita Wall? Meet my husband, Cy Vance."

Her married friend and mother looked up at Cy and did a triple take. Kellie couldn't blame her. The man was too striking.

"How do you do?" She shook his hand. "We've all wondered who the man was to snag our star." Her gaze swerved to Kellie before she whispered in her ear, "Now I understand. Wow, wow, wow."

While Kellie tried not to react, Cy asked, "Are you here alone?"

"No. I'm with some friends."

"You're welcome to join us."

She shook her head. "I wouldn't dream of intruding on you honeymooners, but thank you for the invitation." She gave Kellie one more hug. "Call me when you have time to talk."

"I will. It's wonderful to see you, Anita."

To her relief the hostess called their number and Cy escorted her to their table. Once their order was taken, Cy sat back, smiling at her. "Every friend of yours I've met lights up when they see you."

"Every friend of mine can't stop staring when they meet you," she countered before she realized what she'd said. Heat rose to her face. "They'd all be shocked and horrified if they knew what the real reason was for our being together. For your sake I hope the stalker makes another move soon."

"But not for yours?"

She lowered her head. "That came out wrong. Even if this is the career you've chosen, it has to be harrowing for you while you're forced to bide your time waiting for the next opportunity to present itself."

Their food came. Once they were alone again he said, "You have that turned around. You're the one being tortured mentally and emotionally." He cut into his steak. "Some victims would fall apart at a time like this, but not you. Your courage makes my job a lot easier to handle." So saying, he started eating.

"That's because you have a facility for calming me down. It's a gift, Ranger Vance."

Before she broke into grateful tears, she dug into her meal. They ate without talking. When she turned down dessert, he left some bills with the receipt and ushered her out of the restaurant to his car.

As they drove out of the parking lot, she turned to him. "I want to pay you for my share of the dinner. I don't expect the taxpayers of our state to take care of my bill."

"Didn't you notice that I paid cash for our dinner? It's from my paycheck. Any allowance I get as part of the job, I'm issued a credit card for that account. Tonight was my personal treat, if you like."

Kellie liked it too much. "Thank you. That dinner was delicious."

"I agree. Before this case is closed, I might just treat you again."

He got a chuckle out of her.

"That's better. I know you feel like this is the neverending story, but it will be over before long. Our stalker

Dan is beside himself without his brother. His need to kill again is stronger than ever because they didn't get the job done. In his desperation to finish what they started, he'll reveal himself in some way and that will be his downfall."

"If you say it, then I know it's true."

"I'm touched by your faith in me. How would you like to go to a family party with me on Sunday night?"

The question caught her off guard. "But they'll all think we're married—"

"They know I'm on a case."

"Do your parents realize you're protecting me?"

"Because I'm undercover, they'll figure it out. The point is, my sister is getting married and the parents are inviting a few people over to celebrate the coming event. Because of my job I've been absent from too many family gatherings as it is and would prefer not to miss this one. But I can't leave you alone. Starting tomorrow we won't have backup from the department unless I ask for it. If you don't want to go, we won't."

She bit her lip. "I can see you need a babysitter for me, one armed with a weapon."

"It's all right. Don't give it another thought."

After what he'd just told her? *Ha.* Kellie eyed his arresting profile. "How many sisters do you have?"

"Just Beth, short for Elizabeth."

"Do you have brothers?"

"No. I'm the only one."

"Well, far be it from me to keep you from a party this important. If I had no siblings except one brother,

I know I'd want him there for the most important moment in my life."

Cy looked over at her. "It *is* the biggest thing in her life. I knew I could count on you," he said in a satisfied tone.

Emotional bribery that fed on her guilt went a long way to persuade her. He had no idea how hard this would be on her. They weren't engaged, and she couldn't count on seeing him again after he'd caught the killer. But there was another part of her that was crazy with excitement to go out with him, even if she understood the true reason for being in his company.

They pulled into the garage and he shut off the engine. "Let me have your car keys for a minute." She rummaged in her purse for them. After she handed them to him, he got out and inspected her Toyota, including the trunk. "Okay," he called to her. She started to get out. "But let me go in the condo first."

That was right. While she could forget everything but the joy of being with him, his radar was on alert every second. Kellie waited by the door until he'd turned on lights and told her she could come in. She entered and locked it. They were home for the night, snug and secure.

Despite the menace still lurking out there, she'd never been happier in her life. There was only one reason why, and that reason was walking around, all six foot two of rip-cord-strong Texas Ranger with dark blue eyes and handsome features to die for.

When she thought of Anita and the look on her face

when she saw Cy, Kellie feared it was the same smitten look she'd been walking around with since Bandera.

"Vic brought your laptop back." At the sound of his deep voice, she swung around and saw it on the kitchen table. "The lab has finished with it. Feel free to check your emails and your blog site. Add whatever comes to mind."

The mention of it reminded Kellie of her phone. She'd turned off the ringer. Thank heaven Cy was here. In his presence she wasn't frightened to see who'd called.

After getting it out of her purse, she walked into the living room and sank down on the couch. While Cy was upstairs, she checked her cell. Five messages had been left. One from Cody, who was verifying their trip plans to Rapid City, South Dakota, for the rodeo. She'd call him back. Four came from friends. There was one text message. It came from… *Trixie?*

Kellie felt sick. When she checked it, there was a picture with the text. She pressed on it and saw herself and Cy in his car as they were backing out of her garage. The text read, Plan to say goodbye to your husband, Kellie girl. It'll be payment for my brother. Then I'm going after your horse. Don't forget your turn is coming.

"Cy—" she cried out in panic. Within seconds he came down the stairs. "Look at this! He's a maniac! He's threatening to kill you and my horse!" She handed him her phone so he could see everything.

Without thinking about it, Cy sat down and put his arm around her shoulders to comfort her. He'd been wondering when she'd break down. All this time she'd been so brave, but the threat accompanying the photo of her horse had been the tipping point for her. It was too much. She burrowed into his neck and sobbed.

He brushed the hair away from her cheek. "Awful as this is, it means he's ready to spring into action. But don't worry. Two of the agency's men dressed like local ranch hands are guarding your horses around the clock."

She blinked. "All this time?"

"Yes."

"Oh, thank heaven."

"The stalker doesn't have much more time before you leave for the rodeo next week. I'm convinced he's going to make his move soon. I'll be ready for him," he murmured, pressing kisses to her brow.

One minute she was clinging to him. In the next instant she raised her head to reveal a tear-sodden face. He brushed the moisture from her cheeks with his thumb.

"I—I'm sorry I fell apart like that," she stammered. "How embarrassing."

Cy heard the words, but their lips were only an inch apart, distracting him from his duty to protect her. All that registered was her warmth and beauty, seducing him into wanting a taste of her. It was wrong to give in to his desire, but he'd passed a threshold where chemistry had taken over. He could no more stop what was happening than he could prevent himself from being swept into a vortex.

When his mouth closed over hers, he heard a small moan, then she was giving him access as if she couldn't stop herself, either. For a minute he forgot everything while the wonder of her response had taken hold. One kiss became another and another until it all merged into a growing need that had set them on fire.

He'd never known this kind of ecstasy before, not even with his fiancée. Maybe it was because of the danger surrounding them that the experience of holding and kissing her had surpassed any pleasure he'd known with the few women from his past.

Kellie was exciting from the way she looked, talked, walked, rode a horse and fought her fear. Her smile dazzled him. Her lust for life—her plans for life—thrilled him almost as much as her touch, almost as much as the feel of her body molded to his.

Caught up in a frenzy of giving and taking, Cy unexpectedly heard a familiar voice come into his head. *You realize the two of you will be walking a very thin line.*

Stunned by how far he'd gotten carried away, he lifted his mouth from hers with reluctance. Somehow he managed to let her go and got to his feet. He cleared his throat and stood there with his hands on his hips while he attempted to get his breathing under control. "That wasn't supposed to happen, Kellie. I apologize for betraying your trust, but you have my solemn oath it won't happen again."

She looked up at him through clear blue eyes dominating a flushed face. "It takes two, Ranger Vance. I was right there with you and crossed a line I swore I wouldn't. But I'll tell you this. I enjoyed it."

An honest woman. He smiled, loving her candor. "It was even more exciting for me than watching you round the third can in Bandera and fly straight down the alley."

After running his hands through her hair, Cy could see he'd disheveled it. She smoothed a few strands off her forehead. "It's past my bedtime, so I'll say goodnight."

"I need to keep your phone," he said before she reached for it. Kellie nodded, then stood up and hurried out of the living room.

No sooner had she disappeared up the stairs than Vic called. Cy pulled out his phone and clicked on. "Did you get in to interrogate our prisoner?"

"Yes, but he's not going to give up any information. These guys are real pros, but I have other news you need to see and sent it to your email. I sent the same email to the agents back east who are working on this case."

"How soon can you get here?"

"I'm walking toward the front of Kellie's town house now."

"I'll let you in."

In a few minutes they sat at the kitchen table. Cy handed him Kellie's phone. "Take a look at the message from the sender named Trixie. Dan took a picture of me and Kellie in the car backing out of the garage earlier today."

Vic studied the photo and read the text. He shot Cy a glance. "The loss of his twin has unhinged him."

"Yup. He's starting to take daring risks and is damn good at knowing how to terrorize Kellie. I assume he's armed with a rifle in order to take care of me and Trixie. Then he'll go back to his preferred method to kill Kellie."

"We've got to find him quick."

"Did Janene ever track down that IP address?"

"No. It has her stumped for the moment, but I've received information on the identical-twin birth records from both cities."

"I want to see those, but first let's talk about the photo. Dan was obviously hiding behind the fence this afternoon in order to take it. No doubt he was hidden in the same place when we took his brother out to the van. I'm thinking he's using one of the town houses."

"So am I," Vic broke in. "I'll phone TJ right now to get us a warrant."

They could read each other's minds. "We'll need backup so we can do a thorough search of every town house on this street and the town houses on the other side of the alley. Our lunatic is hiding out here somewhere ready to strike. We need to nab him fast."

"Agreed."

While Vic got on the phone with their captain, Cy opened the email Vic had sent. He studied the statistics for identical twin boys born in hospitals in 1986 when the populations of both areas were smaller. The sum from both cities equaled ten sets, six from Charleston, four from Virginia Beach. Hopefully, the agents at the other end could track down the parents from birth records and make an ID that would help them form a correct profile of the brothers.

Vic ended the call. "TJ's getting the warrant as we speak. He's sending Luckey to guard Kellie so you and I can do the search with the crew. As soon as he gets here, we'll start."

Cy's thoughts were whirling. "I need to tell Kellie

about the change in plans." Since he had her phone, he needed to tell her in person. "Be right back." He got out of the chair and hurried up the stairs with her cell phone.

"Kellie?" he called to her before rapping on her door.

"Yes?" she answered immediately.

"I have to leave for a little while with Vic. But I won't go until Luckey gets here. He's one of my closest friends in the Rangers."

"One of the Sons of the Forty, you mean?"

"Yes. He'll guard you with his life."

"I don't doubt it."

"I'm leaving your phone on the floor outside your door in case you need it. If the stalker calls, let it ring through to your voice mail. I've just put Luckey's phone number in your list of contacts. He'll answer if you call him. Try to go back to sleep if you can, and I'll see you in the morning."

"Be careful, Cy."

He took a deep breath. "Always."

Chapter Seven

I have to leave for a little while with Vic.

Kellie could only imagine what that meant. Instead of lying there shuddering in fear for Cy, she threw back the covers and slid off the bed to get her phone. When she opened her door, she saw her cell but couldn't hear voices downstairs.

Something important was going on and he wanted her out of it, yet he always put her needs first. She believed he was so dedicated, he'd treat any person he was guarding with the same kind of care. That was the problem. Kellie wanted to mean much more to him.

When they'd kissed earlier, she'd never wanted them to stop. She couldn't blame all of it on hormones. This man was different. She was different when she was with him. Kellie had dated a lot of guys over the years, but something had changed when she'd first looked into Cy's startling dark blue eyes.

She picked up her phone and went back into the bedroom. If only there were someone she could talk to about this, but her feelings were too private to divulge even to her family or closest friends. She'd known Cy for only a week. Anyone she confided in would smile and tell her it was natural that a man and woman thrown together in a dangerous situation would grab a little comfort that went along with the hero worship. But in the long run it couldn't be taken seriously.

As she walked over to the bed, more questions ran through her mind. What would it be like to be married to a Texas Ranger? To know that every time he left for work, he was facing danger head-on? When he didn't get home on time, or was involved in a stakeout that kept him away for days at a time, how would she be able to handle it?

Judging by the tension gripping her body right now, she already had the answer to her question. She wouldn't be able to cope. To love Cy meant she would never be at ease when he was out of her sight.

Kellie's mom didn't worry when her husband left the house. She knew he'd walk in at the end of the day and come find her wherever she was. Barring a natural disaster or an unforeseen accident, her mom didn't have to be concerned that she might never see her husband alive again.

Like her mom, Kellie had grown up knowing their husband and father would always be in their lives. She'd never given it a thought. But she did now…

With a tortured sigh, Kellie turned off her phone and lay back, praying this threat to her life would be over soon. If the stalker were caught before she had to leave for South Dakota, she would end her association with Cy cold turkey. That was the only way to deal with her feelings. They never had to see each other again and she could concentrate on getting ready for Finals.

Tomorrow she'd talk to the real-estate agent helping her find the right property to buy. So far she hadn't found the exact thing she wanted. Maybe something else had just been listed on the market. Whether something turned up or not, she'd go on her last four-state circuit of rodeos starting with South Dakota, then Wyoming, Colorado and Oklahoma.

After that she'd come home for three more rodeos in Texas before she left for Las Vegas. Once Finals were over, she'd buy a place to get her new training business started. With the decision made about Cy, she turned on her side. But her mind wouldn't shut off. Being in his arms, being kissed with such hunger, had changed her.

Upset with herself, she turned on the other side. When sleep didn't come, she slid out of bed to get her laptop off the table. The latest scores of her competitors would be listed. Cynthia Lyman from Tombstone, Arizona, was the barrel racer to beat. She'd made the most money for the year, and her last winning time was 13.77.

Kellie needed to do better than that in order to come in first. Her time in Bandera was 14.10. Though she came in second, it wasn't good enough. Once she reached Las Vegas, she'd be competing for ten nights and had to nail those barrels with consistently low scores in the 13s. Focus was everything.

After reading the latest news, she went to her blog. Once she'd thanked people in a general message after reading the latest entries, she posted her schedule of events for the next seven weeks and promised to add to her blog between each rodeo.

Eventually she grew tired and put her laptop on the floor before succumbing to sleep. When morning came, she was surprised to discover she'd slept in until nine. She couldn't remember the last time she'd done that. Emotional exhaustion had to account for it.

Was Cy back?

With her heart in her throat, she showered and dressed in riding clothes and boots. She ran a brush through her hair and put on lipstick before hurrying downstairs.

"Good morning, Ms. Parrish."

Her spirits plummeted to see a dark blond Ranger wearing a polo shirt and jeans seated at the table with his laptop while he drank coffee. He was a close friend of Cy's.

"Good morning. You must be Luckey."

"That's right."

"I take it C—Ranger Vance hasn't come home yet."

"Nope. He's still out working."

She bit her lip. "Have you heard from him?"

"Not yet."

Good grief. What was wrong with her? He wasn't about to discuss Ranger business with her. "I'm going to make breakfast. Would you like some?"

"Sounds good."

"Cy loves bacon and eggs." Cy's name rattled off her tongue. She could have kicked herself for using it.

Luckey's brown eyes smiled. "I think that's an all-around favorite." He didn't miss a thing. Of course he didn't. He was one of the Famous Four she'd heard mention of on the news.

"Good." She got to work and whipped up some biscuits to go with them. Before long they sat across the table from each other while they ate.

"If I'd known that house-sitting Cy's wife was going to come with these perks, I'd volunteer more often."

She shook her head. "Once he catches the stalker, he probably won't be able to live down this fake marriage."

"Cy's a brilliant tactician. That fake marriage caught the first stalker before any of us could blink. It won't be long before he brings the other one into custody. In case you weren't aware, the captain gave the assignment to him because he knew he was the right man for the job."

Kellie knew that already.

"However, I'd like you to know that any of us would have been happy to take your case on after watching you in the Bandera Rodeo."

Luckey was a charmer and very attractive. "You could have no idea how grateful I am for all your help." She got up to pour him another cup of coffee. "I happen to know you were on watch all night long and must be exhausted. If you want to stretch out on the hide-a-bed in the living room, please go ahead while I wash the dishes."

He didn't get up. "If I lie down, then I'll go to sleep. That's a no-no on the job. I'm better off sitting here talking to you."

While she loaded the dishwasher, she asked the first question to pop into her head. "What made you go into law enforcement?"

"I wanted to be a Texas Ranger from the first time I saw a troop of them riding their horses in an Austin parade. I was just a little guy. When I told my dad, he said that we in the Davis family descended from a real Texas Ranger living back in the 1800s. After he showed me my great-great-grandfather's picture, that did it. I was going to be just like him."

"That's a darling story."

His chuckle filled the kitchen.

"Are you married, Luckey?"

"Divorced."

Kellie frowned. "I'm sorry. I shouldn't have asked."

"It's all right. My ex-wife didn't find my occupation darling."

No. She wouldn't. No woman *would* who wanted her husband with her every night of her life. "But if she married you—"

"She thought she could handle it."

With that response, Kellie felt as if someone had just walked over her grave.

He cocked his head. "How come you're not married?"

"I've been too busy chasing a dream."

"And thrilling crowds," he added.

Her mouth broke into a smile. "You're full of it, Ranger Davis."

"I couldn't agree more" came a familiar male voice from the living room. She lifted her eyes in time to see Cy, who walked into the kitchen looking wonderful even though he was tired and needed a shave. How long had he been listening to their conversation? At the sight of him, her heart knocked against her ribs.

She smoothed her palms over her hips. "There's more breakfast if you want some."

"Don't mind if I do." He caught a chair with his boot and sat down by Luckey. If he had any news about the stalker, he wasn't ready to share it with her.

"I didn't know your wife was such a great cook, Cy. Try the biscuits. They're sensational with strawberry jam."

"Yeah?" The two men glanced at each other. Kellie could tell streams of unspoken messages were passing between them.

She poured a cup of coffee for Cy and placed a plate of food in front of him along with utensils. "There's more where this came from."

"Bless you," he murmured, eyeing her with a look that sent coils of heat through her body.

"I'm sure you two have a lot to talk about, so I'm going upstairs. Thank you for watching over me, Ranger Davis."

"It was my pleasure."

Kellie darted out of the kitchen and hurried upstairs. When she reached her room, she fell onto the bed, so relieved Cy was all right she cried tears of happiness into her pillow. Taking a deep breath, she reached for her phone. No call from the stalker. There was only one message. It came from her parents. She should have phoned them last night before she'd gone to sleep.

Without wasting more time, she called them and brought them up-to-date on what was going on. Later in the day she and Cy would drive out to the ranch to exercise the horses. At least that was her plan, but it all depended on him.

"How did the search go?"

Cy looked at Luckey while he ate. "I don't even know where to begin. It curdled my blood when we entered the town house opposite this one on the other side of the fence. According to the landlord, a married couple named Michael and Julie Sanders signed a year's lease in February. When the landlord was shown a picture, he identified Dan as the husband."

"Good grief!"

"No one was home. When we searched the upstairs, we found that the bedroom overlooking Kellie's garage had been made into a shrine. Her pictures were plastered all over the walls and ceiling. Hundreds of them." It had been a nightmarish experience for Cy.

"We found camera equipment and half a dozen guns along with a ton of ammo. One of the rifles has a high-powered scope and was set by the screened window he'd left open. All the weapons are loaded. There's duct tape, pepper spray, handcuffs, ether, everything used in their other murders.

"In the master bedroom Vic found that a part of the closet contained men's clothes. The other half held women's suits and jackets. The upstairs bathroom was filled with makeup and wigs.

"Just yesterday Vic had questioned the owner of a local theater costume shop in town. He remembered selling a lot of women's makeup, including a brown and blond wig, to a man who said he needed them for a play he was producing. When Vic showed him the picture, the owner identified him immediately. The date of the purchase was the first of February."

Luckey shook his head. "That was right before they signed the lease."

"Yup. Those perverts have been holed up there all this time, eying Kellie's every move." Cy hissed the words. "While Denny held down the fort, Dan followed Kellie around the circuit. We found a motorcycle in the garage, so he's out somewhere either on foot or in another vehicle, maybe even a motorcycle."

"No doubt they're responsible for a slug of unsolved armed robberies here in Austin to finance their operation."

Cy's jaw hardened. "We fully expected Dan to walk in on us. When he didn't show up, we left and ordered the other condo renters on both sides of the alley to vacate the premises until further notice. We've organized the crew to stake out his place. After his last phone message to Kellie, my gut tells me he's going to make his move when he gets back from wherever he's been. I'll be his first target. I know how his mind works. He's planning to take me out with the rifle, then he'll break in here for Kellie."

"What do you want me to do?"

"Get some sleep on the hide-a-bed because I'm going to need you later." He got up from the table. "I'll be upstairs catching some sleep myself while I wait for a signal from Kit, who's heading the crew."

"Kit's outside?"

"Yup. TJ wanted the best fresh body to head the stakeout. I told him I wanted Kit. Vic has gone home to get some sleep. After I explain to Kellie what's happening, I'll be in the guest bedroom. She's free to roam around the house, but I don't want her leaving for her parents' ranch today. That will have to wait."

He reached for another tasty biscuit and popped the whole thing into his mouth before taking the stairs two at a time. "Kellie?" Cy knocked on her door.

Before long she opened it. He could see her laptop open, lying on the bed she'd made. She was so beautiful to him, he swallowed hard. When he thought of all the pictures smeared over the walls and ceiling in the other condo, rage for the maniacs who'd been lying in wait for her for almost a year threatened to take over.

"Luckey's asleep downstairs, but we need to talk. Shall we do it in here or in the guest bedroom?"

"Here is fine. Go ahead and use that chair." She walked over to the bed and sat on the side. He brought the chair around so they were facing each other. A quick glance around the room with its piles of soft, colorful pillows on the bed and comfortable accents around the room proved to him a very feminine woman lived inside the cowgirl.

Cy leaned forward with his hands clasped between his legs. "We've tracked down your stalker to his lair. He's not there at the moment. As we speak, a crew from the department has his place surrounded. I don't know how long it will be before he returns. If it extends into days, we'll deal with it. What you need to know is that you're safe as long as you stay in this condo."

She nodded. "I'll phone Dad and ask him to work the horses."

"Good. You're free to move around the condo. I'm going to catch some sleep in the guest bedroom, but I'll be leaving the door open. If there's any activity at all, someone will phone me and Luckey, so you're not to worry about anything. Keep your phone right with you. If the stalker calls, I want you to come and wake me before you answer it. Turn on the speaker and keep him on as long as you can."

"Okay." She stirred restlessly. "I-is he close by?" Her voice was full of fear.

What to say that wouldn't alarm her...? "Yes, but we have everything under control."

"I know that," she whispered and got off the bed to walk around. "What if he has a gun?"

"It won't matter. He'll be surrounded."

Her hands formed fists. "But it *does* matter. Even Texas Rangers with all the protection available have been known to get injured, or worse..."

"That's not going to happen."

Her eyes blazed a hot blue. "He's out to kill you for arresting his brother."

He got to his feet. "I won't give him the chance."

"But if you get shot, it'll be my fault. I couldn't bear it if anything happened to you."

Cy could have sworn that was her heart talking. When he'd agreed to take her case, he'd felt an attraction that had been growing so deep and fast, he didn't recognize himself anymore. TJ had warned him about walking that thin line. Unfortunately he'd already crossed it after meeting her in Bandera and would have pursued her, case or no case.

Get out of her room, Ranger Vance. Now.

"I assure you everything's going to be fine." He put the chair back by the window and left for the other bedroom.

After putting his gun under the pillow, he took off his cowboy boots and lay down, desperately needing a couple hours of sleep. It seemed as if no sooner had his head touched the pillow than he heard a phone ringing. He glimpsed Kellie's face through his eyelids and bolted upright.

She answered the phone and turned on the speaker. "Why do you keep calling me?"

"I like to hear the fear in your voice."

"You like to make people afraid?"

"Why not?"

"That's sick. You're sick, sick, sick!" she yelled into the phone. That brought Luckey from downstairs. Both men listened while she got him going. *Keep it up, Kellie. Stick it to him where it hurts.*

"Does your mother know what kind of person you've turned into?"

Bingo.

"What mother? She didn't want us. We were orphans, but you wouldn't know anything about it with your rich daddy and mommy. You're going to pay for not going out with me. But first I'm going to finish off that husband of yours."

"You don't know who you're dealing with!" Kellie's

lethal tone lifted the hairs off Cy's neck. "Try to hurt him and you'll wish you'd never been born!"

Luckey flashed Cy a secret smile before a maniacal laugh came through the phone. He muttered several obscenities and clicked off.

Kellie looked at Cy. "Did I keep him on long enough?"

"It was perfect. He's ready to explode. That's what I've been waiting for. Let's all go downstairs." He glanced at his watch. To his shock he'd slept seven hours. It was already five thirty in the evening. After putting on his boots, he reached for his gun and followed them out of the room.

"Would you gentlemen like some iced tea?" She'd already gone into the kitchen.

"We'd love it," Luckey answered for them because Cy had made a detour to the living room to phone Kit.

"Any sign of him yet?"

"No."

"He just made another harassing call to Kellie. She pressed his buttons. I think he's going to make something happen as soon as he returns to the town house."

"I'll let you know the minute he shows up. Anything you need and we're ready."

"I owe you for this, Kit."

Cy hung up and walked back in the kitchen. Trust Luckey to get Kellie laughing about something. His friend had a way. "What's so funny?" He'd trained his eyes on her, unable to look anywhere else.

Before she could answer, Cy's phone rang. It was Kit. He turned his back to her. "What's up?"

"The second we got off the phone, a woman with

neck-length brown hair pulled into a stall driving a used blue Sentra sedan. She got out wearing a business suit and heels and has just let herself in the condo."

"We've got him!" Cy blurted with elation. It felt as if he'd been waiting forever for this moment. "He'll be watching from the upstairs window with the rifle. I'll give him ten minutes before I back out of the garage."

"We're on it."

He clicked off and turned to Luckey, who was drinking a glass of iced tea. Kellie was in the background cooking tacos for dinner. "This is it," he muttered. "You know what to do."

"Yup."

Cy hurried upstairs and put on his bulletproof vest. Over it he wore a gray hoodie, and he went back down to the kitchen. "Be sure and save me some dinner."

Kellie's eyes look haunted. "You're leaving now?" He heard the wobble in her voice. "You haven't even drunk your iced tea."

"Sorry. I've got some business to do, but Luckey will enjoy it. Remember he's here to protect you. See you soon."

He opened the kitchen door to the garage and closed it behind him. Once he was in the Subaru SUV, he sat there to synchronize his time to the second with Kit and the crew. He hoped that once he used the remote to open the garage door, the sound would alert the stalker that he was leaving. That was the signal for the crew to move in.

The plan was to back out slowly, giving Dan time to make his best shot.

Five, four, three, two, one.

Up went the garage door. Cy started the engine and let it idle for a minute to draw out the stalker. Then he started backing into the alley. At the point where he turned the car, he braked and shut off the motor. In the split second it took to open the door and roll to the ground, he heard three loud shots fired in succession, shattering the side windows.

Some of the glass grazed his neck and cheek. Moments passed as he stayed down and let the other Rangers do their jobs. Sirens blared as police cars and an ambulance converged in the alley. He got out of the car and saw the street now looked like a war zone. The paramedics ran over to him while he got to his feet and brushed off the bits of glass, but he was waiting for the call from Kit.

When it came, they were the sweetest words he'd ever heard. "Your plan worked perfectly. This stalker was caught in the act. He twisted and screamed while we cuffed him. Now he's on his way to join his twin."

Cy drank in gulps of air. "Thank God."

He couldn't wait to tell Kellie, but he had to ride in the ambulance first while they tended to his wounds, which were superficial. After he'd been taken to the ER, TJ was there to greet him. While Cy sat on the end of the examining table as the doctor put some small bandages over the cuts on his neck and cheek, the captain's eyes played over him with grave concern.

"That was a hell of a thing you did out there tonight, offering yourself up as the sacrifice."

"I was wearing my vest."

"He could have shot your head off."

"I ducked. It was all planned out."

"If you ever try a stunt like that again…"

"You told me this was a high-profile case and you needed it solved ASAP. I just wanted to make sure those two lunatics are put away forever. Trying to take me out added another lifetime sentence to their list of heinous crimes."

After the doctor left the cubicle, the captain said, "I phoned Ms. Parrish and her parents and told them the siege was over. They're probably at her condo right now celebrating."

Cy would have liked to tell her the news himself, but he'd had to follow protocol and get checked over first. "Their relief must be making new people out of them."

His boss nodded. "Thanks to you she's free to live her life fully and win that championship in December. Vic got on the phone to the agents back east. Once again the fame of the Four is going out over the networks for catching two of the vilest criminals wanted by the FBI from coast to coast."

"I'm thinking there may be other murders they've committed. With them both in custody, who knows what information we can get out of them. Hopefully, this will lead to solving some cold cases, too."

TJ flashed him a rare smile. "That's for the detectives to follow up on. What matters is that it took the Texas Rangers to solve this case. Something tells me we'll be hearing from the governor soon. *Again*." He patted Cy's shoulder. "You've done great work," he said in a quiet voice. "I'm glad you didn't become an attorney."

"Amen," Cy whispered. Otherwise he would never have met Kellie. "Don't forget it took the whole team, TJ. But thanks for going along with my unorthodox plan. I believe that was the word you used."

"You flushed them out with your clever sting in record time. According to your buddies, this marriage seems to have agreed with you. What do *you* say?"

"The jury is out where that's concerned."

He nodded. "Vic's waiting in the lounge. When you're ready, he's going to drive you home. Take the day off tomorrow to recover before you write up all the details of the case. That's an order."

"Yes, sir."

After the captain left, Cy got off the table and reached for his hoodie and vest. He found Vic and they walked out to his friend's car. "I appreciate the lift home."

En route to Cy's house, Vic glanced at him several times. "The captain was right. You're damn lucky to have walked away from that shooting."

"If you're going to tell me you wouldn't have done the same thing, I wouldn't believe you. After Dan made his last harassing call to Kellie earlier today, I knew I was his next target. Which means the best move was to play it out on my own terms. While he was concentrated on me, the crew closed in, taking him by surprise."

They grabbed some burgers at a local drive-through, then headed for Vic's house in South Austin. Cy had chosen to live in a secluded neighborhood hidden away in a wooded area. His rustic lodge-style home with exposed wood appealed to him for several reasons. Besides a loft where he had his office, the open floor plan was dominated by a cathedral ceiling with tons of natural light.

When they reached the entrance, it dawned on him he hadn't stepped foot in his three-bedroom house for over a week. Normally after being away on a case, home sounded good to him while he relaxed. But tonight he knew something was missing even before he got out of the car. He knew what it was. Kellie wouldn't be here when he walked inside.

Over the past seven days, they'd spent hours together. When they had to be apart, she'd been constantly on his mind. If it weren't so late, he'd drive over to her town house right now with the excuse that he wanted to collect anything he'd left while working the case.

But before that, he needed a shower and a shave.

Vic turned to him. "You look like death. Go to bed and we'll talk in the morning."

Cy opened the door. "I couldn't have done this without you. I owe you big-time."

"I'll remember that when the captain gives me my next case."

"Good night, Vic." He shut the door and went in the house carrying his vest and pullover. Without turning on lights, he climbed the stairs to his bedroom in the loft located across from his office. He plunked his things in the chair and moved over to the bed to pull off his boots.

The moonlight coming through the window caused the gold band on his ring finger to gleam. He needed to remove it before he went into headquarters in the morning. The boss had told him to take the day off. For the first time since joining the Rangers, the thought of nothing to do all day long sounded like a death sentence.

A whole day without Kellie? He wouldn't know what to do with himself. The captain's question went round in his head.

According to your buddies, this marriage seems to have agreed with you. What do you say?

Cy threw back his head, afraid to answer it out loud. If he did that, it would be tantamount to a confession that could change his whole life. Especially if Kellie didn't answer it the same way.

Chapter Eight

Ten after midnight. No phone call from Cy. No doorbell ringing.

Kellie's parents had left her town house at ten thirty. They'd begged her to go home with them, but she'd told them she was exhausted. After the exciting phone call from the captain of the Rangers, who praised Cy's heroism for leading the team that caught both stalkers, she preferred to go straight to bed. She would drive out to the ranch in the morning.

Luckey had stayed with her until her parents arrived. He'd received a call from one of the other Rangers letting him know Cy had been taken to the hospital but his injuries were minimal.

She didn't believe that for a minute, and the fact that he hadn't tried to make contact convinced her something was seriously wrong. She'd heard the shots and learned what had happened from Cy's superior. But he was trained to gloss over information he didn't want her to know. Luckey had prevented her from going out in back while it was still a crime scene. She recognized he was only doing his job, but it killed her that she had to wait for information that came in bits and pieces.

That was the part of the exclusive Ranger brotherhood that bothered her. Surely Cy had to know she was anxious to hear his voice and make sure he was all right, even if she couldn't see him.

Restless and worried, Kellie paced the floor and then sank down on the couch. Cy's hide-a-bed was still in the living room. He would have to come back to get it, but obviously not tonight.

She glanced down at the rings. He'd be taking those back, too. But she felt as if they'd become a part of her. She would sleep wearing them one last time.

At one in the morning, she took some ibuprofen for a headache and went upstairs to bed. The painkiller helped her to fall asleep, but when she awakened Saturday morning, she realized she'd been crying. She'd had nightmares.

Because of her ordeal, her parents had worried she wouldn't sleep well and might have bad dreams. But oddly enough, it wasn't the stalkers who had filled her mind. Throughout the night she'd wandered endlessly in her search for Cy, unable to find him anywhere.

Thankful to be awake, she got out of bed to shower and wash her hair. If Cy came over this morning, she wanted to be ready for him. After putting on a clean pair of jeans and a plaid Western shirt, she applied some makeup and pulled on her cowboy boots before going downstairs.

While she was in the kitchen pouring herself a glass

of orange juice, her phone rang. Fighting her disappointment that it wasn't Cy, she reached for it. "Mom?"

"Honey? Turn on the news. We'll talk after it's over."

Taking her juice with her, she hurried into the living room and turned on the TV to one of the local stations. Between swallows she watched the breaking news.

"For those of you who've just joined us, last evening our own Texas Rangers finished up a sting that ended in the arrest of two killers on the FBI's most wanted list. Three brutal unsolved murders stretching from Illinois to Tennessee and South Carolina might have turned into four if it hadn't been for our state's bravest. We're standing by for a message from the governor."

Kellie sank down on the couch to listen.

"Today is one of the finest days for the Rangers, who prevented the murder of one of our celebrated Austin citizens, Kellie Parrish. She's the twenty-five-year-old barrel racer who will be competing in the National Finals in Las Vegas in December. She has been stalked by identical twin brothers whose killing spree started four years ago.

"The same rangers who brought down the drug cartel here six months ago took the lead in the capture of these predators. The criminals' names are being withheld as FBI agents in Illinois, Tennessee and South Carolina are putting all the facts together and notifying family members of the women they'd targeted."

A shiver ran through Kellie. The thought of the poor parents and families of the three women who'd been terrorized and killed brought stabbing pain to her heart. Because of Cy, they could now be provided with answers. But those poor women hadn't been blessed to have Cy protecting them.

Without wasting a breath, she phoned her mother. The minute she heard her voice, she broke down sobbing. "Oh, Mom. Cy is so wonderful." She tried to hold back the sobs, but it was pointless. "I don't want to think what would have happened if he hadn't taken my case."

"Then don't, darling. Have you talked to him since last night?"

"No. He had to go to the hospital last night. Maybe he's still there. I have no idea how serious his injuries were. Even if he's been released, I'm sure he has so much to do."

"I don't wonder. How soon are you coming?"

She wiped her eyes with her other arm and took a fortifying breath. "I—I don't know yet."

"Sitting around waiting to hear from him isn't the answer."

Kellie jumped to her feet, hurt by her comment. "What do you mean?"

"The two of you have been living in close quarters throughout your ordeal, pretending to be married. Now that the threat has gone, I'm not at all surprised you miss having him at your side on a constant basis. He's the stuff heroes are made of. Heavens, I'm a little in love with him myself. Please don't tell your father."

"Oh, Mom." She let out a half laugh because her mother knew her so well.

"I'm not surprised you've lost your head, but you've got a championship to win, remember? Ranger Vance isn't going anywhere. Give it time."

Kellie hated it when her mother was right.

"Thanks for the talk. I should be at the ranch within the hour."

After she got off the phone, her mood was completely different. She rushed upstairs for her purse and came back down to write a note at the kitchen table.

Dear Cy,
Words can't express what I'm feeling, so I'm not going to try. I forgive you if you let yourself in to get the rest of your things while I'm not here. The governor gave you a ringing endorsement today. Congratulations. Just know that you will always have my undying gratitude. You saved my life. What greater service can one human do for another?
Kellie

She read it over several times, wondering if she needed to change anything. But no, it said what she wanted to say. Unlike the piece she'd written on the blog about their marriage, this one wasn't over-the-top. Viewing it objectively, she felt she'd hit just the right tone.

Without giving herself a chance to change her mind, she removed the rings and left them on top of the note. After grabbing the extra garage-door opener from the drawer, she hurried out to the garage and climbed in her car.

When she backed out, she saw no sign of the crime scene from last night. But it was out here that the stalker had fired on Cy. Another shudder left her weak before she pulled herself together and started for the ranch.

During the drive, half a dozen messages were left on her phone. She knew she would be inundated by good wishes and concern from her friends for a while, but she wasn't ready to talk to anyone about this except her parents. Then she would take separate rides on Trixie and Starburst, exactly what she needed to sort out her head.

Her left hand gripped the steering wheel. It looked bare without the rings. *How do they feel, Mrs. Vance?* he'd asked, staring at her with his gorgeous dark blue eyes.

They'd felt natural.

Without them, without him, nothing felt natural.

Another two miles and she pulled up in front of the ranch house. Her phone rang again. She glanced at the caller ID and rushed to answer it. "Cy?"

If he hadn't known how she really felt about him, he did now.

"Good morning, Kellie."

He sounded wonderfully alive. She gripped the phone tighter. "Are you still in the hospital?"

"I'm at headquarters. Last night I was only there for a few minutes to have a couple of tiny cuts treated before going home."

"I'm so thankful you weren't seriously injured." Her voice shook. "I heard three shots."

"It's over now." It was obvious he didn't want to talk about it. "If you're still at your town house, I'd like to come over and get my stuff. Vic's coming with me.

We'll take out the hide-a-bed so you can have your house back."

Kellie moaned. If she hadn't left so soon…

"I'm sorry, Cy. I'm out at my parents' house. You still have a door key, right?"

"Yes."

"I can imagine how busy you must be, so feel free to drive over and let yourself in."

After a slight pause, he said, "Sounds good. I'll leave the key and your garage-door opener on the table."

Her eyes closed tightly. She'd purposely left the rings and the note in case something like this happened. "Cy? I want to see you again to thank you. Is there a night you could come over and I'll cook dinner for you?"

"You don't need to do that."

"There's every need. You saved my life."

"Tell you what. The captain has a new case for me. I need to take a look at it. When I know my schedule, I'll call to let you know what night would be good."

So now that he didn't have to guard her, he wasn't planning on taking her to his sister's engagement party on Sunday evening. Already he'd been put to work on another dangerous assignment. That was his job.

For one week out of her life, the two of them had been inseparable. But it was over. He'd never again be exclusively hers. How was she going to bear it?

"I hope you can make it Monday or Tuesday. Cody and I will be leaving for South Dakota on Wednesday."

Another silence before he said, "How long will you be gone?"

The breath froze in her lungs. "Seven weeks."

"Seven?" He sounded surprised. "Without a break?"

"After I leave Oklahoma I'm doing three rodeos throughout Texas with Sally and Manny. It'll be November before I return home." She stared blindly into space waiting for a response.

"If I can't make it either of those nights, will you give me a rain check?"

Kellie had to brace herself to handle the hurt. "Do you even have to ask? Ranger Vance will always have a standing invitation to my home."

"That's nice to hear."

She could hardly swallow. "I'm so glad you're all right. Take care of yourself, Cy. The Famous Four wouldn't be the same without you."

Enveloped in pain, Kellie clicked off before she said too much. Then she turned off her cell. She was glad he hadn't learned she was still at the condo earlier waiting around for him.

The remark her mother had made during their phone call had gotten her out of the house in time to save her from making the biggest mistake of her life!

CY PULLED THE van in front of Kellie's town house with a grimace. "Let's get this done fast." He didn't wait for Vic. After he got out and opened the side door to accommodate the hide-a-bed, he headed for her front door. The key was on his ring.

Vic followed him inside. They made quick work of getting the couch out to the van. In a few minutes he'd restored the living room to its former order. "I'll run upstairs to grab my laptop and any clothes I left."

"While you do that, I'll take down the camera from the garage."

"Good. Be back in a second."

When he came down with his bag, he went into the bathroom to pack the toiletries he'd left. All was done except to leave the key and garage-door opener.

Cy walked into the kitchen and put both items on the table. That was when his eyes were drawn to the diamond and wedding band he'd given her. They were sitting on a note she'd penned. A vise seemed to close around his chest.

He pocketed the rings before reading it. The last lines stood out. *Just know that you will always have my undying gratitude. You saved my life. What greater service can one human do for another?*

Kellie had written this before he'd phoned her. Now that the threat to her life was over, she hadn't been able to remove the rings fast enough. She hadn't mentioned tomorrow night's party, not even a hint that she still wanted to go with him.

So what in the hell did those kisses mean the other night when they'd both come close to losing control? Gratitude had nothing to do with the way she'd melted in his arms, kissing him until he felt immortal. She'd been on fire for him. That wasn't something you could hide.

Vic joined him. "What's going on, Cy? You haven't been the same since you walked into headquarters this morning. If I didn't know better I'd say you've seen a ghost."

Cy lifted his head. "TJ was right. He warned me

that pretending to be married meant I'd be walking a very thin line. At the time I didn't realize how much truth he spoke." *Or how much I wanted it to be real.* He turned to his friend. "That's why *he's* the captain. Let's get out of here."

He walked out of the house, making sure the front door was locked before he closed it. When they got in the van, Vic turned to him. "Come on, Cy. It's me you're talking to. Something's eating you alive. What is it?"

Cy tossed his head back. "I think I've been played."

"By whom?"

"Who do you think?"

"You couldn't mean Kellie."

"Until I read her note, I didn't think it was possible, either. Gratitude is the last thing I want from her."

Vic cocked his head. "I take it you two crossed the line."

"Only one time. After Dan threatened to kill her horse, she fell apart and I comforted her. Things got out of control for a few minutes. That's all."

"Apparently it was enough to turn you inside out."

"Never again," he vowed through gritted teeth.

"Listen to me, Cy. You're too close to the situation and not thinking straight. Try looking at this from her point of view. Before my wife died, I learned a lot from living with her. Not everything is what it seems to be. Kellie had to have feelings for you or she wouldn't have kissed you. But don't be upset because she's grateful to you for saving her life. Both emotions can coexist in the same universe."

He took a sharp intake of breath. "You saw the wedding rings on the table."

"Now that I think about it, I see you're not wearing your wedding band, either. How come?"

"You know damn well why."

"Can't you believe she took her rings off for the same reason?"

"But did she?"

"Only you can answer that question. Has she left you with no hope?"

Cy rubbed his eyes. "It's not like that. She said she wanted to cook dinner for me. I knew it was just her gratitude talking. But the other night I told her my sister's engagement party is on Sunday night. Since I didn't dare leave Kellie alone, I asked her if she'd be willing to go with me and she said yes. But now that the case has been solved, she didn't—"

"Didn't what?" Vic challenged. "Tell you she still wanted to go with you?"

"No," Cy muttered.

"Did you ask her if she still wanted to go? Maybe she was waiting for you to bring it up. You've been joined at the hip for a week in the most dangerous kind of situation, but now that you no longer have to pretend you're married, I'd say she's feeling a damn sight vulnerable... and probably nervous."

He flung his head around. "Nervous—of me?"

"You've been in charge all this time, dictating every move. Maybe she fears *she's* been played."

"*Hell*—"

"Yup. And hell is where you're going to stay till you get this thing straightened out."

Stirred up by Vic's perceptive comments, he started the engine and they took off for the warehouse at headquarters. Once they'd dropped things off, Vic left for home while Cy walked through to his office.

Hell wasn't the place he wanted to be. He sat down at his desk and phoned Kellie. No doubt she was out riding and it would probably go through to her voice mail. If so, he'd wait until he got a live response, even if it took until he went to bed.

In the meantime he opened the file folder on the new case TJ had given him.

Fidel Ravelo is wanted in connection with the armed robbery of approximately $7 million from a security company in North Austin, Texas, that took place two years ago. He allegedly took three security employees hostage at gunpoint and handcuffed, bound and injected them with an unknown, nonlethal substance to disable them further. The FBI is offering a reward of up to $1,000,000 for information leading to Ravelo's capture. He's believed to be in Venezuela, but recent rumors say he's been seen in Brownsville, where he has ties to family.

After studying the specifics, he'd start by talking to the security employees. Maybe one of them could recall a detail that hadn't been included in the report. But he couldn't do any more work today. The captain had told him to go home. Cy decided to take his advice because he could no longer concentrate.

KELLIE FINISHED SHAMPOOING Trixie and rinsed her off. After putting a little conditioner on her tail and mane, she brushed them to make them silky. Her last action was to use a damp cloth to rub her palomino's face. Then she gave her a kiss and some Uncle Jimmy's Squeezy Buns for a treat. She and Starburst chomped them down.

"There! Now you two look beautiful and I'm sure you feel much better." Both horses stood in the late-afternoon sun while she towel-dried them so they wouldn't catch cold. On Monday the vet would come out to look them over and check their hooves before the trip to South Dakota.

"All right, girls. It's time for dinner." She grasped their lead ropes and walked them to their stalls inside the barn. After removing their bath halters, they could eat from the hay nets and drink water.

The exercise had been good for her, reminding her these horses were her children and her passport to a championship. "See you tomorrow."

She could hear nickering and walked to Paladin's stall. Only two days ago Cy had ridden him. The memory of that heavenly afternoon made her ache for him. "You want a treat, too?" Kellie fed him the last of her horsey treats and walked out to clean up the grooming equipment. Once she'd coiled the hose, she headed back to the ranch house.

Today she'd wondered if she would make it through

to evening without Cy, but here she was still walking around. And thanks to him, still alive. Somehow she had to get beyond all this. Earlier in the day her father had told her this was a time for debriefing. By working with her horses, it would help put the horror of her experience behind her. The passage of time would do the rest, but she couldn't hurry the process.

Her mind thought about Cy. Every time he solved a case for the agency, how did he put the horror behind *him*?

She let out an anguished sigh. When she looked to the sun getting ready to set, she noticed the sky was shot through with pinks and yellows. The same sky Cy might be looking at tonight. How long would it take her to stop missing him? Was he missing her right now? Had the magic between them been a figment of her imagination? Those moments in his arms were real enough.

If he were her husband, how would she deal with their separations, knowing that every time he left the house it was possible he might not come back? Under those conditions, how long could the magic last?

"Not very long," she whispered to the air. Kellie didn't have the right stuff to live with a hero like Cy. That was what he was. It took a special type of woman who could compartmentalize her feelings in order to deal with that kind of stress on a day-to-day basis.

Once she reached the ranch house, she went upstairs to her old bedroom to shower. Since she had no appetite, she got ready for bed and reached for her laptop. It was time to draft a disclaimer to put on her blog. She'd known this day would have to come. Who knew Cy would solve her case this fast?

Kellie got to work on it. When she'd finished, she read it over half a dozen times, but she needed another opinion before posting it. Since it was only eight thirty, she reached for her cell phone to call her friend Kathie. Seven messages were waiting for her, including one from Kathie. It wasn't until now she remembered that she'd turned off her phone. The last one was from Cy. He'd called hours ago. She couldn't believe it.

Her hand trembled as she pressed the button and listened. "Kellie? Call me ASAP."

The urgency in his deep voice gave her heart the greatest workout of its life. He'd solved her case and was already working on another one. Why was he calling her now? Had he left something at the town house he'd forgotten and didn't want to be accused of breaking in to get it?

If she didn't phone him back, she'd never know the answer to that question. His call gave her the excuse to talk to him again. Feeling light-headed from emotions bombarding her body, she pressed the digit for his number.

He picked up on the second ring. "Kellie?"

"Hi." She was trying to catch her breath.

"Thanks for calling me back."

"I didn't know you'd phoned until a minute ago. I've been out shampooing my horses and just finished."

"How lucky for them."

She chuckled in spite of her angst. "They love it and they were so good for me. They didn't move."

"That doesn't surprise me. They love you. Horses aren't that different from humans. Rosco P. likes to do tricks for me."

"Rosco P.?" Kellie was charmed down to her toenails by the revelation. "Was he the horse you rode in the Bandera parade?"

"That's right."

"I didn't know that was his name. Sounds like the bumbling character from the old *Dukes of Hazzard* television show with Boss Hogg."

"The very one."

"I adored that series. The way those brothers drove that car around, driving the Boss crazy, was hilarious."

"I got a kick out of it, too."

"What kind of tricks can you get your horse to do?"

"He can bow and do the Spanish walk."

"You're kidding!"

"Nope. Most of the time I use a ball to play with him. For incentive I feed him Rounders Molasses treats."

"Starburst likes those, too." Kellie almost said that they'd have to get their horses together, but she stopped herself in time. "Cy—I'm probably keeping you from your work. Did you forget something at the town house? Is that why you called me?"

"No. I phoned to ask if you want to go to my sister's engagement party tomorrow night. We'd talked about it before, but that was when I was protecting you. Now that the threat is over, we can go without worrying about our undercover lie."

She pressed a hand to her mouth to stifle a cry of joy. He still wanted her to go with him.

"I'd like that very much."

"If it works for you, I'll pick you up at your town house at six thirty. It's a semidressy affair."

"Thanks for telling me. I live in cowboy boots and forget they're not suitable for every occasion."

"Understood. I know you have questions about how everything went down last night. I'll do my best to answer them. See you tomorrow night. I look forward to being with you again, Kellie."

Her pulse raced. "Me, too. And you're right. I'd like a little closure. Good night." *I want to see how serious your injuries are.* She hung up in a daze, suddenly motivated because she knew she'd be with Cy tomorrow night.

In the morning she'd clean her one-stall horse trailer and living quarters to get it ready for her trip around the circuit. Kellie had to put fresh feed and hay on board, plus all her gear and plastic barrels.

She had nine or ten different bits and took them with her along with several pairs of reins and halters. In her dressage training routine she felt snaffles were the best, plus the square mouthpiece O-ring, so her horse's mouth would stay soft and undamaged.

Once the vet came out to check her horses, she and Cody would be ready to go. He and his fiancée would be over on Wednesday to load Starburst and they'd all drive in tandem. What she'd give if Cy were in a different line of work and could travel to the various rodeos with her.

You're crazy, Kellie.

One phone call from him and her head was in the

clouds again. She couldn't afford to forget what he did for a living. He'd dodged a bullet while protecting her, but what about his next case, and the one after that?

By the time she'd given herself another talking-to, a great deal of her excitement had dissipated. A night out with Cy would be wonderful, but she'd pay a price. She just knew it! But it was too late to cancel on him, and she didn't want to.

After turning out the light, she crawled under the covers with her mind made up that it would be their final goodbye.

Before she left for South Dakota she'd post her blog piece. But Kathie deserved an explanation over the phone first. She'd been hurt that Kellie hadn't told her about her marriage. That was something she could fix right now.

Kellie hadn't really been in touch with anyone since the stalker first approached her in Oregon. Cy had made up her whole world and still did.

Knowing she wouldn't fall asleep for a long time, she reached for her cell. While they were on the phone, she could run the blog piece by her friend and see if she had any other suggestions before it went out. When Kellie thought about telling everyone she really hadn't gotten married, she felt so hollow inside, she could hardly stand it.

BY SIX ON Sunday evening, Kellie had showered and shampooed her hair. There was enough natural curl that she blow-dried it into a wavy bob with a side part.

Once she'd applied her lipstick in a tangerine frost color
she loved, it was time to get dressed.

She had several outfits, but in the end she chose
her sleeveless black flared jersey dress with the high
rounded neck. Her tiny black-and-gold puffed teardrop
earrings went perfectly with it. On her feet she wore
black sling-back high heels. Before she left the bedroom, she reached for her black clutch with the gold
fastener.

One last look in the mirror and she realized she
didn't need any blusher. The temperature she was running did it for her. Kellie would be meeting Cy's family
tonight. She needed to look her best for him.

At twenty after six the doorbell rang. Her heart
leaped because he was early. She hurried downstairs
to let him in. How ironic that only two days ago, Cy
had permission to come and go as if he lived here while
he carried out his plans to protect her.

When she opened the door, the tall, spectacular-
looking male in the midnight-blue suit and lighter blue
shirt almost caused her legs to buckle. Kellie had to
hang on to the door handle or she would have fallen.
She noticed a small bandage on the side of his neck
above the collar, but nothing else, thank heaven. He
was here—and he was okay.

Chapter Nine

Cy took in the vision before him. Mounted on her palomino, Kellie Parrish in Western attire was a complete knockout. But tonight the champion barrel racer had taken on a different persona. To say she was dazzling in black was an understatement.

She had a glow about her he hadn't seen before now. The stalker brothers had stolen that radiance from her, but now that they'd been caught, she'd been restored to her former self. Her heart was in those blue eyes, and she was looking at him the way she'd done when they'd kissed each other senseless the other night.

"Hi" was all he could say until his breathing returned to normal.

"Hi," she answered in a soft voice. "I'm ready."

"Make sure both doors are locked."

It brought a smile to her face. "I did."

"Sorry. Old habits die hard."

"I forgive you," she murmured as he walked her to his Audi sports car parked in front of the town house. Once he'd started the engine and they were off, she turned to him. "How long will it take us to get to Dripping Springs?"

"That depends."

"On what?"

"Maybe we'll just drive into the sunset. What would you say to that?"

The blood pounded in her ears. *I'd go anywhere with you.* "I'm not sure your sister would forgive you."

"What if I told you I'm tired of doing my duty?"

He felt her glance. "Your sister isn't a duty."

"True. But the way you're looking tonight, I'm not sure I want to share you with my family. You look stunning, Kellie."

"Thank you," she whispered. "You look better than I feared you would after being sent to the hospital."

He thought he heard a compliment in there somewhere. "I had no choice but to go in the ambulance. Those were the captain's orders. Otherwise I would have come back in the town house to talk to you."

She nodded. "Luckey told me as much."

"Well, Ms. Parrish—we have a half hour of privacy before we reach my parents' home, where you'll be bombarded with questions. Ask me anything you want."

"I want to know how you knew the stalker would come after you in the alley."

"When I realized the stalker had a clear look at your garage in order to take that picture, and to see his brother hauled out to the van in the very same place, I decided he could be hiding out in one of the town houses on either side of the alley. So Vic and I went door to door. We hit the jackpot when we entered the

town house opposite yours through the fence. Those two
criminals had been renting it since February."

He heard her gasp. "I don't believe it. All this time?"

"We found enough evidence inside to help the agents
in winding up the other murder cases back east." Cy
didn't tell her about the shrine. It would horrify her,
and she didn't need the added trauma now that they'd
been incarcerated. "Dan kept a loaded rifle with a scope
by the side of the bedroom window overlooking your
garage.

"After he sent you that last phone message about
getting rid of your husband, I decided to draw him
out. When the team saw Dan return to the town house
dressed like a woman, I figured he would make his
move against me soon. So I set it up and hoped he'd hear
the garage door open. If he hadn't done it when he did,
then he would have tried again and again. It was my luck
that he was so angry, he took the first chance he got.

"I backed the car out. As soon as I turned the wheels,
I knew he'd take a shot if he was going to, so I stopped
the car and rolled out to the ground. Those three shots
shattered the glass. That was it. The team closed in on
Dan, who had no idea they were staking him out, and
took him away."

She lowered her head. "You could have been killed
so easily."

"No. The setup was on my terms. I knew what I was
doing. Those evil twins are going to be sent to prison
for life without parole."

"The governor praised you on TV."

"It was all in a day's work."

"Don't be absurd, Cy. What you did was as great as what the Original Forty did when they saved Texas."

"That comparison is way over-the-top. Just remember that saving you was greater, and I couldn't have done it alone."

"But it was all your brainchild. Sometimes you seem bigger than life. I'm in awe of you."

Cy smiled to himself. He'd take that for a start. "It helped that the target of those killers happened to be a woman who's the pride of Texas. You showed courage under fire and stayed in control while they terrorized you. Kind of like the way you handle Trixie when you race into the arena. Thousands of rodeo fans across the country are in awe of you."

"You're never going to let me thank you properly, are you?"

They were driving into Dripping Springs. Cy took the first turnoff and drove to a neighborhood park with a small lake. After pulling to a stop in an area away from other people, he stopped the engine. He undid his seat belt and turned to her, sliding his arm along the back of her seat. "What is your definition of *proper*?"

He waited while she digested his question, then she undid her seat belt. His heart thudded as she launched herself at him, throwing her arms around his neck. She started kissing his face. Every feature. *"This and this and this!"*

Suddenly her mouth reached his and he forgot everything except the thrill of holding her in his arms once more. She was no longer the woman he had to protect. For the first time, he was free to kiss her and show her what she meant to him without having to hold back his passion. He'd been aching for her since they'd kissed a few days ago.

"I've missed you for the last two nights," he whispered into her shimmering hair. Her fragrance enveloped him.

"It's been hard since you moved out," she admitted. "I know we were only together for a week, but I got used to being with you. To be honest, I feel lost."

"I know the feeling." Cy crushed her mouth again, never wanting this ecstasy to stop. They couldn't get close enough. He would never be able to get enough of her.

"We're going to be late for the party," she struggled to say after he lifted his mouth so she could breathe.

He groaned. "What party?"

"The one I got dressed up for."

"I guess we have to go so I can show you off."

"Does your family know you're coming?"

"I texted them I'd be there."

"Do they know you're bringing someone?"

He cupped her beautiful face in his hands and kissed her thoroughly. "No. It will be fun to surprise them. That is if we make it there."

They gave in to their desires once more before Kellie pulled away from him. "You *have* to go." She moved to her side of the car and fastened her seat belt.

Resigned for the moment that this would have to wait until later, he got the car going and they drove the rest of the way to his parents' home in silence. Before they pulled in the driveway, he saw a dozen cars parked on both sides of the street. Hurricane lanterns with lighted candles lined the walkway to the front door of the spacious rambler.

"Since the wedding and reception will be held at the church, my folks have gone all out for this party." He turned off the car.

"I'm not surprised. Your sister is their only daughter."

"Beth has been doted on. She came along when my parents didn't think they could have another child."

"My parents had to wait a long time before they got me. How old is she?"

"Twenty-three. She has her degree in English. After New Year's, she'll be teaching at a middle school." He got out of the car and went around to help her out. "I'll tell you a secret. She's afraid of horses. Always has been."

Kellie looked up at him in surprise. "Was she hurt by one?"

"No. But she fell off her mount during a ride when she was little. My dad tried to help her overcome her fear, but she wouldn't do it. After that experience the only time she'd try it was if Dad or I took her on rides on our horses."

"Oh... What a shame. Does her fiancé ride?"

"He tolerates it if he has to."

She smiled. "Can you imagine having to tolerate Rosco P.?"

"No." Kellie was so lovely he lowered his head to kiss her mouth once more. "She and Tom are a good match," he whispered against her lips before he walked her to the front door and let them into the foyer.

"Well, look who's here—"

Cy might have known his father's older brother would spot them first. "Your mom said you were coming. We've all been waiting for the man whose name has been in the news for the second time this year. Well done, Cy." He gave him a pat on the shoulder before his glance fell on Kellie.

"Uncle Bruce? Allow me to introduce Kellie Parrish. She's—"

"All of Texas knows who she is." His uncle shook her hand, eyeing her in admiration. "It's an honor to meet our state's leading rodeo champion." He looked back at Cy. "And *your* wife, I understand. You always were a dark horse."

"No—" Kellie blurted, darting Cy an anxious glance. *Hell.* "How many people know about that?"

"Everyone at the party." His uncle smiled at Kellie. "My son's wife, Terrie, reads your blog religiously, and the word spread. Come with me. We're all waiting to meet the two celebrities of the evening."

"I'll handle this," Cy whispered to her and put a hand on her back as they walked into the living room. All the chatting ceased, then everyone started clapping. "Sorry about this, Kellie," he said out of the side of his mouth.

"It was inevitable," she whispered back.

The din died down. "Hi, everyone. I didn't expect a greeting like this when it's my sister's engagement party. We don't want to intrude on yours or Tom's happiness, Beth, so let me just explain a few things so you can all enjoy the rest of the party. I understand you're under the impression that Kellie and I are married. It's not true."

At that remark, expressions sobered. "We had to pretend to be married to smoke out the killer."

"Well, I'll be," one of his aunts exclaimed.

"It turned out there were two of them. Identical twin brothers who'd murdered three other women back east before they targeted Kellie."

Murmurs of horror came from the group. "Those two criminals have been arrested. Kellie is now free to continue traveling the rodeo circuit before she competes in the Finals in Las Vegas in December. Her next rodeo will be in South Dakota this coming weekend."

She tugged on his arm and whispered, "Do you mind if I say something?"

"Go ahead."

"We're together tonight because we're working on a statement to put out on my blog and the newspaper about the lie I told people. It was necessary to my case that the stalkers believe I had a husband. His captain and my parents agreed.

"Ranger Vance's brilliant idea frustrated those killers, who lost focus long enough for him and the other Texas Rangers to close in on them faster than anyone expected. But let me assure you he wouldn't have missed his sister's party for the world. Under the very real circumstances of life and death, I learned for a fact he loves his sister and family more than anything." A few *ohs* of sentiment followed her comment. "That's why I agreed to come with him. We'll finish up police

business after the party. Since I'm the only girl in my
family, too, I know how important this night is to Beth
and her future husband. Please forget we're here now
and go on with your celebration."

Cy already knew he was in love with Kellie, but
her ability to think on her feet under difficult circumstances added to her stature in his eyes. She was a living miracle.

AFTER CY SAID he wanted to leave the party, his mother
walked Kellie to the door. He and his father were behind
them. "You've been through an experience I wouldn't
wish on my worst enemy." Her son looked a lot like his
attractive mother. She had those dark blue eyes, too.

"Cy was heroic in his treatment of me. If my choice
of words sounds strange to you, let me assure you chiv-
alry isn't dead. Because of how he handled everything,
it took away a lot of the horror." Kellie felt her eyes
smarting. "He made me believe in him, that he could
do anything if I went along with his plan. He affected
my parents the same way."

His mother's eyes misted over. "He always did have
the quality that instills confidence. Cy's father wanted
him to go into law, but he had another dream. A dangerous one. To think he saved your life makes me ashamed
that I ever wished he'd find another career."

"Then you can imagine how grateful I am to him."

It was obvious Cy's mother had found a way to live
with it, but Kellie was afraid she would never be able
to get over her fear for his safety. She knew herself too

well. To live in constant agony because of a man's occupation wasn't for her. A wave of deep sorrow washed over her, knowing that after tonight she wouldn't be seeing him again.

"Our family will be rooting for you in December."

"Thank you, Mrs. Vance."

"Call me Annette."

She smiled. "Your daughter is darling and Tom seems like a wonderful man. You must be so happy for her."

"I am. She's never given me grief. Cy has been a different story, but that's because he's definitely his own person."

"I found that out."

The older woman reached out to hug her. Then Cy's father gave her a hug.

"I understand you were the model of bravery during your ordeal. My son grew up esteeming that quality once he found out we had real Texas Ranger blood running in our veins."

"I've heard the story, and the more I learn about Cy and his colleagues, the more I know all the legends about the Rangers are true."

Cy reached her side. "What are you two talking about?"

"You and the Lone Ranger riding your trusty steed Rosco P.," she teased.

His dad laughed and winked at Kellie. "Drive home safe."

"We will. It was a lovely party."

She hurried ahead of Cy to reach his car. But he

overtook her and helped her into the passenger side. After they backed out of the driveway and headed toward Austin, he reached for her hand and wouldn't let go. "You were fabulous tonight."

"Your family is wonderful."

"Everyone thought *you* were wonderful." He squeezed her hand tighter before letting it go to make a turn.

"Beth looked the way every bride-to-be should look. Radiant with no cloud in her sky."

She felt his glance. "You said that with a degree of sadness." Cy was already picking up on her dark thoughts.

"I didn't realize it was that obvious." She changed the subject and they talked about the different relatives and friends she'd met at the party. They kept the tone light, but once they'd reached her town house and had gone inside, he shut the door and put his hands on her shoulders from behind.

"Tell me what was eating at you during the ride home," he murmured against the side of her neck.

This was going to be the hard part. She moved away, forcing him to drop his hands. "Before we talk, I want you to read the draft I've written for the blog. And after that I'd like your opinion on what we should give to the newspaper. The *Statesman* and the *Chronicle* have been asking for an article. My laptop is upstairs. I'll bring it down and we can work at the table."

She tossed her clutch on the couch and rushed away, praying he wouldn't try to stop her. When she'd told herself she could quit Cy cold turkey, that was before she realized she was madly in love with him. This was the kind of love that would never go away, not in a millennium.

CY REMOVED HIS suit jacket and tie. He hung them over the back of one of the kitchen chairs before sitting down in another one. This place had been like home to him for a week. Now he was a guest.

While he waited for her, he pulled out his phone. There were messages from the guys, but those could wait. He listened to the one from the captain. "Call me on my private line ASAP. I have some news on the Ravelo case."

Since Kellie hadn't come down yet, he phoned his boss. "TJ?"

"I'm glad you called, Cy. There was a homicide over in East Austin tonight around ten. It turns out someone shot one of the hostages taken by Ravelo during the robbery two years ago. His name is listed in the file as Jorge Montoya. Go over to the morgue and see what the autopsy revealed before you come into work in the morning."

Kellie walked in the kitchen while they were talking and put her laptop on the table. He stood up and turned his back to her while he finished the conversation.

"I've been studying the case. Maybe Montoya was in on the robbery with Ravelo. But when he didn't get his cut of the take, he gunned for Ravelo and got liquidated by a hit man or Ravelo himself. I'll find out when I'm down in Brownsville."

"Trust you to come up with a better possibility than anything the police have been able to figure out."

"It's a guess."

"Nine times out of ten your guesses beat the hell out of everyone else's."

"Don't I wish. Good night, TJ."

When he hung up and turned around, Kellie had taken a seat at the table. "I'm sorry if I intruded on a private conversation."

He bristled. "You could never intrude. The captain and I were going over a new case."

"So I gathered." She averted her eyes and opened her laptop. "Take a look at what I wrote the other night. Tell me what needs to be added or deleted." She was all business.

Cy moved it around so he could read it. The sooner they got this out of the way, the sooner he could find out what was causing her to pull away from him. At the park before the party, she hadn't hidden anything from him. The old saying that he thought he'd died and gone to heaven had summed it up best. After that, how could she change so fast from the warm, loving woman he was crazy about to someone he didn't recognize?

To all my fans—If you haven't watched the news, then you may not know that I've been the target of two stalker brothers who have made my life a living hell for the past month. The Texas Rangers were called in to help me.

In order to draw these criminals out, I had to pretend to be married in order to trap them. Now that they've been arrested in a cunning sting, I can announce that my marriage was a brilliant piece of fiction that kept me alive until they were caught. Besides my wonderful parents, I owe the Texas Rangers my life.

But I'll have you know that the husband I made up truly is the man of my dreams. Maybe one day... In the meantime, I'll be working hard riding the circuit until December, when I'll be participating in the National Finals Rodeo in Las Vegas. See you there! Long live the rodeo!

He sucked in his breath. "I can find no fault with it."

"Good. I thought I could send the first two paragraphs to the newspapers. But I'll put the entire article on my blog."

"Again I think what you've written is just right. One question, though." He shot her a glance. "Why did you use the word *cunning*?"

"Because you had to fight fire with fire. It's what you do. No one else comes close to your genius. *Cunning* means deceitful, crafty and full of guile. Those words describe the two stalkers who would have murdered me if it hadn't been for you. That's why you're such a brilliant Ranger."

He rubbed the side of his jaw, trying to figure her out. "Why are you suddenly distancing yourself from me?"

She sat back in the chair and stared at him through veiled eyes. "Because you became my hero throughout this reign of terror. My prince, if you like. But when you brought it to an end, I realized you do this every day for a living. You move on from one ghastly, gory case to another, and then another and another. On the phone just now I heard you discussing a hit man and a robbery.

"Those aren't just words to me anymore. A hit man is someone who actually goes out and kills people. Those brothers were planning to kill me. They became real. The whole situation became agonizingly frightening when Dan started stalking me. Then he tried to kill *you*. I've lived through a nightmare and will never be the same again."

"Kellie—"

"Let me finish. The other day Dad brought up the possibility of my getting therapy. I didn't want to hear it, but I think he's right. Forgive me for throwing myself at you in the car. I didn't know any other way to express my feelings. It shows how off-kilter I am. You're a man and you responded like any red-blooded man. But I'm a wreck, Cy."

His stomach roiled. "So what are you saying? That you take it all back? That you don't want to see me again?"

"Yes— No— I'm not explaining myself right. I would love to be with you again and again, but I can't bring myself to do it because—"

"Because what?"

"I'm afraid I'll lose you while you're in the line of duty. The other night you made yourself a target for Dan to shoot you. I was there, and I was dying inside. I went through that experience with you. Don't you see?" She got to her feet.

"I know that when you go to work, you're going to

put yourself in jeopardy laying your life on the line every day, or night, depending on the circumstances." She clung to the back of her chair. "You asked me why I sounded sad tonight. I'll tell you why.

"I saw your sister and her fiancé so happy, and I was so envious. She never has to worry when he goes to work at your dad's law firm that he'll be shot or blown to bits by a bomb or stabbed to death. I know there aren't any guarantees in this life for any of us, but he'll probably live a long full life and raise a family with her.

"I don't see that in your stars, Cy. I'm being honest. I couldn't handle it if anything happened to you. Though I'll never forget you, if I don't see you again, hopefully in time I'll fall in love and get married to someone who's—"

"Safe?" He cut her off.

"Yes!"

"Where's the barrel racer who stares down danger every time she enters the arena?"

"For heaven's sake, Cy. You can't compare that to what you do. I don't care about me. It's you who matters! Just hearing about this new case you're going to work on makes me sick to my stomach. I don't want to think about it. I know someone has to protect us from the evil out there, but I don't want the man I love to be the one who does it."

He grabbed hold of the table, hoping he'd heard her right. "You *love* me?"

She swallowed hard. "What do you think I've been saying all this time? Yes, I love you. I'm madly in love with you. Isn't that crazy? We only met nine days ago, yet I know to the marrow of my bones it's true.

"But I don't want to be in love with you. Your poor parents didn't have a choice when you made up your mind what career to go into, but I *do*. So I'm going to ride away from you while I still can."

"That's not going to solve anything," he said in a grating voice.

"Maybe not, but when I'm off on my rodeo circuit, I'll be spared knowing that you were shot and killed by some lawless felon while I was gone. I don't want to be anywhere around when that happens. Now, I think you'd better go. The vet is going to be out early in the morning to give my horses a checkup."

The fact that she loved him would help him get through all the other things she'd said that he hadn't wanted to hear. She needed more time.

"Will you let me hold you for a little while before I leave?"

She shook her head. "No. I don't dare. Kissing you in the car was a big mistake."

Like hell it was…

"Kellie? Look at me."

"Please don't ask me. I enjoyed the evening with your family. Let's let it rest there with that memory."

"Would it help if I told you I'm head over heels in love with you?"

"For the second time, you mean?" she asked in a sharp tone. "If I recall, you told me you barely escaped marriage the first time around."

"That's because I wasn't ready for a commitment."

"Even so, someone will come into your future who will be the right fit for you. Maybe a woman in law enforcement who can deal with the risks to her own life and yours. They say the third time's the charm."

"You're being intentionally cruel, but it's not working. You and I were on a collision course from the moment we bumped into each other in Bandera."

"That's what they said about the last meteor coming toward Earth. But before it got caught into our gravity, its orbital path suddenly missed us and flew in another direction."

"Your metaphor doesn't apply to us. We got caught in the gravity you and I created together. There's no greater force. You can take off for South Dakota, but we'll never be able to escape each other's pull."

"I pray you're wrong," she said with tears in her voice. "Goodbye, Cy. As I heard Vic say to you, watch your back. Might I add, keep Sylvia close. She gets to go with you wherever you go because she has no issues. She even gets to sleep under your pillow and will be with you to the end. What a lucky woman."

Kellie... Kellie...

He reached for his jacket and tie. "Will you walk me to the door?"

"I'd rather not." She clung to the chair back. "Is this new case going to take you to Brownsville?"

"Maybe, but it's nothing for you to be concerned about."

"You see what I mean? Already I'm sick with worry because there are so many killings down there and you haven't even left my house."

"I'm sorry you heard me on the phone."

"So am I. Forgive me for being so awful to you, Cy. I wouldn't be alive today if you hadn't come to my rescue. Please go before I make everything worse."

She was in so much turmoil, he realized there was nothing he could do right now. "I'm leaving." He crossed through the living room to the door. After opening it, he waited to see if she would call him back, but it didn't happen. The evening had turned into a nightmare of new proportions.

Cy pushed in the night lock and shut the door. After reaching the car, he sat there behind the wheel for a few minutes. Kellie loved him. But after what she'd lived through, if he asked her to marry him, then he needed to get into a different line of work.

The thought of leaving the Rangers tore him up inside.

The thought of losing Kellie ripped his heart out.

Chapter Ten

"This is Lydia Olson from Rider Rodeo Connection in Rapid City, South Dakota, for the Black Hills Pro Rodeo. The reigning champion barrel racer for tonight's win is Kellie Parrish with a 13.90 score. You're just racking up the wins, girl. Congratulations!"

"Thank you so much."

"I had to pull out my cheat sheet to list all your stats. You're a Wrangler NFR Qualifier ten times, a College National Finals Qualifier two times, the National High School Rodeo Finals Qualifier four times, and the Pro Wrangler Finals winner in Oklahoma City, Oklahoma, three times. And this year has been the best for you so far."

Kellie nodded. "It's been a good year for me." A year that had changed her life in ways she would never have imagined, but she didn't want to think about Cy right now. "My horses have been terrific and I'm hoping to do well at Finals in December. There's a lot of money to be won and the competition is tough. You're only as good as your last win, so you can't let down. I've got six more rodeos to go before I head to Las Vegas."

"You've thrilled the folks tonight and I wouldn't be surprised if you come out number one in Las Vegas."

"I'm excited to try."

"Where are you headed next?"

"Cheyenne, Wyoming."

"Well, we wish you luck. Thank you for talking to us for a few minutes. What plans do you have to celebrate tonight?"

"I'm going to go pet my horse before I do anything else. She was perfect tonight."

"There it is, folks! Kellie Parrish, who stunned the crowd on her champion horse, Trixie."

"Thank you."

Kellie left the arena and hurried to the rear of the pavilion to see Trixie. Cody had already taken care of Starburst.

Trixie neighed when she saw Kellie, who rushed up to her and threw an arm around her neck. "You were wonderful, Trixie. Here." She pulled a horsey treat out of her jeans pocket. The palomino gobbled it noisily. Kellie chuckled as she led her by a lead rope out the back of the facility to the trailer.

For the next half hour she went through her routine of removing the saddle and bridle, followed by a brush-down before loading her inside the trailer for the night. Earlier in the day Kellie had mucked out her stall, where she'd provided water and had put fresh hay in the net.

"Good night, Trixie. Dream of grassy meadows and sunshine."

Her horse neighed in response before Kellie shut the door.

"That horse is half human."

"Hey, Cody." Her dark-haired buddy had parked next to her. "How's Starburst?"

"I rode her for a while. She's in good shape. Great job out there tonight. I've never seen you ride better. Frankly, after knowing what you've just been through, I don't see how you stayed so focused."

The determination to erase Cy from her mind had played a big factor.

She smiled at Cody. "I couldn't do any of it without you, but I guess you know that. We've made some good money. Depending on what happens at Finals, we should both have enough to get started on our careers after the New Year."

"That's what Jenny and I are counting on. Want to celebrate with us tonight? We're going to grab a bite and take in a movie."

"Thanks, but I'm exhausted. I'll follow you back to the RV campground and call it a night."

They both started up their trucks and drove the short distance to the outskirts of Rapid City. After checking on her horse once more, she visited Starburst and gave her some horsey treats. Then she went into her trailer and took a shower. Once ready for bed, she phoned her parents. They celebrated her win by informing her they would fly to Greeley, Colorado, in two weeks to watch her performance. What would she do without her loving, supportive parents?

After she got off the phone, she posted a message on her blog to keep her fans informed of tonight's performance. Once that was accomplished, she returned phone calls from Olivia and Sally, who told her Manny was competing at the rodeo in Greeley. Kellie would look forward to seeing them there and introducing Sally's bull-rider-champion husband to her folks.

At last ready for bed, she got under the covers and turned on the radio. But the country-and-western station played the kind of music that talked of breakups and unhappiness. She turned to KBHB broadcasting from Sturgis, South Dakota. Lots of farm news and world news interspersed, but she wasn't able to concentrate and finally shut it off.

In the dark of the night she couldn't kid herself. She'd been hoping she'd hear from Cy all week. It hadn't happened. Kellie hadn't seen him since last Sunday night. They'd parted on such an ugly note, it had left her shaken. Was he deep into his new case?

When she couldn't stand it any longer, she looked up Luckey's number on her contacts list. The temptation to find out what he knew about Cy had been driving her crazy. Tonight she gave in to it and phoned him. The call went directly to his voice mail, but she held off from leaving a message and hung up. She was a fool. Luckey would know she'd called and would probably tell Cy. So much for going cold turkey. She eventually fell asleep, furious at herself for succumbing to the impulse.

The next morning Kellie got up and dressed. After eating a bowl of cereal, she planned to walk both her horses before they all started the drive to Wyoming. On her way out of the trailer, her cell rang. She checked the caller ID and felt a swift surge of adrenaline. It was Luckey. She answered on the third ring.

"Hi, Luckey."

"Hi, yourself. I saw you called last night, but I didn't get a chance to return it until now."

"I shouldn't have bothered you."

"Surely you didn't think I'd mind."

Like Cy, he had those special qualities and charm that made him stand out. "No. I'll be honest. Ranger Vance and I said goodbye last Sunday night. Since then I've been out on the circuit. But I couldn't help overhearing part of a conversation he had with the captain. It had something to do with a case that could take him to Brownsville." She moistened her lips nervously. "I've been a little worried because of all the tension on the border."

"I'm on another assignment and can't discuss any cases, but as far as I know all is well with him."

"I guess I'm having a hard time letting this go. After he saved my life, naturally I don't want to see him injured or worse."

"It's understandable considering he went undercover to protect you. You wouldn't be human if you didn't come out of your experience unchanged. I'll tell you a secret. When I applied to join the Rangers, there was a saying printed at the top. 'Decide that you want it more than you are afraid of it.' I thought about it long and hard before I submitted it."

Kellie had to stifle a moan. "That explains the spirit of the Sons of the Forty."

"It explains why you're a rodeo star," he replied. "Not everyone is driven by the same passion. Since the guys and I saw you at the Bandera Rodeo, we're all planning on you winning the World Championship."

"Thank you for those kind words. For everything," she half whispered. "You've given me a lot to think about. Watch your back, Ranger." She hung up to prevent further conversation.

Decide that you want it more than you are afraid of it. Such a simple statement, yet such profound wisdom.

AFTER HIS FLIGHT from Brownsville to Austin on Saturday evening, Cy went straight to his house to get some much-needed sleep. So far the Ravelo case wasn't opening up for him. If there were any family members still living there, Cy hadn't found evidence of one. He'd been concentrating in the wrong place and would pursue his angle on Montoya's tie-in to the robbery now that he was back.

Sunday morning he got up late and checked his laptop for emails. Nothing from Kellie, no phone calls. She had his cell-phone number, but it seemed she'd meant what she'd said two weeks ago. She didn't want to love him. *Damn* if she wasn't proving it by her silence.

He glanced at her rodeo schedule on the website, then read her latest entry on her blog. Last night she'd had another winning performance in Cheyenne, Wyoming. Two wins in two weeks. Without the specter of the stalkers, she was going ahead full steam on her road to a dazzling championship in Las Vegas.

In a dark mood and feeling empty, he left for the office. On Sundays it was fairly quiet around there and he'd be able to get through the paperwork that had been piling up while he'd been gone. Halfway through it, his cell rang. The caller ID said Bronco Parrish.

His heartbeat quickened and he clicked on immediately. "Mr. Parrish?"

"No. It's Nadine Parrish."

"Hello, Nadine. How are you?"

"I've been fine until just now."

"What's wrong?"

"I'm sorry to bother you, Ranger Vance. Maybe it's nothing, but I found something in Kellie's mailbox. I went over to her town house this morning to check on things and water her plants. Maybe this isn't important, but I thought you should know."

He frowned. "What is it?"

"Besides her usual mail, there was another typewritten envelope with her address, but no return address. It's postmarked two days ago. I brought the mail inside, but I haven't opened it."

"Are you still at her condo?"

"Yes."

"Don't touch it. I'll be right over and park in front."

Cy's mind raced with possibilities as he left headquarters and drove to Kellie's town house. Maybe it was simply a note from a friend, but something in his gut told him that wasn't the case. He reached into the glove compartment and pulled out a pair of latex gloves from a box he kept there.

Nadine had opened the front door and was waiting for him. Judging by the lines on her face, she was worried. They'd all assumed this case was over. He hoped to heaven he was wrong about a third party being involved with the stalkers.

She gave him a hug he reciprocated. By tacit agreement they went into the kitchen and sat down at the table, where she'd left the mail. The white envelope stood out from the rest of the bills and ads.

"Let's see what's in here." He put on the gloves and opened it.

You're a little *fresa* who should have been eliminated a long time ago. No one wants a badass like you around in your skinny designer jeans.

This wasn't the language that came from either stalker. The type was different. If he didn't miss his guess, it was sent by a jealous female. Dan could have been using her, possibly her car. He lifted the typewritten note to his nose. There was a faint smell. Not perfume. Because it had been posted only two days ago, maybe residue lotion had clung to the paper. Kellie's mom eyed him nervously.

"What do you think?"

He didn't show her what was typed. "I'm not sure, but you were wise to call me. I'll take this to headquarters. If you're through here, I'd rather you didn't come back until I've done an investigation. I'll let you know when I deem it safe. Whatever you do, don't tell Kellie. I understand she's come in first at both rodeos so far. Let's not throw her off track unless we have to. If I think she needs to know, I'll get in contact with her."

"I agree. Thank you so much for coming right over."

After Nadine locked the front door, he walked her to her car then got into his own. On the way to the office, he phoned Vic, who'd put on his voice mail. Cy left him a message and asked if he'd meet him at headquarters if at all possible.

The second he got in his office, he opened the paper file on Kellie and searched through the evidence, but he didn't see the report on the Sentra sedan. While he was studying the notepaper already in the file, Vic walked in.

"Hey, Vic—I'm sorry to bother you on a family day."

"It's all right. Jeremy is at his aunt's house playing with his cousin Randy right now. For you to be here on Sunday meant your message was urgent. Have you gotten a break on the Ravelo case?"

"No. That's why I'm back in Austin, but something else has come up and I'm afraid it could be serious. Here's a pair of gloves." Cy pulled them out of the box in his bottom drawer. "Take a look at this. Kellie's mother found it with the mail when she went over to her town house this morning."

Vic put the gloves on and checked the note, then looked at the envelope. "This was mailed two days ago from the Del Valle post office."

"That's only seven miles southeast of here. Where's the paperwork on the Sentra sedan impounded the night of the takedown?"

"Maybe forensics didn't send it up yet, but it should be on the computer. What are you thinking?"

"I'm wondering if Dan had a girlfriend who lives around there and was using her car."

"I took a look at it. A 1999 model that looked like it's been through a war."

"Maybe she found out about Kellie and couldn't stand the competition. This note has a scent. The other notes don't. They're not made of the same kind of paper and the language isn't like Dan's."

His friend picked it up to test. "You're right, but news of the arrests has been all over the internet and TV. If such a person exists, why would she send Kellie a note now?"

"I don't know, Vic. It's just a hunch, nothing more, but I don't like it. I want to find the person who mailed this. For a start I need the name of the owner of that car."

"I'll phone Stan at home. Maybe he can tell us where the report is backed up in the system. I have his home phone number on a list in my office." He pulled off the gloves and tossed them into the wastebasket. "Give me a second and I'll get it."

Vic had been gone only a minute when he came right back and handed Cy a file. "The report was on my desk. I guess they thought you'd be in Brownsville longer, so they gave it to me. It must have been put there after I went home yesterday."

He sat down next to Cy and they pored over it. "The present owner is Martina Martinez with an address in Garfield, Texas. That explains the postmark when they moved the Garfield post office to Del Valle."

"She has a rap sheet for petty crimes starting at the age of fifteen. At the present age of twenty-one, her last known address is 16 Spring Street, and her last known employment is a manicurist job at the Travis County Hair Salon."

"Maybe he hit on her when he went in to get a manicure or another wig or some such thing."

"That's what I'm thinking," Cy murmured. "Her car went missing the night we arrested Dan. I think we both know why she didn't call the police to report it stolen."

"No doubt she stole it off someone else."

"Let's find out right now. I'll drive us."

They left the building and took off. The GPS guided them to a small bungalow in a run-down neighborhood on Spring Street in Garfield. Cy parked two houses away from the actual address and turned off the engine.

"While you knock on the front door, I'll move around the back so any escape is covered."

"Right."

They'd worked together for a long time and could read each other's minds. Cy walked to the rear and planted himself next to the back door. It didn't take long before it opened and the woman they'd hoped to find came flying out as he suspected she would. Cy caught her tattooed arm and forced her hands behind her back to cuff her. She let go with a stream of Spanish curse words, trying to kick him. By this time Vic had joined him. "I've called for backup."

"Good. Martina Martinez, you're under arrest for evading police during an official investigation. You have the right to remain silent until an attorney is present. If you don't have one, the court will appoint one for you."

An older Hispanic woman of maybe fifty hid herself

behind the partially opened door. "What do you want with my Martina? She's done nothing wrong."

Vic's hands were on his hips. "She shouldn't have run when I asked if I could talk to her."

"What do you want with me?" the suspect cried. "I haven't done nothing."

"Where's the blue Sentra car belonging to you?" Cy questioned.

"I don't know what you're talking about."

"Your rap sheet says you're the owner, but it showed up at a town house in Austin. The man driving it has been arrested for murder. The police already have your fingerprints on file from your former arrests. When they match them to the ones found in the car along with his prints, then you'll be going to prison along with the guy for being an accomplice."

"There's no guy!"

"Sure there is. Is he your boyfriend? How about that threatening letter you mailed to Kellie Parrish from the Del Valle post office?"

She tried to spit at him. "You can't prove I sent anything to that spoiled *fresa*."

Convicted by her own mouth. *Fresa* meant "strawberry," a derogatory term she'd written in her note.

"Your fingerprints will be all over that letter when it's examined. What happened? Did he take off in your car to see Kellie and didn't come back? Did that make you so angry you lashed out at her?" Cy heard sirens getting closer by the second.

"Shut your mouth, *chota*!"

Cy had hit a nerve. Nothing could have pleased him

more than to be called a crooked cop. "We'll let you tell that to the judge."

Vic took her other side. They dragged her around to the front of the house while the older woman screamed at them. Neighbors in the area came out of their houses to see what was going on. Two police cars had converged on the scene. The officers took over and put her in the back of one of the patrol cars. After giving information for the incident report, Cy walked back to the car with Vic.

"I'll ask TJ to get a warrant so the crew can search the house for signs that Dan might have stayed there from time to time. Someone needs to take down a statement from the mother."

When they got back to headquarters, Vic left to go pick up his son. He invited Cy to come over to his house later and they'd kick back with a beer. That sounded good since Cy dreaded going home to his empty house.

He went into his office to leave a message on the captain's phone about the arrest of the Martinez woman. Then he phoned Nadine Parrish to give her the news. She wasn't the only one greatly relieved. For a second when he'd first seen that letter postmarked only two days ago, his heart sank at imagining there was still another stalker out there.

The two of them decided Kellie didn't need to know anything about this until her tour of the circuit was over. Before they hung up, Nadine informed him she and her husband were flying to Greeley the next Saturday to watch her compete in the rodeo.

Kellie's mother could have no conception of the kind

of pain he'd been in for the past two weeks. All he could say was he hoped she'd make the best time and he wished her well.

"I'll tell her."

With that phone call over, he was emotionally drained and left for his car. Before he turned on the engine, he received a call from Luckey and clicked on.

"I'm glad to catch you, Cy. Are you still in Brownsville?"

"Nope. I came home when my lead there went dry. It's a good thing I did." For the next few minutes he told his friend about the letter and the arrest of the Martinez woman.

"That must have knocked you for a loop when you saw another note."

"I have to admit it did."

"Does Kellie know about it?"

"Not yet. Her mother will probably tell her when she and her husband meet up with her in Greeley to watch her performance."

"Why not you?"

"Because we parted company two weeks ago."

"As in…"

"I won't be seeing her again."

"Cy… there's something you ought to know."

He inhaled sharply. "What's that?"

"She phoned me last weekend."

"Kellie *what*?"

"Yeah. I was on a case and couldn't answer it. She didn't leave a message. The next morning when I saw that she had called, I phoned her to find out what she wanted. At first she was apologetic for bothering me. Then she asked if you were down in Brownsville.

"I told her I couldn't discuss a case, but assured her all was well with you. She thanked me and then just before hanging up she said, 'I guess I'm having a hard time letting this go. After he saved my life, naturally I don't want to see him injured or worse.'"

Cy bowed his head. In one week she'd broken down to Luckey. To Cy's joy, the ice was cracking. He'd warned her they could never escape each other's pull. After hearing this bit of telling news, the longing for her was so great he knew he had to do something about it. Knowing her folks were flying to Colorado next week gave him an idea, but he'd have to clear it with his boss.

"Thanks for being my friend, Luckey. I owe you."

Chapter Eleven

14.00. Second place for the night at the Oklahoma rodeo. Not good enough.

Cynthia Lyman had taken first with a 13.95.

"It wasn't your fault, Starburst." Kellie threw an arm around her neck and fed her a treat. She'd been losing concentration and there was only one reason why. Instead of getting over Cy, her love for him was stronger than ever. She was dying to talk to him, to be held and kissed. But she needed to nail some first places at the three upcoming rodeos in Texas in order to maintain the highest average. That wouldn't happen if she didn't snap out of it.

The most despondent she'd been since leaving Austin, she walked Starburst back to the trailer and loaded her inside. Once she'd taken care of her, she drove to the RV campground where she and Cody were staying.

There were headlights behind her she could see through the side-view mirror on her truck. Someone else was coming into the RV park. She wound her way through to their reserved area. The lights stayed with her. Maybe it was Cody.

Soon she turned into their spot and could see Cody's truck and trailer ahead in the distance. Her cell rang. She knew it was Cody. He always phoned her when he saw she was back. After stopping the truck, she clicked on without looking at the caller ID.

"I know…you don't have to say anything, Cody. I didn't have a good night."

"14.00 nabbed you a second place. From where I was sitting, you wowed the audience."

At the sound of the familiar male voice, she almost went into cardiac arrest. *"Cy?"* Kellie was trying to comprehend it. "You were in the audience tonight?"

"Yup. I flew into Oklahoma City and rented a car at the airport so I could drive to the arena and watch your performance. I wanted to join you while you were walking Starburst to the trailer, but I didn't want to frighten you. I've probably made things worse by following you. Thus the phone call."

Kellie was speechless.

He'd come all this way to see her.

She forgot everything and scrambled out of the truck. He was moving toward her. She couldn't get to him fast enough and started running. He caught her up in his arms and swung her around like a bride.

"Cy—" But anything else she would have said was stifled by the hunger of his kiss. Delirious with love and wanting, she kissed him back without thinking about anything else. All she could do was show him what he meant to her. They melted together, trying to become one.

"I love you, Cy. You were right about everything. I miss you too horribly to let you go."

"That's all I need to hear. I'm in the middle of a big case and have to be back at the airport in a half hour to catch the red-eye from New York to Austin. It makes one stop here. We don't have much time. Come and get in the car with me. We have to talk fast."

She wanted to scream that it wasn't fair to experience this much rapture, only to have it snatched away in so short a time. But this was Cy's life. Even working a dangerous case, he'd come for her. She had to find a way to deal with it, because he really was her whole world.

After they got into the car, he pulled her to him. She needed his kiss as she needed air to breathe. What they were doing was devouring each other, but there wasn't enough time to pack in all their feelings in a matter of minutes.

"I love *you*, Kellie. You're so much a part of me at this point, I can't live without you."

"I can't either, darling. I've been so afraid of loving you for fear I'd lose you. But Luckey told me something that straightened out my dilemma in a hurry."

"He said you called him."

"Obviously I couldn't bear even a week apart from you. He told me about what was written on the application when he wanted to become a Texas Ranger. It said, 'Decide you want it more than you're afraid of it.'" She looked into those dark blue eyes. "I want you more… so much more you can't even imagine."

"Good old Luckey," he whispered against her lips before driving his kiss deeper. After he lifted his head, he reached into his Western shirt pocket. "Will you marry me for real this time?" He held up a diamond ring.

She let out a cry. "It's the same one you gave me before. I thought it was property from the agency's warehouse."

The smile she loved broke out on his face. "It's not the same one, exactly. But it's the same style, yes. I wanted the ring to look like the one you wore when we pretended to be man and wife. I think I wanted our marriage to be real from the beginning." He slid it home on her ring finger.

Tears filled her eyes to feel it back where it belonged. "So did I. The blog piece I put on about our fake marriage wasn't fake to me. I meant every one of those words you said were over-the-top."

He pressed his cheek to hers. "I said them because I wanted to think you meant them, but I was afraid that dream could never become a reality." He found her mouth and kissed her passionately, over and over again. "Have you put your disclaimer in the paper and on your blog site yet? I've been too busy to look."

"No. I've been holding off. It's because I haven't been able to take back the words I wrote. I'm afraid they're written in my heart forever. I could feel myself falling for you after your captain first brought me into your office at the agency. There you were again, the Ranger I'd bumped into in Bandera. You were the most glorious sight this cowgirl had ever seen, standing there in the sun in your Stetson."

"Someday I'll tell you all the things I thought about you that day, but we don't have much more time. How would you feel about getting married secretly in Fort Worth three weeks from now? I'll arrange to take the weekend off."

"Only the weekend?"

"I can't take more while I'm still on this case. We could be married by a justice of the peace in the afternoon, then I'll watch you win your last rodeo. We'll honeymoon for a day on our way back to Austin. After Finals we'll have a family wedding at the church and a reception."

She burrowed her face in his neck. "I think it's perfect, but I don't know how I'm going to last until Forth Worth without you."

"I'll phone you every opportunity I get."

"If you're undercover, I don't want to know about it."

"That's good. We'll both be happier that way. Tomorrow I'll tell my folks we're engaged."

"I'll do the same and inform the parents we want to be married right after Finals. I'll tell Mom to call your mom. The two of them will get together to plan the wedding."

"My folks have been waiting for this day forever. I have a three-week vacation coming up whenever I want to take it. The last night of Finals will be Saturday, December 12. We could get married on New Year's Day and take off for that long honeymoon you announced on your blog."

She crushed him to her. "I can't believe this is really happening."

"You will." After another kiss, "I have to leave for

the airport now, sweetheart. Come on. I'll walk you to your trailer."

"You don't need to do that. I know you're in a hurry." On a groan, she gave him one more kiss to last until they saw each other again in Fort Worth. "Never forget how much I love you, Ranger Vance."

Somehow she forced herself to get out of his car. She ran to the trailer and opened the back to check on Starburst. The headlights of his rental car shone on her and her horse. When she couldn't see them any longer, she turned to Starburst and half sobbed for joy against her neck.

"He loves me, Starburst. See my engagement ring?"

Her horse nickered in response as if to say she already knew.

KELLIE HAD A hard time keeping her secret from Cody, even though he knew she was engaged for real. On Friday they reached Fort Worth. After getting settled at the RV campground, she told him she had some shopping to do in town and would work out with the horses later in the day.

After several stores she found a lovely oyster-colored two-piece lined wedding suit with long sleeves and pearl buttons. The jacket had lace trim on the collar and around the hem. She wanted to look bridal yet smart and sophisticated for this fabulous man she was marrying. This outfit was for him alone. She bought matching high heels and a beaded clutch bag. A new pair of pearl earrings caught her eye plus new underwear and a nightgown, the kind she'd never worn in her life. All soft lace and tiny straps.

Once she was back in Austin, she'd hunt for a gorgeous wedding dress with her mom. Her parents were thrilled Cy had proposed and were already planning a New Year's Day wedding with his parents.

Excited out of her mind because she was marrying Cy in the morning, she hurried back to the RV park and exercised both her horses. She told Cody she'd be going into town in the morning, but would be back by noon to prepare the horses for the drive to the arena.

That evening she put her children to bed and she got started working on herself. First to wash her hair, then do her nails and toenails.

Cy would fly into Forth Worth in the morning. Everyone would presume he was out of town on a case. They planned to meet in the lobby of the Fort Worth Police Administration Building on West Belnap at 9:30 a.m. He'd arranged everything and Justice of the Peace Wilford Hayes would marry them.

Trust her fiancé to want their marriage to take place at the police bureau. As for Kellie, she didn't care where it happened, as long as it did!

At a quarter to nine the next morning of November 7, she left for the police administration building, not wanting to be late. The parking was in a lot adjacent to the building. She drove in and parked her truck. As she walked out and across the street, she received so many wolf whistles and horn honks, it was embarrassing.

"That's some lucky dude!" a guy called out from his cement truck.

She was almost to the doors of the building when she caught sight of the most handsome man she'd ever seen. He stood in front of the doors holding a small florist box. He was wearing a light gray suit and dazzling white shirt. *Cy.*

"I'm the lucky dude all right."

Those piercing dark blue eyes were alive with desire as they swept over her. "Good heavens you're gorgeous." He pulled her into his arms and kissed her right on the street where everyone could see them. "These are for you. Let me pin them on."

While she stood there in a daze, he undid the lid and fastened a gardenia corsage on her shoulder. People waited to go in until he'd finished and had opened the door for her. He ushered her inside and kept his arm around her waist all the way to the elevator. "If it was your plan to take my breath, you've succeeded."

"I'm out of breath myself. I didn't know three weeks without seeing you could be so long. It's embarrassing how much I love you."

They got out on the next floor and walked down the hall to Judge Hayes's office. The secretary smiled and told them to be seated while she let the judge know they had arrived. Cy put the corsage box on the next seat over and clasped her hand in his.

"If you only knew how long I've been waiting for this moment." The throb in his deep voice resonated throughout her trembling body.

"I *do* know," she whispered back. Kellie would have said more, but the judge came into the outer office. The older man studied them for a moment.

"I believe I'm about to marry two of our state's most famous celebrities this morning. Come into my chambers." In an aside, he asked his secretary to find the other witness and join them. Cy squeezed Kellie's hand a little harder before walking her into the judge's office. He put the necessary papers on the desk. Two women came into the room after them and shut the door.

After the judge made the introductions, he asked Kellie and Cy to stand in front of him and join hands. They reached for each other automatically.

"It's my privilege to marry a fine Texas Ranger and our state's champion barrel racer. If you're ready, we'll begin the ceremony."

"We've been ready for a long time." Cy spoke boldly.

A smile broke out in the judge's eyes. "Is that true?" he asked Kellie.

"Yes."

"I can tell your husband-to-be is impatient."

"Not as impatient as I am, Your Honor."

"All right, then. Let's get to it. Kellie Parrish, do you promise to love him and cherish him and all that other stuff?"

Kellie couldn't help but laugh. "I do."

"Cyril Vance, do you promise to love her and cherish her and all that other stuff?"

Cy looked at her. "I do."

"We both do," Kellie said emotionally. "Forever."

The judge nodded. "Forever it is. I now pronounce you man and wife. Have you got a ring?"

Kellie stared at Cy in concern. He pulled the gold

band out of his pocket and handed it to her. She pushed it onto the ring finger of his left hand.

"Now you may kiss your bride, but make it a short one."

"I'm afraid I can't do that," her new husband said.

"I get your point. Well, don't just stand there—and don't forget you've got a rodeo tonight, Mrs. Vance. After the favor I've granted this superhero here in cutting this ceremony short, I expect a star performance."

"I'll try."

"I do believe you've got him hog-tied, and that's a real feat. According to his captain, who happens to be a good friend of mine, no female has been able to succeed until now. But I can see why she's brought you to your knees, Ranger Vance. If I were forty years younger, you'd have some tough competition. Now, get out of here and live a happy life!"

"Thank you, Judge," she said to him as Cy rushed her into the other room. No bride had ever had such a unique wedding ceremony.

Before she could take a breath, he drew her into his arms and gave her a kiss to die for. "Let's get back to your trailer. I'll drive. If an officer pulls us over, I'll flash my star."

This was a side of Cy she hadn't seen before. He was like a different person. Funny, playful. Life with him was going to be filled with surprises. She almost had to run to keep up with him. They flew down the hall. He didn't want to wait for the elevator. Instead he opted for the stairwell. Before she knew it, they were outside and headed across the street to the parking lot.

"The truck's down there on the right."

"I know where it is. I watched you drive in and park."

That was her Texas Ranger. Always ten steps ahead of everyone else, and he was her *husband*!

"The keys."

She rummaged in her beaded bag and handed them to him. After he helped her into the passenger side, he ran a hand over her thigh and leg before shutting the door. His touch, so unexpected and convulsive, had set her on fire.

On their way out he paid the fee and they took off for the RV park with her directing him. "How soon do we need to leave for the arena?"

She checked her watch. "An hour."

"No matter how high I go over the speed limit, that won't leave us time for a wedding night until after your win tonight."

What?

He shot her a glance. "You couldn't be as disappointed as I am, but I need a whole night to make love to my wife for the first time. Since I'm counting on you clocking the lowest time in your event, I'm going to have to be patient a little longer. While you get ready, I'll hitch the trailer to the truck and do any odd jobs you need doing."

Kellie loved him so terribly, her heart hurt.

Cy spoke the truth. Their wedding night wouldn't be perfect if she couldn't hold him all night long. But they'd wanted to be married today. Even though a price had to be paid, nothing in life had made her this happy.

When they drove up to her trailer, Cody was outside

it checking one of the tires. When he turned and saw the two of them in their wedding finery, a huge smile broke out on his face.

"Well, what do you know? You got hitched and beat me and my fiancée to the punch." He walked over to give her a hug and shake Cy's hand.

Cy wrapped his arm around Kellie. "We didn't want to wait any longer. Would you mind taking a couple of pictures of us with my cell phone? We need to record this day for posterity. One day we hope to have children who will deserve to see the way their gorgeous mother looked the day we got married."

"And their father," she added with tears in her eyes. They hadn't talked about children. There were still so many things they didn't know about each other. Every revelation made her love him more.

He fixed the phone so all Cody had to do was keep pressing the button.

Trust Cody, who behaved like a photographer at a photo shoot. He had them pose this way and that, and of course lined up a few shots of them kissing.

"Yeah, yeah. That's what we want," Cody teased them until she was red in the face.

"No one knows we got married except you, Cody," she informed him. "Where's Jenny?"

"Out shopping. I'll pick her up on the way to the arena."

"You can tell her, of course. Cy and I will be having a big church wedding after Finals. This wedding was just for us."

"You two have been through hell. I'm happy for you."

He handed Cy the phone. "I'm just going to put a little more air in this tire."

Cy reached for her hand and they walked to her trailer. "It's the painted blue key," she said as he looked at the key chain. He unlocked the door and they went inside. For a few minutes the world was shut out.

She heard the sigh that came out of him. He turned to her and removed the gardenias from her jacket. "I wouldn't want to smash these." He put them on a chair, then took off his suit jacket and tie. "How long will it take you to change into your riding clothes?" He'd started undoing the top buttons of his shirt.

"Five minutes."

"Do it now while I hitch up the trailer. That will give us ten minutes to say hello to each other as man and wife before we have to get out of here."

The romantic side to Cy sent ripples of delight through her nervous system. He was excitingly methodical. As soon as he left the trailer, she rushed to change clothes. Tonight she'd wear a new Western shirt with fringe and a new pair of jeans. She had to remember to remove the pearls and put in her gold cowboy-boot earrings.

Once she'd hung up her wedding suit and put on her Western outfit, she pulled on her cowboy boots. Then she put on her cowboy hat so she wouldn't forget it.

"Leave the hat off for a few minutes."

Her heart leaped when she realized Cy had already come back inside.

The burning in his eyes made her legs tremble.

"Come here to me, darling. I need to hold you for a few minutes so I can believe that you're really mine."

Like being underwater, she moved slowly toward him and slid her hands up his chest and around his neck. He lowered his head to kiss her mouth, and the world stood still. She couldn't get close enough. No kiss was long enough. They'd gone beyond words to a place where hearts and desires had taken over.

It seemed as if they'd barely had a moment together when she heard a rap on the trailer door. "Sorry to bother you, Kellie. I'm heading over to the arena. See you soon."

A sound of protest broke from Cy before he put her away from him. But he had to hold on to her so she wouldn't fall. "I shouldn't have started kissing you, Mrs. Vance."

"I'd have died if you hadn't, Mr. Vance."

December 1

"I've been nauseated for the last couple of days, Dr. Shay. I'm supposed to leave for the Finals championship in Las Vegas tomorrow, but I need something to help me get over this flu fast."

"You don't have the flu, Mrs. Vance. You're pregnant."

Kellie came close to fainting. "Are you positive?"

"Your blood test didn't lie."

"But I've been on birth control pills for over a year to regularize my periods."

"Even so, there are reasons why you weren't protected. Women who become pregnant while taking an oral contraceptive either miss one or more doses, or you take a dose at a different time from the normal interval. If you took one in the evening instead of the morning, that can throw things off."

She tried to think back. Had she done either of the things he'd just mentioned? Wait—the day of their marriage she might have taken the pill that night instead of that morning because she was so excited about meeting Cy. Maybe she did miss a dose or two. She simply couldn't remember.

But one thing was certain. Her obstetrician couldn't be wrong. She was going to have Cy's baby. The news filled her with a joy beyond comprehension. But her nausea was so severe, she couldn't possibly compete.

"I'll give you some sample packets of nausea pills. You can take something before bed and see how it affects you. For some women it works after a few days. With others, you just have to wait until the nausea passes with time."

"Thank you."

When she got into her car, she had to sit there for a few minutes before she felt she could drive home to the condo. Once she got there, she lay down on the couch and phoned Cy. She had to leave a message on his voice mail.

"Darling? Please call me ASAP. It's an emergency."

Half an hour later he came bounding through the back door of the kitchen. "Kellie?"

"I'm here on the couch."

He hurried into the living and knelt down by her. "You're pale. What's wrong?"

"I went to the doctor this afternoon. I thought I had the flu. Cy? We're going to have a baby. It had to have happened on our wedding night."

His eyes flared with a light she'd never seen before. "You're pregnant?"

"I know it doesn't seem possible, but the blood test didn't lie. Even though I'm so nauseated I want to die, I'm so happy to be carrying your baby, you just can't imagine."

He looked anxious and vulnerable. She'd never seen him like this before. "I'm so sorry you're feeling ill. What can I get you?"

"Some ice chips? I've taken one of the pills he gave me."

"Anything."

He was gone in a flash and brought some ice back in a cup. She put several chips on her tongue. "Will you phone the parents? We may need to postpone the wedding. Thank heaven the invitations haven't gone out yet."

Cy kissed her lips. "We'll send wedding announcements instead and wait until you're over your morning sickness before we have a reception."

"Will you call Olivia in Colorado Springs tonight? Tell her I have to withdraw from Finals because we're expecting. She'll take care of everything."

"Oh, Kellie—" He made a tortured sound in his throat. "To think my marrying you has caused you to miss the thing you've wanted most in life."

She shook her head. "You're wrong, my love. The first time we bumped into each other in Bandera, I knew I wanted you more than anything else in life. I've won lots of events over the years and have had my thrills. But knowing I'm going to have your baby is a gift beyond price."

"Darling!" Cy put his arms around her.

"I hope our parents will forgive us for getting married without telling them—" she spoke into his hair "—but to be honest, I feel so sick right now, I can't think about that."

"I'll take care of everything. You just lie here. Do you need a blanket?"

"No. The thought of heat makes me sicker. Oh—" she moaned. "You need to call Cody. Tell him he'll get his share of the money even though I didn't compete. I'll send him a check in a few days. They're getting married soon and will need it."

"I'll do it. What else?"

"Call TJ and ask him if he can spare you for twenty-four hours. I need you with me."

She could see his throat working. "As if I'd be anywhere else."

"Those psycho twins you took down changed the very structure of our lives. There should have been a happier, safer way to have met. But I wouldn't trade that week we spent together playing man and wife for anything on earth."

He smoothed the hair off her damp forehead. "I've said this before, but I'll say it again. I thought I'd died and gone to heaven."

"What a story we have to tell our baby one day." She closed her eyes, starting to feel sleepy. "I was the undercover bride of a Texas Ranger. Promise me something?"

"Anything, darling."

"If it's a girl, we're not naming her Sylvia."

While joyous laughter poured out of her husband, she reached for some more ice chips.

Men had it so easy. It wasn't fair. But she wouldn't have it any other way, and she wouldn't have any other man.

* * * * *

Grace hadn't signed up for this. She'd agreed to a professional relationship.

Kissing did not belong in a professional relationship.

She'd committed to helping him. And she had. He now knew his name. Jackson Hawke, billionaire. The truth was he didn't need her anymore. His people could give him the support he needed. In fact, they'd be better qualified than her by far.

But she took pride in keeping her promises.

She liked helping him. Being honest, she admitted he'd helped her, too. In the beginning, the challenge of his situation gave her something to focus on at a time when she was at a loss.

The problem was he kept breaking the rules.

The kiss changed things. Her response changed everything.

HIS
UNFORGETTABLE
FIANCÉE

BY
TERESA CARPENTER

Published in Great Britain 2015
by Mills & Boon, an imprint of Harlequin (UK) Limited,
Eton House, 18-24 Paradise Road, Richmond, Surrey, TW9 1SR

© 2015 Teresa Carpenter

ISBN: 978-0-263-25156-2

23-0815

Harlequin (UK) Limited's policy is to use papers that are natural, renewable and recyclable products and made from wood grown in sustainable forests. The logging and manufacturing processes conform to the legal environmental regulations of the country of origin.

Printed and bound in Spain
by CPI, Barcelona

Teresa Carpenter believes that with love and family anything is possible. She writes in a Southern California coastal city surrounded by her large family. Teresa loves writing about babies and grandmas. Her books have rated Top Picks by *RT Book Reviews* and have been nominated Best Romance of the Year on some review sites. If she's not at a family event, she's reading or writing her next grand romance.

This book is dedicated to Patty, Maria and the gang at the Grab & Go on 6th Street in downtown San Diego. Much of my books are written during lunch. Thank you for your service and your patience. And for not throwing me out when I'm the last one there.

CHAPTER ONE

"G. DELANEY, YOU look beautiful tonight." Chet Crowder slurred the compliment.

Sheriff Grace Delaney glanced down at her khaki uniform, thought of her black cap of hair slicked back for convenience and her lack of makeup beyond a swipe of mascara and a touch of lip gloss, and figured if she needed any further evidence of Chet's intoxication she had proof of it in that comment.

"Is it midnight yet?" the eighty-year-old demanded. "I get a kiss at midnight." The words barely left his mouth when he bent over and puked all over the slick concrete floor.

"It's against procedures to kiss the prisoners." Grace cited policy as she nimbly avoided the deluge, stepping around the mess to escort him to the middle cell.

"But it's New Year's Eve," Chet protested with a burp. "You can make an ex-exception for New Year's Eve."

He didn't have to tell her it was New Year's Eve. Not even eleven o'clock and they already had three D and Ds—drunk and disorderly. Business as usual for the holiday. But not much longer for her. In a little over an hour she'd be handing over her gun and shield, her interim assignment as sheriff at an end.

"Rules are made for a reason," she stated. Her father's mantra, and thus the words she'd lived her life by. He'd been on her mind a lot tonight. "No exceptions."

"You're a beautiful woman, G. Delaney." Chet lumbered across the cell to the cot chained to the wall. "But no fun. That's why I didn't vote for you. Too serious, girl. Need to have a drink and lighten up some."

Grace's shoulders went up and back in instinctive defense against the criticism. It wasn't the first time she'd heard she needed to lighten up. She didn't understand it any more now than she had before. Being sheriff was serious business. Laws were meant to be upheld.

"Go to sleep, Chet. I'll release you in the morning." Well, someone would. She'd be on her way to San Francisco. With her term over and her dad gone she had nothing to stay here for—certainly not the pity job offered by her successor.

Moving to the mop bucket she'd had maintenance leave at the ready, she rolled it over and cleaned up Chet's mess. New Year's was one of two big festive events that got the residents drinking in Woodpark, California, entry to the Redwoods. The other was the annual fair and rodeo at the Fourth of July. She'd been told last year had been tame because of a heavy snowfall, but they'd still had eight citizens sharing cell space.

This year a crisp, clear night promised lots of revelry. Her successor set down the rules for the night. Depending on whether property damage was involved, D and Ds were allowed to sleep it off and be released in the morning. No need to book their guests.

Relaxing her standards made the muscles between her shoulder blades ache. She glanced at the clock. Only one more hour to endure.

She'd just tucked the rolling bucket back into the corner when patrol strolled in with a large man in blue jeans and a bloodstained white T-shirt.

The man's head hung forward, so his chestnut-brown

hair covered his features. He seemed tall, as even with his head and shoulders slumped he topped Mark's five-ten.

"What do we have here?" she asked.

"D and D. I found him walking on the road into town. He reeks of beer and has no identification on him. I brought him in to sleep it off. No hits on his prints. I ran them because he refused to give up his name. I figure we'll get his story in the morning."

"And the blood?"

"It was there when I picked him up. Must have been a brawl when he lost his wallet."

"Did you have medical look at him?"

"Yeah, he has a bump on the head, a small scratch. Nothing serious."

"Why is he in cuffs?"

"Didn't like my questions. Did a little resisting."

She nodded. With the man's size she wasn't surprised Mark had taken the precaution. She pushed the door open on the first cell so the patrol officer could walk the prisoner inside. "Right this way, sir."

"I shouldn't be here." The man's shoulders went back, his head lifted and he slowly turned to pin her with hard eyes. A dark scowl turned even features into a harsh mask. "I haven't done anything wrong."

"We frown on public intoxication in Woodpark." Now that she saw his face he looked vaguely familiar. She'd probably met him around town somewhere.

"I didn't have a drink." His expression shifted from displeasure to confusion and he repeated, "I didn't have a drink."

"What's your name, sir?"

Instead of answering he went to the cot and sat, letting his head fall forward once again.

"What's his blood alcohol level?" Grace asked Mark, leading the way into the open office space.

"I didn't run it. He was staggering and smelled of beer. It's already busy out there with the holiday and we're just letting the D and Ds sleep it off. I didn't think there was a need." He clipped his cuffs back in place. "Do you need me for anything else? I should get back in the field."

"No." Her shoulders tensed at the lack of procedure but it wasn't her department anymore. "You go ahead."

"Hey, if I don't see you again, good luck in San Francisco. You'll do better in the city. We're too low-tech here."

"Thank you." She appreciated the good wishes—she did—but she couldn't help noticing there were few expressions of regret that she was leaving. "Before you go, where are our mystery man's effects?"

"Property locker." He canted his head. "But there's not much—a jacket, chaps, a watch and a belt. If you're hoping to find a clue to his identity, you'll be disappointed."

"Probably." She'd check it out anyway. Not much to do besides monitor patrols and babysit the inmates. The town had less than five thousand citizens. At double duty there were six men on patrol. As a petty officer in the navy she'd been responsible for directing and training three times that many.

She missed the navy—the discipline, the control. She'd given it up to assist her father when he was diagnosed with prostate cancer. No regrets. Even though she'd lost him after seven months. She'd thought she was honoring him when she accepted the town's request to fulfill his remaining term as sheriff. Losing the recent election proved she'd failed to fill his shoes.

She'd lived with her father's exacting demands for thirty years. She didn't need to have him here to know he'd be disappointed.

Hopefully San Francisco would prove a better proposition for her. Or possibly Los Angeles or maybe San Diego. She knew she wanted someplace cosmopolitan. Thanks to the life insurance her father left her, she had half a million dollars to help her make her next life decision.

After hearing from her patrols and checking on her prisoners, she decided to look into the mystery man's property to see what she could find. She located the large plastic bag marked John Doe, the official designation for an unidentified individual, and brought it to her desk.

The strong scent of leather wafted into the room when she opened the bag. She pulled out a jacket, extra large, and chaps, extra long. Both were of fine quality, handstitched. In a smaller bag was a watch. Grace went through the pockets in the jacket, found nothing.

She pulled the chaps over, held them up in front of her and thought of the man in her cell, trying to picture him in this gear. Not difficult at all. Gave her a little thrill actually—a truth she'd keep between her and the mop bucket.

Something didn't measure up with John Doe. Broadshouldered with a lean, muscular frame, his downtrodden mien didn't fit with his physique. Or his protests of innocence, such as they were.

She ran her hands over the chaps, looking for hidden pockets, trying not to think of the leather framing JD's package. Of course she'd looked. She was trained to observe, after all. She found a matchbook from a tavern on the edge of town.

The watch was the real surprise. The heft and materials were quality all the way; the display of mechanics and the movement of gears gave the timepiece a sophisticated appearance. She looked closer—did that say Cartier? It did. And yes, she found similar watches on their website. Her eyes popped wide at the price: seventy thousand and up. Gah. Her next search was of robbery reports.

Nothing hit.

One thing was clear. JD had resources. Whether legitimate or not was another question. No hits on his prints only proved he'd never been caught. Yeah, call her a cynic. But why else wouldn't he want to give them his name? This guy wasn't adding up. He appeared familiar yet Mark hadn't known him.

The leatherwear shouted motorcycle, but where was the vehicle, his gloves and his helmet? Why was he walking along the side of the road?

The 101 ran right through the middle of town. Maybe someone ran him off the road and then robbed him? It fit the evidence. But why not tell them of the crime? Submissiveness didn't suit him, but he could be disoriented. He had a bump on the head. People often forgot events leading up to an accident. Maybe he was hurt more than the EMT was able to determine.

Time for a conversation with JD.

Thump. Thump. Pain pounded relentlessly through his head. Keeping his eyes closed helped marginally. Plus when he opened them there were only gray walls and cell bars to look at.

Man, he'd messed up big, to be laid out in a jail cell with a throbbing head.

Thump. Thump.

Problem was he couldn't remember what he'd done. The squat cop claimed he'd been drinking, but he had it wrong. He wouldn't feel as if he'd tangled with a semi if he had any alcohol in his system. His right shoulder and leg throbbed in time with his head.

At least he had the cell to himself.

Thump. Thump.

He wasn't even sure what map pin he inhabited. If only his head would clear, he was sure it would all come back. Then he'd get out of here and be on his way. Yep, as soon as his head got with the program, he'd explain things to the squat cop and then he'd be gone.

Thump. Thump.

The cell door clanked. He squeezed an eye open, spied the lady cop. He remembered her. The attitude. The uniform. The pretty blue eyes.

"How are you feeling?" she asked in a much friendlier voice than when he arrived.

"Like I was hit by a truck."

"Is that what happened?"

Thump! Thump! Suddenly his head hurt worse. Have mercy, he didn't think it possible. Couldn't people just leave him alone?

"I thought I was here because I was intoxicated."

"You denied drinking."

He had no answer for that. He'd jump on it if he thought she'd let him go, except he wasn't ready to move.

"You were walking when the officer came across you."

"It's not against the law to walk."

"No. But it's uncommon for tourists to arrive by foot."

He didn't respond. It hadn't been a question, after all. The low, husky timbre of her voice might be soothing if not for the interrogation.

"What do you drive?"

Drive? His brows drew together. Hadn't she just said he was walking?

"You were wearing a leather jacket and chaps. Where's your motorcycle?"

Thump! Thump!

He lifted his arm to lay it across his forehead. He gnashed his teeth at the show of weakness, but he had the desperate need to hold his head on, like if he didn't brace it in place it might explode.

"Are you okay?" Her voice hovered right above him and he smelled the freshness of peaches. She'd obviously moved closer.

"Can we do this another time? My head hurts."

"I'm going to check your wound," she warned him, the warm breath of her words blowing over his forearm. "It's possible you're hurt worse than we originally thought. This may hurt."

Her body heat warmed him as she loomed close. He shivered. With the pain racking him, he hadn't noticed how chilled he'd grown.

Thump! Thump! Sharp pain shot across his head.

"Ouch." He flinched away from her probing, all thoughts of the cold chased away.

"I'm sorry." She softly ran her fingers through his hair.

Yes. That felt good. He leaned toward the soothing touch.

"I need you to move your arm. I'm going to check your pupils." She suited action to words and he suffered the agony of a flashlight scorching his retinas.

"Irregular pupils. You have a concussion. I think we need to get you to the hospital," she declared.

"I'd be fine if you'd leave me alone." He dismissed her claim, waved off her hand. "I just need to rest here for a while."

"It's not up for discussion," she stated simply. "I'm obligated to see to your care. It's up to you whether we go in my cruiser or I call for an ambulance."

"I'm not riding in any cryptmobile."

"Then we need to get you on your feet."

"I think I'll just lay here for a while." Just for a bit, until he could breathe without pain and the room stopped spinning.

"I can't allow that. You have a concussion. You're disoriented. You need to be seen by a doctor. It's department policy."

"Well then." She wanted to disrupt him, ratchet up the pain, all to meet department policy? Right. He had fifty pounds on her. He wasn't going anywhere.

"How did you get hurt?"

Thump.

"Where's your motorcycle? Your wallet?"

Thump, thump.

"What's your name?"

Thump! Thump! Thump!

"Will you stop? Your talking hurts my head." So a few details were missing. It would come back once the pounding stopped.

"That doesn't really reassure me. Tell you what, if you stand up, look me in the eyes and tell me your first name, I'll consider leaving you alone."

"I don't want to stand up." Why wouldn't she just go away?

"Don't want to? Or can't?"

The taunt brought renewed pain as he frowned. He put his arm back on his head. Nice as her touch was, her insistence undid any good her soothing brought. Her goal, no doubt. It would take more than pride to drag him to his feet tonight. Possibly a crane would do it.

"Look, I'm not interested, okay? You're a beautiful woman, but I'm injured here."

"I'm not hitting on you." Outrage sent her voice up an octave. "I'm concerned."

"Are you sure? I've never had a cop run their fingers through my hair before."

"So you've been detained before?" She was quick to pick up on the inference.

He just stopped himself from shaking his head. "Just saying."

"That's it. I'm calling for an ambulance."

Everything in him rejected the option of being delivered to the hospital.

"Wait." He opened his eyes. She stood over him, hands on shapely hips, a scowl pinched between her stormy blue eyes. Clenching his teeth against the need to scream like a girl, he shifted to sit, and then pushed to his feet. Holding his shoulders back, he forced himself to meet her poppy blue eyes without flinching.

"Satisfied?"

She ran those cop eyes over him, assessing him from top to bottom. She nodded once as if satisfied by what she saw. It took all his strength not to sag in relief. But he wasn't out of hot water yet.

She cocked a trim black eyebrow. "And your first name?"

He was tempted to lie, to toss her any old name. But that felt wrong. Too easy. The falsehood didn't bother him— being predictable did. She expected him to blow her off. It was what he'd been doing since she'd entered the cell.

Forget that. Now he'd made the effort to get on his feet, he saw the value in getting a doctor's opinion. And some serious meds.

He met her stare-for-stare and confessed. "I can't remember."

"I can't remember." The words seemed to echo through the cell.

Grace blinked up at him. A rare enough occurrence— at five-nine she didn't often have to tip her head back to look a man in the face—but standing at his full height of six-three JD required her to do just that to assess his truthfulness.

Amnesia?

It seemed a stretch. Still, he had a sizable bump on his head and displayed signs of a concussion. It would explain his disorientation and his unwillingness to talk about himself.

Then again it was a tad convenient. Except why bother? He'd been told he'd be free to go in the morning.

"You don't remember your name?" She needed to determine the extent of his missing information.

"No."

"Do you know what year it is?"

He answered correctly.

"How about the President of the United States?"

Another correct response. He swayed on his feet, reminding her that, regardless of the state of his mind, his pain was all too real. She decided to let the doctor sort him out.

"Let's go." She led him to her desk, where she handed him his jacket. "I already made a call for Parker to come drive you. He should be here any minute."

"Oh, joy."

"At least he's familiar to you."

"I'm not dim-witted, you know." He sprawled in her desk chair with his jacket in his lap. "Just memory-challenged."

The corner of her mouth twitched at his show of humor. "All the more reason to stick with what you know until you've seen the doctor."

"I know you, and you smell better."

Now, why did that send a rush of heat to her cheeks? "I'd take you, but my duty is up in thirty minutes."

Probably a good thing. JD had managed to shake her up more than a little over the course of a mere hour.

"Check that." A deep voice announced. She recognized one of her other patrol officers. She stood to see him escorting a happy prisoner toward the back. "Brubaker, the new sheriff, has been monitoring the radio calls. Since I was bringing someone in, he told Parker to stay in the field. He wants you to take John Doe to see the doctor, and I'm to cover the rest of your duty here."

"Who will replace me at the hospital?"

The officer shrugged. "I'm sure Brubaker will send someone."

Right. She clenched her hands at having her control yanked away early. Brubaker had no authority to usurp her orders before midnight. But there was no use arguing.

"Okay," she said to JD. "Let's go." She'd already put her box of personal items in her SUV, so she grabbed her backpack and slipped into her hip-length leather coat.

The effort it took JD to gain his feet showed as it had in the cell, but he managed it and donned his jacket without uttering a sound. He stayed silent on their trip to her hybrid Escape.

In the vehicle he braced his head on a raised fist. "So I'm a John Doe."

"You're familiar with the term?"

"An unidentified person or body. I watch TV, the movies. I guess that means you didn't get a hit on my prints or you'd have a name for me."

"Right on both points." She stopped at a light on Main Street and three women in party hats, winter jackets and heels laughed and joked as they crossed in front of them. The light changed and she pulled forward.

"What happens if I don't get my memory back right away?" He slowly turned his head to pin her with a pain filled gaze. "How do you figure out who I am?"

CHAPTER TWO

HOW WOULD THEY identify him? Good question. Woodpark was a small town with limited resources. They'd have to reach out to a larger city, or perhaps the feds. Grace didn't have the heart to remind him it wouldn't be up to her.

"Let's see what the doctor has to say before we worry about that."

A grunt was her answer.

A few minutes later she pulled into the hospital parking lot. Like the sheriff's office, the emergency center did a brisk business on New Year's Eve. Grace walked to the front of the line.

"Sheriff," the clerk acknowledged her and then glanced at JD. "We're very busy tonight."

"So I see. You're going to have to make room for one more. I have a prisoner with a head wound."

"Take a seat and I'll let the doctors know."

"Of course. Please let them know I'm quite concerned."

She found him a seat in the crowded waiting room. He looked about to protest at taking the last chair, but he sat instead. Whatever his background, he'd learned some manners. That he ignored them was testament to the extent of his injury.

"You sounded worried," he drawled.

"Head wounds are dangerous." She leaned against the wall next to him. "We already know of one complication."

"So it wasn't a ploy to advance our case?" He lifted his gaze to hers and arched a dark brow.

Under the bright lights she noticed his eyes were leaf green. And a hint of red played in his dark hair. She turned her attention back to the front desk. "Maybe a bit of a ploy."

"And calling me a prisoner?"

She allowed a small smile. "Oh, yeah, that was totally a ploy."

He laughed and then groaned and clutched his head.

She sobered. "It's also true. You are a prisoner until morning. No dying on my watch please. You can't imagine the paperwork involved."

"I might be touched if it didn't just pass midnight. You're officially off duty."

A glance at her watch confirmed his claim.

"Sheriff." The clerk had returned. "Dr. Honer will see you now."

Grace checked the door but no sign of her replacement magically appeared. JD walked past her and then stopped.

"Are you coming?" he asked. "I can handle this on my own if you prefer."

"You're in city custody. I'm coming."

She followed him to the back and stood in the hall while he changed into the paper hospital gown the nurse provided. It was a small room. She took heart in the fact he would look silly sitting there, decked out in the flimsy robe. Too bad he didn't use it. When she entered the room, she found he'd stripped down to gray knit boxer briefs.

OMG.

Cough. Cough. Good gracious, she nearly choked on her own tongue as drool flooded her mouth. Swallowing hard she made her way to the corner, trying hard not to stare at all the hard lines and muscular definition on full display.

"You were supposed to put on the gown."

"It tore. Don't worry about it. Turns out I'm not modest."

Of course not. Turned out she had a bit of a voyeur in her.

Confronted with the sight of all that flesh and mus-cle—toned, and tanned, and tantalizing—she missed at first glance that a wound marred his nice six-pack. Still pink and edged with staple marks, the slash ran about six inches long under his right rib cage.

"You've been stabbed."

He glanced down at himself. The action made him sway, so he quickly lifted his head. "Where?"

She moved closer to point. "It looks pretty ragged, which tells me it wasn't a switchblade. Maybe a serrated blade. Or a piece of glass, possibly a metal fragment. Any of that spark any memories?" If shock value had any power to activate his memory, learning he'd been stabbed should do the job.

Leaving her question unanswered, he used long fingers to explore the wound. He flinched a little, indicating the cut was still tender. Or perhaps it was just the thought of being stabbed.

"Does it hurt?" she asked, hoping to get him talking. He revealed so little she had a hard time reading him. Part of it had to do with his missing memories, but she had the sense his reticence went deeper than that, was actually a part of his personality.

"Sore, not painful." Emerald eyes met hers. "It's not from this accident?"

"No." She shook her head as she examined the wound from a safe distance. "I'd say it's a few weeks old. The doctor might be able to tell you more."

As if on cue, Dr. Honer, short and balding, opened the door. He addressed his patient first. "I'll be with you in a minute." Then he gestured to Grace. "Can I see you, Sheriff?"

She stepped into the hall and he pulled the door closed behind him.

"Sheriff Brubaker called." He informed her. "He's not authorizing any care for the prisoner. He's been released instead. An officer is going to drop off his property."

Just dandy. Brubaker, the mayor's brother-in-law—who until today had worked for his wife's insurance agency—obviously didn't care about the liability involved in releasing an injured prisoner. Or worse, didn't know.

One of Brubaker's campaign issues had been her overspending, because she'd insisted the town bring the department's technical capabilities up to the twenty-first century. It didn't surprise her that he refused to spend any funds on a D and D set to walk out the door in the morning. Much simpler and cheaper to cut the guy loose. Even if he was injured.

"Doctor, this man has a head injury, a concussion at the very least. And possible amnesia. He says he doesn't remember who he is. We haven't been able to identify him, as he was missing his wallet when he was picked up walking into town."

"Sounds like he's had a rough night. I'll examine him, of course, but if he has no means of payment and the sheriff's office refuses to pay, I'm limited in what I can do."

"Whatever you can do, Doctor, will be appreciated."

He nodded and pushed the door open. "That's why I voted for you, Grace. You may draw a hard line between black-and-white, but people matter to you. It's not all about the bottom line."

JD sat on the doctor's stool. At five-seven it was the only way Dr. Honer could see his patient. If JD laid on the exam gurney his head would be up against the wall, and if he sat up he'd be out of the doctor's reach unless he bent in half—something his equilibrium wouldn't allow for in his present condition.

After a thorough exam, Dr. Honer announced, "The good news is there doesn't appear to be any neck or spinal injuries. As for the head wound, I'm going to need an MRI."

Concerned by the need for a scan of his brain, she stayed with JD, following him down the hall and sitting with him while he waited to take the test. He sat staring at the wall.

"Are you okay?" the pretty cop asked, her voice low, careful.

"Apparently not, if the doctor wants to do tests."

"The tests could reveal good news," she suggested.

"Doubtful. It's never good news," he declared with a depth of feeling that belied his lack of memory.

What a fool, sitting here in the hall dressed in a freaking hospital gown—the nurse had found a cloth one big enough to fit—while the whole world paraded by. He glanced at his bare wrist and bit back a curse. Everything had been stripped from him. He couldn't even mark the time, except to note it was moving at a slug's pace.

"I hate hospitals. And you know the worst part?" He sent her a sidelong glance. "I don't even know why."

"It must be difficult."

"Frustrating, debilitating, terrifying. The not knowing goes on and on no matter how hard I try to remember."

"Maybe you should stop trying, give your brain a chance to heal."

"Easier said than done. There's just pain and a whole lot of nothingness." He leaned his head back against the wall, amazed at what he'd revealed to her. Who knew? Maybe he was a Chatty Cathy, but somehow he doubted it. More likely her soothing presence lulled him on a subliminal level. "Talk to me."

"Okay." A beat of silence follow as he watched her struggle to find a topic. "About what?" Right, exactly what did you discuss with a stranger who had no memory?

"Why are you still here? According to what I've heard, not only are you off duty, you're out of a job."

"That's right." She chirped cheerfully, the first false note he'd heard from her. "My term as sheriff is up. I'm footloose and fancy-free as of midnight."

"So answer the question. Why are you still here? I really can handle this alone, you know. I'm not stupid, I'm just—"

"Memory-challenged," she finished for him. "I know. But you shouldn't have to go through this alone, JD. You are the victim of an accident and possibly—probably—a crime in our town. It's the least I can do to help you until you can stand steady on your own two feet."

"Why?" She called him JD. He supposed it was better than John Doe, which reminded him of dead bodies.

She blinked at him, black brows drawn together. "Why what?"

"Why is it the least you can do? You don't owe me anything." And with a certainty he felt to his core he knew the generosity she offered wasn't as common as she made it sound. Not in his life. It made him itchy—both grateful and suspicious at the same time.

"For me law enforcement isn't a job, it's a calling." The simplicity of the statement did nothing to detract from her sincerity. "My instincts to protect and serve don't click on and off with the punch of a time card."

"Was that your campaign slogan? If so, I can't believe you lost."

"I didn't really run a campaign. I felt my work should stand for itself."

"So you're an idealist."

"No, I'm a realist."

"Wrong. In the real world a candidate's work should speak to whether they can do the job, but in reality the voters like to be courted. They want to think you care about their opinion, their vote."

"So you're a cynic."

"No, I'm a geek."

She sat up straight, her breasts pushing against her khaki uniform shirt. "That's a clue."

"What?" He dragged his gaze to her face, flushed with excitement.

"You said you were a geek. That's pretty specific. Your brain let that slip, it has to mean something."

"Like what? I belonged to the chess club?"

"I don't know. But no one would look at you and think geek."

"And we're back to me."

"Yes, but we have a clue. Actually we have several. The chaps and leather jacket tell me you were riding a motorcycle. The quality and the expensive watch tell me you have access to money. And now we know you're a geek. A picture is forming."

"Of a motorcycle-riding geek with a fetish for expensive watches? Maybe I don't want my memory back."

"Don't say that. So the clues don't appear to fit together. That's only because we don't have all the pieces yet. It's all part of a bigger picture."

He found himself staring at his bare wrist again. He rubbed his hand across it. "I wish I had my watch now. I hate waiting."

"I'd say we've found another clue, but I don't know anyone who likes to wait. Hang in there." She patted his knee. "The doctor said it wouldn't be long."

Oh, no, she didn't just treat him like a child to be pacified. Even half-dead he couldn't allow that to slide. There were consequences when a beautiful woman touched him, and she was about to learn what they were.

Shifting toward her, he reached for the hand that committed the offense and slowly drew it to his mouth. He turned her hand palm-up and pressed a kiss to the sensitive center, gazing into her eyes the whole time.

She looked a little shell-shocked, leading him to believe the men of this tiny burg were idiots.

Her eyes narrowed and she tugged at her hand, seeking freedom. He held on for another moment. "Thank you," he said, keeping his voice soft, intimate. Finally he released her.

Sparks flashed in her eyes and he braced to be read the riot act. "You could be married, you know."

Not exactly what he expected. And it made him stop and wonder if he had a woman in his life, and the wondering made his head hurt. He realized he was rubbing his hand over the wound below his rib cage.

"I'm not."

"You can't know that for certain."

"No," he agreed. Because she was right. No memories existed to support his claim. "Yet somehow I do."

He wished he knew where the certainty came from. Maybe then he could plumb the source for actual memories, for real recollections. But the more he fought for it, the worse his brain hurt.

Luckily a male tech strolled up. "We're ready for you. Please follow me."

"Wish me luck." He stood, hospital gown flapping around his knees, strangely reluctant to leave her.

"Good luck." She stood, too, tucked her thumbs in her back pockets. "You've got this. After all, you're a smart guy, just memory-challenged."

A smile tugged up the corner of his mouth. "Can you hang for a while longer?"

She nodded. "I'll be here."

More than a little flustered, Grace spent the next long, worry-fraught hour gathering her composure around herself. Memory failed her as to when a man last affected her so strongly. She had no reason to care, but she did.

When JD appeared, she hopped to her feet. He looked so drawn. Exhaustion and pain weighed heavily on him. Without a word she followed him back to the doctor's office and took up her position in the corner.

"Who is the President of the United States?" The doctor started in on the questions needed to determine the extent of JD's memory loss.

JD answered with a scowl, adding, "What is it with you two and your obsession with the president?"

"General questions are used to create a baseline," Dr. Honer said. "It helps to determine if you've forgotten learned elements, a chunk of time or personal memories."

"Well, I should know the president's name. I've met him three times."

Silence fell over the room.

"How do you know that?" she demanded.

JD carefully turned his head around to her. Confusion briefly flashed through his eyes before he blinked it away. "I don't know."

"Do you remember under what circumstances you met him?"

"No."

"Because we might be able to identify you from news reports if we can pinpoint the event."

"I can't recall. But I know I've met him, just as I know I didn't have a drink last night." He turned to the doctor. "How is that possible? To know something but not have the memory to support it?"

"The brain is a marvelous and complex thing," Dr. Honer responded. "We're still learning many of its capabilities. The results of injuries are as varied and unpredictable as the number of people who sustain them. Do you remember anything about your childhood? Where you grew up? Your parents' names?"

"No." JD pinched the bridge of his nose, clearly in pain, clearly exhausted.

"What is the prognosis, doctor?" Grace asked softly.

"As you suspected, Sheriff, he has a severe concussion and a less serious laceration. Though they are in the same general area I don't believe they are connected. Is it possible you were in a motorcycle accident?"

"I can't say, Doc."

"It's probable." Grace spoke up. "He was wearing leather chaps when Porter brought him in."

Dr. Honer nodded his balding head. "The surface bump and laceration aren't significant enough to cause the level of swelling revealed by the MRI or the symptoms you've described. They certainly shouldn't have caused a memory lapse. But if you were in a motorcycle accident, it would explain the additional trauma."

"How so?" JD wanted to know.

"The helmet protected your head, which probably saved your life, but you still connected with the ground with enough impact to shake your head up inside the helmet, causing the brain to ricochet against the skull. Probably knocked you out for a few seconds. An accident would account for the bruising on your hip, as well."

"And the laceration?" Grace asked.

"It had gravel in it, which tells me it most likely happened after he removed the helmet. He may have fallen on his walk into town. Or more likely someone knocked him down."

"More likely?" Grace mused in full sheriff mode. "What makes you say that?"

"There's faint bruising on his lower jaw and on the knuckles of his right hand inconsistent with his other injuries. Since you mentioned he didn't have a wallet on him, my guess is someone ran him off the road and attempted to rob him. He probably came to in the middle of it, fought back and took a right to the jaw. In his condition that's all it would take to put him on the ground, causing the bump and the cut. Double head trauma more than accounts for the possibility of memory loss."

"Does that mean I'll get my memories back once the bump goes away?"

The doctor scratched his cheek. "I'm more concerned with the swelling of the brain. It could be fatal if it reaches the point of critical mass."

"And what are the chances of that?" JD's calmness amazed Grace.

"I'm cautiously optimistic considering the time lapse since you were picked up. You need to remain under observation and have another MRI after a bit, to see if the swelling is increasing or diminishing. It's possible once the swelling goes down that you could regain some, if not all, of your memories."

"What are my options if the swelling reaches critical mass?"

"Some people respond to medication. Worst-case scenario—a hole may need to be drilled into your skull to relieve the pressure."

She shuddered. That sounded scary.

Dr. Honer directed his next comments to her. "I highly recommend he be moved to the city. We don't have the necessary equipment to handle a delicate procedure of that nature."

Great. No way Brubaker would authorize the cost of ambulance service to the city. He'd already released the prisoner. JD was on his own. And her duty ended over an hour and half ago.

She could have left at any time, but she kind of felt invested. She could only imagine what JD must be going through: in pain, dealing with strangers, unable to remember anything of his life, not even his own name. It must be frightening. Yet he handled it with stone-faced grace.

"Sheriff, if I can have another moment?"

"There's no need to leave, Doc." JD halted them, a grim note in his voice. "If it's about me, I have a right to hear it."

"You need another MRI and to be monitored throughout the night, if not the next few days. I've expended all the resources I can at this point."

"I'll drive him." The words were out before she fully considered them, but what the heck, she was leaving town anyway. This just moved her agenda up by a few hours. Her sense of duty didn't end with the removal of her title and paycheck. And it went against every instinct to leave an injured man to take care of himself.

Looking at JD, no one would doubt his ability to handle himself. Though injured, he radiated a quiet intelligence, his stoic endurance testament to an inner core of strength. Which said a lot. Between Dr. Honer's prognosis and JD's memory loss, his whole world was one big uncertainty.

"You can drive him. Good, that's good." Dr. Honer sighed in relief. "Take him to the free clinic on Main. I'll send a referral over, let them know to expect you."

"I can pay." JD stated with certainty.

She and Dr. Honer stared at him, neither wanting to question how he'd pay as it was clear this was one of those things he knew without knowing how he knew. Remembering the seventy-thousand-dollar watch, she tended to believe him. However, a hospital would be much less trusting.

A knock came at the door and the receptionist stuck her head into the room. "Sheriff's department dropped off this property bag for Sheriff Delaney."

"Thanks." Grace took the large, clear plastic bag, checked to make sure it still held all its contents and handed it to JD. "You've officially been released from custody."

CHAPTER THREE

JD ACCEPTED THE sealed bag. He'd been released. He supposed that was a good thing. But where did it leave him?

"Does that mean you won't be driving me to the hospital?" No big deal. He didn't really care for all this medical mumbo jumbo anyway. Especially the whole bit about drilling into his head. He'd take his chances on the swelling going down.

Once that happened, the doc said, his memories might come back. He could feel them out there, as if they were hidden behind a dark curtain in his head and all he had to do was find the lever that worked the curtain.

He'd miss Grace, though. She was the only constant he knew in this new world.

"I said I'd take you, and I will." She assured him. Her gruff tone made him wonder if she was insulted to have her word questioned or if she regretted making the offer in the first place.

She was an odd mixture of duty and concern, with a whole lot of pretty thrown in.

Funny thing, his bruised brain only managed to stay focused on two things: pulling back that curtain and the complex G. Delaney, ex-sheriff, misguided realist, delectable morsel. When he couldn't take the blankness for another second, he shifted his attention to the left and admired the fit of G. Delaney's uniform to her trim body and soft curves.

32   HIS UNFORGETTABLE FIANCÉE

Her question about his marital status served as no deterrent. He wasn't married. The lack of guilt only supported his irrational certainty.

"I have to stop by my house first," she went on completely unaware of his imaginings. "To pick up the rest of my things."

"Keep an eye on him." Dr. Honer directed her. "You know what to watch for with a concussion. Wake him every few hours to check for nausea, pupil variation, incoherency."

"I will."

"I heard you were moving to San Francisco." The doctor went on. "Best of luck to you. And to you, young man. I hope you get your memory back real soon."

What if I don't, he wanted to ask, but he bit the words back. The doctor had done all he could. So JD simply said, "Thank you." He accepted the prescription for pain medicine and followed Grace's curvy butt from the room.

Grace made a last sweep through her small apartment, making sure she hadn't left anything behind. The one-bedroom apartment sat atop the garage of her father's house. She'd already packed her things, which didn't amount to much—a duffel bag and two boxes. She wouldn't be back unless it was to drive through on her way to somewhere else.

After she lost the election, she sold the house and rented back the apartment. Her lease ended tonight.

Her father had brought her here. With him gone she had no reason to stay. The citizens made that clear, casting an overwhelming vote. She got the message. She'd been too hard-core. They wanted someone who would let boys be boys on occasion. Someone connected, like Brubaker.

It baffled her why the town council even asked her to finish out her father's term if they didn't want her to carry on the regimen he'd put in place. He'd trained her, after all. Probably thought she'd have a softer touch, being a woman. But she couldn't be less than she was.

Disappointing, though. She'd thought she'd found the place she wanted to put down roots. Everyone had been so friendly, welcoming her into town when she came to help Dad. She'd mistakenly felt accepted when they asked her to finish his term. The experience made her wonder if she even wanted to continue in active law enforcement.

Finding nothing left behind, she locked up and skipped down the stairs one last time before sliding behind the wheel of her SUV. JD slept in the passenger seat. He'd dozed off on the way to her place and she hadn't bothered to wake him for this stop. He would have insisted on helping but was in no shape for it. Why put them both through that argument?

She believed rules were there for a reason and exceptions created chaos. In the case of the law, it also put people at risk. And if you gave one person an exception, everyone expected to get the same special treatment. Then why have laws?

Her father had been a stickler for discipline and order when she was growing up. Especially after her mother died when Grace was eight. Tightening the reins had been his way of coping. She understood that now. But to a grieving little girl, all the fun in life seemed to have died with her mother.

And that didn't change for a very long time. Still hadn't, if you talked to the townspeople. Grace Delaney didn't know how to have fun.

They were wrong. She liked to have fun as much as the next person. She just chose to do so in less gregarious ways. Hey, when you came off extended hours patrolling shore leave, a little peace and quiet was all the fun you could handle. And a good book or a fast video game was all the company you craved.

The activity of carrying her things down to the car served to revitalize her for the coming drive. Still, in order to help keep her alert, she pulled into the all-night diner and purchased a coffee to go. Though truthfully, JD's presence kept her on a low-level buzz.

He made her usually roomy SUV seem small. His broad shoulders and long limbs took up more than their share of space. The smell of man and antiseptic filled the air. And his heat warmed the car better than her heater.

Thinking of JD, she added a second cup to her order in case he woke up.

Grace carried the coffees to the SUV and headed the vehicle toward Santa Rosa. The clear night and full moon made the drive go fast.

JD stirred every once in a while but didn't wake up. She couldn't imagine what he must be going through. Bad enough to be robbed and left injured and abandoned on the outskirts of a strange town. How much more unnerving it must be to lose his memories, to lose all sense of self.

Except for that one moment of vulnerability before going in for the MRI, he took it in stride. She supposed it was all he could do to handle the pain of his physical ailments.

Not least of which was a stab wound. The doctor concurred with her time frame for the stabbing at less than a month. JD stated he had no memory of the incident. He'd sounded frustrated, an emotion she shared.

He had to be wondering about his life—the circumstances of the stabbing for one, the accident for another. He'd been alone when he met up with Porter, but he could well have a family out there wondering about him. A wife praying for his safe return.

A wife. Her shoulders twitched at the notion. Something

deep inside rebelled at the thought of him with another woman. Which was totally insane. There was nothing between the two of them.

For sugar's sake, they'd spent half their time together on separate sides of the law.

Not that it was an issue. He had no wife. Or so he said in that way of his that was so definite. How could he be so sure of some things, yet have no memory to support his conclusion?

Perhaps the amnesia was a hoax. One big fib to cover a crime.

So his prints didn't hit. There were plenty of criminals that never got caught.

He could have had a falling-out with his cohorts who ditched him and took his ride. Then he could have stumbled into town and unfortunately drawn the attention of a sheriff's deputy. Who would believe a motorcycle thug with a stab wound owned a seventy-thousand-dollar Cartier watch? No one. So he ditched his wallet and claimed to have lost his memory. All he had to do was sweat it out in the drunk tank for a few hours and he was home free.

Except for the do-good ex-sheriff who insisted on taking him to the hospital.

That version made more sense than the motorcycle-riding geek with an expensive taste in watches and a penchant for knowing things he couldn't back up with facts.

And yet she believed him.

The concussion was real. The pain was real. The frustration was real. The occasional flash of fear he tried to hide was very real. She'd been in law enforcement too long not to recognize those elements when she saw them. And there were medical tests to back it all up.

Not to mention the fact if he was a thug, she'd probably be lying on the side of the road back near Woodpark.

Well, he would have tried, anyway. She didn't go down so easy.

The lights of Santa Rosa came into view. She stole a sip of JD's coffee, wrinkling her nose at the lack of sugar. Surprisingly it still held a good heat. And the punch of caffeine she longed for.

No question about it, he was a puzzle, but a legit one.

Still, she'd be smart to take the things he was so sure of with a grain of salt. There was no sense, none at all, in fostering an attraction when neither of them was sure of their future. When neither of them was sure of themselves.

Because, yeah, losing the campaign had really shaken her. Not that she'd ever admit it out loud. She thought she'd been doing a good job, that the community liked her. But the votes hadn't been there. It had left her reeling. And feeling a little lost. She put her heart and soul into protecting and serving the citizens of Woodpark, and they chose a stuffed shirt who was more hot air than action.

Their loss, right? Except the experience threw her off stride, made her question her decisions and her vocation. Which was so not her. She always knew exactly what she wanted, and she went after it with a zealousness that earned her what she sought.

Not this time.

So, yeah, she had more empathy for JD than she might have had otherwise.

In a moment of connection and sympathy, she reached across the middle console and gripped his hand where it lay on his muscular thigh. His fingers immediately wrapped around hers, and her gaze shot to his face.

There was no change in his expression or posture, leaving her to wonder how long he'd been awake.

She pulled her hand free.

"We're about twenty minutes from Santa Rosa," she

told him. "I bought you a coffee. It has a little heat left if you want it. There is cream and sweeteners."

He straightened in his seat and scrubbed his hands over his face.

"How are you feeling?"

"Like I was in a cage fight with a motorcycle and lost."

"You need to choose your sparring partners more carefully."

He barked a laugh. "Yes, I do." He picked up the to-go cup and took a sip. "Black is fine." He stared over at her. "How are you doing?"

Wow. Tears burned at the back of her eyes. She couldn't remember the last time someone asked how she was doing. She blinked, clearing her vision, shoving aside the maudlin reaction to a simple question.

"Fine. The coffee has kept my body alert."

"Ah. And what's your mind been busy with?"

"Nothing. Everything."

"Well that narrows it down. Was wondering if I'm lying mixed in there somewhere?"

"Yes. I discounted it."

Silence met her response. And then in a hoarse voice, he asked, "Why?"

"The evidence supports your claim." She told him truthfully, and more hesitatingly, "And I trust my gut."

"I'm glad." He turned to stare out his window. "Because I'm trusting it, too."

She eyed his profile before focusing on the road again. "Then for both our sakes I hope it holds true."

"Do you have a job lined up in San Francisco?" Now she felt the weight of his gaze on her. "Is that why you're headed there?"

"I prefer the city." Amenity was easier in the city.

"Me, too."

"Another clue?"

"Yeah, let's call it that." He sipped his coffee, then dropped the empty cup into the holder. "Losing the election causing you to question your career choice?"

"My ego took a hit." She lifted one shoulder, let it drop. "I'll shake it off."

She hoped.

"Good. You're better than the lot of them."

"Really." His endorsement tickled her, bringing out a rusty smile. "And you base your accolades on what exactly?"

"On my observations. Everyone we talked to liked and respected you. It was a busy night, a holiday they were working, yet they thought enough of you to remember it was your last day and to wish you well in future endeavors. You would have won the election if you put a little effort into it. They'll be missing you soon enough."

Hmm. What he said made sense. And she liked it better than her version where they were all thinking good riddance. People did like to know their opinion mattered. Maybe she should have campaigned a little.

Too late now.

"Yes, well, on to the next adventure."

"And what will that be? Do you have a job offer?"

"I have options." Her future loomed ominously ahead of her like the fog creeping up on the west side as she took the off-ramp in Santa Rosa. "A town in the next county over offered me an undersheriff position." The city was bigger than Woodpark, but not by much. "And there are always patrol positions in San Francisco."

"You don't sound too excited by those options."

"The undersheriff is a higher rank, but San Francisco holds more appeal. It's a dilemma."

The truth? Neither of them appealed to her.

"The undersheriff position holds some appeal, except

TERESA CARPENTER — 39

for the location. I've seen too much of the world to be happy in a small town."

"Then why run for sheriff?"

Because she thought she'd found acceptance.

She explained how she got the job. "The people were decent for the most part and seemed to like me. For a while I felt like I belonged. But the election results don't lie. I wasn't one of them. The mayor's brother-in-law was one of them."

It was an old lesson, well learned. And yet she'd fallen for it again. The need to belong. As a child she'd suffered with every base change until she learned to Bubble Wrap her emotions. And as an adult she'd stayed in more than one relationship longer than she should have.

Her last boyfriend let her catch him cheating so she'd finally get the hint. Not one of her more stellar moments. Rather than fall into the pattern again, she'd stayed single for the past two years.

"A position in San Francisco holds a lot of appeal locationwise. It's a beautiful place with so much history and culture. The problem is it's an expensive city to live in and a beat cop doesn't make much."

"It would be a step backward for you."

There was that. "I don't mind working my way up, but I really wanted something more, something to challenge my mind."

And she wanted a home. Someplace permanent. She appreciated what she'd seen of the world, and had more countries she longed to visit. But more than anything she wanted a place to come back to, a place to call home.

"I'll figure it out." She pulled into the clinic parking lot. "We're here."

While JD had another MRI she found the cafeteria and got a cold soda. The idea of caffeine didn't bother her. When her head finally found a pillow, nothing would keep her awake.

Figuring she had a few minutes, she took a seat at a table, leaned her head against the wall and fell asleep.

It seemed only an instant later she opened her eyes. She yawned and blinked her watch into focus. An hour had elapsed.

Wondering when this night would end, she did a few stretches—oh, yeah, that felt good—gathered her soda and headed back to emergency. Clear down the hall she heard a ruckus going on and hurried toward the sound.

"You can't keep me here against my will," JD declared. He sat on the side of the gurney facing the doctor, a plump woman in a white lab coat with lovely mocha-colored skin and beaded black braids clipped atop her head.

He was refusing to be admitted at the doctor's request. Stubborn man.

"It's just for observation." The doctor spoke with resigned patience.

"You said there was no additional swelling," JD pointed out.

"No. But you've sustained a severe concussion." The woman responded. "I highly recommend you be admitted for tonight and possibly tomorrow. Head wounds are unpredictable. It's for your own safety."

JD pushed to his feet. "I'm fine. I have the pain medicine the last doctor gave me. I can take care of myself."

"Sir, I really advise against leaving." She shifted her bulk to block his exit. "You need bed rest. Trauma of this magnitude requires time to heal. At this stage just being on your feet walking around could result in more damage."

The mulish look on JD's face revealed what he thought of her suggestion.

"JD," Grace interjected softly, "the night is almost over. Why don't you rest for a few hours and I'll come get you in the morning?" The stars knew it was what she longed to do. He could lie down and be out in a heartbeat. She still needed to find a hotel and check in before her head found a pillow.

His shoulders went back and he gave one slow shake of his head. "I hate hospitals. I've spent too much time in them already tonight. I'll rest better somewhere else. Anywhere else."

She sighed. He meant it. The tension in those wide shoulders, the clenched jaw, the faint flicker of panic in his emerald eyes told her his dislike went deeper than memories. He really intended to leave.

"You've done enough," he told her. "Thank you for all your help. I can take it from here."

It was the wrong thing to say. He tried sliding past the doctor, but she had her moves on, keeping him pinned while signaling to a nurse.

"Sir, we really can't release you without adult supervision. This level of traumatic brain injury results in disorientation and confusion. You represent a danger to yourself and others."

JD did not back down. "I need you to get out of my way."

"Get security." The doctor instructed the nurse.

Time to defuse the situation. "Doctor, we understand your concern. Of course he won't be alone. He's been lucid all night. You've confirmed the swelling hasn't gotten any worse. He's clearly determined to go. Won't causing him mental duress be worse than allowing him to leave?"

Faced with his stubborn determination, the doctor saw the sense in Grace's calm argument. "You'll be with him?"

JD opened his mouth. She shot him a don't-you-dare glare.

"Yes."

"And you'll bring him back in the morning?" The doctor pressed.

Green eyes narrowed. Grace agreed the physician was pushing it.

"I'll see he gets the care he needs."

The woman reluctantly agreed. She noted her concerns on the release form and reiterated her instructions and the symptoms to be concerned over.

"Mismatched pupils, vomiting, excessive sleepiness." Grace rattled off the last of the list. "Doctor, you've been very helpful. I think I should get him somewhere to lie down. Good night."

Taking JD's arm she led him away, not releasing him until they were out the door. "Don't look back." She warned him. "She might change her mind."

"They couldn't keep me against my will." He bit out.

"She's not wrong. With the concussion you're not thinking clearly."

"You told her I've been lucid all night."

"And you have. That doesn't mean you're making good decisions. You should have been admitted. At least for the rest of tonight."

Halfway across the driveway to the parking lot, Grace realized JD wasn't keeping pace with her. She swung around to find him hovering near the exit. She started toward him.

"Do you want me to pick you up?" Dang, she should have thought of that. She'd just been extolling his injuries but she kept forgetting how extensive they really were.

"No." He closed the gap between them. Surprised her when he bent to kiss her cheek. "Thanks for all you've done. I wouldn't have made it through the night without you." He shoved his hands into his jeans pockets. "But I can't take advantage of you any longer. It's time to say goodbye."

CHAPTER FOUR

"Goodbye?" Grace repeated. Then, more forcefully, "Goodbye?"

"Thank you for everything." He turned to walk away.

"Oh, no, you don't." She jumped into his path, pointed her finger toward her Escape. "You don't like hearing the truth so you're just going to walk away? Forget that noise. Get in the vehicle. Now."

He scowled. "You're no longer the sheriff and I'm not your prisoner. I appreciate your help. But I'll be fine. The test tech gave me the address for a local shelter. I can take it from here."

"No." She blocked his attempt to walk by her. "You can't. I just vouched for you in there, meaning I'm responsible for your butt. Like it or not, you are in my care. We'll be sticking together like sauce on spaghetti until I'm sure you've regained your faculties."

Which included the rest of the night at the very least. More likely twenty-four to forty-eight hours. At three-thirty in the morning exhaustion prevented her from thinking beyond that. The night nurse had recommended a nearby hotel. She planned to check in and immediately check out.

This delay was not making her a happy camper.

"I don't like it." He declared. He picked her up, set her aside and headed toward the street. "Good luck with the job search."

In a heartbeat she stood in his way, hand to his chest. "You don't want to mess with me, JD. Get in the car."

He struck out in a defensive move. She countered and they engaged in a brief tussle. He knew karate. And he was good. She was better. And she wasn't injured. In a few moves she had him on one knee. She released him.

"I'm sorry." He ran a hand over his neck. "I didn't mean to fight you. It was instinct."

"I get that. But stop battling me." Weariness dragged at her. "Neither of us has the energy for it. Listen, I can't let you wander off alone. If something happened to you or to someone because of you, I'd feel responsible. There's a hotel a few blocks away. Let's just go there for the rest of the night and see how you're doing tomorrow."

He walked by her toward the parking lot. "Let's go, then. I'm beginning to see why the citizens of Woodpark voted against you."

Grace flinched. Okay, that hurt more than it should have. She'd stood by his side all night and the first time she challenged him he struck out at her. She understood he was upset with the circumstances more than with her. Still, it felt personal.

Following after him, she clicked the locks open. They traveled the few blocks to the hotel in silence. Unfortunately, the hotel the nurse recommended looked small and shabby. Thankfully it had a sold-out sign in the window, taking the choice of staying there out of Grace's hands.

She was tired enough not to care where she laid her head tonight. Still, she preferred not to suffer regrets in the morning. A quick scan on her phone for local hotels brought up several national chains. She went with Pinnacle Express because they were known for their good service. She plugged the address into the GPS while JD called and made a reservation.

Given the need to monitor his health and his attempt

to walk away, she told him to make it one room with two beds. He lifted one brow but didn't question her.

When they reached the room, JD disappeared into the bathroom. She heard the shower turn on as she tossed her duffel bag on the nearest bed. Energy gone, she dropped into the only armchair to wait her turn. She had barely closed her eyes when she heard the door opening. Dragging heavy lids open, she watched him stroll across the room in gray knit boxer briefs.

He moved like poetry in motion. Graceful, muscles flowing with every step. So beautiful that for a moment she wondered if she was dreaming. The ugliness of his scar stripped the dream quality away. She sat up.

More alert, she noticed he moved carefully on his way to the bed. He didn't acknowledge her, simply sprawled out on his stomach and went to sleep. He didn't even cover up but lay with his tight, knit-clad butt facing her and went to sleep. Already soft snores filled the silence.

Shaking her head she set her phone alarm to wake him in a few hours to check him out. Yeah, that was going to be a joyous chore.

Let him sulk.

She wouldn't compromise her principles because he thought he was fine when medical science and personal experience told her his judgment was off right now. Better he be pouting than be dead.

She was reaching for the energy to get up and shower when she fell asleep.

An insistent beeping woke Grace. She opened her eyes to a strange room dimly lit by light from a bathroom. She stretched her neck, working out kinks.

It took a moment to remember where she was—a less than comfortable armchair in a hotel in Santa Rosa—and who she was with—a man she'd known less than six hours. A record for her. She was strictly a third-date-or-longer gal.

She shut off the annoying sound of the alarm and ran her fingers through her hair, taming spiked ends she could feel poking out at odd angles. After one last roll of her neck, she pushed to her feet. Half-asleep, she stumbled to his bedside.

Time to check JD's vitals, to torture him with more questions about his friend the president and what year it was. He was so out of it he hadn't heard the alarm going off.

"JD," she called his name. No movement. She called again, louder. Nothing.

She reached out to shake him then pulled her hand back. He still sprawled across the bed, naked except for the knit boxers that clung to his hard backside. Nowhere to touch besides smooth, bare skin. Fingers curled into her palm in instinctive self-preservation.

Already attracted, touching him seemed risky, almost a violation. But she was no longer a sheriff, just a Good Samaritan no longer bound by strict protocols. Which almost made touching him worse. Duty would drive her to see to his health.

And this was no different. Giving a mental tug at her big-girl panties, she placed her hand on his shoulder and shook. She was seeing to his health.

Uh-huh, so why did it feel as if she was stroking a lover? Snatching her hand back, she stood back and waited.

He didn't move. Dang it.

"JD." She shook him harder. He shifted, moving his head from one side to the other so he now faced her but he continued to sleep. Boy, he was out. Of course he'd had a long day.

Yeah, and hers was growing longer by the minute. Wait, why was she waking him? Oh, yeah, because of the concussion.

Half-asleep, she perched on the edge of the bed, and getting right down next to his ear, she said his name louder and gave him another shake. He shot up, rolling over and sitting up in one smooth motion. His eyes popped open, focused on her. The wanting in them sent a tingle down her spine.

They were face-to-face, eye to eye with nothing but knit boxer briefs and her suddenly inadequate clothes between them.

"Grace," he said.

Flustered and distracted at hearing him use her name for the first time, she was unprepared when he swept her into his arms and pulled her to him.

"Uh, JD." She wiggled and shifted. Trying to push away? If so, she failed. The way he held her, she only succeeded in rubbing her hip against him, causing his body to react. Not good. Her hands went to his chest, ready to push him away. The feel of his skin, the heat under her hands addled her senses.

"Oh."

"Grace," he whispered, and wrapping a hand around her head he pulled her to him as he lowered his head. He kissed her softly, slowly. A gentle caress, sexy but soothing at the same time. Then the contrary man slid his tongue into her mouth and, oh, he tasted good. She fought hard to throttle back her desire, to ease the growing passion. No easy task when all she wanted was to draw him to her for a long sensual snuggle.

He broke off the kiss, nibbled a path along her jaw and nuzzled a kiss behind her ear. She sighed and her body went limp in his arms.

"You're killing me here, JD."

He went still. And then pulled back, slowly disengaging his body from hers. He blinked once, twice. She knew immediately when confusion vanished and he became aware of where he was and what he was doing.

Her cheeks heated when he pushed away from her, not stopping until his back hit the headboard. Could he get far enough away?

"Uh, sorry." He apologized. "I don't usually grab women in my sleep." His dark brows pushed together. "At least I don't think I do."

She cleared her throat, reminded herself he was injured even though her body still reeled from the strength and warmth of his. "Don't worry about it. Concussions—"

He stopped her by blurting out the name of the president.

She frowned. "What?"

He stated the year, then took the phone she still gripped in her hand and flipped it open so the light shone between them. "Are my pupils even?"

Flinching away from the light, she narrowed her eyes to scrutinize him. "Yes."

"Good." He closed the phone and gave it back to her. "I'm all checked out." He slipped from the bed and moved to the other one. "Good night." He slid under the sheet and rolled so his back faced her.

"Good night." Ignoring a misguided pang of regret, she flopped down in the space he'd just left. The bedding smelled of him, held the heat of his body. For just an instant, she sank into a fantasy of what could never be. And moments later she followed him into slumber.

Grace woke to the smell of coffee and bacon. Groaning, she rolled over, slowly opened her eyes and stared into a leaf-green gaze.

"Good morning." JD greeted her with a tip of his mug.

She swung her feet around and sat up on the edge of the bed. The bed she thought he'd gone to sleep in the night before. Now he sat feet up leaning back against the headboard on the bed opposite her. Thankfully he'd covered

the memorable gray knit boxers with his jeans. A white
T-shirt and socks completed his apparel.

Exactly how had things gotten switched around? She
had a vague niggling of something happening in the night,
but she'd been so exhausted she couldn't pull it to mind.
She could only pray it had nothing to do with the erotic
dream he'd starred in.

"Morning," she mumbled.

"Actually, I got that wrong." His mouth rolled up at the
corner. "It's after one."

"After one?" She was appalled. "Why didn't you wake
me? Checkout was at noon. Now I'll have to pay for another night."

"Sorry. I haven't been up long myself. Just long enough
to order breakfast."

Her stomach gave a loud growl at the mention of food.
She covered it with her hand. "The coffee smells divine."

He gestured toward the desk. "I got one for you."

"Bless you." She headed for the desk.

"Bacon and eggs, too."

"Mmm," she hummed her approval and detoured to her
overnight case for her toiletries. She longed for a shower,
yet the growl in her stomach demanded she feed it first.
A shower could wait, but she needed clean teeth to start
her day.

"How's the head?" she asked on her way to the bathroom.

"Better than last night," he answered with a total lack
of inflection.

She stopped and faced him, lifting an eyebrow. "But
not by much?"

"The doctor said it would take time."

"Right." The woman had been sure to repeat it several
times, making sure she included Grace so she would know

the doctor held her accountable for his care. "So still no memory?"

"Not from my past, no."

Meaning what? He was making new memories? Like kissing her? There'd been kissing in her dream. She narrowed her gaze on his face. His expression gave nothing away. Dang it. How did she get in his bed anyway? Exhaustion really knocked her out last night. The last thing she remembered was admiring his tight bum in soft gray.

And then her alarm went off.

And OMG. He'd kissed her. It hadn't been a dream at all. He'd kissed her and then pushed her away.

Without looking at him, she ducked into the bathroom and closed the door. Amnesia looked pretty good right about now. She wouldn't mind losing a few minutes of memory. Actually just a few details.

She inhaled a deep breath, forcing herself to calm down. So he'd kissed her. No need to freak out. He'd come to his senses and apologized. No harm done.

Yep, that was her story and she was sticking to it.

Back in the room and sipping coffee between bites of bacon and eggs, Grace worried over what else might have happened during the night. The fact she still wore her clothes from yesterday was a big clue, and frankly a huge relief. At least nothing too compromising happened between them.

Well, if she discounted the kiss. And she did. Discount it. In fact, in her mind it never happened. A dream never to be discussed or brought to mind.

Yeah, right. Even after brushing her teeth she felt him on her lips.

"I meant to move on to San Francisco today, but since we slept in I think it'd be best to take it easy. Give you a day to recuperate. We'll go shopping, get you another set of clothes."

"Okay, this is not going to work for me." He set his paper mug aside and crossed his arms over his impressive chest.

"What's not working?" She hoped he wasn't going to be difficult again this morning. Afternoon.

"Having you call all the shots." He stood and went to the window, drawing back the drapes to let in the weak afternoon sun. "It was all right when I was near incapacitated. But I'm thinking better now. And I may not know who I am, but I can promise you I'm not the type to happily trail behind someone like a trained puppy dog."

"That's hardly been the case." Puppy dog? More like bulldog. He certainly hadn't been docile last night at the hospital. But given his attempt to leave, she should have expected another bid for independence. "I've only been trying to help."

"I know. I appreciate it. But I'm not a child that needs his hand held. I do, however, need to find out my identity. I called the local police department while I was waiting for breakfast to be delivered. Once the officer got past the idea I wasn't joking, he suggested I take my problem to San Francisco. A bigger police department or the FBI would have more sophisticated resources."

"Yes."

"And you're headed to San Francisco."

"Yes."

"So you've planned to take me with you?"

"Yes."

He nodded. "I want to hire you."

She froze with a piece of bacon halfway to her mouth. "What? Why?"

"I may have no control over my mind, but I insist on having control over my life. Putting a name to my face is only one step to getting my life back. You have resources, connections. You can help me to learn not just a name, but who I am. Where I belong. Tell me about the people in my life. I was stabbed. I need to know if it's safe for me to return to where I came from."

"You don't have to hire me to find that out. I've said I'll help you."

"No. You're used to being in charge. If you're just helping, you're going to feel you have a say in what I do. If I'm the boss, I have the say."

"JD, it's your life. You'll always have the final say."

"You think it's the concussion talking." He crossed his arms over his chest.

"I think you're trying to survive in a world that's suddenly foreign." Not so calm now. She set her fork down. "I'm not your enemy."

"I know." The intensity in his eyes didn't waiver. "We need to do this my way, Grace."

She could see they did. It was his way of making sense of what was happening to him. Of coping. She understood—probably more today than yesterday—the drive to control the areas of his life he could. And he wasn't wrong about her having an opinion. The thing was, him paying her wouldn't change that.

Of course, it would give him the sense of being in charge. Which was all that really mattered.

"I need a job for real."

"This is a real job."

"You know what I mean. The real job hunt needs to come first."

He frowned, but nodded. "Agreed."

"Well, if I agree, we'd need to set a time limit. Say two weeks, and then we reevaluate where things stand."

He hesitated but nodded again.

"Okay. How do you plan to pay me?" She gave in. No need to make things more difficult for the guy. And she knew how to present her case when necessary.

"With this." He walked to the night table between the beds, opened the drawer, and drew out his watch.

She shrank back in the chair. "I can't take your watch."

"Good, because I'm not giving it to you. But the thing is worth a small fortune. It can fund my search."

"You intend to pawn it?"

"Can you think of a better way to get fast cash? I can't continue to live off your charity."

"I can afford it." She assured him. She had a healthy savings account before leaving the navy. And now she had the life insurance money from her dad as well as the funds from the sale of his house. Once she found the right job, she planned to use the money to buy a house and put down some permanent roots.

But she had enough to help out a person in need.

"Save your money, Grace. You're unemployed. I'm not going to mooch off you."

"Well, pawning isn't the answer either. You won't get what the watch is worth. And you can't just sell it. A piece like that would require provenance. Plus, what if it has sentimental value?"

"I don't think so." He set the watch on the desk beside her plate. "Not many people can afford seventy thousand dollars' worth of sentiment. This is a flash piece, meant to intimidate and impress."

"You do know you're talking about yourself?"

"Maybe." He ran a finger over the glass front of the expensive piece. "I like the exposed gears."

"Well, you are a geek."

A small smile lifted the corner of his mouth. "So I am."

"We'll find a jeweler." She lifted the watch and examined the craftsmanship. It really was beautiful. "In San Francisco, not here. You'll get more for it in a bigger city. We'll get an estimate of the watch's value, and I'll buy it off you. When we get you home, you can buy it back if you want to, or I can sell it and get my money back."

With narrowed eyes and a clenched jaw, he looked as if he wanted to protest. Instead he nodded.

"I can live with that deal. Let's get going." He sat on the end of the bed and reached for his boots.

"No." She leaned back in her chair and took a fortifying sip of coffee to prepare for her first battle. "I know you're anxious to move forward, but I'm not ready to walk out the door. I have to shower and change. And today is a holiday. A lot of places are closed on New Year's Day. Plus we're going to have to pay for the hotel for another night anyway, so I suggest we do a little more recuperating today. Maybe shop for some clothes for you. We can put together a plan for when we get to San Francisco tomorrow."

He propped his hands at his sides. "You seem to have missed the part where I'm the boss now."

"Not when it comes to your health." She corrected. Best to be clear with him, because on this she wouldn't bend. "Let me clarify. As far as my services are involved, there's no compromising when it comes to your health. If I feel you're pushing it, I'll call a halt. I said that I'd be responsible for you and I take my duties seriously."

"So I've noticed." He tossed his boot down. "What happened to it's my life and the final decision is mine?"

"Still applies. Except when you're being bullheaded about your health. Today we rest. Tomorrow is up to you."

"You'll make some phone calls, set up some appointments in San Francisco?"

"Of course."

"Okay. We'll shop for clothes today. And put together a plan for tomorrow."

"And rest."

He scowled but nodded. "And rest."

"Good." One battle down. She pushed her plate aside and stood. "I'll shower and then we can go." Carrying her paper mug of coffee, she grabbed her duffel and disappeared into the bathroom.

JD listened to the shower come on and tried not to think of Grace with water streaming over her body. Yeah, not working. He easily envisioned being with her, raising soap bubbles by running his hands over her skin.

Nothing to feel guilty over. He knew he wasn't married or in a committed relationship. One of those odd things he was certain of. But Grace was now his employee.

Best if he kept his distance.

The situation had already created a faux intimacy between them that created a level of trust unusual in an acquaintanceship less than twenty-four hours old.

She didn't quite get the me-boss-you-employee relationship, but he'd work on her. Getting around her unrelenting sense of duty when it came to his health would be a bit of a problem. He was grateful to Grace, but she made rigid look loose when it came to her duty.

Still, as long as he kept his raging headache to himself, she should have no argument with his plans.

A good thing, because he needed to take control of his life. Being at the whim of fate felt wrong. Whoever he was, whatever he did, he hadn't been a follower. Deep in his gut he knew he'd been in charge. The Cartier watch sure seemed to indicate so.

He refused to sit around all day and brood over what he didn't know. But she was right, the holiday hampered them. And he could use a change of clothes.

Bottom line, this hotel room beat the heck out of the hospital. If he had to take another day to heal up, better here than in an antiseptic-scented hell.

He sat on the bed, leaned back against the headboard

and crossed his ankles. A pain pill went down easy with a swig of coffee.

She'd made no mention of the kiss they'd shared. Was that because she didn't remember, or because she preferred not to? Of the few memories he had, it rated right up there at the top. Waking to her bending over him last night had been a temptation he couldn't resist. Her nearness, the electric connection of her caring gaze broke through his defenses and he reached for her, claiming her soft lips in a sweet kiss. And oh, man. The tension they'd both tried to ignore throughout the night simmered over. Burned him up.

She'd been right there with him, her response explosive. He'd been ready to roll her under him and relieve their tension in the most basic way possible. He remembered the smell of her hair, the taste of the tender spot behind her ear.

When she'd moaned that he was killing her, it shocked him to his senses. Her surrender had him immediately backing off. He wanted her willing, not succumbing. If she was resistant at all, he had no business taking their relationship in a sensual direction. It would create unnecessary tension between him and the one person interested in helping him.

The water went off in the shower. And now he saw her running a towel over damp curves and that short cap of dark hair. He may have left her in her lonely bed last night, but the attraction remained alive within him.

He forced his mind away from the erotic imaginings. Instead he focused on the contacts she'd mentioned. He had to believe he'd soon have a name to replace the emptiness in his head.

It was the last thought he had before he drifted off.

Grace exited the bathroom to find JD napping on the bed closest to the window. She closed the drapes and wrote him a note telling him she'd be back shortly. Grabbing her purse and phone, she went downstairs to the lobby to make a few phone calls.

The officer on duty in Woodpark stated a patrol had traveled the road JD had been walking on and there'd been no sign of his motorcycle or wallet.

"There was a report of an altercation at the Red Wolf Tavern including a man fitting JD's description. The bartender said he hadn't been drinking. He'd eaten, paid for the meal, apparently from a big wad of cash, and bumped shoulders with a guy on his way out the door. Got beer spilled on him. The other guy tried to get tough with him and the man fitting JD's description put the aggressor on his knees. The guy backed off and that was the end of it."

"Except for the part where the guy followed JD, ran him off the road and robbed him."

"That's a possible scenario."

Yeah. The probable scenario.

"That's all we've got."

And from his tone, all they were willing to do. JD had been released. Wasn't even in town. The new sheriff would see no reason to expend time or resources on finding JD's property or identity.

So no help there.

Next she called a friend from her boot camp days. Doug worked for the FBI, in the San Francisco office. She considered him their best bet for finding JD's identity because the government had face-recognition technology. The San Francisco Police Department may have it as well, but accessing it wouldn't be so easy. She didn't have any connections there, and it could take a while to get results.

She called Doug, but it turned out he and his wife were visiting her parents in Bend, Oregon, and he wouldn't be back in the office until Monday. Great. She could imagine JD's reaction to the delay. Good news, though. Doug was willing to help once he got back in town.

She sank back in the deep red chair, happy she'd gone with Pinnacle Express. She'd stayed at a few and never had complaints. So much better than the Shabby Inn. She enjoyed the muted grays, the push of red, the modern furnishings and artwork. And the large sleeping rooms, though sharing with a six-foot-plus man sure put large into perspective.

Sitting in the lobby watching families come and go, she felt safe, comfortable. Simple emotions most people in the United States took for granted, but she'd sat or patrolled in plenty of locations that didn't encourage such simple emotions.

Before her father's illness, she'd planned to finish her career in the navy. Now, she was glad to be home, looked forward to finding a place and making it her own.

But first she had to help JD find his home.

With him in mind, she stopped in the gift shop on her way back to the room and picked up a disposable razor, toothbrush, toothpaste, deodorant and a new T-shirt. It wasn't much and wouldn't last long, but it was a start. Shopping didn't strike her as an activity high on JD's list of favorite things to do. Hopefully he'd view a trip to obtain new clothes and a few personal items as forward momentum in his quest.

The selection consisted of shirts with towering redwoods, seascapes and big block letters spelling out CALIFORNIA. She decided on the redwoods, but, of course, there were none in his size.

The man was really running on a bad streak of luck— or she was. Grace hadn't decided which yet.

Given the size of JD's shoulders, his choice of shirt came down to a kelly green with seals frolicking on a beach or a bright red with California blazoned across the chest. She went for the red. The green might work well with his eyes, but he didn't strike her as a seal guy.

Which was only half the truth of why she chose the red. The truth had to do with the fact his green eyes were distracting enough without having them made more prominent by the color of his shirt. Her mind zigged right from thoughts of his gorgeous eyes to forbidden wonderings about his bone-melting kiss.

It started out so soft and grew into a searing melding of mouths, all while he cradled her to his hard body with a surety and strength that kindled a sense of passion and security. He pushed past her defenses until her body ignited, and then he eased off and apologized.

How mean was that?

She'd be a lot happier if she could relegate the incident to a dream rather than to a memory.

The last thing she remembered from the night before was her irritation at his prime body and sulky attitude. She'd been sitting in the chair, waiting for access to the bathroom, when he strolled out in nothing but his underwear and passed her as casually as if he was two and she his mother.

Not feeling motherly, uh-uh, not at all.

Which was why the kiss was so forbidden.

So yeah, the kiss would remain a memory. Because, oh, no, she was not talking to him about it.

He hadn't said anything. Hadn't given one hint they'd spent part of last night in each other's arms. Surely if it meant anything to him, he would have said something.

"Stop it," she said aloud.

"Ma'am?" a voice asked.

She turned to see she'd startled a man and his young son sharing the elevator with her.

She pulled on a smile. "Sorry. Internal argument."

The man nodded, but seemed relieved to get off on the next floor. The two of them gave her odd looks as they exited.

Grace groaned. She squeezed her eyes shut, then opened them and rehit the button for her floor. Regardless of the attraction she had for him, both subliminal and overt, she needed to shut it down. On every level—be it prisoner, victim or her boss—JD was off-limits.

And if the seventy-thousand-dollar watch was any indicator, he was out of her league, as well.

Her savings, the life insurance and what Dad left her put her in good shape financially. Enough so she didn't have to rush into a new job. She could take her time, really weigh her options and choose the right position for her. But she was nowhere near millionaire status.

How much money did you have to have to feel comfortable dropping nearly a hundred thousand on a watch? Lots. And lots.

More than a military brat was accustomed to.

She let herself into the room and found JD still sleeping in his bed. Or was it her bed?

Oh, no. She was *not* going down that tract again. Especially not with him stretched out right across the way.

She gave serious thought to waking him so they could go shopping, getting them both out of the room altogether. But he needed to heal, and the rest did him good in that regard.

Next came the idea of taking off and doing the shopping without him. He shouldn't care. Men rarely cared about missing a shopping spree. Except he would care. He wanted control of his life, which for JD, came down to picking out his own pair of jeans, and whatever else he decided he needed.

She wasn't so desperate to dodge her thoughts that she'd deny him his first steps of independence.

Feeling righteous, she stretched out on her bed and closed her eyes. But they didn't stay closed. She wasn't sleepy, and she wasn't usually the type to nap. Which meant she lay there, staring at the long lean length of JD sprawled in the bed across from her. And he looked good, causing her to have totally inappropriate, lascivious thoughts about her boss.

Unable to take it, she flipped over. Better to stare at the wall. Except she could still smell him. There was no escaping the yummy scent of soap and man.

Sheesh, she was in so much trouble.

Giving up, she swung her feet to the floor. Grabbing shorts and a T-shirt out of her duffel, she stepped into the bathroom and quickly changed. After updating her note, she headed out the door again.

Maybe she could pound him out of her head in the gym.

CHAPTER FIVE

"You were sleeping. I had calls to make and I didn't want to disturb you." She paused to look at a window display of boots. "I left you a note."

He'd seen it. A few words jotted on a hotel notepad stating she'd gone to the lobby, and then that had been crossed off and the word *gym* added. Envy caused his shoulders to tense for a moment. His restlessness told him he led a more physical life, if not manual labor, then he had the use of a gym. He would have joined her when he saw the note, except he had enough smarts to know his head couldn't take the physical exertion right now.

Not that he'd admit that out loud and give Grace any leverage.

Maybe that's what had him in a foul mood. He'd hired her, yet she was still calling the shots. Maybe his ego stung. Yet the explanation didn't fit. His ego may have taken a hit, but his intelligence recognized the reasoning. And accepted Grace had no control over the timing or the fact her friend was out of state.

It was the helplessness that grated on him. He hated it.

For a while after he woke up and read the note, he'd thought she'd abandoned him. That she wised up after his attack in the parking lot and finally left him. It didn't even matter that her duffel was still there. He'd been totally, irrationally freaked.

At least they were finally doing something. Even shopping beat sitting on his hands.

"Good. Because I would never hurt you." He felt compelled to reassure her. "It was an instinctive reaction when I struck out at you in the parking lot last night."

"I know." She met his gaze with confidence before turning those stunning blue eyes back to the boots. "Like any cop, a master-at-arms learns to read people. I wouldn't be here with you if I felt threatened in any way."

"Right." In jeans and a beige sweater all traces of Sheriff Delaney were gone. The loving cling of her sweater over the generous swell of her breasts knocked all thoughts of her uniform from his damaged mind. "As long as we're both clear on that point."

"We are." She pulled wistful eyes away from the tall, black leather boots in the window and moved on. She tossed him a teasing glance over her shoulder. "Are you afraid of me?"

Yes. The answer came without thought, without foundation. Why would he be afraid of her?

"I don't know. When you get your tough on, you're scary."

The corner of her mouth curled up in a pleased smirk. He had to smile. She enjoyed being a tough cookie.

"Of course, the rest of the time you're a marshmallow."

"I am not." Totally outraged she swung into his path. "Take that back."

"Marshmallow."

"Take it back, or I'll leave you here to do your shopping alone."

"Would never happen. You're too nice. You need to help. You can't help yourself."

"Don't test me, JD. I've been trained by the best to do what needs to be done."

He held up his hands in surrender. "You win. You're one

scary dude." He got the words out, but not with a straight face. His lips twitched a couple of times.

"Hmm." She surveyed him with narrowed eyes. "Believe it." She nodded her head to the left. "This shop should have what we need."

He followed her inside the menswear shop. The masculine feel and smell of the place immediately put him at ease. Much better than the hotel gift shop. He stepped in there for a few minutes and was grateful he wasn't wearing frolicking seals.

Grace wandered around, pulled a few things off the rack, but made no attempt to sway him. He saw a few things he liked, and then he saw the price tags.

No. He was not going to allow Grace to absorb any more costs for him. Frustration spiked the pounding in his head to a blinding level. Grabbing her hand, he pulled her from the store.

"Where are we going?" she demanded. "Didn't you see anything you liked?"

"We're finding a jewelry store. I want my own money." He stopped at a directory, scanned the specialty listing and turned back the way they came.

Resistance yanked at his hand as Grace dragged her feet. "We agreed you'd get a better estimate for the watch in San Francisco."

"I need money now." He didn't stop. And he didn't let go.

"You can pay me back." She caught up to him, worked at freeing her hand. He held on.

"No."

"JD."

"No."

"Can we at least talk about this?" She swerved toward the food court coming up on their right. "Let's get some lunch and discuss it."

He hauled her back to his side. "No. We can eat after."

"Okay." A touch of temper vibrated through the word. "You're going to want to stop yanking me around like a yo-yo."

"You'd be fine if you stopped fighting me." He spotted the jewelry store up ahead and quickened his step. "I'm the boss, remember?"

"Yeah, well. I don't usually hold hands with my employers."

"We're a small operation." He ran his thumb over the soft skin of her wrist just to mess with her. "I like to keep things intimate."

He felt the frost in her glare sting his skin but ignored it as they reached their destination. "We're here."

"Good afternoon and Happy New Year's." A tall, thin woman with black hair, a black dress and black pumps greeted them as soon as they stepped inside. "I bet I can guess what you're looking for." She clapped her hands. "And don't you make a lovely couple? Goodness, what beautiful babies the two of you will make together. Engagement rings are right over here."

She headed toward a glass case loaded with glittering diamonds.

JD followed.

Grace continued to yank at her hand.

"There must have been some enchantment in the air this New Year's." The woman rounded the case. "You're the third couple to come in today."

"Oh, no." Grace stated emphatically. She gave a mighty tug to free herself. He let go, and then had to catch her elbow to keep her from falling. Stepping away, she stood at attention. "We're not engaged."

"Oh." The woman—her name badge read Monique— looked back and forth between him and Grace. Finally she nodded and gave them a knowing smile. "Maybe for Valentine's Day?"

Grace's cheeks turned red. "No, not for Valentine's Day."

Monique smirked and held up her hands in surrender. "What can I do for you today?"

"I'd like to get this watch appraised." He unlatched the watch and set it on the glass counter. "It's a Cartier."

"Goodness, a Cartier." Monique picked up the timepiece and studied it. "I've never seen one outside of catalogs. Oh, my, it's gorgeous. Val will love this. He'll be the one to appraise it for you. He's out to lunch but should be back shortly. Do you have proof of purchase?"

"Not on me." He didn't hesitate, didn't look at Grace. "Do I need it to get an appraisal?"

"Not for an appraisal, no. If you wanted to sell it, you would. The owner requires it on high-price items like this."

"Your discretion is admirable."

Monique smiled as if he'd flattered her personally. "Thank you." She held up the watch. "Should I hold on to this for Val to look at?"

"No." JD took it from her. "We'll come back. Thank you for your help."

Placing a hand in the small of Grace's back, he ushered her from the store.

"Wait." This time it was her grabbing his hand. "I know you're frustrated, but it's for the best. I have a contact I trust looking into the resale value. I should hear from him soon. A jeweler could say anything and you wouldn't know any better."

She was right. And it annoyed him that he hadn't thought of the need for information before negotiation. It only made sense. It was a standard business practice and something he should have known.

Maybe the concussion did mess with his head.

"Okay." He agreed.

She nodded her approval and made for the food court.

He didn't budge and she jerked to a stop when she couldn't go any farther.

"What now?

"Not the food court. We're not spending any more money until I can buy."

"That's ridiculous. It's just lunch. And I'm hungry."

"Make it quick, then." He walked to a slated bench and sat. "Because we're doing this my way."

"You're being unreasonable." She sat next to him and drew out her phone and sent a text. "And stubborn. I think we've definitely found your first character trait."

"You say that like it's a bad thing." He let his head drop back and closed his eyes. Immediately the soft scent of her filled his senses. Orange blossoms and a hint of ginger, sweetness with a hint of depth. It suited her. And enticed him. Each breath helped to soothe the pain beating at his skull.

She laughed, not a pleasant sound. "Says the stubborn one."

"Sweet thing, you aren't in a position to toss stones." He opened his eyes to see her glance up from her phone.

"What's that mean?"

"It means you could teach stubborn lessons to a mule. Miss I-Won't-Compromise-On-My-Responsibilities."

Rolling her eyes, she went back to her watch search. "That's called having a sense of duty."

"Yeah, you keep telling yourself that." He propped his head on a closed fist.

"JD?"

A different quality in her voice and a soft hand on his arm drew him around to her. Blue eyes measured him. "Are you okay?" she demanded. "When was the last time you took your pain medicine?"

He stabbed her with a glare. "And I give you exhibit A."

"I'm serious."

"So am I."

She swiveled on her hips to face him. "I can see you're in pain."

Nice hips encased in blue denim. "I haven't been out of pain since I woke up on the side of the road."

"Which is no reason to be a martyr."

"I don't need it." Rather than look at her he turned his attention to the hat kiosk in front of him, to the rows of caps denoting NFL, NBA and other sports teams. He wondered if he had a team he supported.

"Listen, I know you're hot to find out who you are, but knowing your name won't mean a whole lot if you don't have your memories. When you push it, you may be delaying your recovery."

"I can't just sit around doing nothing." The pounding in his head escalated. He pulled his gaze away from the silver fangs on the football cap of the Las Vegas Strikers. Focused on the beige terrazzo flooring instead. "My mind doesn't shut off when I'm not moving around. It's constantly seeking information that's not there. That hurts more than staying occupied."

"Okay. I get that. But you need to rest, to heal, especially in these first few days." She leaned back on the bench and stared out at the post-holiday shoppers. "Obviously the money thing bothers you. I get that, too. You must feel helpless without funds of your own. Why don't I give you an advance until we get it appraised?"

"No." She was too generous, too trusting. How could she know he wasn't making this whole thing up to take advantage of her? As it was, he already owed her too much. Didn't like the fact she was lending him money at all. The watch meant nothing to him. He'd rather sell it and have his own resources.

"Yes." She countered. "It'll only be a few hundred dollars today, because that's my ATM limit."

Not waiting for a response from him, she got up and walked away. About a hundred feet up she stepped into an alcove. A few minutes later she was headed back to him.

The woman had no sense of self-preservation at all. Didn't she understand the risks she was taking with him? She'd been a law enforcement officer. She should know better.

When she held out the money, he folded his arms across his chest and refused to take it.

"Nothing is easy with you. I'm not giving you anything I'm not willing to lose. So far. We may have to work out incremental payments for the watch."

Okay, that made him feel slightly better. But he still didn't reach for the money. His resistance didn't deter her. She rolled the bills up, tucked them in the crook of his elbow and walked away.

"Whatever," she tossed over her shoulder. "I'm getting something to eat."

And she had the nerve to call him stubborn.

He was the one with the concussion, but she was the one not thinking right.

She had no reason to trust him. No reason to put her money at risk. Such generosity of spirit was foreign to him. Who knew who he'd be when he got his memory back? He could be a scumbag willing to prey on gullible fools.

Lord, he prayed he wasn't a scumbag. If that turned out to be the case, better he never regain his memory. Then he'd have a chance to start over. The question then was would his true character bleed through to his new identity?

It was too much to contemplate when his head felt ready to explode.

So yeah, he'd give in, but only on his terms.

He followed her into the food court. Bought a plate of

Chinese food—he had to admit it felt good to have money in his pocket—and joined her at a table in the communal dining area.

"Here." He held his watch out to her.

She just looked at him.

"You've lent me money using the watch as collateral. You need to hold on to the collateral."

She finished a bite of pasta. "That's not necessary."

"Yes, it is." He stared her down.

"All right." She took the watch and buckled it on. "If it'll make you happy." At its tightest point it dangled on her wrist like a bulky bracelet. He'd have to add another notch.

"It does make me happy." He felt it in the easing of the tension in his shoulders, which emphasized the throbbing in his head. Giving in to the pain, he pulled out his prescription bottle.

Grace watched in silence as he popped a pain pill with a sip of soda. At least she didn't gloat. Putting up with stubborn was bad enough.

"So you like Chinese?"

"Yeah. This is pretty good."

"And spicy. Risky, going with the kung pao chicken."

"I can handle it." He dug in, savoring the heat, the garlic, the nuttiness.

"How did you know you'd like it?" She wondered.

He shrugged. "One of those things I know without knowing how."

"So the real you *is* coming through. That has to be good, right?"

Another shrug. Who knew?

She cocked her head to the left. "There's a movie theater. You want to get out of your head? Let's go see a movie. Killing a couple of hours in a dark cinema should occupy you and still be restful."

"Yeah, we could do that." He stood and gathered their trash. "As long as it's not some chick flick."

"I like a good chick flick, but I was thinking something more shoot-'em-up."

"You like action-adventure?"

"I do. And sci-fi. But not horror."

In front of the theater, he surveyed the choices while she did the same.

They both chose the same one, her voice echoing his by a beat. He met her gaze, both brows lifted.

She grinned. And led the way inside, denim hips swaying.

A smile tugged at the corner of his mouth. He liked this idea better by the minute.

The mall shops were closed when they got out of the movie. So she took him to Walmart instead. The break seemed to settle him. And he was able to get everything he needed at prices that didn't make his head hurt, or so he said.

Afterward he wanted to take her to a nice steak dinner. They compromised on a decent dinner, and then she drove them back to their room, where they both fell asleep watching a *Breaking Bad* marathon.

Sunday morning he surprised her by joining her in church. She heard him saying The Lord's Prayer, so he'd been involved in religion at some point in his life.

They arrived in San Francisco midafternoon. Grace booked them into another Pinnacle Express, this time two rooms. JD looked out over the city and said it looked familiar. She refrained from asking how.

Her friend came through with a value for the watch of sixty to ninety thousand, depending on the condition of the watch. Rather than rush out to find a jewelry store, JD suggested another movie, followed by dinner in Chinatown.

Monday morning she knocked on JD's door. He let her

in. The drapes were open to a view of the bay and a slice of the Golden Gate Bridge. He wore his new jeans and a blue knit shirt that brought out the green of his eyes.

"How are you doing this morning?"

He ignored the question. "I told you the city felt familiar. I went downstairs and gathered up some brochures. Nothing stood out to me, except to confirm I know the city. For the last hour I've been scouring the *San Francisco Chronicle*, looking through back articles hoping something would click." He shook his head, indicating a lack of success. "I must wear glasses. It was hard to focus on the computer."

"It's the concussion." When he just shook his head, she moved on. "Are you ready to go?" They had a meeting with her friend Doug at the FBI. "We're a little early, but I don't know the area."

"Sounds good." He closed up the computer.

She considered taking a cab, because driving in San Francisco was insane. Parking was worse and required you have an offshore account. But she preferred to have her own vehicle.

Downstairs JD held the door for her and then walked around to slide in beside her. The roomy Escape felt cramped, with his big body taking up most of the space. His scent filled the air around them. To distract herself from the fact that only inches separated her from him, she watched as he took in the sights of the city.

"Anything look familiar?" she asked.

"All of it." He confirmed. "Just like with the brochures. I know the layout of the town. I can tell you where the theater district is. Where to get great seafood. But I don't know in what context I know it. Whether I lived here, worked here, traveled here. It's all a blank."

"Don't force it," she cautioned him. "The doctor said you should let the knowledge come to you."

"I'm trying." He leaned his head back, closed his eyes.

She glanced at the GPS and saw they were nearing their destination.

"Head for the Pinnacle Hotel," JD said. He opened his eyes and explained, "It's near Union Station, only a few blocks from Golden Gate Avenue, and there's a Sullivan's Jewels in the lobby. I want to see if they can give me a more exact appraisal."

"Okay." Grace checked the Cartier strapped to her wrist and decided they had time. At the hotel she pulled into valet parking, gathered her purse and jacket and exited, handing the attendant her keys before joining JD. He placed his hand on the small of her back and escorted her inside.

"Good afternoon, sir," the doorman greeted him. The Pinnacle Hotel was the five-star version of the Pinnacle Express. The liveried doorman held the door for them to enter.

Inside, a stunning water feature welcomed them. The lobby buzzed with activity as people came and went and stopped to conduct business or simply to chat.

JD didn't linger, escorting her directly into Sullivan's Jewels. The store had a traditional feel. Everything gleamed, from the dark woods and glass display cases, to the gold-and-crystal accessories. And inside the cases: sparkle, sparkle, sparkle.

"Good afternoon, sir." A personable young man in his twenties crossed the floor to greet them. "I'm Christopher. How can I help you today?"

"I'd like to get a watch appraised." JD held up the watch she'd given back to him on the trip across the lobby.

"Certainly, sir. May I ask, was there something wrong with the piece?"

"No. I'm thinking of selling it."

"Of course. We can handle that for you." The young

man assured him. "This way, please." He directed them to a private room furnished with leather chairs and a small table. "Please wait here. Can I get you some refreshments? Water? Coffee?"

"No, thanks. If we could make this quick, I'd appreciate it." JD slid into a leather chair. "We have to leave for an appointment in thirty minutes."

"Absolutely, sir. I'll get with the manager and be back in a few minutes."

"Well, you can't fault the service." Grace sank into her own chair. "He's eager, but I don't get a bad vibe off him."

"It's a reputable store. We'll get a fair appraisal here. Too bad they won't actually buy it. He didn't mention proof of purchase, but I don't see Sullivan's cutting corners."

"Me neither." She sighed, suffering from diamond envy. "We strolled by some gorgeous pieces."

"Huh." She felt his gaze like a touch as it ran over her. "You don't strike me as being big on bling."

"I'm not usually," she agreed. "But I don't generally spend so much time in jewelry stores. All this temptation coming my way, I might become a convert."

"If it turns out I'm rich, when this is over you can pick something out and I'll get it for you as a bonus."

"I'm not hinting, JD. You're already paying me when it's not necessary. I don't need a bonus on top of a wage."

"A bonus isn't about need." Elbow propped on the table, he massaged his temples with one hand. "It's about appreciation."

"Are you okay?"

"I'm fine. I think I've been to this hotel before. My head is throbbing and I've noticed a pattern. My head hurts more when my mind is struggling to assimilate something it recognizes but can't place."

"Wow, that could be helpful." And painful, though it

made sense in a way. "If you think you've been to the hotel, maybe someone at the front desk would remember you."

"Doubtful. Do you know how many people must go through here in a year?"

"You're probably right." But it might be worth a try if time allowed. In an investigation you followed up on every lead. She'd gotten results when the odds were worse. "Why don't you close your eyes while we wait?"

"Don't baby me, Grace."

She rolled her eyes. As if that was possible.

To keep from fussing at him, she texted Doug to let him know she and JD were in the area and would be on time for their appointment. Doug texted back to come on over, he could see them at any time.

"Doug is ready for us when we finish here," she passed on to JD. She snapped a picture of his profile and then requested he look at her. Once he complied, she snapped a facial shot and forwarded both to her friend.

"What are you doing?" JD demanded.

"I sent your pictures to Doug. Maybe he can get started without us."

"Good idea." The news perked him up. "We'll give it five more minutes and then leave. We can always come back."

Christopher returned a few moments later. "My manager is dealing with a delivery. He won't be able to examine the watch in the time you have. I can make an appointment for you, or I can give you a receipt and we'll have the appraisal ready for you when you pick up the watch."

JD showed no reaction as he held out his hand for the watch. "We'll try back after our appointment. I'm not sure how long we'll be."

"Of course. We're open until six."

JD escorted Grace from the store.

"Why didn't you leave it? It would only be for a short while. And we have to come back here for the car."

"This is all I have in the world." He handed her the watch. "I prefer to keep it with me." He made for the front doors. "It would be different if we weren't about to talk to the FBI. I'm hoping they can give me a name and I can learn about who I am without appearing a sick fool in public."

For the love of Pete, save her from the male ego. He didn't want to be at a disadvantage in front of the sales force. She should have guessed this was about control. Hopefully, this meeting would provide some answers.

Sighing, she gave in. They could always come back if the FBI failed to produce his identity.

She tucked her arm through his. "You're not sick, you're memory-challenged."

He grinned at her, the smile flashing a never before seen dimple. And her heart tilted just a little.

CHAPTER SIX

"YOUR NAME IS Jackson Hawke," Doug Allen announced moments after escorting JD and Grace into an interview room. Of average height and weight, with average features and average brown hair in the expected FBI black suit, Doug waved for them to take seats.

JD let the name sink in, waited for it to trigger a flood of memories. All it brought was a sledgehammer beating in his head. An acknowledgment, of sorts, of its familiarity.

"Oh, my God." Grace breathed.

He glanced her way to find her staring at him wide-eyed.

"What?"

"Jackson Hawke. Oh, my gosh, JD. You're a billionaire." Her eyes narrowed as she ran her gaze over him. "You shaved off your goatee. And you're bigger in person. You're not missing." She turned that intense regard to Doug. "He's not a missing person, or I would have put it together."

Billionaire? Goatee? JD ran his fingers over his clean-shaven chin, still reeling from hearing his name. Nothing else seemed to compute.

"No." Doug confirmed. His alert gaze, which was anything but average, landed on JD. "There's no record of a missing-persons report. But he is part of an ongoing investigation in Las Vegas—an assault."

She sat up straighter at that news. "That must be when he was stabbed."

"That matches the report. I have some of the details here." Doug pushed a file across the table. "You doing okay, Mr. Hawke?"

JD clutched for Grace's hand under cover of the table, relaxed a little when her fingers curled around his. "I'm fine. It's a lot to take in."

"I'm sure it is. You're an important man, Mr. Hawke—"

"JD," he cut in. "Please call me JD."

"Of course, JD. I haven't broadcast this news yet, but the tech that helped with the face recognition probably has. I expect my bosses will appear soon. Let me just say now, the FBI is happy to lend any assistance we can. Are you under a medical doctor's care?"

"Better, I'm under Grace's care." He didn't feel like an important man. Didn't particularly want to deal with the FBI top brass. But he was grateful for their help, so he'd do what he had to.

"Those are pretty good hands to be in." Doug joked. "She always had the best scores in first aid."

"You did okay." Grace shot back. The friendship between the two was an easy camaraderie.

"I was better at putting holes in than plugging them up."

"Doug is a crack shot," Grace explained. She squeezed JD's hand, a sign her chitchat was intended to give him time to assimilate all he'd learned. At least that's how he took it. "The military tried to recruit him for sniper duty."

"Yeah, not my thing." Doug tucked his hands in his pockets. "I'm not afraid to use my weapon, but being a sniper is too premeditated for my taste. Your game 'Rogue Target' is pretty intense."

"My game?"

"You were right, JD," Grace answered. "You are a geek. A supergeek. You create digital video games. 'Pinnacle' was your first, some argue your best. It launched you into the big leagues against Sony and Nintendo. 'Unleashed' is currently the number one game in the world, and number two is 'Rogue Target,' which came out last Christmas."

"You own Pinnacle Enterprises," Doug informed him. "An entertainment conglomerate. As well as Pinnacle Games, you own TV and radio stations, Pinnacle Comics, Pinnacle Hotels and the Strikers football team in Las Vegas. Your net worth is in excess of ten billion."

"That's right." Grace tapped a finger off her forehead. "Pinnacle Enterprises. That's why the hotel looked so familiar today. You own it. And the others we've been staying in."

"You have a penthouse suite at the Pinnacle here in town. As well as in Las Vegas and New York. From what I've found, you have no residences outside the hotels. Your official address is your corporate address in Las Vegas."

He had no home. For some reason that rang true.

A knock sounded at the door and it opened to admit a tall man, rounding around the middle. He had sharp brown eyes and steel-gray hair.

"Doug," he said, his voice as deep as he was tall. "I hear we have a celebrity in the house today."

"Yes, sir. This is Jackson Hawke and my friend Grace Delaney. Mr. Hawke is experiencing a memory lapse. We were able to assist him by providing his identity. JD, Grace, this is Ken Case, Special Agent in Charge."

"I'm glad we could help. We've met a time or two at charity events around town."

"I'm sorry. I don't remember you."

"Not a problem." Ken drew out a chair and sat. "I'll be truthful. They were brief introductions. You probably wouldn't recall in any case. How did you come to lose your memory?"

Grace gave a brief rundown of events, managing to get the facts across without making him sound like a felon or a fool. Quite a talent she had there.

"The doctor is hopeful I'll get my memory back within a couple of weeks." JD added in the hopes of minimizing how lame he felt. He was a billionaire, and right this minute he couldn't hold two thoughts together at the same time.

"With the new information from the Woodpark sheriff's office yesterday, my theory is that after the altercation at the Red Wolf Tavern, the man who accosted JD followed him, ran him off the road and robbed him."

Ken nodded, his eyes speculative as they assessed Grace. "It's a likely scenario. Nice to meet you, Grace. Doug has mentioned you in passing. How did the election go?"

"I lost." Blunt and to the point, Grace didn't sugarcoat her response.

"Too bad. I have to think it's their loss." Ken appeared impressed with Grace, too. "Has Doug tried to recruit you to the wonderful world of the FBI?"

"He has." A tinge of red tinted Grace's cheeks. She wasn't immune to the attention of the head man. "And I'll admit I've been tempted. But I've lived my entire life moving at the whim of the navy, first as a military brat and then as an enlisted. For once I'd like to be able to choose where I live and what I do."

"Hard to argue with that." He stood. "If you change your mind, let me know. We'll talk."

"Thank you, I will."

"In the meantime she works for me." JD stood, as well. His head hurt and he was ready to go. "Can I take this report with me?"

"Of course." Doug moved to hold the door.

"Good luck." Ken offered his hand. "I hope you get your memory back soon. I want you to know you can count on the discretion of this office." After shaking hands, he took off.

With the exit in sight, JD subtly ushered Grace in that

direction. Doug walked with them. JD longed to escape, but he owed the man. "Thank you for your help. It's a huge relief to have a name to claim."

They stepped into the hall.

"You're seriously going to pass up a career in the FBI because you're tired of traveling?" Doug nudged Grace in the shoulder. "You were going to do your twenty."

"I know. It's different now I'm out. It's not even the traveling. There's still a large part of the world I want to see. But I want my own place. I want a sense of permanence."

"I know your dad left you some money. Buy a house somewhere, make it your base and come to work for the FBI. You'll have the continuity you want and a great career, as well."

She rolled her eyes at Doug's insistence. "I'll think about it. But don't get your hopes up. I really want a home."

"Sherry gives me that, wherever I am. She was hoping to get together, do some catching up."

JD tensed at the suggestion. Doug seemed like a nice guy, but JD wasn't up to socializing at the moment. Of course, he could let Grace go on her own. Except, no, the idea of being without her cinched the tension tighter.

Impossible. Jealousy was beneath him. He knew it to the soles of his feet. Grace would call it another clue. He just accepted that he didn't envy. He got his own, bigger and better than anyone else's.

Good thing he was a billionaire.

"I would love that, but I can't this trip. Maybe in a couple of weeks. I bet she's getting big. Only two months to go, Daddy."

Doug turned a little pale.

Was it petty of JD to feel a little satisfaction?

Grace laughed. "You'll be fine." She gave him a hug. "Thanks for your help."

"I'm glad I could be of assistance." He shook JD's hand, slapped him on the arm. "Nice to have met you."

"You've met a shell." JD pointed out.

"JD!" Grace exclaimed.

But the bitter comment didn't faze the other man.

"You're in there. And who knows, this may be the better man. Either way, Grace is a pretty good judge of character. If she's willing to put up with you, you must be worth knowing."

JD glanced at Grace. She stood with her hands braced on her hips eyeing the two of them. Finally he nodded. "I believe in Grace."

"So do I." Doug jutted his chin in acknowledgment before reaching for the door handle. "Take care of our girl."

And now he did feel petty.

"That was rude." Grace left him to call the elevator. "And after he went out of his way to help you."

"It was his job to help me." JD—Jackson—slapped the file folder against his leg.

"Maybe. But without his help you'd have had to go through a lot of red tape and waited a week or more for half the information you got." The elevator arrived and she stepped inside. "He didn't have to have the information ready when we walked in the door or give you a copy."

"So he's a good guy." He punched the button for the lobby. "I get it."

"Do you?"

"I said thank you."

"And then you disrespected everything he did with a dismissive comment."

She'd been hurt and embarrassed when he cut Doug off. It felt personal.

And why wouldn't it? Doug was her friend, doing a

favor for her. He'd provided JD with the information he'd been looking for only to take a hit.

JD—Jackson—said nothing.

She reached the glass doors of the building entrance and fisted her way through. JD followed, flinching from the light. He shifted to put the sun at his back.

She spied the frown lines at the corners of his eyes and the anger fizzled away. How could she forget that he was in pain? An hour ago he'd confessed it got worse when his brain tried to connect his past with the present. He must be in agony.

The way he interacted with others without giving away his condition amazed her.

He stood, shoulders back, chin up, braced to take on the world. While speaking with the FBI, he'd handled himself with such quiet confidence she doubted Doug or Special Agent Case noticed he suffered from a massive head injury. Well, until the end when he got surly.

"Come on." She strolled to the quick mart on the corner.

He kept pace. The fact he didn't bother to ask where they were going confirmed her suspicion. It was all he could do to deal with the pain.

In the small market she found a pair of sunglasses with extra dark lenses and carried them to the counter. She started to pay, but JD drew out his new wallet. She'd given him more cash this morning. The clerk removed the tags and JD wore the glasses out of the store.

"Thank you. These help."

"I'm sorry," she said.

"For what?" He started off for the Pinnacle where they'd left the SUV. "You were right. I was rude."

"You were hurting." She caught up to him, and wrapped her arm through his. He stiffened, but she didn't let go. "And, I imagine, a bit disappointed. It would be hard not to hope your memories would come back once you learned your name."

He shrugged. But she saw his jaw tighten.

"You don't have to pretend with me, JD."

He stopped and swung to face her. "What am I going to do, Grace?" His face revealed his distress. "I can't step into the shoes of a billionaire and confess I lost my memory. The whole world would pity me. And that's just the beginning of the problems. I can't run a multibillion-dollar company. Not only would I not know what I was doing, I don't even know who my employees are. Can you imagine the damage I'd do to my own company?"

"The first thing is not to panic." She tugged on his arm, got him walking again. "You don't have to rush into anything. First we'll read through the file, get a feel for who you are. Then we'll go from there. Research your people so you know them when you meet them. It's going to be fine."

A billionaire. Grace kept her gaze facing forward. She would never have guessed. Of course, the hugely expensive watch had been a clue. One she hadn't ignored. She'd done a search for millionaires under forty and went through six months of Forbes magazine.

The problem was he had a reputation for keeping a low profile and protecting his privacy. So there weren't that many photos of him out there to find, except for the odd photo snagged by the paparazzi at social events.

She'd probably looked right at a picture of him while doing her research and not recognized JD.

In all the pictures that came to mind he'd had long hair and a goatee. And his well-toned body must be one of the nation's best-kept secrets, because she'd had no idea he was such a hottie.

Though now that she thought about it, his name had been linked with beautiful actresses and models.

Lucky for her he had no memory of them. Because,

seriously, how did an average girl like her compete with actresses and models? Not that she was actually competing. She was helping him, that was all. They weren't dating or anything.

Good thing. Because he was way out of her league.

He stopped again. Faced her again. "You're going to stay with me?"

"You hired me, remember? I promised you two weeks."

"What about the job with the FBI?"

"I'm not taking a job with the FBI."

"You should. You'd be good at it. Doug wants you to. Case liked you. He'd help you. The job is there if you want it."

"I don't want it."

"Doug had a sound suggestion," he argued, "buy a place, make it your base. It would give you the sense of permanence you crave, yet you'd be free to pursue a career where you can really make a difference."

His insistence gave her pause. Maybe he was trying to give her an out. "So you're releasing me from my promise to help you?"

"No." The denial had no maybe attached to it. He took her hand and began walking again. "But the offer will be there when we're done. You should think about it."

"Maybe I will." How could she not? But it didn't feel right. She craved permanence and to her that meant having a place of her own to go home to each night.

At the hotel he walked right past the valet station. Surprised, she hurried to catch up.

"Where are you going?"

"Supposedly I have a room here. I want to check it out."

"Without any identification?"

"I'm betting they know me. You suggested it yourself earlier."

The law enforcement officer in her cringed at the notion of the hotel letting just anyone into JD's—Jackson's—suite. But then he wasn't just anyone. He was Jackson Hawke. His identity hadn't completely sunk in. She'd taken a billionaire to Walmart. Now that was cringe-worthy.

She matched her stride to his as they crossed the marble floor of the huge lobby. The furnishings were modern, the art abstract. As they drew closer to registration, she noted there was a line to check in both for regular guests and for VIPs. She glanced at JD's profile, wondering what he would do. Would the owner of the hotel stand in line?

"Good afternoon, Mr. Hawke. It's good to see you again." Ah. Saved by the bell. In this case, the bell captain. "May I assist you with luggage today?"

"No, thank you, Watkins." JD replied smoothly. "I prefer to go directly to my rooms."

"Of course. Let me get your key for you." Watkins stepped around the registration desk and quickly returned with a keycard he presented to JD. "We were not advised you'd be staying with us. Your suite is ready as always, but there are no refreshments. I'll take care of that immediately."

"Thank you, Watkins." JD shoved the key into his pocket. "Perhaps you'll join us first. You can tell my companion, Ms. Delaney, of all the hotel's features on the way to our room."

"Certainly, sir." Chest puffed out with pride, he ushered her and JD to the elevators where he inserted a keycard before pushing the button for the top floor. "As with all Pinnacle Hotels, the building is modeled after the silver sphere in 'Unleashed,' Mr. Hawke's first game. It has thirty floors representing the thirty levels of the game. Each floor is smaller than the floor below it, creating the rising pinnacle. We have a shopping mall, a salon and spa, a gym complete with sauna, a pool and some of the best restaurants in the city."

"Everything a girl could want," Grace mumbled, overwhelmed by what JD owned.

"Including diamonds," Watkins agreed. "Sullivan's Jewels has a store in the lobby."

"We noticed." She smiled thinly, her shoulders going back. Was he inferring she was with JD because he could buy her diamonds?

"Watkins," JD said softly from beside her, "You aren't insulting my guest, are you?"

The chill in his voice sent a shiver down her spine.

"No, sir." The man paled. "Never. I cherish my job. Everyone at the Pinnacle does. I would never disrespect you or your guest." He turned to her. "I apologize if I offended. I just know my wife drools over Sullivan's displays whenever she comes by."

"They do have lovely items." She conjured a smile, embarrassed she'd overreacted. "No harm done."

JD lifted one dark brow.

Watkins cleared his throat. "I bought my wife a necklace from one of Rett Sullivan's collections for our twenty-fifth wedding anniversary. She wears it every chance she gets."

"A wise choice, I'm sure," JD stated, letting the poor guy off the hook.

The elevator doors opened feeding them into a large foyer. In the middle of the room, a glass pedestal table housed a towering flower arrangement in various shades of blue. Three archways led deeper into the suite. Watkins pressed a button on a remote, and royal blue drapes opened to display a glass wall highlighting the San Francisco skyline.

"I'll see that refreshments are sent up." Watkins replaced the remote and returned to the elevator. "May I make reservations at the steak house for you both? Or perhaps you prefer sushi tonight?"

"The steak house," JD decided. "At eight."

"Very good, sir. Please call me if you need anything." The elevator doors closed and he was gone.

"I'm sorry if he upset you." JD took her hand.

"It was a foolish reaction." She pulled away, moving toward the skyline. "I guess all this glamour—" she swept an arm out to indicate the posh suite "—is throwing me a bit. I'm not used to penthouse suites."

The slick, modern feel of the furnishings downstairs were repeated here, but where the blue was an accent color downstairs, it dominated here. The chairs and sofa were large, white and built for comfort, despite the sharp lines of their design. A low glass coffee table seemed to float atop a blue rug swirled through with silver and black.

Across the way stood a dining table that looked as if it came from the captain's mess of the *U.S.S. Enterprise* and was large enough to seat half the crew. Beyond was a chef's dream. The gourmet kitchen gleamed with copper and stainless steel.

And all of it opened onto the world.

"This is spectacular, JD. I don't know how to take it all in."

She felt his heat behind her and then he was turning her to face him. He lifted her chin on the edge of his hand until her gaze met his.

"How do you think I feel? I own all this. It blows my mind." He released her chin to run his hand through his hair. "Almost literally. My head feels like it's about to explode."

"I'm sorry. I'm making this about me and that's just wrong." How could she forget this was about him? So she experienced a little discomfort. It was nothing to what he suffered. She cupped his face, stared into his eyes, automatically checking his pupils. They were even but pain lurked there. "We should go back to our hotel, let you rest before we move in here."

Annoyance flooded the green irises. "I told you not to baby me." He retreated to the dining table with his folder from the FBI.

"Then stop making me the bad guy." She gritted her teeth at his obstinacy, swept over and grabbed the folder. "You have a head trauma. Even without the loss of memory, it's going to take days to recuperate. You've learned enough until some of the pain has subsided. With the concussion you probably can't read it anyway. And, no, you probably *don't* wear glasses. I know you don't want to keep hearing it, but a concussion isn't something you can dismiss. It can mess with your vision."

Tucking the folder under her arm, she strolled to the kitchen. She set her purse on the open counter separating the kitchen and dining room and opened the full-size refrigerator. No water, but Watkins had warned them there were no refreshments stocked. In fact, the refrigerator was off, so she turned it on and then moved to the cupboards, where she found a square glass made of fine crystal and ran water into it.

"Drink." She set the glass on the counter. "You need to stay hydrated. I find when I'm taking pain medicine it helps to drink lots of water."

He stalked up to the counter, pushed the water aside and held out his hand. "Give me the folder."

"No."

"I'm the boss."

"Except when it affects your health. Then I have veto power. Veto."

"Grace."

"JD." Shoot, shoot. She really needed to remember to use his name. Now she'd lost her edge. Pretending she hadn't, she lifted her chin and countered. "Jackson."

He pressed his lips together. "You can call me JD."

"No, we both need to get used to Jackson."

He couldn't argue with that, so he didn't. But his hand still demanded the folder. Stubborn.

"Okay." She took a page from the folder, glanced at it and set it in front of him. "Read me the last paragraph."

He picked up the paper, looked at it, moved it forward, moved it back. "It's referencing the Las Vegas property."

"Yes. Now read the address."

He scowled at the paper, then tossed it down. "Maybe I do need glasses."

"No glasses, no contacts. Not according to your California driver's license." She tucked the page back in the folder. "It's the concussion, Jackson. It's not a weakness, it's just something you have to get through. I know it chafes, but right now resting is the best thing you can do to help yourself."

His eyes narrowed and focused intently upon her. Gaze locked on her, he prowled around the end of the counter, the action so predatory she forced her feet not to retreat.

When he got within a foot and kept coming, she planted a hand on his chest. It didn't stop him. He clasped her hand, drew it down to the side and invaded her space.

"What are you doing?" She reared back.

"This." He lowered his head and took her mouth with his.

She stiffened. This was not a good idea. But he stood back, claiming her with his mouth only. He lulled her by taking it slow, keeping it easy. He tilted his head to the perfect angle. His lips were moist, soft, mobile, exerting the right amount of pressure. He lingered, seducing her slowly, until she deepened the kiss by stepping into him.

His arms came around her pulling her against him and his tongue swept over her bottom lip seeking entrance. Closing her eyes, she sank into sensation. Her surrender motivated him to heighten the caress to the next level, building heat and passion until she strained against him, wanting to be closer, needing more.

She forgot to breathe and didn't care. His touch mattered, his taste. A silly thing like air could wait.

He eased back. Chest heaving, he kissed her on the temple. Then released her.

She blinked at him. Was he stopping? Now? Uh-uh. She stepped into him again. This time he caught her hands to keep her from touching him. He shook his head, moved away.

"What the heck, JD?"

He reached for the glass of water and drained it. "You'll have to forgive me. I didn't mean for it to go so far. After days of lacking memories and feeling like an invalid, I needed to do something that made me feel good and that I'm good at."

She went still. "You used me?"

CHAPTER SEVEN

"You used me?" The stricken expression on Grace's face ricocheted through JD.

"It wasn't like that." He tried to dismiss his blunder. "Come on, let's see what the rest of this place has to offer."

He reached for her arm, but she yanked it away.

"I'm sorry, Grace." He shifted closer and she shifted away. He had to make this right. "I didn't mean to use you."

"We talked about keeping our relationship professional."

"Yes." He cleared his throat. "I know."

"So how did you mean it?" She cocked her head, blue eyes icy cold. "Is this one of my duties? Am I to make myself available for the occasional kiss whenever you feel the need to show your prowess? Because, oh, yeah, you are accomplished. I got hot, I got bothered."

"Grace, you can stop. I feel bad, okay?"

"I just need to know what my job duties entail. Am I supposed to moan, to give you audible cues?"

Anger flared. She didn't need to make such a big deal out of a little kiss. So frustration got the best of him and he lashed out, trying to grab a moment of joy at something he was good at. After the kiss in the bed that first night, he knew they were compatible.

He should have known she'd blow it out of proportion. The women he knew would just go with it. Hell, they'd make the most of the moment. But not by-the-rules Grace.

She needed to talk it to death, set parameters, probably write up procedures.

He wanted to order her to forget it, but the heft of that lead balloon wouldn't fly. He had enough brains not to let his defensiveness get the better of him.

"Can't we just put this behind us?" He tried for a charming smile. "I probably have a game console here somewhere. We can play a bit, relax. All very restful stuff."

She simply stared at him. "You know, JD, I've given you a lot of leeway. Let things go because I know you're hurting and that the loss of memory and concussion can make things confusing. But I draw the line at being used as a sensual punching bag. If that's a condition of helping you, I'm going to have to retract my offer of assistance."

"Sensual punching bag?" he repeated, offended by her attitude. "You said it was good."

"I said I got hot and bothered," she corrected, easing some of the burn only to ratchet it back up by demanding, "Is that the point?"

"No. Look." He held his hands up in surrender. "Hands-off. It won't happen again."

"I'm not sure I can trust you. Because it happened before, didn't it? In bed that first night."

He rubbed a finger over his throbbing temple. "It just happened."

"It just happened?" she repeated incredulously. "How? Tell me, JD, how does a kiss just happen?"

"Right. I can see you're not going to be happy until I spill the whole humiliating story."

Arms crossed over her chest, she lifted one dark eyebrow urging him to get to it already.

"I guess you deserve an apology for that, as well." To delay the inevitable he walked around the counter and stood facing her with his hands braced on the marble. "I woke up and you were sitting next to me in the bed. You probably meant to test my vitals, check on the current state of the presidency and so on. Anyway, I was half-asleep and you were there and it happened."

"That's your story? You woke up and it happened?"

"Yeah," he pushed back. His actions had been instinctive. "I was half-asleep and you looked sexy with your hair all mussed up. I reached for you without thinking about it."

With blue eyes narrowed, she studied him as she contemplated his story.

Really? As if he'd make up being a lecherous fool.

"And what happened next?"

Geez, he knew five-year-olds who asked fewer questions. Okay, maybe not, but he wished she'd bury the bone already. How was he supposed to defend himself properly when it hurt to think?

"Once I came to my senses, I broke it off. You checked my vitals and I moved to the other bed." He glanced away, and straightened the folder on the counter. "That was the end of it."

"That's everything?"

"I apologized."

"An apology isn't always enough. You can't be doing this, JD."

"I've said I'm sorry, and I am. I don't want you to quit. I know ours is a professional relationship. And I respect that. But I'll tell you this, having you around calms me. You ground me in a world out of control. Ever since I realized my memory was gone, it's all about getting it back, finding my identity. Everything is focused out.

"Kissing you is something I did for me. It brought me peace. It brought me joy. It took me out of myself and into you. And I am sorry if it hurts you, but it just may have saved my sanity. So do I regret it? No."

"I don't know what to say to that. Because a kiss involves two people, JD. It can't just be about you."

Oh, no, she didn't. He leaned halfway over the counter. "Don't pretend you weren't right there with me."

Flames flared in her eyes, confirmation she couldn't deny her full participation. She picked up her purse, and swung the strap over her shoulder. "I think we need a break from each other. I'm going back to the other hotel. I'll stay there tonight and bring our stuff over in the morning."

She swung around and headed toward the arch leading to the foyer.

No. This wasn't what he wanted at all.

"Grace," he called out. "You don't have to go."

"I really do."

But she stopped and came back. His spirits lifted. She wasn't leaving him, after all.

She grabbed the folder. "I'm taking this with me." Without waiting for a response she headed out again. "Enjoy your steak dinner."

A moment later the door closed with a distinct thud.

He wasn't feeling any joy now.

Wait, the women he knew? That was strange. Not that the women in his past had little in common with Grace— he was getting used to the certainty without foundation. But he'd experienced no pain with the thought.

If Grace was here, she'd probably claim it was a sign of his mind healing.

Testing, he tried focusing on his last girlfriend; he opened his mind and tried to picture her here. Pain shattered through his head. Nausea curled in his stomach. Dots danced before his eyes. He dropped onto a dining room chair and lowered his head between his knees.

Sweet merciful dog biscuits. As the ringing in his ears began to fade, he conceded. Maybe he did need to rest.

* * *

Grace let herself into the Pinnacle Express hotel room and tossed her purse on the bed. She needed this time alone. JD had her so off-kilter she didn't know how to act.

Her mind buzzed, refusing to settle on a single thought. She was flustered. And a master-at-arms never got flustered.

She hadn't signed up for this. She'd agreed to a professional relationship.

Kissing did not belong in a professional relationship.

She dropped into the armchair and looked out on the pool. It was empty, the cool weather chasing most guests away. But in the far corner a small family enjoyed the bubbling spa.

Her bubbling emotions were much less fun.

The memory of their first kiss rolled on the screen in her head. The temptation of him sprawled nearly naked on the bed, the surprise of him reaching for her, the tenderness in his touch, the sensual feel of his mouth on hers. And him pushing her away.

Except she wasn't one for self-deception. And she didn't miss the fact he was the one to pull away in both encounters. She obviously had no restraint when it came to him. And, just as obviously, he did. So she'd given in to her instincts to flee, to put time and distance between them. If she was smart, she'd keep going.

Yet she'd committed to helping him.

And she had. He now knew his name. Jackson Hawke, billionaire. The truth was he didn't need her anymore. Sure, he felt vulnerable, but he had grit and fortitude. He'd be fine. His people could give him the support he needed to find his way in the corporate world. In fact, they'd be better qualified than her by far.

But she took pride in keeping her promises. And she

understood the desire to prep before putting yourself in an unknown situation.

She liked helping him. Being honest, she admitted he'd helped her, too. In the beginning the challenge of his situation gave her something to focus on at a time when she was at a loss.

The problem was he kept breaking the rules.

The kiss changed things. Her response changed everything.

She'd worked with men too long not to know they pushed the limits at every opportunity. She'd been kissed on the job before, but she'd managed to correct the misguided fool's perception of their relationship and still work effectively with him.

Not with JD. No chance of pretending he hadn't melted her insides. He'd called her on that bit of self-deception.

Best to end their connection now. The obvious chemistry between them would only complicate their working relationship. Because unlike the other instances of men crossing the line with her, she actually liked kissing JD. A lot.

She pushed to her feet and began gathering JD's things into the bag he'd bought. Cheap things he'd probably never use. Another reason to end things between them. They were from different worlds. He was high finance, glitz and glamour at its peak. She was a military brat, a law enforcement officer with an uncertain future.

And she hadn't missed the fact he had no residence beyond hotel suites. They really had nothing in common.

So why did she miss him so much?

JD missed Grace as soon as she walked through the door. She was the only constant in the short memory of this life.

Jackson Hawke, billionaire. How freaky was that?

He wandered the suite, taking in the luxurious accommodations. There were three bedrooms and five bathrooms, including a master bath as big as the sleeping rooms he and Grace had stayed in the past few nights.

It all felt so foreign.

More familiar was the computer room, which looked like a James Bond command center. And the media/game room, furnished theater-style in dark gold, deep brown and comfortable leather. Sliding into the center seat, he ran his hand over the console. Oh, yeah, he felt right at home.

Too bad he had no one to share the moment with.

Missing Grace, he continued to wander. He found a closet with a full wardrobe of clothes. Everything from jeans to a tuxedo. All in his size. Poking around, he pulled open a drawer and found a safe. He pressed the switch at the bottom and a palm plate lit up.

He stared down at it.

"Here goes nothing." He placed his palm on the plate. Tumblers clicked and the plate beneath his hand lifted.

Guess that settled the doubts percolating in the back of his head that the FBI had made a mistake. Something eased in him at the confirmation. Flipping the lid, his eyebrows popped up to his hairline. Cash, lots of it, filled half the box, which was about the size of a large laptop computer but about eight inches deep. A few pieces of masculine jewelry were tossed in the other half, including another watch—expensive, but not as nice as the Cartier. Under the jewelry were some papers, but he didn't bother looking at them.

He wouldn't be able to read them anyway.

Ah, score. No need to be able to read to recognize the passport he plucked from a plastic sleeve at the back. His brows rocketed again when he opened it to find it nearly full with stamps from foreign lands. It appeared he was well traveled.

He looked around to share it with Grace—actually

walked into the next room looking for her before he recalled she'd left. So he reached into his pocket for a phone.
Only he didn't have one. Damn concussion, messing with
his head. It wasn't the first time he'd blipped on something
so obvious. This one, like the others, he'd keep to himself.

Missing Grace, and grumpy over the fact he couldn't
contact her, he returned to the closet, did a quick count
of the cash—three hundred thousand dollars—snagged
a bundle worth five thousand and then closed and reset
the safe.

A knock came at the door. He answered to find housekeeping had arrived to stock the suite. He left them to it
and headed downstairs. At the concierge desk Watkins
came to attention.

"Mr. Hawke, how can I help you?"

"I have a few things I need. I'm hoping you can help
me."

"Of course."

JD laid out his requests and received the same com-
pliant response. Yeah, he could get used to this. When he
finished, he gave Watkins a few bills to cover the costs
and another for a tip.

Then he strolled across the lobby to Sullivan's Jewels.
Maybe he could find something that would help Grace
accept his apology. But he'd have to be thoughtful about
it. He didn't want to upset her and end up owing her another apology.

Grace's cell phone rang startling her from a light doze as
she watched TV. "Hello."

"Hi, Grace." A deep male voice came down the line.

"JD?" Her heartbeat quickened. A reaction she dismissed as surprise. She didn't think he had her number.

"Yeah. I had Watkins pick up a phone for me."

Of course he did. "Did you need something?"

"Yes. I was wondering if you had a chance to read through the file."

Her gaze went to the file open on the bed next to her. "I flipped through it. Doug gave you the highlights. I'll do a search for your key personnel tonight and we can go over the information tomorrow."

"How about tonight? Come back, join me for dinner."

She hesitated, tempted to do just that. The very fact she wanted to explained why she couldn't. "I think it's best if we take this time apart."

"So you said." He sounded disappointed. Or was that wishful thinking? "Let me know if you change your mind."

Grace stormed into Jackson's suite. She powered right through the foyer into the living area. The fact he wasn't there blasted her ire further up the scale.

"Jackson Hawke, show yourself." The sharp demand rolled through the rooms.

"You're back." He appeared in the arched doorway.

"You have some nerve." She tossed her purse on the white couch. "How dare you have me evicted from my room at the Pinnacle Express hotel?"

"Did they upset you?" A frown drew his reddish brown eyebrows together. "I expressly requested they not upset you."

"Oh, the manager was very nice." She paced in front of the window. "As he threw me out of my room. How can that be anything but upsetting? I was so embarrassed."

"They were instructed that you were being upgraded to this hotel. Why would that be embarrassing?"

"Oh, I don't know," she mocked. "Maybe because they now think we're romantically involved and that I'm available at the click of your fingers." Seeking calm she drew in a deep breath, let it out slow. "What's the deal, Jackson?"

"I wanted you here. I owe you a nice steak dinner."

"It was a gross misuse of your authority. I was coming back in the morning. There was no need to go to such drastic measures."

He drew closer until he invaded her space. He stopped short of touching her, though his fingers twitched as if he wanted to. "Why are you calling me Jackson?"

"It's your name." And her way of calling to mind the differences between them. Her chin lifted. No need for him to know that.

"I didn't want you spending your money over there when there's plenty of room here. The place has three bedrooms. We can be apart in separate rooms."

"It's not the same."

"I know. That's the other reason I did it." Giving her a sad smile, he gazed into her eyes and confessed, "I was lonely without you."

Her anger deflated like a pinpricked balloon.

"You were out of line," she declared, unwilling to let him charm her so easily.

"I won't do it again." His fingers feathered over her hand, before he pulled back. "Not without warning you first."

She narrowed her eyes, reproaching him.

He shrugged. "It's the best I can do. And seriously, I couldn't enjoy my steak dinner without you."

"You could have changed the reservation to tomorrow."

"I considered it. But I wanted you here." He held his hand out toward the doorway. "Come, let me show you the rest of the suite."

Her eye landed on his new phone. She picked it up. "You need to be careful what you do. The hotel may let you slide on the bill, but you're still going to need money until you can get new identification and new credit cards. I leave you alone for a few minutes—"

His finger on her lips shushed her. "How about this—

you don't treat me like a child, and I won't treat you like a sensual punching bag. Fair trade?"

An argument sprang to her lips. She bit them together, holding it back.

"Fair trade."

"Good." He smiled and, wrapping his fingers around hers, led her out of the room. "Now, let me show you what I've found."

She tried to work her hand free, but it was a halfhearted attempt, and he ignored her as he moved through the suite showing her bedrooms, an office that rivaled British Command, a media room with a full-size billiard table and finally a master suite to die for.

"OMG." The bathroom took her breath away. The walls were made of glass, thick bricks on the bottom to obscure visibility and preserve privacy, but the top part was clear, blue-tinted glass. The huge walk-in shower was made of quartz rocks and lush, overhead greenery. Multiple showerheads promised a luxurious drenching. When you took a shower, you'd feel as if you were at the top of a waterfall looking down on the world. "Dibs on the shower."

He laughed. "I've already used it. It's quite spectacular."

She poked her head in a sauna. "Is this what you wanted to show me?"

"No. I saved the best for last." He disappeared back into the bedroom. She slowly followed, her feet reluctant to leave the bathroom oasis.

Inside the bedroom he'd disappeared altogether. "Jackson?"

"In here." His head popped out of a closet.

She joined him, stopping on the threshold to blink and take it in. Okay, maybe owning a house was overrated. Maybe she didn't need to own the ground under her feet to consider the space she occupied as home. Because, seriously, she could live in this room.

"Wow. Just wow." Forget sleek and slick in here. Warm wood and creamy marble welcomed her inside. Suits lined one side split by a three-way mirror, while shoes filled the opposite side and down the center ran a marble-topped island with a sink at one end and drawers on all sides. Three chandeliers lit the room and a chaise lounge provided a spot to sit. "I think I'm in love."

"And I think that's the most girlish thing I've heard you say."

"I'm a girl," she defended her reaction.

"Mostly you're a cop."

"Seriously? You're going to go there after the whole kissing incident?"

His expression was total innocence. "I didn't say you weren't pretty."

She scowled, as mad at herself for the surge of pleasure as she was at him for the asinine comment. Shaking a finger at him, she advised, "You may want to stop while you're ahead."

"I'm ahead?" He grinned, flashing his dimple.

"Better watch it," she cautioned. "You didn't care for the consequences the last time you provoked me."

Jackson sobered. "You don't strike me as the type to run from your problems."

"I'm not. But I'm not a martyr either, so I do believe in stepping back to cool off. An occurrence that shouldn't be necessary in a professional relationship. At least not often."

"Okay, okay." He raised his hands in surrender. "Message received. We'll keep it professional. Now, look."

He grabbed her hand and drew her next to him where he stood over an open drawer in the island. She shook her head. The man needed a pamphlet on respecting people's boundaries.

She glanced in the drawer. Oh. "It's a safe." With a palm plate lock. She looked up at him. "Did you try to open it?"

"I did. Watch." He placed his hand on the lock.

She held her breath.

It clicked open.

She grinned around a rush of air. How horrible would it be if he'd only been a Jackson Hawke look-alike? Yeah, it might have been rough explaining their presence in a billionaire's personal suite to the San Francisco Police Department.

And then he opened the safe and all thought left her head. She stared at a stack of cash easily equal to a quarter of a million dollars.

"Good gracious," she breathed clasping her hands behind her back to keep from touching. "Jackpot for you."

"And the cash isn't all that's in here." He pulled out a passport. "This will work for ID right?"

"Yes, it will."

"Good. I had Watkins contact my people in Las Vegas to let them know I lost my wallet. He reported I'd have replacement cards in the morning."

"Sounds like you're all set." She was right, he had done just fine without her. And she wasn't sure how she felt about that.

CHAPTER EIGHT

"Do NOT EVEN think of dodging out on me," he whispered in her ear. "I know that's what you're thinking."

"It's something to consider," she countered, for her benefit as well as his. "You did all this on your own. And you have people now that can help you."

"Which is why I need you now more than ever." He reached for something deep in the vault. "No need to sell my watch." He glanced down at her. "It does have sentimental value now. And I'm keeping the provenance papers on my person, just in case."

"Hopefully nothing like this will happen to you again."

"Hopefully. But I have the stab wound, too. So obviously stuff happens."

"I guess. But you can't live your life based on fear."

"I don't intend to, but there's such a thing as precaution. I'll carry the papers for a while. And I got this for you." He handed her a four-inch square jeweler's box with the name Sullivan's scrawled across the top. "For all your help."

Again her hands went behind her back. "I can't take that."

"Of course you can. I can afford it. I'm getting the sense that being rich comes naturally to me."

She sent him a droll stare. "Being rich and being a jerk are not the same thing."

"Ouch. I probably deserve that."

"No probably about it."

He ignored her. Instead he ran his hand down her arm and pulled her hand around to place the box in her palm. "I want to do this for you. You don't really understand what your help has meant to me. I'm bad at verbalizing it, and yeah, I've messed up a couple of times. I'm nobody to you, a stranger, yet without hesitation you stepped up to help me. Paying my way when you didn't have a job yourself and there were no apparent means of me being able to pay you back."

"There was the watch," she reminded him. "I didn't do anything anyone else wouldn't do." She set the box on the counter and edged away from Jackson until she stood across from him. "And you are paying me."

"You don't even understand how special you are. Let's be clear, I'm paying you for your knowledge and your connections. There's no way to fully pay you for your compassion, your patience, your faith in me. This," he said, pushing the box toward her, "is a mere token of what you deserve. My hope is you'll know my gratitude whenever you wear it. And because it seemed right, it's Cartier."

"Jackson." She stared at him helplessly. A Cartier? It was too much. Of course it was too much. She couldn't take it. Could she?

"It'll go to waste if you don't take it. I'll put it back in the safe and it'll stay there forever."

"No." Her hand moved protectively toward the package before her mind engaged and she curled her fingers closed. But the thought of his gift languishing, forever unopened, seemed wrong. "That would be a waste. You should return it or give it to someone else."

"It isn't meant for someone else. It wouldn't have the same value. It's for you, or no one."

"Oh, give it to me already." She held her hand out palm up.

His eyes lit up. Knowing better than to say anything, he grandly placed the package in her grasp.

"You are never to tell me how much this cost."

"Rest assured it was below ninety thousand."

Her gaze flew to his face. "It better be well, well below."

"You said not to tell you."

"Oh, my gosh. You are evil." Opening the box, she peaked inside and forgot to breathe. "Oh, my. Oh, JD." She lifted out a thin rope of diamonds set in white gold. "It's beautiful."

"Let me." He took it from her, wrapped it around her right wrist and connected the clasp. "It looks good on you."

"It would look good on a cat." She moved her arm, admiring the flash of the diamonds in the light. It really was too much.

"No going back." Again he seemed to read her mind. "And it'll go really good with the little black dress I got you to wear to dinner."

"What? Oh, no, nothing more." She was talking to his back. "I'm not taking anything else from you."

"Not even the shower?" he said over his shoulder. "Everything is laid out in your room."

"Everything? No. No. No." She dogged his heels. "Jackson, I'm serious. No more."

"I'll be in the game room when you're ready." He stopped and gave her a wink. "Our reservation is at eight." He turned into the game room leaving the door open behind him.

Grace dug in her heels determined not to chase after him any farther. She was an intelligent, competent woman, not a witless fool. He had no power over her. She'd wear an outfit of her own choosing.

Don't look, she warned herself as she entered her room and headed straight for the bathroom. *Pay no attention to the clothes on the bed.*

She might have made it, except the room itself stopped her. Done in white, gold and silver, the decor took her breath away. Decked out all in white, the bed appeared to float. Above it, large gold discs drew your attention up. A silver geometric design in the white carpet was repeated on the ceiling trim. In front of the window a modern sofa and chair in a soft silvery-gold invited her to come sit and relax.

No way was that possible with the clothes strewn across the bed.

Of course she looked.

And her feet betrayed her by taking her closer. Oh, my. He'd gone with the classic little black dress. It lay stretched across the white down-filled duvet. And he nailed her taste to a T. The dress had a boatneck with three horizontal strips of sheer mesh between the neckline and bustline and then again at the bottom of the slightly flared skirt ending with the mesh a few inches above the knee. The dress managed to be both sexy and conservative at the same time.

A pair of peep-toe heels sat on the floor, and a tiny black patent-leather purse rested next to the dress on the bed, along with a box and a bag from Victoria's Secret. For a woman who'd spent a good part of her life in uniform, the ensemble was irresistible.

Still, her resolve may have held except she kept remembering the exotic waterfall shower in Jackson's bathroom. The devious man had connected the two, making her feel she had to wear the dress to have use of his facilities. Heights had never bothered her, and oh, how she longed for a top-of-the-world experience.

And by gosh, she meant to claim it.

If that meant wearing the dress, she'd wear the dress and wear it well. Her legs were one of her best features.

Shouldering her duffel, she left the lovely room and headed straight for Jackson's bathroom. She closed and locked the door. Using the control panel on the outside of the shower she keyed in the number of shower panels—all—and temperature—hot—she wanted. Then she checked out the contents of the Victoria's Secret bag. Shampoo and conditioner and body wash and lotion, all in her favorite orange-blossom scent. Nodding, she stripped and stepped inside.

Water washed over her from all sides.

Heaven.

Well worth a small slice of her pride. For which he'd pay. Oh, yeah, she'd make him sweat for forcing the issue, for stealing kisses and ignoring the rules. And get dessert, as well. Sweet.

The shower grotto ran about seven feet long and five feet deep. About four feet of it was glass bricks topped by clear glass. The other three feet was a stone wall made up of smooth multisize rocks that curved around to create the side of the grotto. A stone bench followed the curve.

Water rained down on her, hot and steamy. She stood on smooth rocks while green fronds draped over the top and sides of the glass partition. The glass bricks came to her bust, safeguarding her modesty. Moving up to the glass, she looked down. The magnificent city spread out before her. In the distance the ocean reflected the clear blue sky and rippled with whitecaps. To her left the Golden Gate Bridge spanned the water to Oakland.

The intoxicating scent of the luxury soaps and shampoos only added to the experience. And made her hair and skin so soft. She never wanted to leave.

The only thing missing was a man to share it with.

Immediately a picture of Jackson sprang to mind. Even in their bare feet he'd tower over her. His broad shoulders would shield her from the brunt of the spray as he kissed her neck.

She turned so the water pulsed against her neck.

And lower. She imagined his hands smoothing away bubbles and his mouth on her body.

When her blood heated to the temperature of the water, he moved them away from the glass to the wide bench and his mouth and hands slid lower yet.

A knock at the door interrupted her fantasy. "Let me know if you need anything." Jackson called out. "The control panel inside the shower includes a phone feature. I plugged my new cell number in for you."

Her eyes popped open.

"I'm fine," she nearly snarled.

Resting on the edge of fulfillment, she glared at the door. What lousy timing. But apropos. She had no business fantasizing about him. Especially after the hands-off speech she gave him.

In retaliation for her traitorous imaginings, she flipped the hot water off first. An icy blast of water hit her heated body. She shivered and quickly keyed off the cold.

"Brr." Outside the grotto she reached for a towel from the stack on a nearby shelf. The thick terry cloth was warm to the touch and the size of a small blanket. She sighed as the warmth enveloped her.

Using a smaller towel—also warmed on the heating rack—she dried her hair and recalled Jackson's comment about being accustomed to wealth. Hmm. More likely it was too easy to give in to the seduction of luxury.

It was okay for him to immerse himself in this world. He belonged here, after all.

She, on the other hand, needed to take care she didn't succumb to the temptation of what couldn't be.

Jackson shot a tiger and swung across the ravine on a tree vine that dropped him short of the opposite side so he fell into a raging river. He caught a ride on a floating log and made it to the other side, but he had a strenuous climb ahead of him.

"I'm ready," Grace announced from the back of the room.

"Me, too. Ah, cagey croc." A crocodile morphed from a log to attack him. "Just one minute," he muttered to Grace as his avatar went after the croc.

"Take your time."

He caught sight of her as she rounded the front of the seats. That brief glance he got of her legs demanded a full-blown perusal. He sat back, ran his gaze from the pink-tipped toes peeking out of her black pumps, up smooth, shapely legs. The dress clung in all the right places, and yes, one of the sheer mesh strips perfectly framed a nice view of her cleavage. A pretty sheen highlighted her lips and eyes. And sweet merciful peaches, she'd mussed her black hair so she looked as if she'd just made love.

"Smokin'."

Amusement lit up her blue eyes. "Me? Or the game?"

"Kak." The game sounded, then announced, "Raptor, you have lost your first life."

"What?" Shifting back to the monitor he saw the croc had eaten him. "Pisser."

"Oh, did you die? Hate when that happens."

"Humph." He might be annoyed with her, except damn, smug never looked so good. "Do you play?"

"Sure. You want to go a round?"

"I'll take you on." The game allowed for a player to play individually or against one or more players. He nodded to the seat next to him, as he reached for the control pad. "Fair warning, I created the game."

"Not now, Jackson." Her hands went to her shapely hips. "We have reservations, remember? Plus, I'm hungry."

"Right. Right." He surged to his feet. "May I say how stunning you look?"

"No, you may not." She turned on her heels and headed out. "That would only be bragging. You coming?"

Following after her, Jackson slowly shook his head. For someone who looked so soft, the woman had no give in her.

The steak-house restaurant went against the futuristic theme of the hotel, going instead with rich, dark woods, marble counters and fine crystal. They offered their clients privacy and range-fed beef. He saw Grace seated and ordered them each a nice glass of wine.

She sipped the wine, savored it on her tongue, then set the glass down.

"Shall I order for you?" He offered.

"I'm a big girl. I can order for myself." She opened the menu and began to scan the choices.

His menu remained on the table. While killing time earlier, he'd checked out the menu online. Better to struggle over the words in his suite than at the restaurant. He hadn't used the top-of-the-line unit in the office. It was password protected, and his head wasn't spitting out any clues to what it might be.

He could not wait until his memory returned.

He'd bought a new tablet at one of the stores in the attached shopping mall. He applauded his decision to make the mall part of the hotel. Travelers often had unexpected needs. He'd certainly found it handy.

He'd enjoyed shopping for Grace. Enjoyed seeing her in the things he'd bought.

The lighting was muted to heighten the sense of privacy, yet as she moved her head to read the menu, light flickered from one spiked tress to the next. She bit her lip in indecision, and he sucked in a breath. White teeth dented plump flesh. It was all he could do to stay in his seat.

More as a distraction than out of need, he opened the menu.

He wouldn't act on his desire. He respected her too much.

Needed her too much, come to that. No matter what she believed.

The waiter appeared. Grace surprised Jackson by ordering the rib eye. He would have pegged her as a salad girl. She kept surprising him. He liked that.

When they were alone again, he sought for a topic of conversation. Easy. "Tell me what you found in my file."

She sat back on her bench seat, and clasped her hands on the table in front of her.

"You were a foster child. Mother died when you were five. Your father was unknown. There was a note in the file that a friend may have knowledge of who he was, but they were unable to locate the friend so no investigation was lodged."

"So I just went into the system?"

"Yes. From what I read, you were passed around to several homes, longest stay was two years. You were quiet and smart, kept to yourself for the most part, but suffered some bullying. A few incidents of cyber retaliation—quite creative, I must say—got you expelled. So you went to three different high schools."

"How many homes overall?"

"Nine."

"Over thirteen years?" It was a lot. He waited for emotions to come—loss, anger, resentment—but he felt nothing. Only the pounding in his head.

"Obviously you had a tough childhood. I can relate, to a degree. Being a military brat, I know how it feels to be uprooted and moved to a new home every few years. How hard it is to start over again and again. You learn to protect yourself."

"I don't remember any of it," he confessed.

She laid her hand over his. "That may be a good thing. With this background, if you lost your memory but remembered your childhood, you would have found it difficult to accept help, however honestly offered."

The food arrived, saving him from the need to reply. He'd also gone with the rib-eye steak and paired it with shrimp. His mouth watered at the aroma coming off the plate. He cut into the steak and found a warm, pink center. The meat melted in his mouth. Across the way he watched Grace savor her first bite and bit back a groan at the ecstatic expression on her face.

She caught him staring and a rush of red rose in her cheeks. She gave a sheepish smile. "It's good."

While they ate, she shared more of what she read in the file. He'd done a stint in juvenile detention for hacking into a school to change grades. Not just his own, apparently, but every student who took English with Mrs. Manning, who he stated was a frigid old crow who got her jollies putting down students to make herself feel superior.

"It sounds like I was doing the world a service. The report seems quite detailed."

"The FBI is thorough."

"So it appears. Can we move past my school years? At least skip to college."

"What makes you think you went to college?"

The question drew his attention away from the peekaboo view of her cleavage. "I didn't go to college?"

"You tell me," she prompted. "Do you remember anything about college?"

He gave it a beat, two. Nothing. "Quit playing with me, Grace."

"Okay. I'm just testing your memory. Despite the hacking incident, you earned a scholarship to Berkeley. You attended for two years. You created your first game there. And it was all uphill from there. As Doug said, you made your first million by the age of twenty-two and your first billion when you were twenty-seven. You own companies and/or properties in fifteen countries. Your net worth is in excess of ten billion. You were *Look* magazine's Man of the Year and *People*'s Sexiest Man Alive the year you made your first billion."

"Very thorough. No wife?"

"No wife. No kids. You were right about that. You're a bit of a player. You've been connected with actresses, models, high-powered executives. Mostly short-term. You have a couple of long-term relationships." She arched one black eyebrow. "If you consider a year long-term."

He lifted one shoulder in a half shrug. "Sounds like I have commitment issues. With my childhood and bank-roll, can you blame me?"

"We all have to grow up sometime. And love has to do with trust not your bank account."

"Says the woman who's never been married. How many long-term relationships have you had?" His life was an open book, or more precisely an open file, to her. Turn-about was fair play.

Her pretty lips pursed as she contemplated him. "Three," she finally answered. "If you consider a year long-term."

He laughed. "Gotcha."

"We're talking about you, not me."

"I'm sounding like a sad character. Properties all over the world but no home. Replaceable women. I hope I have good friends."

"I don't know about that, but I did an internet search, and you have a lot of influential acquaintances."

"That's reassuring." The sarcastic comment slipped out. He tried hard not to whine. But the whole situation tore at his patience.

"Sorry."

He shrugged. "Not your fault. Anything about the people I work with?"

"You have four people in your top echelon. Your legal counsel, Ryan Green. Financial advisor, Jethro Calder. And security executive, Clay Hoffman. The three of them go back to your foster days with you. Your associate Sierra Ross is a Harvard attorney. I've just started looking into them. I'll have more tomorrow."

"Good." He finished his wine and asked, "What about the stabbing? You haven't mentioned that."

"Are you sure you want to hear this tonight? We can go over it tomorrow, when you're more rested."

"I want to hear it now."

"Okay. Well, according to the report, you stated a woman you were dating went wacko when you refused to let her spend the night. Her name is Vanessa Miller. She began by throwing things at you, and when you tried to restrain her, she stabbed you with a piece of broken metal frame. Sometime during the altercation, you were able to activate a panic button. She slipped away while security was seeing to you."

"A real winner. I guess I can really pick them." Every word she spoke drilled a nail into his skull.

"Don't judge yourself too harshly." She gave him an out, sympathy strong in her voice. "Dating is a difficult prospect these days. I imagine it's even more so for a man in your position."

He imagined so, too. Truly, how could he know for certain if his date was into him or his money?

"Have the police apprehended her?"

"No. They suggested you beef up your security. Instead, you decided to take a vacation. You took your Harley and went off the grid. That was three weeks ago. Does any of this strike a chord with you?"

Pain streaked down his neck when he shook his head. "It's like hearing a story that happened to someone else.

But if the throbbing in my head is anything to go by, it's dead-on."

"Are you okay?" She leaned forward to study his eyes. "Do you want to head back to the room?"

A glare sent her back into her seat.

"I'm just saying I'm ready when you are."

"You need dessert," he insisted. He wouldn't be the reason her meal was cut short. She deserved this treat for all she'd done for him.

"I don't want dessert."

"All women want dessert. Order some anyway."

Blue eyes narrowed on him. "First of all, I'm not all women. Second, I couldn't even finish my steak. We can leave now."

"I'm fine. And I saw you drooling over the chocolate mousse cake when you were looking at the menu. You know you want some."

As if summoned, the waiter appeared. "May I get you anything else tonight?"

"The lady would like dessert." Jackson answered before Grace could send the man away.

Her eyes flashed with annoyance but she smiled at the waiter. "I'll take a piece of the chocolate mousse cake." She turned her saccharine sweet smile on Jackson. "To go, please."

Leave it to her to find a way around him. Fine with him. He'd been staying for her anyway. The waiter quickly returned with the boxed dessert and the bill. Jackson charged it to his room.

In the elevator on the way to the suite Grace dropped a bomb. "Here's something you need to know. A few years ago you started a foundation for displaced teenagers. They're having a big fund-raiser three days from now. You're scheduled to be there, and from all accounts it's something that's pretty important to you."

"I guess that starts our clock ticking then, doesn't it?" Hearing about his childhood, he was proud of the fact he'd also created a way to help. Which meant facing the world whether he had his memory back or not.

"I'll make sure you're ready," she promised.

He keyed them into the suite. Inside, a handful of pink message slips had been placed on the foyer table. He picked them up and waved them for her to see. "I hope you're right, because ready or not, the world has found us."

CHAPTER NINE

SHE TOOK THE pink message slips from him and returned them to the table. "These can wait until tomorrow. I'm ready for our game. Prepare to go down."

Over the past hour she'd seen how rehashing his past had aged him before her eyes. Pain etched lines around his eyes and a clenched jaw drew tendons tight in his neck. The world may be knocking on the door, but it could wait until tomorrow. Tonight he needed to relax. Whether he liked to admit it or not, he was still healing.

"Now, that's just crazy talk." The tension visibly drained from his shoulders. "Nobody beats the master." Without glancing at the messages he headed for the game room.

"I don't know." She trailed behind him, pretending she didn't notice the nice fit of his dress pants over his firm posterior. "The master is broken. I think I've got a shot."

He stopped suddenly and swung around. Her reflexes were excellent and she stopped short of running into him, but they were still nose to chin. The predatory light in his eyes rooted her to her spot. She could show no weakness.

"Your trash talk won't get to me. I'm not broken, I'm memory-challenged."

She groaned.

"Hey, my instincts and reflexes are as sharp as ever. I've got this."

"Yeah, you keep telling yourself that," she tossed back. He seemed to thrive on the competition. "Just know there will be no mercy when you start whining that you have a concussion." She slid past him, deliberately knocking his shoulder with hers. "I'm going to change. I want to be comfortable when I kick your butt."

"Hmm," he mused, "probably for the best. You'd only distract me in that getup."

"Nice try." She exaggerated the sway of her hips, smiled when she heard him groan. "Five minutes, Hawke. Don't go to sleep on me."

"Babe, I'll be warming up your seat."

In her room she wasted no time kicking off her heels and trading out the dress for jeans and a comfortable sweater. After pulling on a pair of soft socks, she strolled down the hall to claim her seat.

"You're a hoot, Hawke." With her hands on her hips, she stared down at the deep candleholder with three flames flickering merrily about. "This is how it's going to be?"

"I promised you a warm seat." He slouched in his seat, his hands on the control.

"Very funny." She moved the candleholder to the credenza where the reflection of the flames danced on the wall and then dropped down beside him. Scrolling through the avatars, she chose her favorite, a shaggy-haired redhead with more muscles than curves who went by Ruby.

The big screen was split into two separate viewing areas. In "Unleashed," the characters have been dropped in a remote part of the Amazon to be hunted as live prey. The player can save himself if he reaches civilization in the form of the Amazonia Resort and Conservation Range near the origination of the Amazon River in Peru. Many routes ended in dead ends or insurmountable dangers. If the hunters didn't get you, the environment probably would.

She and Jackson would be playing the same game but running their own course. They could well run into each other in a kill-or-be-killed scenario. They each started

with three lives and two weapons of their choice. She went
with a nine millimeter and a machete. Jackson had a fish-
ing knife and a crossbow. She noticed both were silent
weapons.

"Okay, here are the rules, we'll play nine levels."

"Nine." He muttered a curse under his breath. "That's
a tease."

"We're not going for a marathon here. I just explained
I have work yet to do tonight. So, whoever has the most
points at each level wins that level. Whoever wins the most
levels wins the game."

"No way. Speed is an element of the game. I don't want
to be twiddling my thumbs while you wander about col-
lecting points. Whoever finishes level nine first is the winner."

"Okay, you're on. First to finish nine wins." It wouldn't
change how she played. Rushing is what lost the game for
most players. "Man up, Hawke, we're wasting time. I have
searches running on your entourage. I want to do an initial
read-through tonight."

"I have my choice." He flicked his thumb and a tall wiry
kid, who looked a lot like Where's Waldo? minus the hat,
emerged from the shadows.

"Slippery Syd? You're kidding me. I thought for sure
you'd choose one of the muscle-bound behemoths."

"A common mistake many players make. This guy is
tough, smart and versatile."

She eyed his profile as he set up the game. "So you do
remember how to play."

He sent her a sidelong glance. "I was born knowing."

"Bragging does not equal skill." Squirming in her seat
she got set for the go. "I can promise I'll make you work
for it."

"Babe," he said, as the game started, "I won't break a
sweat."

"Honey, you're going to crash and burn."

At least she hoped so. He kept discounting his concussion, but she counted on it, both to slow down his reflexes and his cunning. She had skills—a girl had to do something to fill the long nights—but he was Jackson Hawke. Her bravado was all bluff.

This may not meet the definition of rest his doctor would recommend, but in her opinion it was better than letting him brood on what was missing in his head or on what he faced in returning to his life without his memories. Playing may require him to use his brain, but it wasn't the part that caused pain every time he had a thought that challenged the block in his head.

Playing relaxed and energized him. Winning would give him confidence to face his friends and associates. Not that she'd let him win. Her avatar slid past a coiled snake, snagged the knapsack that would garner her fifty points and hopefully some ammo and rappelled out of the pit.

She'd disciplined herself to use his real name earlier, for her benefit, but also for his. He needed to get used to hearing and reacting to the name. That's also why she'd switched to his last name to razz him about the game.

Out of the corner of her eyes she saw Slippery Syd taking on an anaconda in level three. Good luck, pal.

If she could get past the sleeping jaguar to get the first aid box on the other side of him, she'd have enough points to advance to level three, as well. One wrong move and she'd be back at the start of level two. She went up and then, by hopping from rock to rock, made it past the napping cat to snag her prize and move up in the game.

While the game reset her at level three, she shook her hands and flexed her fingers.

"Congratulations," Hawke taunted, "you're only half a level behind."

"A quarter level," she corrected. "And that can change in a heartbeat."

As she spoke, he missed his footing on a jump and landed in the river. Piranhas were on him in an instant and he lost his first life.

"Poor Slippery Syd. Now we're even again." Her level three started and she had a plan. There was antivenom on this level she may need later. She'd make for that before Hawke could get there and then advance straight to level four.

As the game went on, they continued to jab good-naturedly at each other. He combined quick wit and easy flirting to make her laugh. She kept striking at his ego, but it had little effect. Her barbs bounced off his thick hide.

No doubt she could distract him by responding to his flirtation. But uh-uh. They'd already been down that road, and she wasn't encouraging him. Her sanity and ability to do her job depended on her restraint.

But, oh, how he tempted her.

He was funny and quick. And he smelled good. Such a distraction.

He reached the ninth level right ahead of her and they were both down to their last lives. She decided to forgo any attempt at points or resources to go straight for the finish line.

She chanced a quick look at his screen and determined he'd made the same decision. Dang, he must have muscle memory for this game because he seemed to know right where to go.

Don't rush, she cautioned herself. *Sure and steady will win this game.*

Stealth was needed on this level as the hunters were close. At one point she saw Slippery Syd ahead of her on the path to the waterfall. If he continued straight, he'd get to the top faster than her, but he'd be exposed. She chose

to go farther down the river, under cover of the foliage.
The ascent was less severe but longer.

She had to hope he made a mistake.

Because she was watching him reach the waterfall sum-
mit, she walked right into a hunter. He had his sights on
Slippery Syd, but when she stumbled into the clearing,
he immediately turned his gun on her. Ruby dove to the
ground expecting the kill shot. Instead there was a thump.
She slowly lifted her head to see a bow bolt had taken out
the hunter. Slippery Syd had saved her.

And he'd also won. Except a shot rang out, echoing on
both screens. And Slippery Syd fell, his last life taken by
a hunter. Because he'd revealed his position to save her.

Next to her, Hawke cursed.

No fair. He'd had the win. She made a mad dash and
wild jump, windmilling her arms and legs in an attempt
to reach a ledge on the rock face of the waterfall. Ruby
missed and fell, suffering the same fate as Slippery Syd.

"You didn't have to do that." Jackson admonished her.

"I kind of did." She assured him. "The win is yours."

"You had more points."

"And you reached more levels faster."

"I'm not claiming a game I didn't win."

"Fine, we'll call it a draw." She tucked her control pad
into the sleeve on the front of her seat. "I look forward to
the rematch." His insistence said a lot about his sense of
fair play. One more thing to admire about the man, when
there were already so many.

"I'm ready if you are." His slumberous gaze rolled over
her, suggesting he was ready for more than a friendly
game.

She licked her lips, suddenly wishing he was just JD,
someone in her sphere she might actually have a chance
at having a relationship with, someone who might stick
around and build a home with her. From the number of

stamps in his passport, Jackson was a jet-setter. Out of her reach and out of her league.

"Oh, no." She rose and backed away. "Shall we say tomorrow night, same time, same place? Ah… I…uh, have some reading to do. I'll see you at breakfast."

Whipping around, she fled temptation.

Grace jerked awake. Something had broken her sleep, but what? She'd left her door ajar an inch or two in case Jackson called out. Was that what woke her? Was he in distress? She sat up.

Then she heard it, a hoarse call sounded from down the hall.

Jackson!

She pushed the covers aside and, not worrying over the fact she wore only an oversize white T-shirt and Tweety pajama shorts, she raced down the hall.

Another shout.

She reached his door and found it slightly open, but by less than an inch. Knocking, she called out, "Jackson? Are you okay?" She waited a beat and then repeated, "Jackson?"

A low moan leaked through the crack in the door. Waiting no longer, she knocked again and pushed into the room. A three-inch swath of light from the bathroom illuminated the room.

"Jackson." He sat up in bed, bare to the waist where the covers pooled around him. He slumped forward, head cradled in his hands. She sat on the edge of the bed and placed her hand on his blanket-covered thigh. She realized he was shaking. "What is it? Do you need a pain pill? Or a doctor?"

"No." And more emphatically, "No." But he didn't release his head. He cursed. "I'm fine. You can go back to bed."

"I don't think so. Tell me what's going on."

"Nothing. Stupid nightmare." He groaned through gritted teeth. "Maybe I will take a pain pill." He reached for a bottle on the nightstand.

"I'll get you some water." She went to the bathroom and returned with a glass of water. He took the pill and she placed the bottle and glass on the bedside table. "Tell me about the dream."

He rolled one bare shoulder. "It's gone. Go to bed. I'm sorry I woke you."

Ignoring him, she reclaimed her spot on the bed, curling one leg up under her. Men were such babies when it came to being in pain, physical or mental. And dealing with them was much the same as dealing with an infant. You knew something was wrong, but it was up to you to figure out what.

"I've heard it's good to talk about a nightmare right after. It's supposed to help release its grip on you."

He laid his hand on top of hers on his leg. Only then did she realize she'd been petting him. "Fair warning, if you don't leave my room, I'm going to get a grip on you."

Knowing he meant the sexual threat to chase her away, she dismissed the warning. The medicine would help, but he was in no shape to make love. "I'm not worried. I'm pretty sure I could knock you down with a feather."

"Babe," he drawled, his voice low and sleep-roughened, "it would be a mistake to equate down with out."

Okay. A shiver of awareness rolled down her spine.

"When you say gone, do you mean the dream is over and done or you don't remember the dream?"

"Does it matter?"

"No," she acknowledged, watching him closely. At least the shaking had eased under the hand he held to his thigh. Evidence the pain pill was working. Good. "I imagine it would be disconcerting either way."

"All I remember is being stabbed and then waking up to crushing pain in my head."

"Interesting. Perhaps it wasn't a dream, but a memory. Maybe that's why your head hurts. You said that happens when a memory tries to come through."

"Maybe."

Seriously? Could he be more stubborn? "Did you get a sense of the woman at all? I'd really like to have more than a driver's license picture to go on as we get ready to head to Las Vegas."

"I'm with you on that." He ran his thumb over the back of her hand. "One of the first things I want to do is go in and talk to the detectives, get an update on where things stand."

"Good idea." He'd already mentioned his desire for more information. But the heat in his eyes told her his mind had shifted away from the conversation to more basic functions. Maybe he wasn't as debilitated as she thought. Time to go.

"Ah, you look like you could sleep now." She tried to ease her hand away from him. "I'll just go."

His hand tightened on hers and she tensed. Then he released her and she thought for a moment she was free. But in one quick move he circled her waist in his big hands, pulled her up and over him and then turned so she was under him. In the space of a few seconds she went from sitting on the edge of the bed to blinking up at a man with wicked intentions on his mind.

"So, Delaney, where is this feather you were talking about?"

His molten gaze rolled over her curves, touching on the skin where her shirt had ridden up at the waist, lingered on the dark shadow of nipple under white cloth and traced the flow of shoulder into neck exposed by the stretch of her collar.

"Huh?" She dragged in a much-needed breath. Sweet potatoes and pecan pie, she was in so much trouble. If just the feel of his eyes set her on fire, what would happen when he actually used his hands on her?

She couldn't risk finding out.

"Okay," she said, wincing because it was more of an aroused croak, "I get the message." She wiggled to the right, gained a few inches of space. "I'll see you in the morning."

"Uh-uh." He dragged her back and hooked a leg over hers to keep her from squirming away. "I gave you your chance to get away." He buried his nose in her hair, and moaned softly. She almost echoed the sound. He smelled so good, of citrus and spice and a touch of woodiness that made her mouth water. "You didn't take it, which tells me you are right where you want to be."

"We really shouldn't do this." His hand landed on her stomach right where the shirt left her bare. Pure instinct had her arching into his touch. Still, she fought for reason. "I'm listening now. I'll go."

"Too late." The heat of his breath on her throat sent a shiver racing through her. "I take my threats seriously. Unlike you, since there is no feather to knock me away with. Ah, the things I could do to you with that feather."

To demonstrate he trailed his fingers, featherlight on the cotton of her shirt, up her torso, along the side of her breast, over her collarbone, where skin met skin and she lost her battle to contain a moan. When he reached her neck, he flipped his hand to use the back of his fingers to lift her chin to the perfect angle to receive his kiss.

Oh, so soft, his mouth settled on hers. She opened for him instantly. His tongue met hers in a dance of wonder. Not a passionate tango, but a slow waltz of turns and holds and the occasional lunge. She sighed and went boneless beneath him.

"Stop," she pleaded. No matter how good this felt, she worked for him. "You have to stop."

"Careful." He nipped her chin with his teeth. "Or I will."

"Oh, you're evil."

"Because I insist you admit you want me as much as I want you?" He fondled the lobe of her ear with his tongue. Her entire lower body tightened. "Or because I don't agree we need to keep business and personal separated? Yes, I'm a bad, bad man."

His hand went to the bottom of her T-shirt, and bunching it, he pushed the fabric upward. Looking her in the eye, he demanded, "Yes or no?"

She knew what she should say, what her dad had taught her, what her career and all her training warranted. Yet never had she yearned for a man more. His strength tempered by his vulnerability got to her on a visceral level. Arching into him as he drew her closer, her eyes fell shut on a sigh.

"Yes. Oh, please, yes."

She expected her clothes to disappear, for him to jump on her offer. And her. Which, oh yeah, she was more than ready for. Instead, he leaned down and soft lips opened over hers. His tongue sought hers and now they tangoed. He led with authority, a true aficionado who seduced with desire and demand. Senses dazzled, she followed every synchronized twist and slow, passionate pivot, sinking into the bedding and drawing him to her.

Her clothes did disappear somewhere along the line, and she reveled in his touch on her flesh. She fought past blankets to reach him, to rid him of whatever he wore, only to find smooth, unencumbered skin. Oh, my. Long and lean, he was beautiful, marred only by the nearly healed wound on his abdomen. Her fingers went to the scar.

"Learning the details of what happened probably sparked your nightmare. Won't you talk to me?"

He was silent for a beat then he sighed. "I can't recall much, mostly emotions—confusion, anger, shock. It gives me a massive headache to think about it," he stated dismissively. His fingers closed over hers, pulling her hand away from the scar. "Does it offend you?"

Surprised by the question, she blinked up at him. In the shifting of his gaze she saw the geek lurking behind the stud. "No." She squeezed his hand and then freed herself to caress the scar with her thumb. "I was a master-at-arms in the navy. I've seen much worse. But that doesn't mean it's not still raw. It won't hurt you to make love?"

He grinned, confidence fully restored. "Babe, my head bothers me more than that little cut. Fortunately, you gave me a pain pill. I'm primed and ready to go, and I can't think of a better way than in your arms. Such a sweet armful. I may have no memory, but I know spectacular when I'm curled up next to her in bed."

Ah, so smooth and yet her heart still melted.

"Still wishing I had a feather, though."

"Would you forget the feather?"

"Not going to happen," he assured her. "I'll just have to improvise some more." He continued to tease her, drawing a single finger between the valley of her breasts and then to a peak, where the light touch tormented her into arching into his touch, demanding more.

Instead he shifted his attention, moving his imaginary feather lower.

"Stop," she said around a giggle, grabbing his hand at her waist. "Well, we've learned you aren't inhibited."

"I'd say not, as I consider feather play to be quite tame."

Have mercy. It made the mind boggle at what he would find to be kinky.

He nuzzled her neck, using his tongue to dampen her skin, and then blew gently in a new form of sensual teasing. The shift from the heat of his mouth to the cool of his breath brought goose bumps to her skin and the desire to get closer. She bowed her neck, giving him better access.

"And you are quite skilled."

She felt him grin against her skin. "So happy you're pleased."

"Oh, I am. But I have to wonder." She moved her hands around from his back and trailed her thumbs slowly, oh, so slow, down his sides. "Are you ticklish?"

"Let's not find out." He bucked up, grabbed her hands in both of his, anchored them to the bed and took her mouth again, slowly lowering himself onto her, linking them in the ultimate dance. Where thought surrendered to sensation and bodies communicated without words.

No longer teasing, he twirled her between moments of utter tenderness, when she felt cherished and special, to sweeps of passionate intensity that drew the wanton out of her. Oh, yeah, she liked that, liked demanding he please her, liked hearing his groans when she pleased him.

Touch for touch, kiss for kiss, her heart raced to the beat of his as pleasure spiraled past excitement and joy to euphoria. And she clung to him as they both plunged into bliss.

Grace curled up in Jackson's arms. Her life had changed forever. She loved him. Crazy, of course. She was a former public servant and he was a billionaire. She wanted to put down roots and he lived in hotels. She craved order and he created games that thrived on chaos.

There was no future for them. She accepted that, but she could have now. She could have his back and make sure he got the rest he needed to heal. And grab every moment possible with him before he got his memory back and didn't need her anymore.

She had her head on straight when she met Jackson in the first-floor restaurant for breakfast. She admired the

French-bistro vibe as she ordered fresh fruit and a crois-
sant. Between bites of strawberries and buttery, flaky
bread she filled him in on his senior staff.

"They're quite an impressive bunch." He flipped
through the reports she'd given him. He still couldn't read
well, but there were pictures so he could put faces to names.

"You're pretty impressive, too." She handed him her
last packet, a file on him he could read when his vision
improved. "You have to remember you're not working at
your normal speed. When I had a concussion, it took me
four weeks to feel right again. I know people where it
took months."

"So you keep saying."

"Because you're expecting too much from yourself too
soon."

He pushed his plate of unfinished eggs aside. "I don't
have a choice, do I? Two days from now I have to be back
in Las Vegas to face a room full of people as a man I have
no idea how to portray."

"Actually, sooner than that." She faced the front of the
restaurant and over his shoulder she saw two men approaching. "Bogies at six o'clock. Jethro Calder and Clay
Hoffman are headed this way. That's your financial advisor and your head of security."

Both men were tall, dark and handsome. Not exactly a
cliché she could rattle off to Jackson. The executives were
about the same height—easily six feet, maybe an inch
or two over—and wore expensive business suits. Jethro
Calder wore navy blue with a pin-striped tie. He had short
black hair and his picture failed to show the depth of his
blue eyes. Clay Hoffman carried more weight, in the form
of muscle mass, and wore black on black with no tie. His
hair and eyes were dark chocolate-brown.

Both were larger-than-life characters, confident, asser-
tive, intimidating. And Jackson put them both to shame.

"Maybe we should have responded to those message slips, after all."

"And said what? Jackson can't come to the phone right now because he doesn't remember who you are?" He chugged a sip of coffee as if it was a bracing shot of fine whiskey. "I'll handle this."

"Jackson," Jethro Calder greeted him as the two men arrived at the table. "You're a hard man to get a hold of." He felt comfortable enough with the boss to pull out a chair and join them at the table for four.

Clay was more direct as he took his seat. "What the hell, Hawke? You can't go off the grid without letting me know. I've had men looking for you for the past two days." His dark gaze narrowed in on Jackson's jaw. "Is that a bruise?"

"I knew this trip was a bad idea," Jethro tossed in. He grasped Jackson's chin to turn his head for a better view of the bruise. "What happened to you?"

Jackson pulled away and held up a staying hand. "First of all, Grace, these Neanderthals work for me. Jethro Calder and Clay Hoffman, this is Grace Delaney."

Two assessing gazes landed on her.

"Ma'am." Clay nodded at her, his dark eyes already having cataloged everything about her, from her shoe size to her short crop of hair. "How long have you and Jackson been friends?"

"Not long," she assured him. She'd only brought her wallet downstairs. She pulled out an old business card, flipped it over and wrote her social security number on it before calmly handing it to him.

"You don't have to do that, Grace," Jackson's protest had a bite to it. He nailed his men with an intent stare. "She's with me. That's all you need to know."

"I have nothing to hide," she soothed him. "He'll check me out anyway. This just makes it easier for everyone."

"Sheriff of Woodpark?" Clay mused.

"Ex-sheriff, actually. My term ended on the thirty-first."

"Hmm." He tucked her card into his pocket as he turned back to Jackson. "Tell us about the bruise."

Jackson simply lifted one dark eyebrow.

The security exec didn't back down. He rolled his impressive shoulders and pinned Jackson to his chair with an intense stare. "Protecting you is my job. I can't do that when you take off on your own. I need to know what happened to determine if you need additional medical care."

"He does," Grace said.

"I don't." Jackson sent her an admonishing glare.

The two men looked back and forth between them.

"Which is it?" Jethro asked.

"He has a severe concussion. And he left the hospital against the doctor's recommendation." Her gaze never left Jackson's during her revelation so she saw the flash of hurt quickly replaced by irritation.

"You're supposed to be on my side."

"Always." She made it a promise. "Which is why your health comes first. He's handling himself." She flicked her gaze to Clay. "But he should definitely see his physician when he returns to Las Vegas."

"Maybe you need to start from the beginning." Clay directed the comment to his boss.

Jackson sighed. Showing his aggravation, he crossed his arms over his chest. "As she said, I have a concussion. Our best bet is someone ran me off the road and stole my wallet and my motorcycle. I don't remember much about the incident."

Grace hid her surprise. She hadn't expected him to be so forthcoming.

"An officer took me to the sheriff's office, where I met Grace. She's been an angel."

He ran a finger over the back of her hand on the table. Dang the man. The deliberate gesture was obviously meant to solidify the impression they were a couple. She narrowed her eyes in a what-the-heck look and he moved his head in a sideways just-go-with-it gesture. She didn't like where this was going, but she left her hand where it was.

"She went with me to the hospital and then drove me to Santa Rosa for more tests. And, no, I didn't want to stay overnight for a pounding head. You know how I am about hospitals."

"Concussions can be dangerous."

Uh-huh. Grace applauded Clay's warning. Vindicated at last. Perhaps his associate could actually get Jackson back to the doctor. She'd caught on to his game. He was giving them just enough truth to placate them without revealing the true extent of his injuries.

"Believe me, Grace isn't letting me overexert myself."

"Does the sheriff's department have any leads on your motorcycle?" Jethro asked.

"Not as of yesterday." Graced fielded the question. "It would be helpful if someone could forward the license and vehicle identification numbers to the sheriff's office. Jackson was a little slim on details."

"A concussion can mess with short-term memory." Clay played right into Jackson's version of events.

"What brings you two here?" Jackson changed the subject. "Any fires I need to know about?"

"No. We have things covered," Jethro assured him. "Development is eager to have your input on the new game, but mostly we were concerned at not hearing from you for nearly a week. Especially after recent events."

"So they haven't apprehended Vanessa yet?"

Jethro glanced at Grace before answering. "No."

Jackson gave a grim nod. "Sorry to give you a scare. I guess with this head thing I forgot it had been so long since I checked in."

"Yeah." Clay leaned back in his chair. "I can see you've

been distracted. We have the corporate jet. Do you want to catch a ride with us back to Las Vegas?"

"No."

"Jackson." Both men spoke at the same time.

He shrugged. "I want another day with Grace."

"I think we should go," Grace inserted. Jackson scowled, but she nodded subtly. "Your people need you. It's time for us to join the real world. It had to happen sometime." Grr. She turned her hand over and threaded their fingers together. "We'll still be together."

His fingers tightened on hers. "You heard the lady. I guess we're headed home to Las Vegas."

CHAPTER TEN

GRACE HIGHLY RECOMMENDED flying by private luxury jet. The one they traveled on had a seating area—better than the normal first class—a living room area, with a big-screen TV and wet bar, and a bedroom area. Both bathrooms had small showers. The appointments were luxurious, the seating comfortable.

The flight took less than two hours. And then she and the three men were in a limousine headed for the Las Vegas Pinnacle Hotel, the showpiece of the Pinnacle properties.

Her jaw dropped as she walked hand in hand through the lobby with Jackson. Just like San Francisco the hotel followed the theme of the game, but to a much larger degree. She felt as if she'd walked into a city wrestled from the desolation of the apocalypse and jazzed up as only Vegas could do.

"This is too cool." Jackson leaned down to whisper in her ear. "I want to shake these guys and explore."

Jethro and Clay walked ahead of them, leading them to the elevators.

"I want to shake these guys and talk." She held up their joined hands and nodded to them significantly. They hadn't been alone since breakfast. His executives joined them in the suite while they packed up and then they'd been on the road.

"We will," he assured her.

Clay walked past the bank of hotel elevators, turned

right and pushed through a door marked Private. Down a short hall was a bank of service elevators. He stopped in front of the first one and used a keycard to activate the call button.

"I called ahead and requested a new set of keys for you. Since you lost your wallet, we recoded all the locks just to be on the safe side. Sierra will have yours upstairs." The elevator arrived and he used the keycard again to access the penthouse level.

"So Jackson has a secret elevator?" Grace asked. "How covert."

Clay looked down his nose at her. "It's a matter of security."

"Because of the woman who stabbed him?"

He lifted a dark eyebrow, showing his surprise that Jackson had confided in her about the attack. "She's a good example of why precautions are necessary."

"Ms. Delaney," Jethro cut in. "Once we reach the penthouse, Jackson's associate will escort you to your room. We have to catch him up on business matters."

"She'll be staying with me," Jackson declared.

Shock rolled across Jethro's face. He sent a questioning glance Clay's way. Trained to show no emotion, Clay masked his reaction. Their surprise was quite telling. Obviously Jackson didn't normally allow his companions to stay with him in his suite. He really did hold himself apart.

No wonder the two men didn't know what to make of her. She didn't fit in his world and he wasn't acting himself. Tension tightened through her shoulders. All her arguments against putting on a false romantic front just took a hit. If they wanted to avoid suspicion, Jackson's pretense of a relationship was their best bet.

People did crazy things when they were in love. His uncharacteristic behavior would make his staff all the more suspicious of her, which gave them the added bonus of switching their focus from Jackson to her.

Uh-huh. Just because it was a brilliant strategy didn't mean she'd let him get away with launching it without talking to her first.

The hotel suite matched the owner's suite in San Francisco. She imagined in everyday life the familiarity gave Jackson a false sense of homecoming. In these unusual circumstances, it helped with his charade.

She led the way into the living room and a spectacular view of the Las Vegas strip opened up before her. The hotel rooms resembled each other, but the views were singular. No pretending you were in the same place when the view was on display.

Then again, a push of a button could fix that problem.

A slim blonde in a chic navy dress and an older gentleman, round in the middle and bald on top, waited in the living room. Jethro took care of introductions.

"Grace, this is Sierra Ross, Jackson's personal assistant. And Dr. Wilcox, his personal physician. Sierra, Doctor, this is Jackson's new friend, Grace Delaney."

"Hello." To cover Jackson's sudden tension, Grace broke away to shake hands. "Dr. Wilcox, I'm glad to see you, though I'm sure you know Jackson isn't."

The man laughed and patted her hand before releasing it. "Oh, I'm aware I'm not his favorite person. A necessary evil at best. But he sends me a stellar bottle of brandy for Christmas every year, so it's a trade-off."

"Don't be upset, Jackson." Sierra brought her brooding boss into the conversation. "Clay mentioned you had a concussion and that Grace recommended you see Dr. Wilcox. I thought it best to bring him here."

"It's fine." Jackson strolled forward and held out his hand. "Thank you for coming, Doc. Do you mind if we get this over with?"

"No problem." The doctor patted his arm after shaking hands. "Shall we go to your room?"

"That works." Jackson came to her. "You'll be all right on your own?" He kissed her on the temple. Up close his displeasure seared her. He whispered, "When I'm done, we need to talk."

"Yes, we do." She lovingly ran her hand down his chest while talking through gritted teeth. "Do yourself a favor, be frank with the doctor. You might be surprised at how he can help you."

"Do you want to come with me?"

"No. You're a big boy. And I agree with your first instinct. These guys would find it odd if I joined you. It's obvious you don't let women get too close."

"Yeah, well, the last one I dated stabbed me. And come to think of it, you're probably armed."

She didn't respond and his eyes went wide.

"You are armed, aren't you?"

"Shh. Not at this moment. But yes, I own a gun. If your man hasn't confiscated it."

"I should have known." Anxiety clouded his gaze. "I'm supposed to be a genius, and it doesn't occur to me that a woman who is ex-military, ex-sheriff would carry a gun."

"It's the concussion." She brushed the hair from his eyes, watched heat push back the anxiety. "Talk to the doctor. Let him help you."

He sighed. "Okay. But it's going to cost you." And he kissed her. In front of everyone. His mouth covered hers in a soft claiming. It lasted only a moment. A hot, sensual moment that stole her breath and had her hooking an arm around his neck to get closer, to extend the caress that ended way too soon.

No, the kiss didn't last long, but the power of it reached all the way to her tingling toes. She slowly opened her eyes to find him smiling down at her.

"These guys are smart. It has to look real to fool them."

Grace sank back on her heels. "Oh, your strategy is working. All too well." Best she remember it was all for show. "Go away now."

He left with the doctor and she found herself alone with his cohorts. Pretending a confidence she only half felt, she chose a chair and sat.

"Would you care for some coffee?" Sierra rose from the futuristic sofa as she made her way to the bar where a carafe and cups were situated. "I must say I've never seen Jackson so attentive."

Before Grace could respond to the leading comment, the suite door opened and a man walked in. Sweet merciful angels, he was gorgeous. Of mixed heritage, he had light brown skin and dreamy gold eyes. He wore his black hair skull close.

"Sorry I'm late." He stopped in front of her. "You must be Grace."

His eyes weren't so dreamy now. They raked over her, assessing every little detail. Jackson's chief counsel made no secret he questioned her presence here.

"And you must be Ryan. Nice to meet you."

"Really? Has Jackson told you a lot about me?" He spread his arms wide, asking, "About us? We can't say the same about you."

"Oh. Well, our relationship is still very new." She gave a half shrug. "Don't blame him. He's not totally himself at the moment."

"Exactly." Jethro jumped on her response. "So you can understand our concern that he's taken up with a stranger."

"I would think you'd be happy he had someone to help him in a moment of dire need. Or is your concern only of a professional nature? Is Jackson simply your boss, or do any of you look on him as a friend?"

The room bristled with hostility.

Clay surged to his feet. "We've been a team for ten years. You have no right to question our loyalty to him."

She relaxed as the others nodded, confirming his impassioned declaration. "Good. Then we all have Jackson's best interests at heart."

"Do we?"

"Ryan, gentlemen, why don't you all have a seat?" Sierra suggested as she poured two cups of coffee—one black, one with two sugars. "And Grace can tell us more about herself."

The men sat, all of them perching on the edge of their chosen seat. All focused their attention on her.

Great. She'd always longed to have the undivided attention of three of the most powerful men in corporate America.

Not.

Yet here she was. Nothing for her to do but bluster her way through it.

"You mean in addition to what you've all read in the report Clay had done before we ever touched ground in Las Vegas?" She met each person's gaze straight on. She had nothing to hide. The secrets were Jackson's, not hers. "I think you all have a fair idea of who I am."

Sierra joined them in the living area. She handed one cup of coffee to Ryan and kept the other.

"You grew up a navy brat. Speak four foreign languages—French, German, Italian and Japanese."

"Are they really foreign if you live there?" she asked rhetorically.

"Joined the navy at the age of seventeen with your father's permission. Your military record is clean. You received several commendations and were accelerating well through the ranks until you quit to care for your ailing father, a retired Senior Chief Petty Officer." Jethro ran through her history as if reading a list. Probably because he had. "Finished your father's term as sheriff in Woodpark when he passed. Ran for sheriff yourself but lost."

"Why is that, Grace?" Clay demanded. "What did you do to upset the good citizens of Woodpark?"

Being it was a question she'd asked herself more than once, the query threw Grace as her confidence took a hit. He knew right where to strike to make her question herself. But she quickly regrouped. She'd done her best for the people of Woodpark. It wasn't her skills that had been in question.

Now she inhaled a deep breath, fought back her insecurities and projected a calm she didn't feel to attempt to put them at ease.

"I did my job." The point wasn't to sell herself to them, but to let them know she wasn't a threat to Jackson. She crossed her legs. "But that's not what you really care about is it? What you really want to know is what my intentions are regarding your boss. The answer is I have none."

"None." Ryan infused the word with skepticism.

"None," she confirmed. She ran a finger down the crease in her jeans. "Look, we met under unusual circumstances, which caused us to bond quickly. At first I didn't know who he really was. He needed help and I was happy to put Woodpark in my rearview mirror. Bottom line, we all agree he's not his usual self. I don't expect our relationship to last past his full recovery. But it's not every day a girl gets romanced by a billionaire. I'm just enjoying the time we have together."

She knew immediately it was the right note to strike. The men looked at each other and relaxed back in their seats.

"He has a lot of money." Jethro stated the obvious.

"He does." She left it at that. She had no designs on Jackson's money, but the more she tried to convince this group of that fact, the less credible she'd sound.

"A lot of women lose sight of the man for the money." Clay observed.

"I knew the man first, his money doesn't interest me. But the trappings are fun. I've never flown in a private jet before."

"So we all agree this will be a short-lived affair."

"No." A deep voice stated from the archway near the foyer. Jackson stood there. "We are not in agreement. My relationship with Grace is none of your business. I'll thank you all to stay out of it."

"Jackson," Sierra sought to appease him, saying, "we're only looking out for you."

By the jut of his chin she'd failed. "I don't need you to look out for me. Grace is the last person I, or you, need to worry about. My money is safe from her. Grace." He held out his hand to her, a demand to join him.

She made her way to his side, took his hand. "Don't overreact," she warned him.

"I won't let them intimidate you."

"I can handle myself. These are the people you rely on daily, who will be here for you long after I'm gone from your life."

"You're the one I know. The one who is here for me now. I won't let them hurt you."

"They haven't." Only he had the power to do that.

But that was her problem.

The fact she loved him changed nothing. Yes, having him take her side reinforced that feeling, but as far as this group was concerned their relationship didn't go beyond a fun time. Couldn't go beyond that. She *was* enjoying their time together, and that was all there could ever be between them.

"Hmm." His gaze flicked to his associates, skepticism clear in the green depths. Had he heard more than she thought? A hand in the small of her back urged her through the archway. "Let's go."

"Jackson," Ryan hailed him. "Are you leaving? I wanted to get with you."

"Later. I need to take my lady shopping."

Shopping? Grace hid an inner grimace. She just got this crew on her side and he probably wiped all her hard work out with that one statement. Not to mention, shopping for what?

"I'm not letting you buy me another thing," she muttered for his ears only.

On the other side of him Ryan said, "I thought you'd want to catch up on what we've done while you've been gone."

"Jethro indicated everything was under control." Jackson threaded his fingers through hers. "After what I overheard, I need to spend the next few hours showing Grace I want her here." Jackson released Grace to walk over and hand Sierra his phone. "I lost my old phone in the accident. Can you update all my contacts and then send me the itinerary for the foundation gala?"

"Uh, sure." Sierra looked shell-shocked. As did the men, to a lesser degree.

Jackson came back and reclaimed her hand. As he led her through the archway, he tossed a final comment over his shoulder. "Grace's number is in there. If anyone needs me they can call her number."

Fury fueled Jackson's pace into the elevator and then to the front desk.

"Good afternoon, sir." A young man dressed in the dark blue-and-black hotel colors greeted him.

"Do you know who I am?" Jackson demanded.

The young man's eyes widened as if he'd been presented

with a sudden pop quiz. He cleared his throat. "Of course, Mr. Hawke. It's good to have you back with us."

Jackson nodded. "I'd like two keys to the penthouse suite." He drew Grace forward. "This is my guest, Grace Delaney. She is to be treated with respect. Anything she asks for is to be charged to me."

"Of course. Welcome, Ms. Delaney."

"Thank you." Next to Jackson, Grace tensed. She twisted her hand in his seeking freedom.

He held on. He always held on.

"You need to calm down," she murmured softly when the clerk looked away to deal with the keys.

"I'm fine." He seethed with indignation on her behalf. She'd done nothing but help him and those self-satisfied blowhards upstairs treated her like a money-grubbing groupie.

"No, I'm fine," she argued. "*You* are overreacting."

"Don't tell me how to feel." Pain spiked as the high emotions sent the blood pounding through his head. He didn't care. Bring on the hurt. He wouldn't allow Grace to be disrespected. His so-called entourage better get behind the notion real quick or they'd be looking for new jobs real soon.

"Here you go, Mr. Hawke. Is there anything more I can help you with?"

"Thank you, no." With keys in one hand, her hand in the other, he headed back to the elevator and the shops down below but changed his mind halfway there and went for the front door instead. He'd had enough of this fishbowl.

A valet immediately appeared. "Hello, do you have a ticket?"

"No." But Jackson automatically patted his pocket, which reminded him he held the keys. He dropped one in his pocket and handed the other to Grace. "Just bring something around," he said.

"Excuse me, sir," The valet, a man in his late twenties with sideburns and a goatee, protested. "You need a ticket. Or would you like a taxi?"

Great. Just when he counted on his identity to work for him, he gets the one valet who doesn't know who he is.

"Mr. Hawke." The concierge bustled up. His name tag read R. Schultz. "I have this, Pete. What can we do for you, sir?"

Finally. "I have vehicles here, right?"

"Yes, sir." The robust man took the question in stride. "You have six vehicles housed here in a private section of the garage."

Six? Jackson figured he had something besides a motorcycle, but six? What did he do with six vehicles? Never mind, he didn't even want to think about that.

He nodded for the concierge's benefit. "Have something brought around, would you?"

"No preference, sir? Perhaps the Ferrari or the Hummer?"

"Something simple, please," Grace spoke up. "Mr. Hawke isn't feeling himself this afternoon."

Jackson's neck twitched. He dropped Grace's hand. He didn't care to have his condition advertised to the world. Something he'd let her know once they were alone.

"Of course." Schultz waved Pete over and passed on the request. "Your car will be right here. I hope you feel better soon, sir."

"Thank you." Jackson gave him a generous tip. And when Pete pulled up in a sporty BMW, Jackson tipped him well and prepared to slide behind the wheel.

"Jackson."

Hearing his name, he paused to see Jethro striding toward him. His associate extended a slim leather wallet toward him. "If you're shopping, you'll need these. Sierra had your cards replaced."

Jackson accepted the wallet, nodded and slipped into the driver's seat. He wasted no time putting the car in gear and pulling away from the hotel.

"There was no need to mention my health." He gritted out between clenched teeth as he pulled out on Las Vegas Boulevard known the world over as The Strip.

"I wouldn't have had to if you hadn't looked like you were about to explode." She adjusted the seat belt over her middle. She stared straight out the windshield, her profile perfectly capturing her mood with the proud jut of her chin.

"Someone needs to be upset over how you were being treated. I won't have them disrespecting you."

That brought her head around along with the full force of her ire. "I told you I can handle myself. It may not have looked like it back there, but I won that skirmish, and you wiped it all out with your stupid comment about going shopping."

"Don't call me stupid. I'm a genius, after all." Being a billionaire was hard work, so many elements to juggle. The money was good, but sometimes he wished he could go back to being JD.

"I didn't call you stupid. I said your comment was stupid. There's a difference."

"Not from where I'm sitting." He inched the car along, overshadowed by the marble columns of Caesar's Palace on one side and the Eiffel Tower on the other. "I heard them all but call you a gold digger." He gave her a brief glance. "You're important to me. They're not."

"Yes, they are," she said with exquisite gentleness. "You just don't remember them right now. And yes, they want to protect you. Were they out of line? A little. Was I insulted? No." She waved her hand at him saying, "Billionaire," and then at herself continuing, "Peon. What are they supposed to think?"

"That I can take care of myself. That I have the intelligence to choose a companion I can trust."

There was a beat of silence as she did him the courtesy of not mentioning the woman who stabbed him.

"Okay," he conceded, "so they may have a small reason for concern."

She laughed, a soft chuckle that invited him to join in the fun. "See, you are a smart man. Please tell me we aren't really going shopping."

"Yes, we are. Unless you have a ball gown tucked away in that duffel bag of yours."

"Uh, no." He felt her studying his profile. "Why would I need a ball gown? Because of the gala? I'm okay. I have the black dress you bought."

"You can't go in the black dress."

"Why not? It's a beautiful dress."

"And you looked beautiful in it. But didn't you see the posters at the hotel? They showed everyone dressed up in monkey suits and long gowns. You might ordinarily get away with wearing the black dress, but you'll be my date so you'll have to wear something spectacular."

"Humph." She settled back in her seat. "The things I do for you. Well, you're not buying it."

"Actually, I am." She could argue all she liked, he was firm on this.

She huffed. "We're not going through this again."

"Nope. Because as you said, you're doing this for me. That means I pay."

"I can afford my own clothes."

"I can afford it more." He sent her a quick, emphatic glance. "Resign yourself, Grace. I'm not letting you pay for anything more while you're helping me. At the very least I can cover your costs."

She stared out her window, tapping on her armrest. "I could point out your friends would then be right about me."

"Come on, Grace, don't do that." He rolled his neck, working on the tension building there.

"Instead I'll ask, why is it so important to you?"

He spotted a billboard advertising a mall in Caesar's and maneuvered a U-turn while he considered how to answer her. Instinctively he sought to protect himself, then he remembered she'd been his advocate before he knew he needed help. She was his one constant since losing his memory.

Bottom line, he trusted her.

He waited to answer until after he left the car with the valet and led her inside the mall.

"I have so little control over anything right now. My memory is shot. I'm supposed to be a genius, yet I feel as though it takes forever to process anything."

She looked ready to protest but he'd heard her argument enough times to know what she'd say. So he shook his head and cut her off. "I know it's the concussion, but it's still my reality."

"I know it's tough." She stopped, forcing him to come to a halt, forcing him to face her. The compassion in her blue eyes almost undid him. "Time will help. It's really only been a few days."

"On top of everything else, I'm a billionaire and I live in a hotel. There's nowhere I can go, nothing I can do where I'm not recognized. And if that's not enough, I have an entourage standing by to critique my every move."

Invading his space, she cupped his face in her hands and read him. He stood still under her intense regard, but it took an effort. Finally she nodded and surprised him by brushing her soft lips across his cheek. He almost missed what she said next. "You need to give yourself a break."

She stepped back and swiped at his cheek where her lips had rested. "I'm sorry. I shouldn't have done that."

Suddenly he fought a minor battle between pulling his

head away to keep her from brushing the kiss away and the desire to lean into her touch. "You can put your lips on me anytime you want. The professional standard is yours, not mine."

"And it's a good standard." With her hands on her hips, she seemed to waver, then set her chin. "Back to my point. You need to relax, not take everything so seriously. Remember, you chose not to tell anyone about your memory loss. If you want to change your mind, you can. People would understand."

"No." Because she'd opened the door to it, he leaned down and kissed her silky cheek, inhaling her clean, orange-blossom scent. The tension coiled deep in him eased a little more, allowing him to breathe freely. He linked his fingers with hers and started walking again. "The only thing worse than being stared at would be being stared at with pity."

"Compassion and empathy are not pity."

"Yes, they are."

"You could tell your royal guard. Much of their protective posturing was because they care about you."

"Maybe," he conceded. "They seem decent enough. But I'm still peeved at them for their treatment of you." He spied a boutique with evening wear in the window and veered in that direction. "I'd have to know them better first."

"You really don't need to worry over every little move, every little detail. Letting your staff believe we're involved was a brilliant move. What they don't attribute to your concussion, they'll attribute to your infatuation."

"Ah, about that—"

"Don't pretend you came up with the idea on the spur of the moment. You had it planned out before Clay and Jethro ever showed up."

He shrugged. He should have known she'd figure it out.

"A romance allows us easy access to each other without anyone questioning it."

"You could have discussed it with me. Whoa." Grace caught sight of their destination, of bold colors and daring necklines of the dresses in the window and dug in her heels. "Not this place. It looks expensive. Let's try one of the department stores."

He tugged her forward. "I like this place. I can afford expensive."

"But I probably won't have occasion to wear the dress again. Just because you can afford expensive doesn't mean you should waste your money."

"Nothing spent on you is wasted." He pointed to a dress in the window. "The red would look stunning on you."

She bit her bottom lip as she studied the gown, her gaze slowly turning wistful.

"Let's see if they have your size." He drew her inside.

The place smelled nice, like a beautiful woman. It was well lit and spacious. Most of the merchandise was modeled by mannequins for a full three-dimensional effect. An older woman in a black suit came forward to greet them. She displayed no sign of recognizing him and he relaxed.

"Hello, I'm Eileen. What type of occasion are you shopping for?" she asked.

"We'll be attending the Hawke Foundation Gala for Displaced Youth," Grace responded.

"Oh, yes." Eileen nodded. "We've sold several gowns to people attending. It sounds like it'll be a lovely event. And for such a worthwhile cause. Wait, that's tomorrow." Her eyes went wide, but she smiled. "That just means we work harder."

"We want to see the red dress in the window." Jackson got down to business.

"I don't know, Jackson," Grace vacillated, "it's so extravagant. I don't think I could pull it off."

"My dear," Eileen enthused, "the dress would be striking with your dark hair and light skin. It just came in today, and I know it won't last long."

"Try it on," he urged Grace. The longing in her eyes told him what she wanted better than her mouth did.

There she went, chewing her lip again, but she gave in. "Okay, but let me look around. Maybe try on a few simpler dresses, too."

"Go ahead. I'll wait here." He dropped into a chair in a seating area set up in the middle of the store. Let her have some fun. If he had his way, they'd be leaving with the red dress. "Oh, Eileen, she's not to know the cost of anything."

CHAPTER ELEVEN

"I WANT TO APOLOGIZE for the third degree we put you through yesterday." Sierra said as she sipped her second cup of coffee. Behind her the Las Vegas strip dazzled the senses.

"I understand." Grace responded.

The two of them sat at the dining room table. The counter between the kitchen and dining room held a full breakfast buffet. The men had just left for a morning meeting and had taken Jackson with them.

He'd brushed them off completely yesterday. Mostly her fault. After they finished shopping, she decided he could use a break, so she directed him east to Hoover Dam. He relaxed on the drive. As she hoped, being in control of something— even a vehicle—bolstered his floundering confidence. When she suggested they take the tour, he jumped on the chance. He'd been as excited as a child, and as inquisitive. He'd loved it. He'd been in a much better place when he got home last night.

"It isn't personal." Sierra assured her.

"It's very personal," Grace corrected her. "But I get it. He's been away and the last gal he was seeing hurt him."

"She did, more than he knows."

"What do you mean?" Grace pushed her plate away and reached for the last of her coffee.

Sierra studied her for a moment obviously calculating how much she should share. "I don't know what to make of you." She confessed. "You're nothing like the women Jackson usually chooses. He likes tall, beautiful and dim."

"Really?" Surprise sent Grace's eyebrows rising. "I would think he'd get bored with dim rather quickly."

"Oh, he does," Sierra assured her. "But he says he wants to be able to relax when he's with a woman, not talk."

"Hmm." Grace decided she preferred her version of Jackson.

"Right?" Sierra demanded as if she'd been awaiting validation of her opinion. "Okay, dim is probably overstating it. And in all fairness, next to him most people fall short on the IQ range."

"Perhaps it's a form of self-defense for him. Maybe dim—for lack of a better word—equates with lack of calculation. So he feels he can trust their emotions more."

Sierra stared at her for a moment. "I never considered that, but you may well be right. Not that he gives his trust. He's the most guarded man I know. And the other three aren't far behind. I understand the foster care shuffle will do that to you."

"The four of them are lucky they found each other," Grace stated.

"Yes, they were all in the same house late in their teens. A good home run by an older couple known for taking on tough cases. They became a family. I met them in college, except Clay, who joined the marines. He joined them in the business later, after it was more established."

"I was a military brat," Grace told her. "So I know how hard it is to pack up and leave the familiar for the unknown. You learn not to expose yourself to the hurt of leaving friends behind by putting up guards."

"Yes. It's created a bond between them that won't be easily broken. But the wealth they've accumulated hasn't made relationships easy, especially for Jackson. Being a billionaire always raises the question of whether the

woman is with him for the man or the money. His reticence is as much self-preservation as it is habit."

"But Vanessa got to him."

"Yes, and by hurting him physically she messed with
his mind. Any emotional advancement he'd made in the
past few years was shot to heck. He went off by himself
while the police investigated and we didn't see him for
weeks. We've been worried."

"It must have been traumatic. Some alone time is probably just what he needed."

"Obviously. He seems happy. I've never seen him be
with anyone like he is with you. I really don't know what
to make of it."

"And how is that?"

"Open. Accessible. He doesn't generally allow his companions in the penthouse. He has a suite on a lower floor
he uses when he's keeping company."

Did he? Interesting. No wonder his inner circle was so
freaked-out.

"I wouldn't make too much of it." Grace downplayed
the importance for Sierra's sake. "We've been through a
lot together the past few days. When the novelty wears
off, I'll be on my way and things will get back to normal."

Sierra wagged a finger at Grace. "That would make the
guys happy. But I'm not so sure it would be for the best. I
think you're good for Jackson."

"Hmm. And what about you? Who's the guy?"

"What do you mean?"

"You wouldn't be telling me all this if you didn't have
romance on the mind. Who are you on the fence about?"

Flustered, Sierra tried to wave Grace off. "I'm not seeing anyone right now."

"But you want to." Grace prompted her. "Who is he, a
coworker, friend of a friend? No, then they could champion him. Someone you met at an event?" Grace contin-

ued to guess. "Or through work?" Ah, a blush. "That's it. Not a coworker then, but maybe a vendor?"

"Okay, you got me." Sierra tried to hide a smile. Oh, yeah, she was in serious crush mode. "He works for the city. He's in charge of juvenile activities. We've been working together on the foundation gala. We've had coffee a couple of times. He seems really nice."

"And you're wondering if he's interested in you, your money or your connections?"

Eyes wistful Sierra nodded. "It's so hard to know when your emotions are engaged whether you're being played or not."

"So check him out," Grace suggested. "You have the resources. As I know from experience."

"I couldn't." Sierra got fidgety. "The reports we draw are pretty inclusive, because we deal in large amounts of money on business deals, and this is a highly competitive field so we want to be sure of who we're hiring. But this is personal. I don't want to violate his privacy in that way."

"So don't run a report. Do a social search." Grace got up to get her computer from the living room. She set it on the table and pulled up the biggest social media platform on the internet. "What's his name?"

"Oh, we can't do this." Sierra moved her chair closer. "We shouldn't do this, should we?"

"We should. A woman needs to be careful in this day and age. A man, too, as Jackson's experience shows."

Sierra gave the name Nick Collins. Grace typed it in.

"This takes patience," Grace explained as she clicked through pages, cut and pasted information.

Sierra leaned forward to read better. A few minutes later, Grace handed her a report that held public details of his career, community involvements and relationships. "It's by no means a comprehensive report, but you'll have a good sense of who he is."

"Obviously he has some issues." Disappointment filled Sierra's voice. "This was very helpful, Grace. You're easy to talk to." Sierra set her coffee cup aside. "No wonder Jackson and Ryan like you so much."

More than surprised by that, Grace had to smile. "Ryan likes me?"

"Oh, yes. You stood up to him. Presented your arguments as if you didn't care if he accepted them or not, and got Jackson to agree to Dr. Wilcox's examination without putting up a fight. Ryan was quite impressed."

"Really?" Surprising, but Grace would take it. If Ryan liked her, all the better for Jackson. This whole situation was hard enough on him. He deserved any break he could get.

"Really. And that's not easy to do. Well, I've wasted enough time on this." Sierra stood and gathered her dirty dishes. "I have to get to work. Thanks for the help. If you're interested, I have friends who would pay for the same info."

"Sure. I'm happy to help."

Sierra nodded. "Let me know if you need anything."

"I will, thanks."

Sierra carried her dishes to the kitchen. "Don't worry about the cleanup," she advised. "I'll let housekeeping know we're done." With a final wave, she departed.

With time to kill, Grace decided to do another search. She went to her room and grabbed the file on Jackson. Doing the search for Sierra had given her some ideas for finding his father. Social services hadn't been able to find his mother's friend twenty-nine years ago. But times had changed. She typed in the friend's name and hit Enter.

Grace's phone rang. She pulled the cell phone out of her pocket but didn't recognize the number. She began to hit

Ignore, but remembered she had job feelers out. This time with Jackson was only temporary.

"This is Grace Delaney."

"Hello, Grace Delaney, should I be congratulating you?"

"Doug!" Happy to hear her friend's voice, she sank down on the sofa and looked out over the Strip. "Why would you congratulate me? Did I get a job I don't know about?"

"Not unless you're ready to join the FBI," he responded.

"I've actually been giving it some thought. I've really enjoyed the profiling and background work I've been doing for Jackson. I might be interested in an analyst position with the FBI."

"We always need good analysts. I'll pass the word. But what I'm talking about is your upcoming wedding. The tabloids have announced you're engaged to Hawke."

"Seriously?" she asked, her heart clenched at the news. How she wished she could dismiss his revelation as sheer craziness. She and Jackson had known each other for only a week. But the truth was she'd fallen, and fallen hard. "Well, I can promise you any rumors of an engagement are greatly exaggerated."

"I'm glad to hear it," Doug said. "So how come I don't believe you?"

Because he knew her too well. "Maybe because I wished it was true?"

"You've fallen for him."

She nodded, though he couldn't see her. "Foolishly, I have."

"Why foolish? You'll make a great billionaire's wife."

Her heart squeezed even tighter. "Ah, that would require the billionaire to have feelings for me."

"So what's the problem? The man I saw clearly held you in high regard."

Hope bloomed, but she blocked it. She needed to be

realistic. "I think you're confusing desperation for a connection. I was the only person he knew in a world gone crazy."

"I don't know. He was jealous of me. That points to a connection if you ask me."

"Jealous?" She forced a laugh. "You're imagining things."

"There must be something there, or the tabloids wouldn't have the two of you getting married."

"There's...chemistry."

"Ah." Silence beat down the line. "If you love him, you have to fight for him."

"Fight for who?" she demanded, raw emotion tearing through her. "Jackson has his name thanks to you, but his memories are still defunct. When he gets them back, I'll just be another memory."

"It's not like you to be a defeatist."

"No, I'm a realist." And an emotional mess. "He lives in hotels, Doug. And you heard me the other day. The only thing I'm certain of is a need for a home, for permanence."

"So get him to buy you a house. He's a bachelor, Grace. And travels a lot for business. Just because he doesn't have a home doesn't mean he doesn't long for one." A call sounded in the background. "Listen, Sherry needs me. Stay strong. The next time we talk, I hope I'll be offering congratulations for real."

"Give Sherry hugs from me. I'll think about what you said," she promised.

"I hope so, because you deserve to be happy. And I'm talking to Ken Case about that analyst position."

The line disconnected and Grace dropped her phone on the couch, staring unseeing out the picture window. Doug made it sound so simple. Fight for Jackson, get him to buy the home they both longed for. So perfect.

Yet so far out of reach.

* * *

Jackson sat at the head of the conference table, listening to the conversation flowing around him. He'd admitted to Grace to being nervous about reporting to work, but diving back into his life was both exhilarating and challenging. He found it fascinating, and luckily much of the knowledge was there, even if the details and people were still blanks.

Again and again he looked around for Grace, wanting to share something with her, but dragging his girlfriend into a meeting would be pushing it.

Other than that, the plan was going great. Her preparations, sourced onto his new cell phone, put all the pertinent info he needed at his fingertips. Names of department heads along with pictures, descriptions of his games, a list of ventures and properties he owned. No one questioned him looking at his phone.

It worried him sometimes that he'd become so dependent on her. Everything he'd learned since arriving in Las Vegas pointed to self-reliance. More, it was clear he kept women at a distance.

He couldn't imagine relegating Grace to her own suite. The best part of his day was waking with her in his arms. But would he feel the same way when his old life caught up to his new one?

His past, losing his mother so young and being in nine foster homes before finding a home with Mama Harman, was a memory bomb waiting to explode. How could he know how he'd feel once those memories returned?

He couldn't. But he knew he wanted Grace by his side when that time came. She'd helped him through every mishap so far. He trusted her instincts, trusted her to put him first. Getting his memories back wasn't going to change that. No matter what those memories held.

The meeting wrapped up and Jackson met Grace in the lobby.

"Hi. Oh. Where are we going?" she demanded when he simply wrapped an arm around her waist and swept her along. "I thought we were going to go over the game plan for the gala tonight. I have the profiles for the invited VIPs. I also asked Sierra for a list of the coordinators and their assistants and did brief profiles on them. And I included the roster of your executives, with the pictures attached."

"Excellent. I can look at them in the car." A large black SUV pulled up as he urged Grace through the door.

"It's going to take you a while to go through that." She slid in when he held the door open for her but stopped him from closing her in. "There are more than forty profiles for the VIPs alone."

"I'm good with facts and faces." He shut the door and rounded the vehicle. Inside the partition was up between them and the driver. "I will admit things seem to take forever to absorb. Took me nearly an hour to get through the file the FBI did on me when I was finally able to read it."

"An hour?" Her pretty blue eyes widened with amazement. "It took me all afternoon."

"I've found I'm a fast reader." He flipped through the file on the tablet she'd handed him, squinting, as his vision still blurred occasionally. That had been the only problem in the meeting earlier. It helped that she used a large font. These profiles included both personal and business details. "I'm amazed you were able to put this together so quickly."

"Yeah, well, I'm good with facts and faces, too." She gave him a rundown of her report. As the gala was a fundraiser, she'd sorted the VIP profiles based on net worth. While he read, she fell silent as the wonders of the Strip caught her attention. Once they left the excitement behind, she turned to him. "Where did you say we're going?"

"To police headquarters. I made an appointment with the detective investigating my case."

"Are you sure you want to do this today? With the gala

tonight? You're bound to see or hear something that makes your head hurt."

"Knowledge is worth the pain. We're here. And I want to get through this." He hopped out of the SUV. She was waiting on the other side. He took her hand and led the way inside to the information desk. "We're here to see Detective Hunt in Special Investigations," he told the clerk.

The woman directed them to the third floor and Jackson led Grace to the elevators.

She turned concerned eyes on him. "I'm just worried it'll ruin your mood for the gala tonight."

"And it may help me to remember." He pushed the up button. "You're always talking about my mind providing clues. Well, this is what my mind is prompting me to do."

"Okay." She squeezed his hand once they were inside the elevator. "But don't expect too much. They probably won't be able to tell you much more than was in the report."

Her concern touched him. He bent and kissed her softly. "I'm glad I have you with me."

A bright sheen came into her eyes and for a heartbeat he thought she might cry. The very notion of his stalwart Grace in tears made his heart twist. But she smiled and the moment disappeared.

She started to say something when the elevator doors opened onto the second floor and a woman who looked to be in her fifties stepped on.

"Good morning," she greeted them with a smile and pushed Five.

From a distance he heard Grace respond. The woman's scent, an Oriental perfume with touches of citrus and rose, hit him the minute the doors opened. His head spun and pain exploded behind his eyes. He knew that perfume. From a long time ago. It belonged to someone important. Someone who represented warmth and comfort. He had the strongest desire to grab the woman and hold her close.

"Jackson." Grace pulled on his hand.

He didn't budge. The woman smiled kindly.

"Jackson!"

He blinked at Grace. "What?"

"We're here." She drew him off the elevator. "Are you okay? You look like you just saw a ghost."

The doors closed behind him. He swung around but the woman was gone.

"Jackson, you're scaring me."

"I'm fine." He spotted a bench against the wall down the way and made his way to it. "Do you have one of my pain pills with you?"

"Yes." She sat next to him and dug in her purse. "Here." She presented him with a tiny white pill and a bottle of water. "What happened back there?"

"I did see a ghost. Or, more accurately, smelled one." Head reeling, he chased the pill with a sip of water and watched her brow furrow in confusion. "That woman's perfume struck a chord. I think my mother wore the same scent."

"Oh, Jackson." Her hand covered his knee. "What makes you associate it with your mother? Did you have an actual memory?"

"No. It was more like emotions that seemed to be from a long time ago. Sensations of love and warmth and happiness. But there was no memory, no face to go with the feelings."

His frustration with the lingering amnesia echoed between them.

"I think that's enough for today," she suggested again.

"No. Don't you get it? I need knowledge. If my brain won't provide me with the facts of my life, I'll get them any way I can." He surged to his feet. "Come on, we have an appointment."

He started down the hall but soon realized she wasn't

with him. Turning around, he spotted her right where he left her. Arms crossed over her chest, she stood with her head cocked watching him. Damn it. He wanted her with him.

He retraced his steps. "Aren't you coming?"

Those watchful blue eyes never shifted from his face. "You've already had a traumatic event. I'll go with you, but only if I get to call a halt if it looks like it's getting to be too much for you."

"Yeah, all right." He grabbed her hand, determined not to leave her behind again.

Her hand moved but her feet didn't. When he came to a stop, he turned to glare at her down the length of their two arms. Her expression hadn't changed. "Promise me."

He gritted his teeth, disliking having limitations placed on him. But the one true thing he knew was Grace cared about him. It was the foundation of his world. "I promise."

She nodded. "Okay then, lead the way."

A few minutes later Detective Hunt stood to greet them. "Mr. Hawke, welcome back. And this must be Ms. Delaney."

"Please call me Grace. Thank you for seeing us on such short notice. I'm sure you can understand Mr. Hawke is anxious to get an update on the investigation. Do you have anything new on the assailant?"

"Not much." Hunt gestured behind them with the file in his hand. "Why don't we take this to a conference room?" A few feet down the hall, he opened a door and ushered them inside. "My partner is on a call regarding another case. She'll join us if she can."

Jackson nodded and sank into one of the cushioned seats. He reached for Grace's hand before giving Hunt his full attention. "What more have you learned about Vanessa? Tell me you are close to apprehending her."

Hunt opened the file, flipped through the pages. "Vanessa Miller's family has money. She gets a monthly allowance and all her household expenses are paid. She has no close friends. Interviews with her neighbors revealed she has a bad temper and sometimes gets violent. We got a search warrant for her home and found a prescription for an antianxiety medication. After talking to her doctor, we determined she has a psychotic explosive disorder."

"That doesn't sound good," Grace spoke up.

"No. People suffering from the disorder can be fine for long periods of time, and then something will set them off and they become verbally and physically abusive. It means she's capable of overreacting to the point of violence over any little thing. The medication is supposed to help, but she's known to go off it, which of course increases the chances of episodes. Your company has security on her residence 24/7, with instructions to contact us if she's spotted, but she hasn't returned to her home."

"You stated she has no friends or employers. What other avenues are you pursuing?" Jackson asked.

"We've interviewed the guests at the party where you met. Nobody particularly remembers her and nobody admits to inviting her. We talked to her neighbors. She's been involved in several disputes so we went out and spoke to the responding officers. Seems she is well-known for blowing up and then being very contrite. Always pays bigger and better for any repairs needed. Still, people are afraid of her and tend to give her a wide berth. She put her maid in the hospital for trying on a pair of shoes, but again she was really sorry, and the family paid the woman off, so no charges were ever filed."

The more Jackson heard, the angrier he got. "If she's such a menace, why hasn't she ever been charged or put in a care facility?"

"Unfortunately, it's not that easy," Grace said. "Unless she actually breaks a law there's nothing the police can do but take a report. Sometimes accumulative reports will build a history supporting action or adding to charges if any are ever brought."

Hunt nodded. "The family should do something, but they've set her up in the house and pretty much washed their hands of the situation."

"I am pressing charges," Jackson declared. "Someone who can lose their temper and stab a guy needs to be put away."

"I'm glad to hear it." Hunt shuffled the papers back together, and a picture slid out. Jackson automatically reached for it as he listened to Hunt. "A lot of men are too embarrassed to admit a woman hurt them."

Forget that. "I think my reputation can survive it."

"Good, good. Have you remembered anything more you think can help us?"

Jackson exchanged glances with Grace. She gave a subtle nod that he took to mean she thought he should reveal his condition to the detective. He responded with a negative shake of his head. He couldn't see where confessing his vulnerability helped the situation.

"No, nothing new." He casually looked down at the picture. It wasn't the driver's license shot, which was what he'd seen before. This was a candid picture of a woman at a party. She had lighter hair, animated features and was dressed in a minidress sipping a martini.

Seeing her in the context in which they met triggered something in his mind.

He dropped the photo to grab his head as pain streaked from temple to temple and thunder pounded behind his eyes. He knew her. Vanessa, pretty, fun, crazy. Images, thoughts, memories began to crowd his mind, of her, of his past, his friends, his company. Everything.

It was too much. Too fast.

"Jackson?" Grace's voice sounded as if she was shouting in a tunnel.

"Mr. Hawke?" Hunt sounded the same.

"I'm okay." Jackson tried to say but it came out as a croak.

He wanted out of there. To be home. And alone until he sorted everything out.

Tension radiated off Jackson. That and the fact his grip nearly crushed her knuckles told Grace something was wrong. She hid her anxiety behind a polite smile.

"It's the concussion," she explained to Hunt. "He was in an accident a few days ago. Is it possible for us to have the room for a few minutes?"

"Of course, take your time. A last word of caution, Mr. Hawke. Vanessa knows she's done wrong. If she follows her pattern, she could be waiting for you to resurface in order to apologize. But she's clearly unstable. Do not engage with her. And your security people should notify us immediately if they see her."

"Thank you, Detective." Grace pulled her hand free to move to the door, a gesture meant to hurry the detective along. "We'll take every precaution. And I'll personally pass your message on to security."

"Tonight's gala is a public event. We're concerned she may take the opportunity to get close to Hawke."

"I'll have Sierra add you and your partner to the guest list."

"Thanks. Let me know if you folks need anything more, otherwise I'll see you tonight." Hunt gathered up his folder and left the room.

Grace closed the door behind him then rushed back to Jackson's side.

"Jackson, what is it? What's wrong?"

She got a groan in response. So not good.

She dug in her purse for another pain pill and the water bottle. The doctor had said Jackson could take two pills if necessary. He'd refused to take more than one and she'd practically had to force-feed the few he'd taken. But he gave her no argument about taking a second pill. He shoved it in his mouth and swallowed on a gulp of water.

Wanting to do something more, she began massaging his temples. He stiffened but didn't ask her to stop. After a bit she shifted her fingers to the top and then the back of his head, working down until she used her thumbs along the chords at the base of his head leading to his neck. He moaned and the tension lessened through his shoulders.

"You remembered something," she guessed. It's the only thing she could think of that could incapacitate him like this.

"I remembered everything." His voice was rough as if squeezed through a vise.

Everything?

"Congratulations." Joy for him washed through her along with a pinch of dread, but now wasn't the time for celebrating or anticipating the end. The surge of intel had obviously overloaded his senses. She needed to get him home so he could rest. His brain needed to shut down for a while in order to absorb everything. "Do you think you can move?"

"Yes. Just give me another minute." He reached for the bottle and drank it dry.

She used the time to call his driver and instruct him to meet them at the front doors.

Jackson pushed to his feet. He gave her a small smile as he reached for her hand. "If I fall, don't let them take me to the hospital."

"Someday you're going to have to tell me what that's about." Grace opened the door and they started down the hall. When he swayed, she wrapped her arm around his waist. His arm automatically went around her shoulders. "Lean on me. I'll get you out of here."

CHAPTER TWELVE

JACKSON LOOKED LIKE a billion dollars. The cut of his tux, the straight line of his posture, the jut of his chin, all spoke of confidence and determination, both elements Grace saw every time she looked at him. But there was more tonight. There was a surety of self that had been missing until now.

He was in his element, among his people. And he was thriving.

Still, she kept an eye on him, watching for any sign of distress or fatigue.

She'd tried to talk him out of attending the gala. He'd crashed this morning when they returned from meeting with the detective. Slept for hours. She woke him around four and suggested skipping the event or merely putting in a brief appearance.

He refused to hear of it. Said he was fine and proved it by pulling her with him into the grotto shower for a lovely interval. She'd been forced to agree he was fine indeed.

The memory brought a touch of heat to her cheeks.

Hard to believe making love with Jackson could get better. It had. The man knew his way around a woman's body. She had no doubt he'd made a thorough study of it at some point in the past.

He laughed at something said in the group he was speaking with and then wished them well and broke away. Several people had joined the group after he did, and she'd ended up standing somewhat behind him. Now she watched as he moved off without her toward the next group.

She slowly followed in his wake. He'd been solicitous all evening, keeping her within hands' reach. Until now. Maybe she should have been the one to beg off the event.

He stopped suddenly and swung around. A frown drew his dark brows together until he spotted her. The approval in his eyes as he walked back to her almost made up for his leaving her behind.

"There you are. I missed you."

She shook her finger at him. "You forgot me."

"A momentary blip. I'm told that can happen when you have a concussion."

"Oh, now it's convenient to have a concussion. I can't believe you're using it as an excuse to me."

"Hmm. Have I told you how beautiful you look tonight?"

Oh, how sly. Of course she knew he meant to distract her. And he knew just how to get to her. The dress was strapless in a deep true red, the fitted, drop-waist bodice hugged her curves to the hips, and the full ballroom skirt, completely covered in ribbon roses, flowed around her when she moved.

She'd never felt more like a woman, or more beautiful. Except in his arms.

Because she wasn't mad, just a little sad to see the end creeping up on her, she let him off the hook.

"You did." She swished the skirt back and forth and smiled up at him, enjoying the spark in his eyes as they lingered on her. "Thank you. For the dress and for insisting it was the right one. I'll never forget this night. I feel like Cinderella at the ball."

"Good grief, does that make me Prince Charming? I don't think I can live that one down."

"Not so." She straightened his already perfect bow tie.

"JD may have stumbled a bit here, but Jackson is in his element. These people are lining up to eat out of your hand. You are every bit the prince of all you survey."

He glanced around at the crowd surrounding them. And there was just a little surprise in the gaze he turned back to her. "I suppose you're right." He wrapped an arm around her waist and pulled her to him. "I guess I'm just used to them versus me."

"I'm sure that's true in some cases." She leaned against him. "But not always. Tonight they're all backing you. This is a good thing you're doing here. And you don't need me hampering your progress. Why don't I find a quiet corner while you work the room for a while?"

Concern flashed into his green eyes. "Are you not feeling well?"

"I'm fine." It warmed her that his focus went to her first. "I just think you can move around easier without me tagging along."

"Absolutely not." He planted a soft kiss on her upraised mouth. "You saved my butt by interpreting Japanese for Mr. Watanabe. We were struggling without his interpreter."

"You were doing fine."

"I wasn't kidding when I said I missed you. My head is a mishmash of old and new. You help to ground me between the two. I can be myself with you."

It meant a lot that he felt that way. Love welled up causing her throat to tighten. She blinked back tears. Oh, yeah, the end was zinging at her with the speed of a bullet. But she could have this last night.

She cleared her throat and lifted onto her toes to kiss his cheek. "Okay, but if Cinderella's feet start to hurt, Prince Charming is going to carry her shoes."

"It's a deal." He kissed her again, lingering over the caress long enough to make her toes curl. Then he released her but kept hold of her hand as he headed toward another group of people.

He'd gone only a few steps when Clay intercepted them. "Jackson, I'll be shadowing you for a while."

"You've been shadowing me all night, Clay. What's changed?"

"A bit of a disturbance in the tunnel from the casino."

"What kind of disturbance?"

"Someone trying to break in. My men are handling it, and Hunt and his partner are headed over to check it out. It's probably nothing. But it means I'll be shadowing you from a foot away rather than ten."

"Do they think it's Vanessa?" Grace asked.

"Wouldn't that make the night a true success?" Clay fell into step with Jackson. "We should know soon."

"I can help if you need an extra hand," she offered.

"You're not going to need an extra hand, are you, Clay?" Jackson made it clear her assistance would not be tolerated.

"You do know I'm trained to handle situations like this."

"Yeah, I do. And I appreciate your willingness to help. But I won't risk you."

"That's just ridiculous." She tugged at her hand, wanting free of the bullheaded man.

"Don't care." He held on tight.

She threw up her free hand in frustration and looked to Clay for help.

He shrugged. "Works for me. I'm counting on you as a last line of defense."

"Ha." She smirked at Jackson.

He glared at Clay. "What the hell?"

Clay remained stoned-faced. "You're my number one concern. I'll use what tools I have to ensure your safety."

Jackson stepped right into her space and cupped her face, forcing her gaze to his. "How much would I have to pay you to get out of law enforcement?"

She blinked at him. What was he talking about? "It's what I do, who I am."

"You could learn something new with what I'm willing to pay. The thought of you getting hurt flays me."

The intensity in his expression shouted the truth of his words.

"I'm good at what I do," she reassured him. "And you were the one encouraging me to join the FBI."

"I was wrong. You should teach kindergarten or become a florist."

"A florist?" she repeated confused with where this was going. Seriously, she killed off cacti, something he didn't know about her, but still. She brushed the hair back at his temple. "Is your head hurting? Maybe we should take a break."

A pleading look toward the other man had him stepping forward.

"Jackson—"

"I don't need a break." Jackson ignored Clay. "I need for you to be safe."

"I am safe, right here by your side. You know as well as I do Clay isn't letting anyone get past him."

"And what about next week or a month from now? I have a scar to remind me things happen you never expect. Working in law enforcement comes with an expectation of being harmed in the line of duty."

"True. But I'm not taking money from you to change careers, so can we get back to enjoying the night?"

"Okay."

Yeah. He'd taken the hint in her tone and backed off.

"But the subject is not closed."

Or maybe not.

"I have confirmation," Clay broke in. "They just apprehended Vanessa."

* * *

Early the next morning, Grace woke to Jackson leaning over her. His lips caressed her cheek. "Sleep in. I have things to catch up on."

And then he was gone.

But there was no going back to sleep. Too much had happened yesterday for her mind to settle back into slumber. Not when she knew a difficult decision loomed ahead of her.

She was so happy for Jackson that Vanessa had been found and incarcerated. And still dread lay lead-heavy in her stomach.

His concern over her welfare touched her, but it also worried her. It would be different if they were a real couple, but her time with Jackson was more fantasy than reality. Their relationship was temporary at best.

She'd be a fool to let a fleeting lover influence her next career choice. Yet it would be too easy to do, considering she loved him. She'd known as soon as he regained his memory that her time with Jackson was limited, but with Vanessa still at large she'd figured she had a little extra time. Now that excuse was gone. She should make the break sooner rather than later.

Being a kept woman wasn't her style.

No, the fantasy only worked as long as she had something to bring to the relationship. Jackson no longer needed her, so it was time to go.

Just forming the thought in her head broke her heart. But it was for the best. She loved Jackson but not his transient lifestyle. She'd compromised in that regard for too long. She may be undecided with what she wanted to do for employment, but finding a place to put down roots was the one constant her soul never wavered on.

And for all his professions of missing her and his bar-

gaining to find her a safer career, the longer the evening
wore on, the more distant he became. Sure, he shackled
her to his side, but he drew her into the conversation less
and less. And for the past hour he sat her on a bar stool
and completely ignored her while he talked to a group of
old cronies several feet away.

It gave her a chance to observe him. He laughed, he
talked, he listened, but always he maintained his distance.
His stance, the angle of his head and the extra inches between him and those he conversed with shouted a need
for space. And people gave it to him, happy just to have
his attention.

His attention had been full-on when he made love to her
last night, but his early disappearing act just confirmed
he was reverting to his old ways. With each passing hour,
the Jackson she knew morphed into the Jackson he used
to be, which by all accounts meant a lack of emotional
commitment.

What she'd learned from reading his file and talking
with Sierra revealed a man shut off from the world. He
lived in hotel suites, kept women and the world at a distance, and 90 percent of the work he did was in his head.
His associates were his family, the company his home.

She couldn't live that way.

The man she knew wasn't quite so closed off, but with
his memory back she had no doubt he'd soon revert to his
former self. Too bad. The signs were there that he longed
for more. He'd created the facsimile of a home by having
all the penthouse suites designed the same. And his work
with the foundation showed he had a heart.

He just wasn't willing to risk it by letting anyone too
close.

So sad, because the man she knew was warm and generous, intelligent and funny. He'd make a great dad.

Good gracious, now she was thinking of children? That

settled it. She threw back the covers and made her way to the bathroom for one last shower in her own personal grotto.

She needed to leave, and she needed to leave today. Before she completely lost her mind.

As Grace zipped up her duffel bag, a text sounded on her phone. Jackson, letting her know he was wrapping up a meeting and would be up in the next few minutes.

She blew out a breath. Showtime.

Carrying her bags into the living area, she set them down near the archway. Being a bright guy, Jackson was sure to get the meaning and start the conversation for her.

A few minutes stretched into twenty and then thirty. More to occupy her hands and mind than because she was hungry, she worked in the kitchen, putting together a snack tray of veggies, fruit and cheese. After a while, she heard Jackson come in.

"I'm in here," she called out.

"Sorry, that took longer than I anticipated. This looks good." A kiss landed on her cheek as he snagged a broccoli floret before opening the refrigerator for a bottle of water. "I've been thinking this morning. I've come up with the answer to your career decision."

A sinking feeling settled on top of the dread she already sported.

"I'm not going to work for you."

"Way to undermine a guy." His Adam's apple bobbed as he drank. "Why not? It's the perfect solution."

So not perfect. Silly her, she longed for a proposal, not a job offer.

To give herself a moment, she carried the tray to the living room and set it on the glass coffee table. Jackson followed on her heels.

"You can work with Clay on our internet security team.

Electronic games are a highly competitive field. Espionage is rampant, but there's little chance of being physically hurt."

"Cyber security isn't really where my talents lie."

"You're being modest. I've seen your work, remember. The reports you've done for me, the profiles you put together for the gala have all been efficient and thorough. Top-notch." He reached for a piece of apple and spotted her luggage. His brows narrowed into a frown. "What's this?"

"I commandeered the suitcase you bought in Santa Rosa to hold the dresses you gave me. I didn't have the heart to squash them into the duffel bag."

"What are you doing, Grace? This sounds like goodbye."

"It is. You're home, Jackson. You have your memory back. You don't need me anymore." She thanked her years in the navy for managing to deliver the message in a strong voice.

A scowl drew his dark brows closer together. "That's not true. I have my memory back, but I'm still having headaches from the concussion."

"Dr. Wilcox can help you with those. And your friends will keep you from doing too much."

"Vanessa—"

"Has been apprehended. She's no longer a threat."

He cupped her cheek in his hand, ran his thumb over her chin, his touch nearly reverent. His eyes entreated her to stay. "I'm not ready to let you go."

Just for a moment she leaned into his hand, savoring the comfort of his touch, knowing this was the last connection they'd have.

"I don't want to go." The words squeezed past the lump in her throat. "Which is why I have to go now."

"That doesn't make sense."

"But it's the way it has to be."

"No," he argued, "there's another way. Come work for me."

Her head began shaking before he finished the sentence. "That's not a good idea."

"It's a great idea," he corrected, his voice going husky with his enthusiasm. "You're already working for me. You can just continue to do so. It's perfect."

"Except I don't want to work where a job has to be created for me. I want to be useful." Could he truly not see how he cut her each time he made the offer?

"You are useful. I couldn't have made it through the last week without you."

"But these were special circumstances. You don't need me to stand over your shoulder to do your business."

"Maybe I do." He broke away to pace. "Your notes saved me at my meeting yesterday. I've been vulnerable, not myself."

"Wrong." She wouldn't let him use his vulnerability against her, because he was so much stronger than his ailments. He'd proven that again and again. "You have been yourself. Pride, stubbornness, intelligence, determination, confidence—all those elements are you. The difference is your shields were down for a while. You've been more open to the world around you, allowed people to get closer. Experienced things like a regular man again."

"I'm not a regular man," he proclaimed with conviction. "I can't allow myself to be vulnerable."

That he believed that made her sad.

"Yes, you can. It takes a strong man to be open to being hurt. If nothing else, this experience has more than proven how strong you are. I hope that now you've regained your memory you'll take the lessons you learned this last week and apply them to your life going forward. Not all women are like Vanessa. They're not going to stab you. Give yourself a chance to be happy."

"Having you work for me will make me happy."

"Stop, Jackson." She couldn't take any more of this. His persistence chipped away at her determination. "Why are you doing this?"

"I told you, I'm not ready for you to go."

"Why not?" Her breath held in the back of her throat as she waited for his answer.

He struggled for words. And when he found them, they shattered her world. "Because I owe you."

She closed her eyes against the pain, then immediately opened them. Nothing to do about the fact they were overly bright. Forcing a smile, she began backing away, suddenly in full retreat.

"Wrong answer. Ah...huh." She cleared her throat. "But it's all good. An honest answer is never really wrong, is it?"

"Wait." He grabbed her hands and held on. "It is if it makes you leave. What did I do wrong?"

"For a smart man you can get some silly ideas. You don't owe me anything. I helped you because I wanted to, not for what I could get out of the experience."

"No." Shock rolled over his face. "I didn't mean that. You know I don't believe that. I want you to stay. We're good together."

"Oh, Jackson. We are good together, but we're nothing alike. I want roots, you want room service. I'm boots and jeans and you're a tuxedo and Italian leather. I need goals, schedules and order. You're spontaneous, creative and thrive in chaos. We are good together, too good. Which is why I can't stay. You think a few weeks together will allow you to work this attraction out of your system. But a few weeks together will only make it harder for me to go. Because it's more than chemistry for me. I love you."

He stopped his pursuit of her so suddenly he rocked on his heels. "Huh?" Wide-eyed, he stared at her, apparently stunned stupid.

Now there was the reaction a girl wanted when she revealed her love. Proof she was right to leave. Never again would she settle for less than love. And she wanted more than the emotion, she wanted the words and dedication that proclaimed she was valued above all else.

"Don't worry about it." She squeezed the words past the constriction in her throat, the pain in her heart. "My problem, not yours." Time to go. Her purse, she began a frantic search with her eyes. She needed her purse. "Listen, I want to thank you. This wasn't all one-sided. I learned a lot in the time we spent together." About herself, about a world she had no place in. "I met some really great people." She met his gaze straight on, because she wasn't a coward. "And a wonderful man."

She crossed to where he was still stuck in the middle of the room. "I've loved my time with you. I'll cherish it forever. Best it ends before it turns into something we both regret." She kissed him softly on the mouth. "Have a happy life."

"Sir," Jethro's assistant interrupted his meeting with Ryan, Clay and Sierra. "The manager of the hotel just called to say security has been dispatched to the owner's suite. There are sounds of destruction and breaking glass."

Clay's phone beeped as they all pushed to their feet. He met Jethro's gaze as they went through the door together. "Where's Hawke? He's alone? Are you sure? Where's Ms. Delaney?" The group stepped onto the executive elevator. "Okay, I'm on my way. Knock. If he doesn't answer, go in. If he's unhurt, I want you to pull back and wait for me."

"What's going on?" Jethro demanded. "Sounds like Jackson is trashing his suite."

"Where's Grace?" Sierra asked.

"She took a taxi to the airport twenty minutes ago."

"Okay, guys, that's not a coincidence."

"Come on, Sierra." Ryan shook his head. "It's not like Jackson to freak out over a woman."

"His relationship with Grace has been un-Jackson-like from the beginning."

"True," Jethro acknowledged as the elevator doors opened on the hallway outside Jackson's suite. Four security officers stood at the ready guarding the open door.

"Mr. Hawke is alone, sir," the head officer reported. "The room is trashed but he appears unharmed."

Clay nodded. "The four of you can go."

A crash came from inside the suite, followed by a foul curse.

"It's best if I go in alone," Jethro stated. The others nodded and he braved the threshold.

In the living room Jackson stood with hands on hips silhouetted against the Las Vegas skyline. Slices of fruits and vegetables were scattered at his feet amid shattered glass. Behind him the room looked as if a tornado had swept through—the coffee table was upended, furnishings were askew and the bar reeked of alcohol from broken bottles.

"You've made quite a mess here, buddy." Jethro joined Jackson at the window and, like him, stared out over the city. "Feel better?"

"No."

"Want to tell me what happened?"

"Grace left." Two words, devastating impact.

"I heard."

"I asked her to stay, to be with me."

"You proposed?"

Jackson heard the shock in Jethro's voice. Right. Why would he even go there? "No. I offered her a job."

"Oh."

"She said she loved me." The truth of that still rocked him.

"Ah."

He turned to stare at his friend's profile. "What does that mean?"

"Nothing. What did you say?"

Nothing. He'd frozen. Too surprised and confused by the declaration to act. Ever since he'd regained his memories, he felt out of sync, as if he was a round peg trying to fit in a square hole. He cherished what he had with Grace, but it was so far from who he was he didn't know how to reconcile JD with Jackson. Except to know he wasn't ready to let her go.

"She left. Why do the people I care about always leave?"

"At least you've known love, Jackson. My mom threw me in a dumpster."

That shocked Jackson from his fugue to focus on his friend. "Good Lord, Jethro, I never knew."

"Yeah, I don't share the fact my mom considered me trash very often. But for you I feel the need." He turned to face Jackson. "Not everyone leaves. Clay, Ryan and I are still here. You're my family, our family. We'll always have your back. The women in your life haven't left voluntarily. Your mom and Mama Harman died. And you knew when you started with Lilly how it would turn out. She was a year older than you, and there's no give in the foster world. Eighteen and you're out."

Jackson wanted to argue it hurt just the same, but his mother had loved him. He remembered her hugs, her laughter, how she had listened to him and read to him. Somehow he'd allowed the sadness of losing her to overshadow the love. The same with Mama Harman and Lilly.

But when placed against the stark knowledge of Jethro's experience he got some perspective. Maybe his recent experience allowed him to be more open to the truth. Grace's influence softened him, allowing him to trust again. He had been lucky to have love in his life. Still, the pattern was too entrenched in him to be easily shifted.

"Dude, you know I look on you as a brother. And you might be right about the rest, but Grace left." The admission cut deep.

"Did she?"

"She's not here, is she?"

"Jackson, Grace didn't leave you. She turned down a job offer."

"She knew I wanted her to stay."

"But did you give her a reason to stay? I've never seen you with anyone like you are with Grace. You've been different since you've been back. Happier. She's been good for you."

No denying that. From the moment he'd opened his eyes in a jail cell, alone and unknowing, to the long, duty-bound night of the gala when she'd stood by his side supporting and encouraging him. Her determination, intelligence and loyalty grounded him during a difficult time. Without her he'd have been lost.

Without her he would be lost.

"You're saying don't mess this up."

"That's what I'm saying."

"I'm going to need a plant."

The two-hour flight to San Francisco gave Grace plenty of time to suffer a few regrets. Pride sent her running, but had she flown from the only man she'd ever love? Shouldn't she have grabbed what time she could with him? He may not love her, but she knew he cared.

And that was the problem. Too often she'd accepted an inequitable relationship, even with her own father. This time she couldn't do it. She loved him too much to compromise. Respected herself too much to trade her pride for a few months' charade.

Doug had suggested Jackson might long for a home as

much as she did, but the way he froze when she said she loved him shouted just the opposite.

No, she'd been smart to end it before her heart got more engaged.

Or so she thought until she walked into the garage at the San Francisco Pinnacle to find Jackson leaning against her SUV. Her traitorous heart rejoiced at the sight of him.

"What are you doing here?"

"I live in a tuxedo world, but I like jeans, too. If you remember, that's what I was wearing when we met."

She blinked at him. "Seriously? That's what you want to say to me?"

"Yes. I run a billion-dollar organization." He blocked her when she tried to walk around him. "Believe me, I value organization as much as I do creativity."

"Jackson, this is futile."

"I'm not going to apologize for the room service. I'm sure you'll come to appreciate it."

"Doubtful, since we won't be together." She tried again to get around him, shutting her ears to his sensible arguments. She'd made up her mind. Again he blocked her.

"I'm not giving up on you, Grace."

"I'm sure there are any number of people able to play cyber cop for you."

He flinched. "I deserve that. But give a guy a break. I've had a lot to assimilate the last couple of days, and I'm told a concussion can cause confusion and disorientation."

"You keep throwing my words back at me." Why did he persist in doing this? She didn't know if she had the strength to say no a second time.

"What can I say? You're a smart woman."

"You're not making any points here."

The elevator dinged and a couple stepped out. They whispered to each other and laughed as they passed. It was a vivid reminder of everything Grace wanted. And Jackson didn't.

"I'm tired, Jackson. I really don't want to do this again." She deserved to be loved. Unless he had three little words to say, she didn't want to hear it.

"I could also point out that I don't trust easily, yet I invited you into my inner sanctum. I haven't done that in ten years."

She blinked again, the impact of his statement catching her unawares. She'd been so upset by the offer she hadn't seen it from his side, hadn't acknowledged the import of it. Still, nothing had changed. He'd offered her a job when she longed for so much more.

"Jackson—"

He placed a finger over her lips. "We agree we're good together. We can work out any differences, explore them, exploit them, rejoice in them."

"You're going to a lot of trouble to recruit a new employee."

"Forget the job." He leaned down and kissed her softly. "It's yours if you want it, but I'm talking a lifetime commitment. I need you in my life. The job was my way of keeping you with me. But I have a better way." Reaching behind him, he grabbed something off the hood of the SUV and presented it to her.

She stared at the plant, a charming little houseplant, some kind of ivy if she wasn't mistaken. "What's this?"

"The first plant for our new home." There was just the slightest shake to his voice. "I want to put down roots with you, Grace Delaney." No shake now. "In Las Vegas, or San Francisco if you want to pursue the position with the FBI. Wherever you want, as long as we're together."

"I think I'm going to start my own business as a private security consultant specializing in profiles and some private investigations. Including you, I've already had four clients. And I found your father."

"My father?" He looked perplexed, then laughed. "That's wonderful." He framed her face. "You're wonderful. Will you marry me?"

This time she blinked back tears. The words were right, the gesture perfect. Dare she hope? For so long she'd believed home was associated with a person. It was how she grew up moving from base to base with her father. But as an adult that never proved true, so she thought she could find home in a place. With his words she realized home followed the heart, and she hadn't found it because she hadn't found the right man. Until Jackson.

But it would only work if he felt the same.

"Why?" she whispered, too afraid to hope.

"Oh, baby." He took the plant and set it aside before pulling her into his arms. He tilted her chin until their gazes met. "Because I was happier staying with you in an economy hotel and having no money than I've ever been as a billionaire. Because you get me. Because I trust you. But most of all, because I love you."

Joy burst through her. She threw her arms around his neck and kissed him with all the love in her heart. He immediately deepened the kiss with an urgency and passion that echoed her emotions. When he lifted his head, she grinned up at him.

"Right answer."

"Does that mean yes?"

"That means yes."

* * * * *

MILLS & BOON®

The Italians Collection!

2 BOOKS FREE!

Irresistibly Hot Italians

You'll soon be dreaming of Italy with this scorching six-book collection. Each book is filled with three seductive stories full of sexy Italian men! Plus, if you order the collection today, you'll receive two books free!

This offer is just too good to miss!

Order your complete collection today at
www.millsandboon.co.uk/italians